QUR'AN AND SCIENCE IN DEPTH

by Christian Prince

Qur'an and Science in Depth

Acknowledgments

Table of Contents

Introduction

وَإِذَا تُتْلَىٰ عَلَيْهِمْ آيَاتُنَا قَالُوا قَدْ سَمِعْنَا لَوْ نَشَاءُ لَقُلْنَا مِثْلَ هَٰذَا ۙ إِنْ هَٰذَا إِلَّا أَسَاطِيرُ الْأَوَّلِينَ

Qur'an 8:31

And when Our verses are recited to them, they said, "We have heard (something like it before). If we willed, we could say same as your(Qur'an) like this. This is nothing but legends of the ancients."

In Volume 1 of *The Deception of Allah*, we spoke about Islam as a system and exposed what it stands for, from the beginnings of Muhammad until he became one of its prophets.

The Qur'an and Science in Depth is the name I found is better   because most of the book is about refuting Islamic scientifically claimed Qur'an, even though it's a book made to complete The Deception of Allah V 1.

In this 2nd volume, we will go deep into the errors of the Qur'an and debunk the Muslims
Muslims claim
 false claims about the Qur'an and its unfounded science.

But before we begin, some Muslims might wonder why we are doing this work if Islam is already false for us in the first place. The reason is to help the Muslims understand what Islam is all about so they would find out the truth because us Christians have been commanded to love even those who see us as enemies.

> **Luke 6:27** - *"But I say to you who hear, Love your enemies, do good to those who hate you."*
>
> **Ephesians 4:32** - *Be kind to one another, tenderhearted, forgiving one another, as God in Christ forgave you.*
>
> **Mark 11:25** - *And whenever you stand praying, forgive, if you have anything against anyone, so that your Father also who is in heaven may forgive you your trespasses."*

For Christians, the answer is in the Bible.

> *Matthew 7:15-20*
> *"15 Beware of false prophets, which come to you in sheep's*

clothing, but inwardly they are ravening wolves.

16 Ye shall know them by their fruits. Do men gather grapes of thorns, or figs of thistles?

17 Even so every good tree bringeth forth good fruit; but a corrupt tree bringeth forth evil fruit.

18 A good tree cannot bring forth evil fruit, neither can a corrupt tree bring forth good fruit.

19 Every tree that bringeth not forth good fruit is hewn down, and cast into the fire.

20 Wherefore by their fruits ye shall know them."

It's a must then for every Christian to keep watch as it says, "beware of false prophets." This is to protect the Christians and at the same time save those who are being deceived, as we ought to love the whole world, including the Muslims. We should care for them in the same way that we care for our fellow Christians.

1 Peter 5:8 NKJV

"Be sober, be vigilant; because your adversary the devil walks about like a roaring lion, seeking whom he may devour.

Note that when I say "Muslims
Muslims claim
claims", I do not mean all the Muslim people but just those who come with such claim."

Let us further look into the Muslims
Muslims claim
claims, expose the contradictions of the Qur'an, as well as reveal its false claims and so-called miracles. (Some say I already answered this in *Volume 1*, which I invite you to read).

Qur'an 3:54

"Plus, they deceived and Allah deceived and Allah is the best of deceivers."

Allah the Deceiver

There are Muslims who claimed that my translation of Qur'an 3:54 was incorrect. As *Volume 2* is a continuation of *Volume 1*, allow me to take some time to prove that their claim is as false as their god Allah. Let us use the Muslims

Muslims claim
translations for the verse below and analyze it.

وَمَكَرُوا وَمَكَرَ اللَّهُ ۖ وَاللَّهُ خَيْرُ الْمَاكِرِينَ

Qur'an 3:54, Yusuf Ali's translation
"And (the unbelievers) plotted and planned, and Allah too planned, and the best of planners is Allah."

1. Look at how the Muslims intentionally changed the words as this text should've read: "And (the unbelievers) *makaro* (they plotted) and Allah ***makr'*** (also plotted), and the best of ***makr*** (plotters) is Allah" (Qur'an 3:54).

The word for both parties is makr but notice that only the unbelievers' act was translated as plotting. The fact is that the same word makr was used for both Allah and the unbelievers. Therefore, they deliberately changed the meaning of the verse in order to cover up the act of their god as the word plotted from the English dictionary means:

noun, verb, plot·ted, plot·ting.
noun
- a secret plan or scheme to accomplish some purpose, especially a hostile, unlawful, or evil purpose: *a plot to overthrow the government.*

Now we understand why Muslims try to cover the truth and the disgrace of their god who is scheming an evil plan.

Muhammad Favorite prayer plot for me and do not plot against me.

> *"The Prophet used to do supplication, saying: "My Lord, aid me and do not aid against me, and grant me victory and do not grant victory over me, plot for me and do not plot against me, guide me and facilitate guidance for me, grant me victory over those who transgress against me.*

Grade : **Sahih** very strong Hadith
Reference : Jami` at-Tirmidhi 3551
In-book reference : Book 48, Hadith 182
English translation : Vol. 6, Book 45, Hadith 3551

If Muslims refuse to accuse Allah of doing evil plan (Makr/Plot) then how Muhammad make it his major prayer?
And take note this is prayer today is one of most used supplicant

Muslims do even in TV show and Radio.

Qur'an 2:253, Yusuf Ali's translation

Those apostles We endowed with gifts, some above others: To one of them Allah spoke; others He raised to degrees (of honour); to Jesus the son of Mary We gave clear (Signs), and strengthened him with the holy spirit. If Allah had so willed, succeeding generations would not have fought among each other, after clear (Signs) had come to them, but they (chose) to wrangle, some believing and others rejecting. If Allah had so willed, they would not have fought each other; but Allah Fulfilleth His plan.

Tafsir Ibn 'Abbas, Trans. Mokrane Guezzou:

"(and some disbelieving) in the Scriptures and messengers. (And if Allah had so willed it, they would not have fought one with another) they would not have differed with one another in the matter of the religion; (but Allah doeth what He will) with His servants."

Read this with me: "If Allah had so willed, they would not have fought each other; but Allah Fulfilleth His plan."

So who's plan is it to make people fight each other? It's Allah's plan. And how can it be achieved? By planning and deceiving. And why is it that human beings don't just have one belief? Because it is Allah's plan.

Qur'an 5:48, Yusuf Ali's translation

To thee We sent the Scripture in truth, confirming the scripture that came before it, and guarding it in safety: so, judge between them by what Allah hath revealed, and follow not their vain desires, diverging from the Truth that hath come to thee. To each among you have we prescribed a law and an open way. If Allah had so willed, He would have made you a single people, but (His plan is) to test you in what He hath given you: so, strive as in a race in all virtues. The goal of you all is to Allah; it is He that will show you the truth of the matters in which ye dispute;

Note here that I'm using the Muslims
Muslims claim
translation so they can't say that I'm trying to make it look bad. "He

11

would have made you a single people, but **(His plan is)** to test you in what He hath given you: so, strive as in a race in all virtues. The goal of you all is to Allah; it is He that will show you the truth of the matters in which ye dispute;"

How did Allah deal with mankind? He played with them – some me he made believers, some he made infidels, and some he made Christians and Jews. Since Allah decides each individual's faith in advance according to his plans, he then can deliberately appoint them a "wrong" faith. Therefore, it's Allah who makes one believe in the wrong path. How can that not be an act of deceiving?

> *Qur'an 6:107, Muhammad Pickthall's translation*
>
> *"Had Allah willed, they had not been idolatrous. We have not set thee as a keeper over them, nor art thou responsible for them."*

Why are they **idolatrous?** Because it is **Allah's will**.

> *Qur'an 6:112, Mohsin Khan's translation*
>
> *And so, We have appointed for every Prophet enemies - Shayatin (devils) among mankind and jinn, inspiring one another with adorned speech as a delusion (or by way of deception). If your Lord had so willed, they would not have done it; so, leave them alone with their fabrications.*

From the above verse, we can understand the following:
1. Appointed for every Prophet are enemies: the devils (*shayatin*).
2. For what use? For "inspiring one another with adorned speech as a delusion."
3. In what way? By **deception**.
4. Therefore, devils are Allah's employees and they've been hired to fulfill his plan, which is to deceive.
5. "If your Lord had so willed, they would not have done it…"

> *Qur'an 16:93*
>
> *And if Allah willed, He could have made you all one belief, but he deceives whom he wills and guides whom he wills. However, you shall certainly be accountable for what you had done.*

> *Qur'an 16:93, Mohsin Khan's translation*

"but He causes to err whom He pleases and guides whom He pleases;"

Clearly, it's Allah who leads us towards the right path or the wrong path: to be guided or deceived.

So it's not Satan who made us not to believe in Islam but rather it's Allah as it says, "but he deceives whom he wills and guides whom he wills."

Now let us aim and shoot the head of the beast and not go around it. We will go to Qur'an and read:

Qur'an 4:142-143, Muhammad H. Shakir's translation

142 Surely the hypocrites strive to deceive Allah, and He shall requite their deceit to them, and when they stand up to prayer they stand up sluggishly; they do it only to be seen of men and do not remember Allah save a little. 143 Wavering between that (and this), (belonging) neither to these nor to those; and whomsoever Allah causes to err, you shall not find a way for him.

Tafsir al-Tustari's translation

Annabel Keeler and Ali Keeler:

The hypocrites try to deceive God, but it is He who causes them to be deceived...

It's strange that Muslims get angry with us for stating, from their own Islamic books, that Islam is based on deception when we can give numerous stories about Muhammad himself deceiving others. He even deceived a Muslim individual whom he happened not to appreciate very much. Let us read the following hadith:

Sahih Al-Bukhari, Book 59, Hadith 369

Reported Jabir's Ibn 'Abdullah: "Allah's Messenger said, 'Who is willing to kill Ka'b Ibn Al-Ashraf, who has offended Allah and His Messenger?' subsequently, Muhammad Ibn Maslama got up saying, 'O Allah's Messenger! Would you like me to kill him?' The Prophet said, 'Yes, I would,' Muhammad Ibn Maslama said, 'Then allow me to say a false thing to deceive Ka'b.' The Prophet said, 'You may say it.'"

If you commit no sin Allah would kill us

> *Sahih Muslim, Book 037, Hadith 6622*
>
> *Abu Huraira stated that the Messenger of Allah (may Allah pray on him and salute him) said, "By Him, which in his Hand is my life, if you mankind were not to commit sin, Allah would sweep you out of the world, and He would exchange you with people who would perform sin and seek forgiveness from Allah, and He then would forgive them."*

Allah will kill only those who do not commit sins. This is a clear proof that the Qur'an copied the Biblical story of Noah's flood and inserted as Qur'an 11:40–44. The Biblical story speaks about God destroying the "bad ones" and rescuing the good people. However, what we read from the above hadith is Allah doing the opposite. This goes against the logic of punishment and reward, or punishment given exclusively to the bad individuals, as we read the following Qur'anic verse:

Qur'an 11:44

> *"And it was said: O earth! Swallow up your water and to the sky Be. Clear your clouds, And the water was made to sink and the judgment was completed, and it (Noah's ship) came to rest upon A-Judi, and it was said: A far elimination for the wrongdoing folk."*

At the same time, it's a contradiction to the story of Lot who is considered a prophet of Islam. According to Lot's story, Allah made rocks rain on his people (Lot's) as a punishment for their sins, as we read in Qur'an 15:59-74.

This story was also taken from the Bible with Muhammad's own fabricated tale added to it. If we go to the Bible in the Book of Genesis 18:26, we would notice that the God of the Christians and the Jews is willing to refrain from His punishment even if there were only 50 righteous people in the entire city. Whereas the god of Islam, according to the above hadith of Sahih Muslim, book 037, Hadith 6622, "Allah then would kill all the good ones and replace them with bad ones." Read with me the following Biblical verse:

> *Genesis 18:26 - KJV*
>
> *"And the LORD said, If I find in Sodom fifty righteous within the city, then I will spare all the place for their sakes."*

From reading the above hadith, we can gather the following ideas and understand the mentality and nature of Allah – how he thinks, what he wants and seeks, what cheers him up, and what angers him:

1. Allah needs our sins.
2. Our sins bring Allah joy and he rejoices when we ask for forgiveness.
3. Allah would not hesitate to punish us by death if we had not sinned, or, if we had not given him joy by asking him for forgiveness of our sins.
4. Deception is one of Allah's tools, which is the same tool that Satan uses. In order for Allah to deceive us, he plays the game of *good cop bad cop*, wherein he's the good guy and we're the bad guys. It constitutes of us chasing him by begging for his forgiveness and him causing us to sin, repeating the whole scenario over and over again. This is how Allah enjoys this world and rewards himself: by causing disorder and deception so that we would try to please him by asking for forgiveness.
5. The God that we have as Christians did not create us to make us ask for forgiveness, but He created us to share His glory with us. This is why we've been taught to refer and talk to Him as "our Father." Our Father is the opposite of the god of Islam. He would not wipe us off if we did not commit sins just so He could replace us with a sinful community. It's never been about His needs but it's all about Him loving us and inviting each individual to have a personal relationship with Him.

The plot of Allah against you

If you have the Deception of Allah V 1, if you go and read about Islam and destiny from there we quote;

Destiny in Islam

> "Afterwards, it (the Angels) will be breathed the soul into his body. So, a man will do the deeds of people of heaven and only the distance of an arm is between him and the heaven, then what has been written by the angel supersedes, and so he starts doing deeds of the people of hell fire and enters hell fire. Identical a person may do deeds and work of hell fire subsequently the deeds which are written to him by the angels will be in command to surpass, so he will change to do the work of the people of paradise, so he enters paradise."

Sahih Al-Bukhari, Book 55, Hadith 549 and

Sunan Abi Dawud 4708 Book 41, Hadith 4691
Grade: correct (Al-Albani)

- I think this is a clear explanation, made by Muhammad himself, showing that what is written concerning you is what will take effect over what you do all your life. No matter how bad or how decent you were as a person, at the end it's what is written for you that will be the final design, not your bad or good deeds. This is one madness of this belief. Who would trust Allah after reading this? Where is the justice?
- What is the benefit of praying, giving to charity or doing good, when the order of Allah is to kill the Christian, Hindu, Buddhist and the Jew?
- At the end, it is not what you do, it is what Allah plan or plot for you will be done, regardless it's your wish or will or not.

John 3:16 - KJV

For God so loved the world, that he gave his only begotten Son, that whosoever believeth in him should not perish, but have everlasting life.

In conclusion, Allah is literally a sick god suffering from low self-esteem symptoms. He is moody, unpredictable, and is filled with anger. No one can or could understand him. He does things based on his selfishness and egotistical interests. We are victims of his deception, which for me is a clear observation that he is nothing but Satan hiding behind the name *Allah.*

Finally, the Plan of Allah to Deceive the Christians

Qur'an 5:14 Yusuf Ali translations

"14 From those, too, who call themselves Christians, We did take a covenant, but they forgot a good part of the message that was sent them: so we estranged them, with enmity and hatred between the one and the other, to the day of judgment. And soon will Allah show them what it is they have done"

In order to make me hate my brother in Christ, you would have to deceive me because that is an evil thing to do. But why is it that Allah hates the Christians so much?

John 15:18-27King James Version (KJV)

"18 If the world hates you, ye know that it hated me before it hated you.

19 If ye were of the world, the world would love his own: but because ye are not of the world, but I have chosen you out of the world, therefore the world hateth you."

Revelation 12:9King James Version (KJV)

9 And the great dragon was cast out, that old serpent, called the Devil, and Satan, which deceiveth the whole world: he was cast out into the earth, and his angels were cast out with him.

We end the topic of Allah deceptions with this verse translated by Muslims:

Qur'an 14:4 Muhsin Khan

And We sent not a Messenger except with the language of his people, in order that he might make (the Message) clear for them. Then Allah misleads whom He wills and guides whom He wills. And He is the All-Mighty, the All-Wise.

Islam is based on psyche and selfishness

Let's start with some recognizable facts about Islam which Muslims hardly notice:

1. The cross is an enemy should be destroyed.
2. Christians should pay Jizya with being humiliated and subdued. But Muslims in Christians lands should not be under same rules and should be treated with respect.
3. The ringing of church bells is offending to Muslims but the call of prayer of Muslims is not!
4. You eating pork is offending to Muslims, although them forcing you not to eat it and not to eat nor drink in public during the fasting hours of *Ramadan* (month of fasting) should not offend you.
5. Attacking your Book and calling you names such as "pig" and "monkey", as stated in Qur'an 2:65, 7:166 and 5:60, should not be offending.
6. Calling you names and considering you to be dirty, as stated in Qur'an 9:28, is not offending but you should never say to Muslims what they say to you, otherwise you're an Islamophobe.
7. A Muslim man can marry your Christian sisters, but if a Christian man were to marry a Muslim woman, he would be executed and

she would be slain.

8. If a Muslim is killed by a non-believer, the unbeliever should be killed; but if a Muslim killed a non-believer, the Muslim would never be killed for Muhammad said so in the following hadiths:

- Sahih Al-Bukhari, Book 3, Hadith 111
- Sahih Al-Bukhari, Book 52, Hadith 283, and
- Sahih Al-Bukhari, Book 83, Hadith 50:

"...The prophet said, that no Muslim should be killed as punishment for the killing of a disbeliever...."

9. Muslims can occupy your land; they call it *Fateh* (opening). Whereas if you try taking your land back, you will be labeled a crusader. Even Westerners by their growing ignorance will humiliate you.

10. Muslims have the right to pray inside Western public schools. The governments in the West provide them with special prayer rooms and there are even certain schools that made bathrooms especially for Muslims. Christians, on the other hand, cannot use the word *god* or pray in these same government establishments.

11. The violent individual is praised by the hypocrites in our government. We see people like George W. Bush, Barack Hussein Obama, and many other liars who shamelessly told their nation that Islam is peace and just and that *Jihad* means self-struggle, which are all falsification.

I wanted to point these facts out as many see them but do not really take notice or recognize them. Maybe, this will be an eye-opener for the reader and show that what I'm trying to expound on is not about Christianity being right and Islam being wrong. Rather, it's about Islam being fraud as well as being a threat to humanity because of its deception and violence with them enforcing themselves onto others. Islam is not based on humanity's value but instead based on the fact that if you do not accept the Qur'an, I will kill you (Qur'an 9:29). Absurdly, someone like me is labeled an Islamophobe!

Qur'an 9:29

Fight those who believe not in Allah nor the Judgment Day, nor forbid what Allah and His Messenger ordered to be forbidden, nor accept the religion of truth (Islam), of the People of the Book (Christians and Jews), until they pay the Jizyah with willing submission, and feel themselves humiliated and subdued.

In the Deception of Allah Volume 1, I've delved into Muhammad's early life up until the time he became a member of Allah's prophets, as he gave himself this position. Let us now study Muhammad's life more in depth and figure out what this man was about.

Muhammad & poverty

Muhammad as a man had a very hard life. He grew up an orphan, had no father and did not receive the care of his mother. Islamic books speak about his mother's death; Muhammad was eight years old when she died. Before that, Muhammad had never known or met his real father who lived an open sexual life with many women. Unable to feed him as his mother produced no breast milk, she gave him to a Bedouin woman who nursed him from the time he was a baby up until he reached 4 years old. Before she passed away, Muhammad lived with his mother for two years. He had no other relatives except for his uncles and his grandfather who later died when Muhammad was 8 years old. That volatile environment at an early age made him an unstable man. He grew with the woman who nursed him for four years, then two years with his mother, and for two more years with his grandfather before moving to his uncle's house who was a father to many children, struggling to survive. Of course, there is nothing wrong with being poor as Our Lord blessed the poor ones. However, this life made Muhammad dream of a new one where he could be a master, not a follower; an employer, not an employee. But how? How could Muhammad escape from his sad life where his people ate lizard for survival? Muhammad was sick of it. He wanted to eat what the wealthy people ate.

> *Sahih Muslim, Book 021, Hadith 4788*
>
> *Ibn 'Umar narrated that there were some men with Allah's Apostle (may Allah pray on him and salute him) from among his companions. Sa'd was one of them. It was served to them the flesh of the lizard when a lady among the wives of Allah's apostle (may Allah pray on him and salute him) said, "It is the flesh of the lizard." Thereupon Allah's Messenger said, "Eat, for it is lawful, but it is not my diet."*

From this hadith, we would notice how bad life was in Mecca. It explains why the Arabs called it "*Mecca*" which means the land of death where you have to work hard for your water and living. As we look it up in the Arabic dictionary Maqaies **Al-Lugha**: "*it's called Mecca for the scarceness of water in it and it says it's a place where the unjust is destroyed and Mecca crushes him as one who crushes bones.*"

So, the Arabs thought that the unjust individual will end up in Mecca where there is no water and where he will be destroyed.

.ويقال: سمّيت مكّة لقلّة الماء بها، كأنّ ماءها قد امتُكّ

.وقيل سمّيت لأنها تَمُكُّ مَن ظَلَمَ فيها، أي تُهلِكه وتَقْصِمُه كما يمكُّ العظم

From here, we would understand why Muhammad always wanted to be with the rich ones, instead of being with poor individuals like 'Umar, Abu Baker and Uthman. To prove this argument, we will go to the Qur'an.

> *Qur'an 80:1-4*
>
> *1 Muhammad gave someone a dark look and turned away.*
>
> *2 Because the blind man came to him.*
>
> *3 What could inform thee, but that he might grow in blessing.*
>
> *4 Or take to consideration and so the reminder might profit him?*

Let us see what is behind these verses from the interpretation of Ibn Kathir, print. 2002, Vol. 8, p. 319:

> *More than one of the academics of Tafsir spoke of that one day where the Messenger of Allah was addressing some of the great leaders of the Quraysh, hoping they would embrace Islam. While he was speaking in direct conversation with the leader, Ibn Umm Maktum came to Muhammad. He was of those who had accepted Islam in its beginnings.*
>
> *He (Ibn Umm Maktum) then started asking the Messenger of Allah about something and urgently carried on asking him. The Prophet ignored the blind man in order to pursue his conversation and make great men of (rich) Quraysh leaders accept Islam. He looked daggers in the face of Ibn Umm Maktum and turned away from him in order to face the other man. Therefore, Allah revealed, "He looked daggers and turned away from the blind man. And how can you know that he might become pure" meaning, he may achieve purification and cleanliness for his soul. "Or he might receive rebuke, and the admonishment might profit on him" which means he may accommodate admonition and stay away from what Allah forbids. "As for him who thinks himself not needing God, to him, you serve;" meaning, you face the rich person so that perhaps he may accept Islam. "It is not your duty to make him pure" meaning, you are not responsible for him if he does not achieve purification. "As for him (the blind man) who arrived at you jogging and is fearful" meaning, he is searching for*

you, and he comes to you so that he may be guided by your answers. "About him you did not bother to take care of his needs and your attention was somewhere else." which means he was very busy. Here Allah commands His Messenger not to leave anyone out without guidance. Rather, he should treat people equally, the noble and the weak, the poor and the rich, the master and the servant, the men and the women, the young and the old. Then Allah will guide whomever He chooses to a path that is straight.

End of Ibn Kathir's interpretation.

From this Qur'anic story, we see the real face of Muhammad. He knew that the success of his claim as a prophet was in the hands of the rich men, and not in the hands of the poor women and men and like that blind man.

The chapter itself shows us how bad Muhammad's image turned out after that incident to the point he had to create a chapter, which is insignificant if you read its entirety. It was made just to clear his acts again as if it was his god Allah correcting his unaccepted behavior.

I interrupted this story to explain how important it was for Muhammad to be surrounded by wealthy men and how he dealt with the poor ones. From this point on, it will lead us to his marriage to Kadija, a wealthy widow who had two husbands 20 years older than Muhammad prior to marrying him.

Muhammad's wife number one: khadija

We will get the story about this marriage from two sources:

Ibn Kathir: Al Bidayah Wa'nihayah: Hafiz Ibn Kathir Arabic Vol. 3, p. 467/468, print year 2002 by Dar Al-'Alam Publishing.

Book of Al-Tabakat Al-Kubra by Muhammad Ibn Sa'ed, Vol. 1, p. 88/89/132:

Abu Al-Majaz reported that Khadija said, "'to her sister go to Muhammad and mention my name to him as a wife to marry', and as she said:'her sister came to Muhammad and he said, 'to her as Allah wishes so they conspired to complete the marriage between Muhammad and Khadija and make it happen, so they made Khadija's father drink until he became so drunk and made him marry Muhammad to Khadija and clothed Khadija's father when he was drunk in new clothes so

21

when he woke up he said, 'where did these clothes come from?' they told him 'Muhammad gave it to you' so he got so angry and he said to Muhammad 'we never liked you'. He took his sword and Muhammad's family took theirs. After the issue was resolved between both families. Muhammad Ibn 'Umar reported in another story that Khadija made her father drink wine until he got drunk and she clothed him in new clothes and slaughtered a cow.

Below is the original text in Arabic for the above translation:

البداية والنهاية
إسماعيل بن عمر بن كثير القرشي الدمشقي
دار عالم الكتب
سنة النشر : 1424هـ / 2003م

page 467/468
[الطبقات الكبرى - ابن سعد]
الكتاب : الطبقات الكبرى
المؤلّف : محمد بن سعد بن منيع أبو عبدالله البصري الزهري
الناشر : دار صادر - بيروت
- الصفحة١. محمد بن سعد - ج 1994طبعة العام ،89 / 88/132
الطبقات الكبرى لابن سعد » ذِكْرُ تَزْوِيج رَسُولِ اللهِ صَلَّى اللهُ عَلَيْهِ

أبا مجلز حدث أن خديجة قالت لأختها انطلقي إلى محمد فاذكريني له أو كما قالت وأن أختها جاءت فأجابها بما شاء الله وأنهم تواطؤا على أن يتزوجها رسول الله صلى الله عليه وسلم وأن أبا خديجة سقي من الخمر حتى أخذت فيه ثم دعا محمدا فزوجه قال وسنت على الشيخ حلة فلما صحا قال ما هذه الحلة قالوا محمد كساكها ختنك محمد فغضب وأخذ السلاح وأخذ بنو هاشم السلاح وقالوا ما كانت لنا فيكم رغبة ثم انهم اصطلحوا بعد ذلك قال أخبرنا محمد بن عمر بغير هذا الاسناد أن خديجة سقت أباها الخمر حتى ثمل ونحرت بقرة وخلقته بخلوق وألبسته حلة.

From this story, we would learn the following:

1. Khadija and her family are not the kind of people who are equal to Muhammad.
2. Muhammad planned a conspiracy and deceived Khadija's father. He made him believe that it was a real marriage blessed by him using the new clothes he was wearing as proof.
3. Muhammad had no problem with wicked activities and with fooling anyone as long he could get what he wants.
4. If Muhammad were an honest man, he shouldn't have accepted such a way to make Khadija his wife.
5. And if Khadija were an honest woman, she shouldn't have cheated and fooled her father.
6. Muhammad knew in advance that in no way or in any circumstances would Khadija's family accept him. Not only because he was poor but because his family was not from the noble Quraysh community.
7. Muslims claim Muhammad was an honest man and he was well-known to be so in Mecca. If that's the case, how then can a

faithful man agree to be part of a cheat?

8. At the same, up until today in the 21st century, Arab men do not accept marrying older women. So why did Muhammad do so? Is it because of the money?

9. Arab men like marrying virgins and young women. Was Muhammad a different kind of man?

What kind of women does Muhammad think are the best to marry?

+ Sahih Al-Bukhari, Book 62, Hadith 16
+ Sahih Al-Bukhari, Book 62, Hadith 172
+ Sahih Al-Bukhari, Book 34, Hadith 310
+ Sahih Al-Bukhari, Book 41, Hadith 589

Reported Jabir bin Abdullah: "While we were going back from an invasion with the Prophet, I was rushing my slow camel. A rider came from the rear end of me and punched my camel with a spear he had with him, and then my camel started running as fast as it could. Notice the rider was the Prophet himself. He said, 'Why are you in such a rush?' I replied 'I am newly married'. He said, 'Did you marry a virgin or a widow?' I responded 'A widow'. He said, 'Why didn't you marry a virgin so that you may play with her, and she with you?' When we arrived to the city of Medina and wanted to enter, the Prophet said, 'Wait until the night falls, for the lady of uncombed hair may comb her hair and the one who's not seen her husband in a while, may shave her pubic area.'"

We would also read in Sahih Al-Bukhari, Book 52, Hadith 211, the following:

Allah's Messenger asked me whether I had married a virgin or a widow and I replied that I had married a widow. He said, "Why didn't you marry a young virgin who would have played with you, and you would have played with her?" I replied, "O Allah's Messenger! My father died and I have some young sisters, so I thought it not proper that I should marry a young girl like them who would in neither case teach them manners nor look after them. So, I married a widow so that she may serve them and teach them manners."

This hadith proves that there is no way that Muhammad is in love with Khadija, an old widow. As you see, he is advising a man to marry a young one and a virgin over a widow. But this hadith needs a deeper look:

- ➢ Muhammad is insane about marrying young girls.
- ➢ Notice that the young girls means children, not young women. "Why, hadn't you married a young virgin who would have played with you, and you would have played with her?"
- ➢ It's about having a child as a wife.
- ➢ This explains Muhammad's marriage to 'Aisha when she was six years of age.

Sahih Al-Bukhari, Book 58, Hadith 234

Narrated 'Aisha: "The Prophet engaged me when I was a virgin at the age of six. We moved to Medina and stayed at the home of Bani-al-Harith bin Khazraj. Then I got unwell, and my hair fell down. Later, my hair grew over again and my mother, Um Ruman, came to me while I was playing in a swing with some of my girlfriends. She called me, and I went to her, not realizing what she wanted to do to me. She seized me by the hand and made me stand at the door of the house. I was exhausted catching one's breath then, and when my breathing became alright again, she took some water and rubbed my face and head with it. Afterwards, she took me into the house. There in the house I saw some Ansari women who said, "finest wishes and Allah's Blessing and a good luck." Then she delivered me to them, and they prepared me (for the intercourse). Unexpectedly, Allah's apostle came to me in the morning and my mother handed me over to him, and at that time I was a girl of nine years of age.

- As we see, Muhammad had brain disorder to the point that he was encouraging a man to leave his happy marriage to get himself a baby wife!
- What would a Muslim say if that widowed wife was his daughter and Muhammad was telling his son-in-law to leave his daughter (the widow) and look for a new baby virgin?
- A young wife who would play with him and he would play with her is an excuse to justify their choice of sex. Is that what men look for in a wife? Is that the reason men get married?
- Pedophiles have difficulty relating to people their own age. Therefore, they find themselves attracted to children.
- It's very clear that if Muhammad had to choose a wife, she would pick someone like 'Aisha, a six-year-old girl rather than Khadija. It's very clear that Khadija was more of a moneybag and a mother to Muhammad than a wife.

Muhammad & brain disorder

- Put his saliva over the body of a dead man?

The Prophet came to (the grave of) `Abdullah bin Ubai after his body was buried. The body was brought out and then the Prophet put his saliva over the body and clothed it in his shirt.

Reference: Sahih al-Bukhari 1270
In-book reference: Book 23, Hadith 32
USC-MSA web (English) reference   : Vol. 2, Book 23, Hadith 360

The Deception of Allah Volume 1 "Muhammad Possessed with Devils".

Sahih Al-Bukhari, Book 73, Hadith 89

*Narrated 'Aisha (Muhammad's child-wife): "The Prophet continued for such-and-such period imagining that he had slept (had sexual intercourse) with his wives, when in fact he had not. One day he said to me, 'O 'Aisha! Allah has enlightened me regarding a matter about which I had asked Him. There came to me two men, one of them drew near my feet and the other near my head. The one near my feet asked the one near my head, 'What is wrong with this man?' (asking about Muhammad). The second man replied, 'He is under the effect of black magic.' The first man asked, 'Who activated magic on him?' The other replied, 'Lubaid Ibn Al-'Asam.' The first man asked, 'What substance did he use?' The other responded, 'The strip of the pollen of a male date tree with a comb and the hair stuck to it, kept under a stone in the well of Zarwan.' Then the Prophet went to that well and said, 'This is the same well which was shown to me. The tops of its date-palm trees look like the heads of the devils and its water looks like the Henna extract'. Afterword's the Prophet commanded that those things be taken out. I said, 'O Allah's Apostle! Won't you expose the magic object?' The Prophet replied, 'Allah has healed me and I hate to circulate the evil among the people.' 'Aisha added, 'The magician Lubaid Ibn Al-'Asam was a man from the tribe of Zuraiq, an **ally** of the Jews."*

Below is the original text in Arabic for the above translation.

صحيح البخاري » كتاب الأدب » باب قول الله تعالى إن الله يأمر بالعدل والإحسان وإيتاء ذي القربى
باب قول الله تعالى إن الله يأمر بالعدل والإحسان وإيتاء ذي القربى وينهى عن الفحشاء والمنكر والبغي يعظكم لعلكم تذكرون وقوله
إنما بغيكم على أنفسكم ثم بغي عليه لينصرنه الله وترك إثارة الشر على مسلم أو كافر
5716 حدثنا الحميدي حدثنا سفيان حدثنا هشام بن عروة عن أبيه عن عائشة رضي الله عنها قالت مكث النبي صلى الله عليه وسلم

كذا وكذا يخيل إليه أنه يأتي أهله ولا يأتي قالت عائشة فقال لي ذات يوم يا عائشة إن الله أفتاني في أمر استفتيته فيه أتاني رجلان فجلس أحدهما عند رجلي والآخر عند رأسي فقال الذي عند رجلي للذي عند رأسي ما بال الرجل قال مطبوب يعني مسحورا قال ومن طبه قال لبيد بن أعصم قال وفيم قال في جف طلعة ذكر في مشط ومشاقة تحت رعوفة في بئر ذروان فجاء النبي صلى الله عليه وسلم فقال هذه البئر التي أريتها كأن رءوس نخلها رءوس الشياطين وكأن ماءها نقاعة الحناء فأمر به النبي صلى الله عليه وسلم فأخرج قالت عائشة فقلت يا رسول الله فهلا تعني تنشرت فقال النبي صلى الله عليه وسلم أما الله فقد شفاني وأما أنا فأكره أن أثير على الناس شرا قالت وليد بن أعصم رجل من بني زريق حليف ليهود

Now, by studying the previous hadith we would learn that:

1. Muhammad had sexual issues.
2. He cannot perform a normal sexual life and witness of this is his most beloved baby-wife 'Aisha.
3. He made up a story to solve the issue or come up with an excuse.
4. However, this story creates a new problem for Muhammad and Islam.
5. Possessed with Devils. See The Deception of Allah Volume 1.

Muhammad's hallucinations

Pay attention to what the hadith reads: "There came to me two men, one of them drew near my feet and the other near my head. The one near my feet, asked the one near my head, 'What is wrong with this man?'"

Hearing voices of two men talking when no one had spoken.

1. In the Muslims
   Muslims claim
   translation of this hadith, they added this sentence: "This is the same well which was shown to me **in the dream**."
2. The fact is that the previous Arabic hadith didn't mention "**in the dream**" as they have been added.
3. The answer is easy. They added the words "**in the dream**" to cover Muhammad's **hallucinations** of seeing patterns like two men, a comb and hair stuck to it, hearing voices, and seeing objects that aren't there.

Sahih Al-Bukhari, Book 54, Hadith 438

Reported 'Aisha: "Al 'Harith Ibn Hisham asked the Prophet, 'How does the God Almighty's inspiration come to you?' He (Muhammad) answered 'In all these methods The angel sometimes comes to me with a voice which is the likeness as sound of a ringing bell, and when this state withdraws from me, I remember what the angel had said, and this type of God Almighty's inspiration is the most difficult task on me; and often the angel comes to me in the shape of a man and talks to me, and I understand and remember what he told me."

- "The angel sometimes comes to me with a voice which is the **likeness as sound of a ringing bell**." How did the angel come to him in the shape of a man and why would he come to him with a sound of a bell, which no one else can hear but Muhammad alone? What's funny is that Muhammad said in another hadith that angels do not accompany people with a sound of a bell!

Sahih Muslim, Book 024, Hadith 5277

Abu Huraira stated Allah's Messenger (may Allah pray on him and salute him) as saying: "Angels do not accompany the travelers who have with them a dog and a bell".

- Another example of Muhammad's madness and contradictions:

Sahih Muslim, Book 024, Hadith 5279

Abu Huraira stated Allah's Messenger (may Allah pray on him and salute him) saying: The bell is the melodious instrument of Satan.

1. But he said that the angel came to him with sound of a bell!
2. Of all the Muslim prophets, why was it only Muhammad that heard sounds of ringing bells?
3. Why is inspiration, which comes with the sound of a bell, the most difficult task for Muhammad? **"Inspiration is the most difficult task on me"**.

Sahih Muslim, Book 030, Hadith 5765

'Aisha stated that Harith Ibn Hisham, that he questioned Allah's Messenger (may Allah pray on him and salute him): How does the inspiration come to you? He said, sometimes, it comes to me the likeness of the ringing of a bell, until it's like destroying me and that is the most difficult task for me and when it is over, I retain that inspiration, and now and then an angel in the shape of a human being comes talking to me, and I was aware of whatever he spoke.

And below is the original text in Arabic for the above translation:

(الترمذي 2333) ، مسلم الفضائل (2عن عائشة رضي الله عنها أن الحارث بن هشام رضي الله تعالى عنه البخاري بدء الوحي (
). سأل رسول الله صلى الله عليه وسلم كيف (474) ، مالك النداء للصلاة (6/257) ، أحمد (934) ، النسائي الافتتاح (3634المناقب (
يأتيك الوحي؟ فقال : أحيانًا يأتيني مثل صلصلة الجرس ، وهو أشده عليّ ، فيقصم عنّي وقد وعيت منه ما قال : وأحيانًا يتمثل لي
الملك رجلًا فيكلمني فأعي مايقول . . . الخ

The hadith below has a lot of fabrication in the translation. Those that are between the two brackets are not part of the hadith at all, but Muslims had to add these to make you believe that this is the angel who came to Muhammad:

The hadith according to Muslim's translation:

> *Narrated Abu Ishaq-Ash-Shaibani: I asked Zir bin Hubaish regarding the Statement of Allah: "And was at a distance Of but two bow-lengths or (even) nearer; So, did (Allah) convey The Inspiration to His slave (Gabriel) and then he (Gabriel) Conveyed (that to Muhammad). (53.9-10) On that, Zir said, "Ibn Mas'ud informed us that the Prophet had seen Gabriel having 600 wings."*

The Hadith above is from the Qur'an but for sure, Muslims all agree that in that verse and this hadith, Muhammad saw an angel. because the smart one who speaks Arabic, will notice immediately that this can't be a story about seeing an angel, since the correct translation is:

> *"And was at a distance Of but two bow-lengths or nearer; So, He did convey The Inspiration to His slave." (53.9-10)*

However, I will leave this topic for another time so we can go ahead with Muhammad's Angels.

Allah Sent Sexy Gay Angels to Lut city!!!

From the book of Al-Bidaia Wa Al-Nihaia By Imam Ibn Kathir Vol (1) Page.41

> *"Allah sent his angels to people of prophet lot the angels came in the image of handsome men to the city of Sodom. This was intended for Allah to test his people so that he would use that as a proof against them when he would send them his punishment." And the angel Gabriel use to come to the prophet in may Allah pray on him in many looks or shapes, some time he come in the look of Dahia Al Kalbi(a very good looking man use to come to Muhammad a lot),and some time he come as an Arabian man, and some time in his real look as Allah created him with 600 wings the distance between each is the same distance between east and the west! and he came to him in this way (with 600 wings) twice."*

Its funny to learn that the good god of Islam sends handsome, **gay**

angels to seduce men on earth and have sex with them so that Allah can take it as a proof against them!
I wish I could make a movie about it so that Muslims would see how silly and insulting this story is. And for Muslims who might not believe it, please buy the book of Ibn Kathir or visit this very Islamic Arabic site.
http://islamport.com/w/tkh/Web/927/41.htm

أن الملائكة تبدو ا لهم في صورة شباب حسان إمتحانا و اختبار ا حتى قامت على قوم لوط الحجة و أخذهم الله أخذ عزيز مقتدر *
) وتارة في اوكذلك كان جبريل يأتي إلى النبي صلى الله عليه وسلم في صفات متعددة فتارة يأتي في صورة دحية بن خليفة الكلبي (
.صورة أعرابي وتارة في صورته التي خلق عليها
له ستمائة جناح ما بين كل جناحين كما بين
المشرق والمغرب كما ر آه على هذه الصفة مرتين

(Sahih Al-Bukhari, Volume 4, Book 54, Number 458)

Narrated Masruq: I asked Aisha "What about His Statement: "Then he (Gabriel) approached And came closer, And was at a distance Of but two bow-lengths Or nearer" (53.8-9) She replied, "It was Gabriel who used to come to the Prophet in the figure of a man, but on that occasion, he came in his actual and real figure and (he was so huge) that he covered the whole horizon."

After reading the above texts, is the bell a good sound or a satanic sound?

What we understand from this is that the angel, or who Muslims call angel, came to Muhammad in two shapes:

Gabriel has 600 wings.
Sahih Al-Bukhari, Book 54, Hadith 455
Arabic Sahih Al-Bukhari, Book of Tafsir Al-Qur'an, Suret Al
Najem, Vol. 4, p. 1841, Hadith 4576

Reported by Abu Ishaq-Al-Shaibani: "I asked Zerr bin Hubaish concerning the Statement of Allah in Qur'an 53, 9-10: 'And was at a distance of but two bow-lengths, or nearer; So He conveyed the inspiration to His slave'. On that, Zerr said, 'Ibn Mas'ud informed us that the Prophet had seen Gabriel having 600 wings.'"

http://www.usc.edu/org/cmje/religious-texts/hadith/bukhari/054-sbt.php

Below is the original text in Arabic for the above translation.

صحيح البخاري   » كتاب تفسير القرآن   » سورة والنجم ،   » باب قوله فأوحى إلى عبده ما أوحى »
] باب قوله فأوحى إلى عبده ما أوحى1841ص: [
4576 حدثنا طلق بن غنام حدثنا زائدة عن الشيباني قال سألت زرا عن قوله تعالى فكان قاب قوسين أو أدنى فأوحى إلى عبده ما
أوحى قال أخبرنا عبد الله أن محمدا صلى الله عليه وسلم رأى جبريل له ست مائة جناح

This hadith has a big problem. It says that the one who came down inspired Muhammad, which means that he did not talk to him, because inspiration dose not invlove talking, If the angel Gabriel inspires that will contradict the teachings of Islam, in which inspirations come only from Allah, tin that case the angels can only speak to prophets but do not inspire.

This would prove my point that it cannot be an angel: "So He conveyed the inspiration to His slave." If it's an angel, how can Muhammad be called **His slave**?

Note that in the Muslims
Muslims claim
translation to the hadith, they added many false words that aren't even there to cover this issue as we would see in this link:
http://www.searchtruth.com/book_display.php?book=54&translator=1&start=0&number=455#455
This is why I posted the hadith up in Arabic to prove their deception because if the one who came down called Muhammad his slave, it must therefore be Allah and it would also mean that Muhammad lied because he said that he has never seen his god as stated in the Qur'an:
Qur'an 6:103

لَا تُدْرِكُهُ الْأَبْصَارُ وَهُوَ يُدْرِكُ الْأَبْصَارَ

[103] *Vision reach Him not, but He sees all.*

But for now, we will focus on Gabriel, the 600-wing angel.

- How was Muhammad able to see the one no one can look at in his true shape? Is it because of the strength of his light?
- How was Muhammad able to count his 600 wings? That would mean Muhammad was looking at the angel for many hours while Gabriel was on standstill. And this is the angel Gabriel's true form or shape, as we see in Sahih Al-Bukhari, 4, Book 54, Number 455:

Narrated Abu Ishaq-Ash-Shaibani: I asked Zir bin Hubaish regarding the Statement of Allah: "And was at a distance Of but two bow-lengths Or (even) nearer; So did (Allah) convey The Inspiration to His slave (Gabriel) and then he (Gabriel) Conveyed (that to Muhammad). (53.9-10) On that, Zir said, "Ibn Mas'ud informed us that the Prophet had seen Gabriel having 600 wings."

صحيح البخاري » كتاب تفسير القرآن » سورة والنجم » باب قوله فأوحى إلى عبده ما أوحى
مسألة: الجزء الرابع
[باب قوله فأوحى إلى عبده ما أوحى1841ص:]

4576 حدثنا طلق بن غنام حدثنا زائدة عن الشيباني قال سألت زرا عن قوله تعالى فكان قاب قوسين أو أدنى فأوحى إلى عبده ما
أوحى قال أخبرنا عبد الله أن محمدا صلى الله عليه وسلم رأى جبريل له ست مائة جناح

Which is a very clear contradiction to Qur'an chapter 35 verse 1. لا تدركه الأبصار وهو يدرك الأبصار
This verse states that angels only have either two or three or four wings.

Qur'an 35:1

"All praise is due to Allah, the Originator of the heavens and the earth, the Maker of the angels, apostles flying on wings, two, and three, and four; He increases in creation what He pleases; surely Allah has power over all things."

trans/ of Muhammad shakir
http://www.searchtruth.com/chapter_display.php?chapter=35&translator=3#1

Which means:
1. They are not sent in the form of men as messengers but they are **messengers with wings**.
2. Angels are messengers that have **two or three or four wings.** Some would have two or three or four pairs of wings. This means that the maximum wings Allah Angels can have is **eight wings.** So how did Muhammad come up with 600?

Sahih Al-Bukhari, Book 54, Hadith 457

Reported Aisha: "Whoever stated that Muhammad saw His Lord (Allah), is committing a great sin for he only saw Gabriel in his genuine shape in the way he was created covering the whole horizon."

Sahih Al-Bukhari, Vol. 6, Book 60, Number 378

"'Aisha added "But the Prophet saw Gabriel in his true form twice" Qur'an 5:67

So what we understand is Muhammad has seen the angel Gabriel in his true shape. But this story creates a problem:
- **Gabriel is so large "covering the whole horizon".** With such a size, it means he will hide the sun and will be seen from hundreds of miles away. But how come it was only Muhammad who have seen him?
- How was Muhammad able to see the angel in his true form when the Qur'an says no one would be able to as Allah always sends his angels in the shape of men, as stated in the following Qur'anic verse:
Qur'an 6:9, Yusuf Ali's translation

"If We had made it an angel, We should have sent him as a

man, and We should certainly have caused them confusion in a matter which they have already covered with confusion."

This is clear statement from Allah or the veers maker, as long as Muslims claim that Allah is the author of the Qur'an. Whenever he sends his angel, he would always send him as a man because if he doesn't, **"We should certainly have caused them confusion."**

See the Muslim translation of Ibn Kathir's interpretation:

http://www.qtafsir.com/index.php?option=com_content&task=view&id=10 22&Itemid=61#3

By the way, there is not even one honest Islamic translation but we will use it because even after their makeup, we can still expose the errors. This is why I'm using the original Arabic.

Tafsir Ibn Kathir, Vol. 3, p. 242

"If an angel was sent to them, he would come in the shape of a man. This is because they (humans) will not be able to look at the angel due to the strength of his light."

Below is the original text in Arabic for the above translation.

تفسير ابن كثير

إسماعيل بن عمر بن كثير القرشي الدمشقي

" تفسير القرآن العظيم » تفسير سورة الأنعام » تفسير قوله تعالى " ولو نزلنا عليك كتابا في قرطاس فلمسوه بأيديهم

242الجزء الثالث صفحة

عن ابن عباس في [قوله : (ولو جعلناه ملكا لجعلناه رجلا)] الآية . يقول : لو أتاهم ملك ما أتاهم إلا في صورة رجل ؛ لأنهم لا يستطيعون النظر إلى الملائكة من النور (وللبسنا عليهم ما يلبسون) أي : ولخلطنا عليهم ما يخلطون . وقال الوالبي عنه: ولشبهنا عليهم .

So angels are made of light and this light is so strong to the point that you wouldn't be able to see. This why Allah had to send his angel as a man as we saw in Ibn Kathir's interpretation, which matches this following hadith:

Sahih Muslim, Book 042, Hadith 7134

'Aisha reported that Allah's Messenger (may Allah pray on him and salute him) said, "The angels were created of light, and the jinn's were created of blazing fire (fire with no smoke), and Adam was created as he had been described for you."

Below is the original text in Arabic for the above translation.

صحيح مسلم» كتاب الزهد والرقائق » باب في أحاديث متفرقة

حدثنا محمد بن رافع وعبد بن حميد قال عبد أخبرنا وقال ابن رافع حدثنا عبد الرزاق أخبرنا معمر عن الزهري عن عروة 2996 عن عائشة قالت قال رسول الله صلى الله عليه وسلم خلقت الملائكة من نور وخلق الجان من مارج من نار وخلق آدم مما وصف لكم

This means that Muhammad lied about seeing the angel in his true look or form with 600 wings. And as long as Islam is based on the story of Allah's inspiration given to Muhammad through the angel Gabriel, we can prove that Muhammad lied about this angel through his own words, contradicting himself and his claimed god. Therefore, Muhammad is surely a false prophet due to his falsification or due to his hallucinations.

Muhammad is the only universal prophet:

One of the Muslims
Muslims claim
 claims is that Jesus and Moses were prophets sent to the Jews. And same as Jesus, Muhammad was the only prophet to the world. I will show you that Muslims don't even read their own book which contradicts every word they claim.

Islam and the racism

If Muhammad is the universal prophet for all of mankind, then Muslims should explain why their prophet considers the black Africans as trouble makers that even the sky and earth are disgusted with their (black Africans) behaviors and voices. Let us look at references from Muhammad's own words.

Muhammad's prophecy towards the black people

The book of Kanz al-'Ummal by Alî Muttaqî al-Hindî, vol. 11, p. 177.

31117 - Narrated by Ibn Abbas from the prophet that Noah said, "don't be happy that you brought the sons of Ham they are cursed by Noah, peace upon him, I swear by him whom my soul in his hand, I see them (the black ones) as nothing but the Devils traveled between the flags of Tribulations, they have unclear voices in their chest, and the voice of a zebra, storms blow because of their act and the earth is troubled because of their acts, they have no respect to my own people and to my religion, the one who reached that time, they should cry on Islam if they can cry."

Below is the original text in Arabic for the above translation.

كنز العمال - للمتقي الهندي
المجلد الحادي عشر >> تتمة الفتن من الإكمال(11/177)

لا تفرحوا بجلب بني حام الملعونين على لسان نوح عليه السلام، والذي نفسي بيده! لكأني بهم كالشياطين قد داروا بين -31117
رايات الفتن لهم همهمة وزمزمة، تهب السماء وتعج الأرض من أعمالهم، لا يرعون عن حرمة ذمتي ولا ملتي، ألا! فمن
أدرك ذلك الزمان فليبك على الإسلام إن كان باكيا.
عن حذيفة قال : إذا رأيتم أول الترك بالجزيرة فقاتلوهم حتى تهزموهم أو يكفيكم الله مؤنتهم ! فانهم يفضحون 31298 (11/219)
الحرم بها فهو علامة خروج أهل المغرب واتقاض ملك ملكهم.
المجلد الحادي عشر >> تتمة الفتن من الإكمال كنز العمال ـ للمتقي الهندي(11/414)
إن الله تعالى خلق خلقه فجعلهم فريقين فجعلني في خير الفريقين ، ثم جعلهم قبائل فجعلني في خير قبيلة ، ثم جعلهم بيوتا 31949
فجعلني في خيرهم بيتا ، فانا خيركم قبيلة وخيركم بيتا.

Tabari, Vol. 2:21 – The Ham offspring (Africans) are all those black and curly-haired, while the Japheth offspring (Turks) are all those who are full-faced with small eyes, and the Shem offspring (Arabs) are those who have handsome faces with beautiful hair. Noah prayed that the hair of Ham's descendants would not grow beyond their ears, and that whenever his lineage meet the children of Shem, the succeeding would enslave them.

Racism to Asians

Sahih Muslim, Book 041, Hadith 6959

Abu Huraira reported Allah's ambassador (may Allah pray on him and salute him) his statement The Last Hour would not come until the Muslims fight with the Turks- people whose faces would be like hammered shields wearing shoes made of hair.

Below is the original text in Arabic for the above translation.

صحيح مسلم - كتاب الفتن وأشراط الساعة ـ لا تذهب الأيام والليالي حتى يملك رجل يقال له الجهجاه
حَدَّثَنَا أَبُو بَكْرِ بْنُ أَبِي شَيْبَةَ وَابْنُ أَبِي عُمَرَ وَاللَّفْظُ لاِبْنِ أَبِي عُمَرَ قَالاَ حَدَّثَنَا سُفْيَانُ عَنْ الزُّهْرِيِّ عَنْ سَعِيدٍ عَنْ أَبِي 2912 5184
هُرَيْرَةَ أَنَّ النَّبِيَّ صَلَّى اللَّهُ عَلَيْهِ وَسَلَّمَ قَالَ لاَ تَقُومُ السَّاعَةُ حَتَّى تُقَاتِلُوا قَوْمًا كَأَنَّ وُجُوهَهُمْ الْمَجَانُّ الْمُطْرَقَةُ وَلاَ تَقُومُ السَّاعَةُ حَتَّى تُقَاتِلُوا
قَوْمًا نِعَالُهُمْ الشَّعْرُ

Sahih Al-Bukhari, Book 56, Hadith 787
Arabic book Hadith 3394

Reported Abu Huraira: that Allah's Messenger said, "Judgment Day will not be demonstrated until you fight a nation wearing shoes made from hair and until you fight the Turks who will have small eyes, red faces and flat noses; and their faces will be like level shields. And you will find that the best people are those who hate the obligation to fight them most of all, until they are chosen to fight. And the people are of different natures: The best of the people who were before the Islamic period were the best ones in Islam also. A time will

come when any of you will love to see me instead of your
families and wealth to be doubled."

صحيح البخاري ـ كِتَاب الْمَنَاقِب ـ فتنة الرجل في أهله وماله وجاره وتكفرها الصلاة
حَدَّثَنَا أَبُو الْيَمَانِ أَخْبَرَنَا شُعَيْبٌ حَدَّثَنَا أَبُو الزِّنَادِ عَنْ الْأَعْرَجِ عَنْ أَبِي هُرَيْرَةَ رَضِيَ اللَّهُ عَنْهُ عَنْ النَّبِيِّ صَلَّى اللَّهُ عَلَيْهِ وَسَلَّمَ قَالَ 3394
لَا تَقُومُ السَّاعَةُ حَتَّى تُقَاتِلُوا قَوْمًا نِعَالُهُمْ الشَّعَرُ وَحَتَّى تُقَاتِلُوا صِغَارَ الْأَعْيُنِ حُمْرَ الْوُجُوهِ ذُلْفَ الْأُنُوفِ كَأَنَّ وُجُوهَهُمْ الْمَجَانُّ
الْمُطْرَقَةُ وَتَجِدُونَ مِنْ خَيْرِ النَّاسِ أَشَدَّهُمْ كَرَاهِيَةً لِهَذَا الْأَمْرِ حَتَّى يَقَعَ فِيهِ وَالنَّاسُ مَعَادِنُ خِيَارُهُمْ فِي الْجَاهِلِيَّةِ خِيَارُهُمْ فِي الْإِسْلَامِ
وَلَيَأْتِيَنَّ عَلَى أَحَدِكُمْ زَمَانٌ لَأَنْ يَرَانِي أَحَبُّ إِلَيْهِ مِنْ أَنْ يَكُونَ لَهُ مِثْلُ أَهْلِهِ وَمَالِهِ

A'hkam Al-Qur'an, by Imam Al-Qur'tubi, print year 1999,
Beirut Lebanon, Vol. 8, Chapter 9:49, pages 87, 88:

"Attack them [the Romans] so you can get the blond girls, so
that Al-Jed said, to him [to the prophet] "do not practice
sexual temptation on us". The prophet said to the people, who
is your leader children of Salama? They said, Al-Jed Ibn Qais.
But he is cheap and coward. The prophet said, and what is the
solution for someone he is it cheap and coward? From today
your leader is Bisher Ibn Al-Bar'a Ibn Ma'rror.

Below is the original text in Arabic for the above translation.

أن رسول الله صلى الله عليه وسلم قال : اغزوا تغنموا بنات الأصفر . فقال له الجد: إذن لنا ولا تفتنا بالنساء وهذا منزع غير الأول ،
[من سيدكم 88وهو أشبه بالنفاق والمحادة . ولما نزلت قال النبي صلى الله عليه وسلم لبني سلمة ـ وكان الجد بن قيس منهم: [ص:
يا بني سلمة ؟ قالوا : جد بن قيس ، غير أنه بخيل جبان . فقال النبي صلى الله عليه وسلم : وأي داء أدوى من البخل بل سيدكم الفتى
: الأبيض بشر بن البراء بن معرور . فقال حسان بن ثابت الأنصاري فيه

Actually, if we study the last hadith, we would find the evil side of
Muhammad very obvious. He did not tell his men to fight the *Kfar*
(unbelievers) who don't believe in Allah. He did not even say that the
goal of the war is to make them believe in the true God. Instead, he used
sexual temptation by saying that those who would attack with him will get
the blond girls. And when one of the men (leader of his tribe) told
Muhammad not to tempt them, exposing the true face of Muhammad, the
latter did not hesitate to get rid of him and force a new leader on this
tribe. Suddenly, the one refusing sexual temptations becomes a bad
leader, a cheap leader, and a coward.

The Devil is black!

The one who will destroy the Kaaba is a black man from Ethiopia, before
the Last Hour:

Sahih Al-Bukhari, Book 26, Hadiths 661, 665, 666

Reported Ibn Abbas: The Prophet said, "As if I were watching
him, a black person with skinny legs tearing out the stones of

the Kaaba one after one."

The same story can be found in Ibn Kathir's interpretation and Sahih Al-Bukhari by following this link:
www.qtafsir.com/index.php?option=com_content&task=view&id=301&Ite mid=36

Below is the original text in Arabic for the above translation.

538صحيح البخاري» كتاب الحج » باب هدم الكعبة ص:
حدثنا عمرو بن علي حدثنا يحيى بن سعيد حدثنا عبيد الله بن الأخنس حدثني ابن أبي مليكة عن ابن عباس رضي الله عنهما 1518
عن النبي صلى الله عليه وسلم قال كأني به أسود أفحج يقلعها حجرا حجرا

We would learn from the hadiths above the following:
♦ It is so clear that Muhammad considers every black person ugly and evil to the point that even Satan himself is black and the one who will destroy the Kaaba is black too.
♦ He described the Turkish people in a very degrading way. Not only did he mention their ethnic group but he also described their facial attributes and the clothes they wore. In case you do not know, the Turkish before can be called true. They were pure Asian nation.
♦ Then we see Muhammad encouraging Muslims to fight the white blond to get the blond women, which meant that he loved the white race but only wanted from them the blond women. That explains why Muhammad promised his men that the *Hoor* (beautiful, white females with big black eyes), which Allah promises every Muslim in heaven, are going to be so white to the point they'll be able to see through their bones.

No black individual, male nor female, will enter heaven

Qur'an 55:72

"Hoor (beautiful, white females with big black eyes) jailed inside their tents."

Sahih Al-Bukhari, Book 54, Hadith 476

Reported Abu Huraira: "The Prophet said, 'The first group (of Muslims) who will enter Paradise will be glittering like the full moon, and the batch next to them will be shining like the most brilliant star in the sky. Their hearts will be as if the heart of a single man of [as if they are one man], for they will have neither hatred nor jealousy among themselves; everyone will have two wives from the hooris, who will be so beautiful, pure, white and transparent to the point the marrow of the bones of their legs will be seen through their bones and their flesh.'"

1. Now, shouldn't we ask ourselves why Allah never promised black women for the Arab men in heaven? These are the reasons:
2. No black individual, male nor female, will enter heaven.
3. It's very obvious that Allah did not consider black women attractive. As a matter of fact, having black skin is a curse as in the Judgment Day, Allah says in the Qur'an that he will make all the Muslims white and all infidels black, for it is a punishment in Islam to be black while it's a reward to be white. As we see in:

(Qur'an يَوْمَ تَبْيَضُّ وُجُوهٌ وَتَسْوَدُّ وُجُوهٌ *3:106)*

Qur'an 3:106 Mohsin Khan's translation

[106] *"On the Day (i.e. the Day of Resurrection) when some faces will become white and some faces will become black; as for those whose faces will become black (to them will be said): 'Did you reject Faith after accepting it? Then taste the torment (in Hell) for rejecting Faith.'"*

Now you might ask yourself how did Muhammad come up with the word *"Hooris or Hoor"*? As long as Allah is the one who chose this word in the Qur'an, this word should then be unique, as what is found in heaven cannot be found on earth.

Sahih Al-Bukhari, Book 93, Hadith 589

Sahih Al-Bukhari, Book 60, Hadith 302, 303

Reported by Abu Huraira that the prophet said, "Allah revealed 'I have prepared for my good servants (in heaven) as no eye has ever seen and no ear has ever heard and no man can ever imagine'".

The fact is that it is not. The promise of the *Hooris* is false as even the name itself already had existed long before the time of Islam. This can be proved in the book of Jame' Al Baiyan fe Tafsir Al Qur'an, Year 310, Islamic, Vol. 6, p. 451.

[7128] *"the Arabs called the women who live in villages and cities hooris for they are white".*

Below is the original text in Arabic for the above translation.

" تفسير الطبري " تفسير سورة آل عمران « القول في تأويل قوله تعالى " فلما أحس عيسى منهم الكفر قال من أنصاري إلى الله
الجزء السادسص451
. " إن لكل نبي حواريا ، وحواري الزبير " - 7128
يعني خاصته. وقد تسمي العرب النساء اللواتي مساكنهن القرى والأمصار " حواريات " وإنما سمين بذلك لغلبة البياض عليهن

And that is why the promises of Allah fit with the mentality of the Bedouins in their condition as desert inhabitants, as He promises them to have no heat in the heaven.

> *Qur'an 77:41, Yusuf Ali's translation*
>
> *As to the Righteous, they shall be amidst (cool) shades and springs (of water).*

Surely, if Muhammad was speaking to someone living in Alaska, he would not promise him cold. Or if Muhammad was speaking to Europeans, he wouldn't promise them blond women but tanned ones. Therefore, Arabs always longed to have white women as no blond women existed in Arabia. Muhammad promised the Bedouin men blond women and what they miss in their lives. As showed to you earlier, he was encouraging the men to fight for them to get the blond women and then exaggerated the description of those *hooris* since he knew how much Arab men dream of having sex with white women. So he promised them women who are so white that they'll even be able to see through the their bones, which is by the way very disgusting. Imagine yourself looking at an x-ray photo of a woman's live body, seeing everything in it move like the blood running, the food being processed, and everything else.

> *Qur'an 3:106 Mohsin Khan's translation*
>
> 106 *"On the Day (i.e. the Day of Resurrection) when some faces will become white and some faces will become black;"*

Now I want to explain a little bit more about this chapter which speaks about faces turning black or white, because Muslims might try to fool you and say that it is just metaphorical. I will prove that it is not. Let's read:

> *Tafsir Al-Baher Al-Mu'he't, Vol. 5, p. 148*
>
> *The interpretation of the chapter of Yunis*
>
> *"Their faces would be black for reality not a metaphorical so it's going to be the color black".*

تفسير البحر المحيط » تفسير سورة يونس » تفسير قوله تعالى للذين أحسنوا الحسنى وزيادة ولا يرهق وجوههم قتر ولا ذلة [ص:
الجزء الخامس148]
الغشاء . وكون وجوههم مسودة هي حقيقة لا مجاز ، فتكون ألوانهم مسودة .

Tafsir Ibn Kathir:

"On the Day the Day of Resurrection) when some faces will become white and some faces will become black; as for those whose faces will become black (to these it will be said): "Did you reject faith after accepting it Then taste the torment in Hell fire? for rejecting Islam. 'And for those whose faces will become white, they will be in Allah's mercy (Going to Paradise), therein they shall dwell forever.)

http://www.islam-universe.com/tafsir_ibn_kathir/3.8983.html

Al ShifaV.12 p.64

"Anyone who says that the Prophet was black should be killed."

. من قال: إن النبي ـ صلى الله عليه وسلم ـ كان أسود يقتل :وقال أحمد بن أبي سليمان صاحب سحنون

We know some Muslims today like the "Nation of Islam" claim that Muhammad was black, however this is absolutely false, and its punished in Islam to say so about Muhammad by death, for it is considered as an insult the white man Muhammad.

> *Abu Hurayra described the Messenger of Allah, may Allah pray on him and salute him, with the words, "He was of medium height, but nearer to being tall. He was very white with a black beard" Al-Adab Al-Mufrad Book 47, Hadith 1155*

Later on, we will give further explanations on Qur'an 27:82 which is the story of the beast.

Let's continue with Islam and racism.

My Muslim friend

Muslims are not allowed to associate with nonbelievers in any way or in any means even if its biological father or brother.

Muslims might say to you that this is not true. They might even say that they are allowed to marry whether Jews or Christians. As a fact, the Qur'an says it is forbidden to befriend your own family members as long as they are none Muslims we see in: Qur'an 9:23

but before I show you the Qur'an I will show you clear evidence from Islamic official sites, where Muslims ask their leaders for guidelines regarding the accurate understanding of Islam;

this is ben taking from this site where Muslims ask for the right answers from their holy leaders;
we quote

***

http://islamqa.info/en/59879

"59879: What is meant by taking the kuffaar as friends? Ruling on mixing with the kuffaar?

First:

Allah has forbidden the believers to take the kaafireen (disbelievers) as friends, and He has issued a stern warning against doing that.

Allah says (interpretation of the meaning):

"O you who believe! Take not the Jews and the Christians as Awliyaa' (friends, protectors, helpers), they are but Awliyaa' of each other. And if any amongst you takes them (as Awliyaa'), then surely, he is one of them. Verily, Allah guides not those people who are the Zaalimoon (polytheists and wrongdoers and unjust)"

[al-Maa'idah 5:51]

Shaykh al-Shanqeeti (may Allah have mercy on him) said:

In this verse Allah tells us that whoever takes the Jews and Christians as friends is one of them because of his taking them as friends. Elsewhere Allah states that taking them as friends incurs the wrath of Allah and His eternal punishment, and that if the one who takes them as friends was a true believer he would not have taken them as friends. Allah says (interpretation of the meaning):

"You see many of them taking the disbelievers as their Awliyaa' (protectors and helpers). Evil indeed is that which their ownselves have sent forward before them; for that (reason) Allah's Wrath fell upon them, and in torment they will abide.

81. And had they believed in Allah, and in the Prophet (Muhammad) and in what has been revealed to him, never would they have taken them (the disbelievers) as Awliyaa' (protectors and helpers); but many of them are the Faasiqoon (rebellious, disobedient to Allah)"

[al-Maa'idah 5:80-81] "

End of quote

***

That being said still the Muslim can be nice to you in order to make you convert to Islam as a way of deception but not for any other reason! We quote from the same site;

***

"Based on this, it is not permissible for a Muslim to feel any love in his heart towards the enemies of Allah who are in fact his enemies too. Allah says (interpretation of the meaning):

"O you who believe! Take not My enemies and your enemies (i.e. disbelievers and polytheists) as friends, showing affection towards them, while they have disbelieved in what has come to you of the truth"
[al-Mumtahanah 60:1]

But if a Muslim treats them with kindness and gentleness in the hope that they will become Muslim and will believe, there is nothing wrong with that, because it comes under the heading of opening their hearts to Islam. But if he despairs of them becoming Muslim, then he should treat them accordingly. This is something that is discussed in detail by the scholars, especially in the book Ahkaam Ahl al-Dhimmah by Ibn al-Qayyim (may Allah have mercy on him).

Majmoo' Fataawa al-Shaykh Ibn 'Uthaymeen, 3, question no. 389"

End of quote

***

Qur'an 2:221

"Do not marry from the non-believing women up to the time that they believe: A slave woman who believes is better than a non-believing woman, even though she attracts you. Nor marry your girls to unbelievers up to the time that they believe: A man slave who believes is to a greater degree than an unbeliever, even though he interests you. Unbelievers will be cold for the hell-fire. However, and Allah, He called to heaven and forgiveness, and forgive your sin by His permission, maybe they shall remember."

Later on, Muhammad figured that if he allowed Muslim men to marry Christian and Jewish women, it would give him the chance to increase the number of Muslims. At the same time, Christian men and Jews would be short of women and their number would decrease. So Muhammad

41

changed his mind again and allowed them to marry from the Christian and Jewish women but forbade Muslim women to marry Christian and Jewish men. This shows that the purpose of allowing these marriages is just to create more Muslim babies because the babies would always belong to the father. As the fathers are Muslims, the babies will be of same faith. **So, he came up with Qur'an 5:5 and said, "it is lawful for you to marry from the People of the Book's chaste women."**

And we did speak in *The Deception of Allah Volume 1*, that Muslims cannot take us as friends and protectors even if we are from their own family members as stated in You can't be a friend to your own mother or father or brother if they are not Muslims.

Qur'an 9:23 Pickthall

O ye who believe! Choose not your fathers nor your brethren for friends if they take pleasure in disbelief rather than faith. Whoso of you taketh them for friends, such are wrong-doers.

Qur'an 9:113.

It is not for the Prophet, and those who believe, to pray for the forgiveness of idolaters even though they may be family members (even though they should be near relatives) after it hath become clear that they are people of hell-fire.

Having said that, I will not mention it again but I will support my point with one more verse.

Qur'an 58:22

"You shall not find from the people who believe in Allah and the latter-day anyone who will be befriending those who act in disapproval Allah and His Messenger, even though they are their own fathers, or their sons, or their brothers, or their family."

We would understand from the previous verse the following:
1. A Muslim can only befriend Muslims.
2. He is forbidden to befriend his own family including his brothers, sisters, father, and mother. Qur'an 58:22/9:23
3. If he is not allowed to associate with his own family just because they did not accept Islam, ask yourself if a Muslim is allowed to have real friendship or any kind of real relationship with you being an outsider, when even his own family has no chance of such thing.
4. Is it not racism to block or dissociate from people who are close

to you or from those who want to partner with you just because they are from a different color, ethnic, or religious background?

This is a total contradiction to the teaching of Jesus Christ that is to accept strangers as our own family. Otherwise, you don't deserve to be in Heaven.

> *Matthew 25:35 - KJV*
>
> *For I was an hungered, and ye gave me meat: I was thirsty, and ye gave me drink: I was a stranger, and ye took me in:*

Now remember that the reason why we are talking about the racism of Islam is not only to expose racism but to expose the false claims of Muhammad being an international and universal messenger. In the coming verse, we will see very clear racism and hatred to the point that Muhammad divided the world into two kinds: filthy and clean. **"infidels are filthy."**

> Qur'an 9:28
>
> *"O ye who believe! Truthfully, the infidels are filthy; so let them not, after this year allow them not to approach the Sacred Mosque. And if ye fear poorness soon will Allah enrich you, if He wills, out of His for Allah is All-knowing, All-wise.".*

You will notice in this verse that Allah told the Muslims not to be afraid of being poor. Muhammad made this chapter so as not to kill the business in the city as the entrepreneurs and merchants at that time were Jews and Christians. Actually, this is the reason why when Mecca became empty of Christians and Jews after Muhammad had killed them, he needed to create a source of income for the city. And so, he enforced the *Hajj* wherein it's a must for every Muslim, at least once in his lifetime, to visit Mecca. If he can afford it, he should do it every year. So, imagine how much money that would generate to the Muslims in Mecca as these visitors would spend money on food, hotel, transportation, gifts, etc.

Muslims in America always try to fool the African-Americans using the history of slavery in the West as their tool to make them hate their own country and hate Christianity. Muslims try to convince them that Christianity is the reason and that those who did it were the Christians. Muslims ignore the fact that the black Africans' sufferings have nothing to do with Christianity and the teachings of the Bible.

The Bible says with clear words that all of us are descendants of one man. At that same time, all of mankind is equal in the sight of God as we read:

1 Corinthians 12:13 - KJV

For by one Spirit are we all baptized into one body, whether we be Jews or Gentiles, whether we be bond or free; and have been all made to drink into one Spirit.

1. Our Lord loves the entire world with no exception:

John 3:16 - KJV

For God so loved the world, that he gave his only begotten Son, that whosoever believeth in him should not perish, but have everlasting life.

2. Our Lord made man in His image which means, when you discriminate the image of a man, you discriminate the image of God. As we read:

Genesis 1:26 - KJV

26 And God said, Let us make man in our image, after our likeness: and let them have dominion over the fish of the sea, and over the fowl of the air, and over the cattle, and over all the earth, and over every creeping thing that creepeth upon the earth.

3. Unity of nature and equality between all ethnic groups, gender, free or slave, as we read:

Galatians 3:28 - KJV

28 There is neither Jew nor Greek, there is neither bond nor free, there is neither male nor female: for ye are all one in Christ Jesus.

4. Education, salvation, love for all the world and all the nations, and all are invited to the Kingdom of God with no exception as we read in:

Matthew 28:19 – KJV

Go ye therefore, and teach all nations, baptizing them in the name of the Father, and of the Son, and of the Holy Ghost:

5. If you remember in *The Deception of Allah Volume 1*, pages 29 to 32, we spoke about the *Pact of 'Umar*, which forbids

Christians to learn the Qur'an or Islam, and forbids them to dress like Muslims. Christians are not allowed to use Muslim **names**, and Christians cannot bury their dead next to Muslim graveyards as Christians and Jews are dirty. Therefore, if all of this is not racism, what is? What would Muslims say if New York City made a sign and put in practice **Qur'an 9:28** intended for the Muslims only? Instead of forbidding the Christians, Jews, and infidels and calling them dirty, NYC would exchange these groups or names by applying them to Muslims and the sign would read: **"Muslims are not allowed to enter the city of New York for they are unclean."** If you look at the United Nations which is supposedly the biggest organization to defend human rights, you will notice how quiet they are about Islamic racism and anti-human right rules. You will notice that not even one European or Western country or government exposes or complains or acts to stop such ugly racism.

6. Imagine if U.N. would make it a crime to insult Islam. And the proposal was made by the Pakistani government with the majority of 23 members out of 47 nations as part of the Human Right Counsel approve that law which is a very clear violation of the right of criticism of free speech and the right of freedom of religion. According to the U.N. Human Right Counsel, I would be a criminal for criticizing Islam. At the same time, we are free to insult all the other religions with no exception.

7. When you enter Saudi Arabia, there are two kinds of residencies: one for the Muslims which have their outside covered white, and one for the non-Muslims which have their outside covered brown. As non-Muslims are dirty and Muslims clean, imagine if in USA or Canada or Australia, we would give immigrants Green cards or Residency cards based on their ethnic groups or religious background, and dividing them into two categories: dirty and clean. This is how ugly the truth is but nobody dares to speak about it. Someone like me speaking about it is surely risking his life. How many people on this earth are willing to risk their lives to say the truth as Martin Luther King did?

8. **You can work in Saudi Arabia but you cannot die!** One of the things people who go to work in Saudi Arabia need to know is that the Islamic law of the Saudi government forbids non-Muslims to be buried in the Kingdom. To avoid having non-Muslim graves in the land of Saudi Arabia, Islam forbids the burial of non-Muslims to keep it holy as the dead infidels will make it unclean. Imagine if we forbade the burial of Muslims because some racist individuals might think they are dirty.

You can read more about it in this article from *The Wall Street Journal*:
http://www.hvk.org/articles/0402/78.html

Free women & Slave women

> Yahya related to me from Malik from Naf'i that Abdullah ibn Umar said, "When the slave divorces his wife twice, she is unlawful for him until she has married another man, whether she is free or a slave. The **waiting period** of a free woman is three menstrual periods, and **waiting period** of a slave-girl is two menstrual periods. (Muwatta' Malik, Book 29, Hadith 29.17.50)

A free man must not marry a slave-girl

> "Malik said, "A free man must not marry a slave-girl when he can afford to marry a free-woman, and he should not marry a slave-girl when he cannot afford a free woman unless he fears fornication." (Muwatta' Malik, Book 28, Hadith #28.12.29)

Free-woman did the slave-girl in order to stop her husband from sleeping with slave-girl

> 'I have a slave-girl and I used to have sexual-intercourse with her. My wife went to her and suckled her breast. When I went to the girl, my wife told me to watch out, because she had suckled her!' Umar told him to beat his wife and to go to sleep with his slave-girl because kinship by suckling was only b(Muwatta' Malik, Book 30, Hadith 30.2.13)y the suckling of the young.' "

1. The man is married but yet he had the right to rape his slave-girl.
2. The poor slave-girl not only the man can suckle her and have sexual-intercourse, but she is on-call for all his house members, even female's ones.
3. Beat your wife!
4. Suckling a woman make her unlawful.

The fact 'Umar is wrong here about suckling young one because there was a chapter in the Qur'an about suckling and adult.

Breast Suckling for Adults in Islam!

(Sahih Muslim, Book 17, Hadith 31) (p. 1452)

"'Amrah reported that she heard Aisha discussing fosterage which (makes marriage) unlawful; and she (Aisha) said:

There was revealed in the Holy Qur'an ten clear suckling's, and then five clear (suckling's)."

but the Hadith above dose not show its meant for adult, then let us read this one.

But where is the verse in the Qur'an about Adult Breast-Suckling?

The Goat ate the Qur'an!

'the verse of stoning and of suckling an adult ten times was revealed, and they were written on a papers and kept under my pillow. When the Messenger of Allah expired and we were busy with his death, a goat entered and ate it (the pages).'
(Sunan Ibn Majah, Hadith 1944)

'A'isha reported that Sahlaa bint Suhail came to Allah's massager (Allah pray on him) and said: Messenger of Allah, I see on the face of Abu Huzaifa some bad thoughts on entering of Salim (who is slave) into (our house), whereupon Allah's Apostle said: Suckle him. She said: How can I suckle him as he is a grown-up man? Allah's Messenger smiled and said: I already know that he is a old man 'Amr has made this addition in his narration that he participated in the Battle of Badr and in the narration of Ibn 'Umar he said: Allah's Messenger laughed. (Sahih Al-Bukhari-Book 008, Hadith 3424)

in Muslim's made translated text, they changed the words to make Muhammad order look more modest, so instead of "I know he is an old man" they change it to "I know he is a young man" search the hadith in Muslims sites to see the fabrication in the translations

This is why I am posting the Arabic text as as its, and the underlined words is where it says "old man"

يا رسول الله إني أري في وجه أبي حذيفة من دخول سالم وهو حليفه فقال النبي صلى الله عليه وسلم أرضعيه قالت وكيف أرضعه وهو **رجل كبير** فتبسم رسول الله صلى الله عليه وسلم وقال قد علمت أنه **رجل كبير** زاد عمرو في حديثه وكان قد شهد بدرا وفي رواية بن أبي عمر فضحك رسول الله صلى الله عليه وسلم

Even Aisha, Muhammad's favored young wife used to do it in order to permit stranger men entering her private rooms.

Sahih Muslim Book 9, Hadith 2023 Arabic

(Sahih Muslim Vol. 3, Book 9, Hadith 1947) Eng

It was narrated from Zaynab bint Abi Salamah:

that the wives of the Prophet all differed with Aisha and refused to allow anyone with ties of breastfeeding like Salim, the freed salve of Abu Hudhaifah, to enter upon them. They said: "How do we know? That may be a concession granted only to Salim."

In Islam forbidding to look at woman's face, or shake her hand, but you can hold her breast and suck her nipples?

***

Muhammad the universal prophet

We now continue with the Muslims
Muslims claim
 claims about Muhammad being the only universal prophet, which is false. As an example, the story of Moses in the Qur'an tells that Moses was also sent by Allah to other nations and not only to the Jews. Notice here that Christians strongly believe that Moses was a Prophet for the Jews. Muslims today claim the same as we believe about Moses being a Messenger only to the Jews.

If Moses was sent to the Jews only, how would Muslims answer this verse in their Qur'an:

Qur'an 10:75-76

75 Then afterwards We (Allah) sent, Moses and Aaron to Pharaoh and his chiefs with Our Signs. However, they were arrogant: they were people in crimes, 76 when the Truth did come to them from Us (Allah), they said, "This is indeed obvious sorcery!"

1. Allah sent two messengers to Pharaoh.
2. Allah wanted Pharaoh to believe in him.
3. To make Pharaoh believe, Allah showed him signs which meant miracles.
4. So if Moses is a Prophet sent only to the Jews, why did Allah himself say, "I sent the two prophets to Pharaoh"?
5. In verse 76, it's clear that Allah wished to send them the truth (Islam) but they rejected it.
6. What's funny is that the Islamic Moses of the Qur'an later on got

angry and asked Allah not to make Pharaoh a Muslim!

Qur'an 10:88

Moses prayed: "Our Lord! Thou hast indeed bestowed on Pharaoh and his chiefs' brilliancy and wealth in the present life, so they might deceive men from Thy Path. So, our Lord, destroy the features of their wealth, and send hardness to their hearts, so they will not believe so they will see the painful punishment."

From Tafsir Al-Jalalayn, we would read the following:
"And Moses said, "Our Lord, You have indeed given Pharaoh and his council brilliancy and riches in the life of this world. Our Lord, You have given them this, so that they may lead mankind astray, as a result thereof, from Your way, from Your religion Islam."

And here we go again. Allah, who is the god of the Muslim Moses, tells us why he made Pharaoh rich and gave him power: so he might deceive his nation! This right here is another reason why I named my book *The Deception of Allah*.

Qur'an 7:136

So We did revenge from them: We drowned them in the sea, because they rejected Our Signs and failed to accept and believe our warning.

Qur'an 73:15

We have sent to you, as a messenger an apostle, to be a witness concerning you, the same as We sent an apostle to Pharaoh.

Qur'an 10:83

"However, none believed in Moses except the offspring of his people, because they (Egyptians) fear of Pharaoh and his chiefs, lest they should persecute them."

As you see, it's clear that Allah wanted Pharaoh to become a Muslim so he sent Moses the Messenger of the Jews! And when Pharaoh rejected Islam, Allah drowned him.

So Muslims have a false claim when they say that all other prophets were meant to be sent to their own nation when their Qur'an contradicts that as we see in verse:

Qur'an 14:4

And We never sent a messenger save with the language of his nation that he might make the message clear for them. Then Allah sends which He will astray, and guides whom He will. He is the all Mighty, the Wise.

So, Allah sends his messengers only <u>from</u> the same nation to be sure that he speaks the same language, "We never sent a messenger save with the language of his nation". So if Muhammad can't be a messenger for a nation with a language different from his, therefore that means then he cannot be a messenger for the whole world but only for those who speak Arabic.

But Moses is not an Egyptian and his language is not the same with Pharaoh's. Based on this verse, if Moses' tongue was Egyptian, he must've been an Egyptian prophet. Therefore, he cannot be a prophet to the Jews. This is a contradiction to Allah's statement.

Muhammad can't be a prophet to the world, because he do speak Arabic only and that is one more contradiction refute all Muslims claim about Islam & Muhammad is for all the world not only for the Arab.

Allah sends Muhammad 7 Qur'ans?

www.islamweb.net

فتاوى إسلام ويب

عنوان الفتوى	:	معنى حديث " إن هذا القرآن نزل على سبعة أحرف"
رقم الفتوى	:	5963
تاريخ الفتوى	:	السبت 29 رجب 1421 2000-10-28

السؤال: ما هو نص الحديث الذي يقول (في ما معناه) إن القرآن نزل على سبعة أحرف؟، و ما هو تفسيره؟، و ما هي درجته؟ وهل لغة قريش هي لغة القرآن؟ أم أن لغة أهل البادية هي لغة القرآن؟

الفتوى: الحمد لله والصلاة والسلام على رسول الله وعلى آله وصحبه أما بعد:

فإن نص الحديث المسئول عنه هو ما جاء في الصحيحين من حديث عمر بن الخطاب رضي الله عنه قال: سَمِعْتُ هِشَامَ بْنَ حَكِيمِ بْنِ حِزَامٍ يَقْرَأُ سُورَةَ الْفُرْقَانِ عَلَى غَيْرِ مَا أَقْرَؤُهَا. وَكَانَ رَسُولُ اللهِ صلى الله عليه وسلم أَقْرَأَنِيهَا. فَكِدْتُ أَنْ أَعْجَلَ عَلَيْهِ. ثُمَّ أَمْهَلْتُهُ حَتَّى انْصَرَفَ. ثُمَّ لَبَّبْتُهُ بِرِدَائِهِ. فَجِئْتُ بِهِ رَسُولَ اللهِ صلى الله عليه وسلم. فَقُلْتُ: يَا رَسُولَ اللهِ إِنِّي سَمِعْتُ هَذَا يَقْرَأُ سُورَةَ الْفُرْقَانِ عَلَى غَيْرِ مَا أَقْرَأَتَنِيهَا. فَقَالَ رَسُولُ اللهِ صلى الله عليه وسلم: "أَرْسِلْهُ. اقْرَأْ" فَقَرَأَ الْقِرَاءَةَ الَّتِي سَمِعْتُهُ يَقْرَأُ. فَقَالَ رَسُولُ اللهِ صلى الله عليه وسلم: "هَكَذَا أُنْزِلَتْ". ثُمَّ قَالَ لِي: "اقْرَأْ" فَقَرَأْتُ. فَقَالَ: "هَكَذَا أُنْزِلَتْ. إِنَّ هَذَا الْقُرْآنَ أُنْزِلَ عَلَى سَبْعَةِ أَحْرُفٍ. فَاقْرَأُوا مَا تَيَسَّرَ مِنْهُ".-وفي رواية- على حروف كثيرة لم يقرئنيها رسول الله صلى الله عليه وسلم. وثبت فيهما أيضا من حديث ابن عباس أن رسول الله صلى الله عليه وسلم قال: "أَقْرَأَنِي جِبْرِيلُ عَلَى حَرْفٍ فَرَاجَعْتُهُ فَلَمْ أَزَلْ أَسْتَزِيدُهُ وَيَزِيدُنِي حَتَّى انْتَهَى إِلَى سَبْعَةِ أَحْرُفٍ". هذا هو نص الحديث. وأما درجته فهي في أعلى الصحة كما هو واضح.

"'Umar may Allah be pleased with him said that he heard Hishaam ibn Hakeem may Allah be pleased with him reciting Soorah Al-Furqaan in a way that was different to 'Umar's recitation, which he had learnt from the Prophet. Therefore 'Umar may Allah be pleased with him was angry and seized him and dragged him to the Prophet, and told him what had happened. The Prophet, ordered Hishaam may Allah be pleased with him to recite the chapter and so he recited it the same way that 'Umar may Allah be pleased with him had heard him reciting. Then the Prophet, said that it was a correct recitation. He also ordered 'Umar may Allah be pleased with him to recite and the Prophet, judged his recitation as correct too. He then told them that the Qur'anhad been revealed to be recited in seven different ways. (Sahih Muslim Book 004, Hadith 1782), (Sahih Muslim Book 006, Hadith 2589)*

From this Hadith, we understand:

1. It is it clear that none of the Muslims heard about the seven Readings before, otherwise they would have not accused one another about the wrong reading.
2. Muhammad had to come with the 7 dialects as an excuse in order to cover his unmatched Reciting because each time he recited the same verse, he couldn't repeat it in the same order. Therefore, Muslims copied each reciting as often as Muhammad differently spoke them.
3. Why did his god send 1 book to be recited in 7 different ways, which means with different words and sentence? Do Arabs need that much number of same book and all live in the same Village? In such small population, the Qur'an is still not clear?
4. Would it have been better if Allah had sent the book in 7 different languages in addition to the Arabic one?
5. That would make the Qur'an clear for 7 other nations and not only for a small village like Mecca.
6. Where are the other 6^t readings of the Qura'n right now? We only know of 1...perhaps 2?
7. Why didn't Allah send the Torah or the Gospel in 7 reading? Why was only the Qur'an sent 7 times?

Stubborn Muhammad wanted seven Allah wanted one!

> *"Ubayy b. Ka'b reported that the Apostle of Allah Allah pray on him was near the tank of Banu Jhifar that Gabriel came to him and said: Allah has ordered you to recite to your people the Qur'an in one dialect. Upon this he said: I ask from Allah forgiveness. My people are not capable of doing it. He then came for the second time and said: Allah has ordered you that you should recite the Qur'an to your people in two dialects. Upon this he (Muhammad) again said: I seek forgiveness from Allah, my people would not be able to do so. He Gabriel came for the third time and said: Allah has ordered you to recite the Qur'an to your people in three dialects. Upon this he said: I ask pardon and forgiveness from Allah. My people would not be able to do it. He then came to Muhammad for the fourth time and said: Allah has commanded you to recite the Qur'an to your people in seven dialects, and in whichever dialect they would recite, they would be right. (Sahih Muslim Book 004, Hadith 1789)*

> In this story you see how clear it is the fabrication, what kind of prophet is enforcing his god, and insisting that his people will not understand one kind of reading?
> It took his god three rounds of negotiation, to convince him that it would be better to give Qur'an in seven dialects?
> If the 7 dialects is made to make Qur'an clear to Arab in the little town, how come Allah did not make Qur'an in other seven languages instead of seven Qur'an for less than 2000 people village?
> I have one simple challenge for the Muslims: Provide us one verse was seven dialects, the answer they don't have any.so its not important no more? It disappeared?
> Then the question would be, if in the time of Muhammad His people were not capable of reciting the Qur'an How they would be capable of reciting and understanding today? If we put on mind that **today** Arab didn't speak the same Arabic which was used for the Qur'an on the time of Muhammad 1400 years ago.

***

Qur'an and its science

Answering Muslims

Please note that cannot post all the claim scripts, due to length of it, instead you can go and visit the link for each claim if so you could read the whole article or claim. I think the answer itself is enough for you to understand what the claims are about and how to refute them.

On **Harun Yahya's** websites (http://miraclesoftheQur'an.com and www.harunyahya.com), and the good thing he even posted this note in his site "All materials can be copied, printed and distributed by referring to this site www.harunyahya.com".
However, we advice you to read the full article from his site, which I will provide a link to it, to avoid copy rights issues.

Mr. Harun has made numerous claims about the Qur'an. I will show the readers how each of these claims are false and that Mr. Harun's false claims were meant intentionally to deceive you. You will read below some of his claims taken from his Website. In this book, I will also expose the real meaning of these Qur'anic claims which Mr. Harun is using to deceive readers. In order to be able to convert as many people as they can into Islam, even by means of deception.
***

53

....

Muslims claim

claim about space and universe science

We live in an expanding universe
The sun will expire after some time
The expansion of the universe
http://miraclesoftheQur'an.com/scientific_02.html

Edwin Hubble with his giant telescope.

In the Qur'an, which was revealed fourteen centuries ago at a time when the science of astronomy was still primitive, the expansion of the universe was described in the following terms:

Qur'an 51:47
And it is We Who have constructed the heaven with might, and verily, it is We Who are steadily expanding it.

End of claim

My answer

We live in an expanding universe

Muslims show in videos how Allah already knew about this scientific discovery 1400 years ago. The fact is that the Qur'an never said this. Let us look at this verse together:

Translation of Royal Aal al-Bayt Institute for Islamic Thought, Amman, Jordan

Qur'an 51:47

And we built the heaven with might, and verily We are powerful.

Here we can tell how the translators lied about the translation. The word they base their claim on is *Mus'uon* موسعون. The fact is that this word is about the power of Allah, that he can do more.

54

Qur'an 51:47

And the sky we have built at the hands of "great strength" and
Al-Qur'an 51:47

تفسير *Tafsir Al-Jalalayn*

{وَالسَّمَاءَ بَنَيْنَاهَا بِأَيْدٍ وَإِنَّا لَمُوسِعُونَ {47
"وَالسَّمَاءَ بَنَيْنَاهَا بِأَيْدٍ" بِقُوَّةٍ "وَإِنَّا لَمُوسِعُونَ" قَادِرُونَ يُقَال : آدَ الرَّجُل يَئِيد قَوِيَ وَأَوْسَعَ الرَّجُل : صَارَ ذَا سِعَة وَقُوَّة"

Mus'uon (as to say: some men support "strong" and more men say it is
with capacity and power.

In Sahih Al-Bukhari, Book of Tafsir Al-Qur'an, p. 1837, (Arabic)
explanation of Al-Zariat (Adh-Dhariyat chapter) we read this:

صحيح البخاري
كِتَاب تَفْسِير الْقُرْآن - سُورَةُ وَالذَّارِيَاتِ -
لَمُوسِعُونَ أَيْ لَذُو سَعَةٍ وَكَذَلِكَ عَلَى الْمُوسِع قَدَرَة يَعْنِي الْقَوِيّ"

Mus'uon means the one with the ability and the one who has the ability
of doing, meaning "the strong one".

For the sake of argument, let's say they did not lie about this false
discovery in their Book. Let's see if we find that this scientific discovery
existed in the Bible thousands of years before Islam.

Isaiah 40:22 NKJV

"stretches out the heavens like a curtain, and spreads them
out like a tent to dwell in."

Job 26:7 - KJV

"He stretches out the north over empty space;
He hangs the earth on nothing."

We don't see the Christians making noise or having a party about such
an amazing discovery in their Book!

I can speak about a discovery if I were the first one to have found it. Not
when it's 3,000 years later! Anyway, the Qur'an does not talk about any
expansion of the universe. It's a pure lie.
....
Muslims claim

The sun will expire after some time

To read the claim in full, please visit this link:
http://www.miraclesofthequran.com/scientific_100.html

And the sun runs to a fixed resting place. That is the decree of the Almighty, the All-Knowing. (Surah Ya Sin, 38)

"... My Lord encompasses all things in His knowledge so will you not pay heed?" (Surat Al-An 'am, 80)"

End of claim

My answer

The sun will expire after some time

First, I'll show the deception of Muslims into promoting their religion.

In the same verse (Surah Ya Sin, 38), Mr. Harun tried to prove that the sun will expire. He also used the exact same verse to prove the rotation of the sun. Here is Mr. Harun's claim:

The helio-centric system

http://miraclesoftheQur'an.com/scientific_104.html
The positions of the Sun and Earth are revealed as follows in Surah Ya Sin:

> And the Sun runs to its resting place. That is the decree of the Almighty, the All-Knowing. And We have decreed set phases for the Moon, until it ends up looking like an old palm spathe. It is not for the Sun to overtake the Moon nor for the night to outstrip the day; each one is swimming in a sphere. (Surah Ya Sin, 38-40)

End of Mr. Harun's quotation

....

First of all, we have questions to Mr. Harun:
From where did he get the word rotation or rotating? You can go read all the translations of the Qur'an, even the ones made by Muslims and Mr. Harun himself. They don't say that.

The claim cannot be true for both. The verse talks about the sun's rotation as we quoted from Mr. Harun, "As stated in verse 39 of Surah Ya Sin, in addition to rotating around its own axis once every 26 days, the Sun also moves through its own course." Is it the day's rotation or is it about the expiration of the sun? Mr. Harun, I think as all who make up many falsifications, forgot what he said in the other claim.

They are quoting these verses to prove the everyday run of the sun and of the moon until the judgment day. They are even trying to make it a scientific discovery. The Bible speaks about the sun disappearing before judgment day in the following biblical verse:

Mathew 24:29 - KJV

Immediately after the tribulation of those days shall the sun be darkened, and the moon shall not give her light, and the stars shall fall from heaven, and the powers of the heavens shall be shaken:

Mr. Harun fabricated the translation of this chapter to make it sound totally different. Let us read this and expose the corrupted interpretation of the Qur'an by Muslims themselves.

"He makes night merge into day and day merge into night, and He has made the Sun and Moon subservient, each one running until a specified time. That is Allah, your Lord. The Kingdom is His. Those you call on besides Him have no power over even the smallest speck. (Surah Fatir, 13)" Harun Yahya's translation.

But that verse used the term **specified time** – "Each one running until a **specified time.**" Allah also explains how he made the day and the night and how the day would overtake the night until the Resurrection Day. Nothing of Mr. Harun's claims are true and this is the proof from Tafsir Al-Jalalayn.

"He, Allah, makes the night overtake to enter, into the day, so that it becomes longer, and He makes the day overtake into the night, so that it becomes longer, and Allah has harnessed the sun and the moon, each, of them, moving, in its course, to an appointed term until the Day of Resurrection."

Tafsir Ibn Kathir

"On its fixed course for a period" (its fixed course of location), which is underneath the Throne, further point of the earth another edge anywhere it goes. It is beneath the Throne, it and all of creation, because the Throne is the roof of creation, and it is not a sphere as many astronomer's claim. It is a dome supported by legs, carried by the angels, and it is above

the world, above the heads of people. When the sun is at its highest point at noon, it is in its closest position to the Throne, and when it runs in its fourth orbit at the opposite point to its zenith. It became in the farther point of the Throne, then it rests (stops moving), and after it asks Allah's approval to rise again. As acknowledged in the hadiths by Sahih Al-Bukhari reported that Abu Dharr, may Allah be pleased with him, said, "I was with the Prophet in the Mosque at sunset, and he said,"

You would read more proof later in Sahih Al-Bukhari (Arabic) book the Start of Creation, p. 1171, Hadith 3027; Sahih Al-Bukhari, The Book of Exegesis of the Qur'an, Hadith 4474.

And this is what another chapter in the Qur'an also states:

Qur'an 36:37-40, Muhammad Pickhall's translation

37 A token unto them is night. We strip it of the day, and lo! they are in darkness.

38 And the sun runneth on unto a resting-place for him. That is the measuring of the Mighty, the Wise.

39 And for the moon We have appointed mansions till she return like an old shriveled palm-leaf.

40 It is not for the sun to overtake the moon, nor doth the night outstrip the day. They float each in an orbit.

1. The Qur'an speaks about the daily course of the sun around the earth. It's not about the end of time but rather the sun's 24-hour course.
2. Therefore, it's an incorrect science in their false Book.

Muslims have this long article explaining that the sun will not live forever using it as a scientific proof. But real scientific discovery has already been written in the Bible long before Muhammad was even born! The verse is only talking about the sun's daily route from one point to another and I will prove that from Muhammad's mouth.

The sun will change its course

This is a prophecy made by Muhammad in Sahih Al-Bukhari, The Book of Tafsir Al-Qur'an, Hadith 4474. You will see that the <u>sun will not disappear</u> forever, instead it will appear from the <u>West</u> changing its course and direction. All of us know that the sun is not moving anywhere for us to have day and night.

The sun will not expire on Judgment Day according to Muhammad and this is the proof:

Sahih Al-Bukhari, Book 54, Hadith 422

Reported by Abu Huraira: The Prophet said, "The sun and the moon will be folded up on the Day of Resurrection."

So as we see, the sun will stop giving light because it will be "folded up" and not that it will expire. Therefore, Muhammad thought the sun was more like a board and Allah folds it as if it's a piece of cloth. This is why the sun will not give its light anymore.

Sahih Al-Bukhari
Chapter Al-An'am 6:158, Book 60, Hadith159

Stated by Abu Huraira: "Allah's Messenger revealed 'The Judgment Time will not be demonstrated until the sun rises from the west: and when the people see it, then whoever will be living on the face of the earth will have the belief, but that is the time when their faith will do no good to a soul and will not be accepted unless the person believed prior to that day.

As you see in the last hadith, the sun will not expire but will only change its direction which is impossible for a very simple reason: the earth is moving in a 24-hour course around the sun causing the sunset and sunrise (as it appears to us) to happen and not because of the sun's direction. This proves once more that Muhammad and his god Allah were ignorant as, according to Muslims, whatever Muhammad spoke of was an inspiration. We see that in Qur'an 53:4: **"It's nothing but inspiration We sent down to him"**. Therefore, it's Allah who taught him about the sun and made him believe it's the sun that moves around the earth.

If you read the claim of Mr. Harun, he said, "the above verse **may be** a reference to the Sun's energy one day coming to an end."

So, is all of this **true or not**? Even Mr. Harun himself does not present it as a fact ABOUT HIS Qur'an but **as maybe.** Isn't it funny that this is the science of "maybe"? I think Mr. Harun used the words "maybe" on purpose to cover himself from being exposed in case someone decides to study carefully his claims. If that were the case, he would justify himself by saying he had stated "maybe."

As a matter of fact, I am so thankful for the Muslims
Muslims claim

claims because as long as they agree with the death of the sun and the expanding of the universe as stated in other claims, how then can they explain this fairy tale story as something told to Muhammad by Allah's angel?

Sahih Al-Bukhari, Book 24, Hadith 553

It was reported by 'Abdullah Ibn 'Umar "The Prophet revealed, 'A man keeps on asking others for something until he comes on the Day of Resurrection without any fragment of flesh on his face.' The Prophet added, 'On the Day of Resurrection, the Sun will come near (to mankind) to such an extent that the Sweat will reach up to the midpoint of the ears, so, when all the people are in that phase they will ask Adam for help, and then Moses, and then Muhammad will intercede with Allah to judge among the people. He will go on until he holds the ring of the door of (Eden's heaven) and then Allah will proclaim him to the best rank with the privilege of intercession, And all the people of the gathering will send their glorifications to Allah.'"

As we see here, this is the last day of mankind on earth. After the destruction of the earth, how will the sun get close to the earth and make it so hot? Obviously, according to Muhammad's statement, the earth is a lot bigger than the sun, therefore the sun is the one that would get close as we can read in another hadith. Muhammad said:
"The sun will get close to the earth to be at a one mile distance." Referenced in:

Qur'an 83:6, Ibn Kathir's interpretation

The Messenger of Allah saying, On the Judgment Day, the sun will draw near to his slaves (mankind) until it is a mile or two away from them. Then the sun will burn them, and they will be submersed in sweat based upon the amount of their deeds,

---

إِذَا كَانَ يَوْمُ الْقِيَامَةِ أُدْنِيَتِ الشَّمْسُ مِنَ الْعِبَادِ حَتَّى تَكُونَ قَدْرَ مِيلٍ أَوْ مِيلَيْنِ قَالَ فَتَصْهَرُهُمُ »
الشَّمْسُ فَيَكُونُونَ فِي الْعَرَقِ كَقَدْرِ أَعْمَالِهِمْ، مِنْهُمْ مَنْ يَأْخُذُهُ إِلَى عَقِبَيْهِ، وَمِنْهُمْ مَنْ يَأْخُذُهُ إِلَى
رُكْبَتَيْهِ، وَمِنْهُمْ مَنْ يَأْخُذُهُ إِلَى حَقْوَيْهِ، وَمِنْهُمْ مَنْ يُلْجِمُهُ إِلْجَامًا

Sahih Al-bukhari (Book 24, Hadith 553)
or in Sahih Muslim (Book 40, Hadith 6852)

"the sun would draw so close to the people that there would be left only a distance of one mile."

The sun would be moving closer towards the earth, in Sahih Al-Bukhari book of Al-Zakah V2 hadith 1405, PAGE 536/537(Arabic book)

Sahih Al-Bukhari (Book 24, Hadith 553)

"Narrated 'Abdullah bin 'Umar The Prophet said, "A man keeps on asking others for something till he comes on the Day of Resurrection without any piece of flesh on his face." The Prophet added, "On the Day of Resurrection, the Sun will come near (to, the people) to such an extent that the sweat will reach up to the middle of the ears, so, when all the people are in that state, they will ask Adam for help, and then Moses, and then Muhammad (p.b.u.h) ." The sub-narrator added "Muhammad will intercede with Allah to judge amongst the people. He will proceed on till he will hold the ring of the door (of Paradise) and then Allah will exalt him to Maqam Mahmud (the privilege of intercession, etc.). And all the people of the gathering will send their praises to Allah."

صحيح البخاري» كتاب الزكاة » باب من سأل الناس تكثرا

الجزء الثاني

باب من سأل الناس تكثرا

1405 حدثنا يحيى بن بكير حدثنا الليث عن عبيد الله بن أبي جعفر قال سمعت حمزة بن عبد الله بن عمر قال سمعت عبد الله بن عمر رضي الله عنه قال قال النبي صلى الله عليه وسلم ما يزال الرجل يسأل الناس حتى يأتي يوم القيامة ليس في وجهه مزعة لحم وقال إن الشمس تدنو يوم القيامة حتى يبلغ العرق نصف الأذن فبينا هم كذلك استغاثوا بآدم ثم بموسى ثم بمحمد صلى الله عليه وسلم وزاد عبد الله بن صالح حدثني الليث حدثني ابن أبي جعفر فيشفع ليقضى بين الجمع كلهم وقال معلى حدثنا وهيب عن النعمان بن راشد عن عبد الله بن مسلم أخي الزهري [فيمشي حتى يأخذ بحلقة الباب فيومئذ يبعثه الله مقاما محمودا يحمده أهل 537الخلق [ص: عن حمزة سمع ابن عمر رضي الله عنهما عن النبي صلى الله عليه وسلم في المسألة

The hadith from the mouth of Muhammad which states that the sun at the end of time will get a mile or two away from us is more than enough to destroy all the previous claims as well as the science of the Qur'an, which again exposes Muhammad as a false prophet.

1. If the sun gets one mile away from us, we will not only burn and

sweat. The earth will already be destroyed long before the sun arrives to such distance: **"On the Judgment Day, the sun will draw near to his slaves (mankind) until it is a _mile or two away from them."_**

2. It's so clear that when Muhammad said, "Then the sun will burn them" he did not mean *it will kill them*. It's about mankind being in high heat because it says after the burn, they will sweat: "and they will be submersed in sweat based upon the amount of their deeds." One more mistake!

3. "The sun will draw near to his slaves (mankind)." This means the sun will be moving towards the earth as it will be immobilized.

4. The sun will be so close, two miles maximum, and it will be so hot that we'll sweat a lot. So now, where is the sun's death? And the sun is moving?! Notice also with me that the sun will not move further away from the earth but would instead come towards us, which is the opposite of what science states.

5. What's funny about this hadith of Muhammad is that the more deeds you have, the more you will be punished!

The everyday course of the sun where the sun sets and rises.

Qur'an 13:2

God, who raised the heavens without any pillars that you see and then He mounted the Throne and the sun and the moon all run to an arranged time, He regulates all affairs, explains the Signs, so in meeting your Lord, that ye may believe.

تفسير *Tafsir Al-Jalalayn*

God is He who raised up the heavens without visible pillars and employ, the sun and the moon, each running for a limited time, until the Day of Resurrection.

Qur'an Yaseen 36:38

وَالشَّمْسُ تَجْرِي لِمُسْتَقَرٍّ لَّهَا ذَلِكَ تَقْدِيرُ الْعَزِيزِ الْعَلِيمِ

And the sun runs to its resting place. That is by the order of Allah, the Almighty All-Knowing.

Does the sun really run an appointed time (every day), or is it about the end of the sun?

Muhammad himself will expose Harun's misleading claim.

- Qur'an 36:38
- Sahih Al-Bukhari (Arabic), Book the Start of Creation, p. 1171, Hadith 3027
- Sahih Al-Bukhari, The Book of Tafsir Al-Qur'an, Hadith 4474

  Abu Zerr reported, "Once I was with the Messenger in the Mosque at the time of sunset. The Messenger of Allah said, 'O Abu Zerr! Do you know where the sun goes?' I responded 'Allah and His Messenger know better.' The prophet answered, 'It goes and prostrates underneath and bows down under Allah's Throne; will it ask Allah the authorization to bow down, but he will not accept, then Allah will order it to go and rise back from where it came from, and that is Allah's Revelation. And the sun runs on its fixed course for a term.'"
  (Sahih Al-Bukari Book 54, Hadith 421)

حَدَّثَنَا مُحَمَّدُ بْنُ يُوسُفَ حَدَّثَنَا سُفْيَانُ عَنِ الْأَعْمَشِ عَنْ إِبْرَاهِيمَ التَّيْمِيِّ عَنْ أَبِيهِ عَنْ أَبِي ذَرٍّ 3027 رَضِيَ اللهُ عَنْهُ قَالَ قَالَ النَّبِيُّ صَلَّى اللهُ عَلَيْهِ وَسَلَّمَ لِأَبِي ذَرٍّ حِينَ غَرَبَتِ الشَّمْسُ أَتَدْرِي أَيْنَ تَذْهَبُ قُلْتُ اللهُ وَرَسُولُهُ أَعْلَمُ قَالَ فَإِنَّهَا تَذْهَبُ حَتَّى تَسْجُدَ تَحْتَ الْعَرْشِ فَتَسْتَأْذِنَ فَيُؤْذَنُ لَهَا وَيُوشِكُ أَنْ تَسْجُدَ فَلَا يُقْبَلَ مِنْهَا وَتَسْتَأْذِنَ فَلَا يُؤْذَنَ لَهَا يُقَالُ لَهَا ارْجِعِي مِنْ حَيْثُ جِئْتِ فَتَطْلُعَ مِنْ مَغْرِبِهَا فَذَلِكَ - لِمُسْتَقَرٍّ لَهَا ذَلِكَ تَقْدِيرُ الْعَزِيزِ الْعَلِيمِ 1171وَقَوْلُهُ تَعَالَى وَالشَّمْسُ تَجْرِي «-ص

where is the resting place of the sun? It's underneath the Allah Throne but what underneath of Allah Throne? It's the water and that can be proven by the coming verse:
Qur'an Hood 12:7
Allah, may He be exalted, says (interpretation of the meaning): "And He it is Who has created the heavens and the earth in six Days and His Throne was on the water, that He might try you, which of you is the best in deeds"

This movement of the sun and the moon will repeat itself until Judgment Day. This means that the sun's movement is connected to Allah's order, not to a natural phenomenon. Maybe we still need more proof on how and what Allah means by the running of the sun and the moon. We will go to a verse in the Qur'an which speaks of Alexander the Great.

Qur'an 18:86

Until he reaches the setting of the sun and finds it sitting in murky water, and there he found people, we said, to him (Alexander the Great), "Either torture them or do good to them!"

Tanwîr al-Miqbâs min Tafsîr Ibn 'Abbâs

﴿ حَتَّىٰ إِذَا بَلَغَ مَغْرِبَ ٱلشَّمْسِ وَجَدَهَا تَغْرُبُ فِي عَيْنٍ حَمِئَةٍ وَوَجَدَ عِندَهَا قَوْماً قُلْنَا يَٰذَا ٱلْقَرْنَيْنِ إِمَّا أَن تُعَذِّبَ وَإِمَّا أَن تَتَّخِذَ فِيهِمْ حُسْناً ﴾

Tanwîr Al-Miqbâs min Tafsîr Ibn 'Abbâs

"When he reached the setting place of the sun, the place where the sun sets, he found it setting in muddy water."

Notice here that he did not say the sea or the ocean but muddy water! Some translations say muddy springs! To get the real meaning of this, we better go and see what Muhammad said about it.

Read again Sahih Al-Bukhari, Book 60, Hadith 326.

According to this hadith, it's so clear that the sun moves from location to another and has a resting place! Is that what science tells us or is Muhammad telling his own made-up story? Surely, this is a clear mistake in the Qur'an and one more proof that the Qur'an cannot be from the real God.

Sahih Muslim, Book 004, Hadith 1275

As long as the sun has not risen yet; but when the sun rises, standstill from prayer, because it (the sun) rises between the horns of the devil.

Sahih Muslim, Book 004, Hadith 1807

The Messenger of Allah saying: "Do not start the prayer at the time when the sun is rising, nor when it's setting, for the sun rises from between the horns of Satan.

1. Note that its says, "for the sun rises from between." This is about a location and not only timing.
2. So at that point, the sun will be located between the two horns of Satan.
3. Look at how he is telling them fairytale stories and scaring them to the point that they even have to stop praying!
4. Whether the sun rises from between Satan's horns or not, why do they have to stop the prayer?
5. Where is the science of Muhammad coming from? It must be coming from the god of Disneyland!
6. Even stars have a setting place. All of them retreat, not only the sun.

Qur'an 52:49

{ وَمِنَ ٱللَّيْلِ فَسَبِّحْهُ وَإِدْبَارَ ٱلنُّجُومِ }

And glorify to him at night and at the retreat of the stars.

Interpretation of "The great interpretation by Imam al-Tabaraani"

He said, {That prayers of the dawn; because Allah after that, saying: (and in the setting of the stars); is meant by the sunset prayer and dinner, either one.

Based on their understanding of their own book as written in Islamic books, the phrase "is meant by the sunset prayer and dinner, either one" means that Allah had the star (sun) to set or go to sleep under his throne.

The places of the stars

Qur'an 56:75

{ فَلَا أُقْسِمُ بِمَوَاقِعِ ٱلنُّجُومِ }

I swear by the setting-places of the stars!

Explanation of Preserving Adler Al-Mason / Alsamen-Halabi (year 756 Islamic).

By the locations: of where **stars set** at the Western part of the world.

1. Do stars move up and down (rise and lower) from the earth?
2. "Setting-places of the stars." Where are the stars' setting-places located?
3. The word "setting" has exactly the same meaning as the previous verse stated in Qur'an 18:86 with regards to the sun sitting in a murky water which means not moving after it arrives to a station (under Allah's throne).
4. Why did the All-mighty god swear by a location of any thing!

In Tafsir Al-Tabari, Vol. 23, p. 147, print year 1973 Beirut, Lebanon:

Qur'an 56:75, Chapter of Al-Waqi'a

"Narated by Ibn 'Abed-Al-A'la from Mu'tamer from his father from 'Ekramah, he said, "that the Qur'an was sent down all of it, and it was located and placed where the stars set or locate, and Jibrel (Gabriel) was grabbing it one by one (verse by verse) and all of Qur'an sent down in the Night of Power

(Al-Qader)."

http://www.islamweb.net/newlibrary/display_book.php?flag=1&bk_no=50
&surano=56&ayano=75

147الجزء الثالث والعشرون تفسير الطبري تفسير سورة الواقعة ص:
حدثنا ابن عبد الأعلى قال : ثنا المعتمر ، عن أبيه ، عن عكرمة : إن القرآن نزل جميعا ، فوضع بمواقع النجوم ، فجعل جبريل يأتي
بالسورة ، وإنما نزل جميعا في ليلة القدر.

The original text in Arabic for the above translation.

As we see here, Allah sent down his Book and placed his verses according to the location of the stars! And each time the angel Jibrel (Gabriel) needed to give Muhammad one of it, he would go to that location and grab one or few verses, then come back to deliver it to Muhammad!

One more mistake in the Qur'an!
Allah swears by the place and location of the stars but at the same time, Muslims are posting to us articles and studies of scientists saying that everything in this **universe is in constant movement**!

Mr. Harun said, "Scientists have only recently unraveled the structure of the sun and discovered what goes on inside it. Before that, nobody knew how the sun obtained its energy or how it emitted heat and light."

We do not know how he got this result. However, we will teach him how to find the truth about Islam and make him understand heat and cold. Is heat coming from the sun or from the fires of hell based on Muhammad's teachings?

Is heat from the sun or from hell fire?

Sahih Al-Bukhari, Book 10, Hadith 512

Reported by Abu Huraira: The Messenger of Allah said, "In very hot weather delay the middle day prayer until it becomes cooler because the severity of the heat is from the harrowing of Hell-fire. The Hell-fire of Hell complained to its Lord said: 'O Lord! My parts are eating my construction, destroying one another.' So Allah allowed it to take two breaths, one in the winter and the other in the summer. The breath in the summer is that period when you feel the extreme severe heat and the breath in the winter is at the time when you feel very severely cold'".

So here we go again to expose the falsehood:

The story proves that Allah considers hell fire as a living creature that gets hot and even complains about its heat.
Our heat on earth is not from the sun but from hell fire. Not only heat from hell but even the cold which is contrary to the function and duty of hell itself. This makes it clear that the sun's absence has nothing to do with cold in Allah's science but it's the breath of hell in winter. I am sure that Muslims wished the books of hadiths had never existed as each time, Muhammad's words would prove their false statements and deception. At the same time, they not only prove that Islam is nothing but fairytale stories but point out that Muhammad is not trustworthy because of his falsifications.

Let us see how we can connect the dots and make an image of Muhammad's understating of this universe and find out where he got his information by answering the next claim.

\-

Muslims claim

The end of the universe and the big crunch

http://harunyahya.com/en/Kuran_Mucizeleri/27224/The_end_of_the_univ erse_and_the_big_crunch
This is how this scientific hypothesis of the Big Crunch is indicated in the Qur'an:

> *Qur'an 21:104*
>
> *That Day We will fold up heaven like folding up the pages of a book. As We originated the first creation so We will regenerate it. It is a promise binding on Us. That is what We will do.*

In another verse, the heavens were described as this:
> *Qur'an 39:67*
>
> *They do not measure Allah with His true measure. The whole earth will be a mere handful for Him on the Day of Rising the heavens folded up in His right hand. Glory be to Him! He is exalted above the partners they ascribe!*

End of claim

\-

My answer

Qur'an 21:104

If we read carefully what Mr. Harun himself quoted from his Qur'an "That Day, We will fold up heaven like folding up the pages of a book. As We originated the first creation so We will regenerate it. It is a promise binding on Us. That is what We will do."

This means in clear words from his god himself, that at the end of the time, Allah will deal with the universe in the same manner when he created the sky. The sky means the space, planets, stars and all other elements in the universe.

The world started by big-bang and will end with big-bang?

That will destroy both claims, because the big-bang was not as its described as a folded book.! We will talk about the big-bang in few pages afterwards.

Allah is saying that he will fold up the heavens on that day (Resurrection Day) just as pages are folded in a book, which is the same thing that he did when he created the sky in the beginning of the universe. This means that the skies are like pages of a book and Allah is opening and closing the book by folding up the pages but the book has never been destroyed. Some Muslims say that the Qur'an approves the *Big Bang* theory which is a false claim because as you can see, Allah in these verses spoke about folding up the heaven in the same way he created it and I don't think the Muslims would say that folding up the heaven is an explosion. That would be really funny.

Mr. Harun again is like a fish swimming in the sand trying to create water because there is no water, it is only his imagination and fantasy. To show you that this is not just my own interpretation of the verse but is a very Islamic understanding, let us go to the book of Ibn Kathir:

Let's read together Ibn Kathir's interpretation, Vol. 5, p. 382-383:

Qur'an 21:104

Reported by Ibn Abbas that Allah said, "Allah will fold up the seven skies and whatever creations and creatures live in it, all of which will be folded up by his right hand, and that will be equal to the size of the sand in his hand". And He (Allah) says: "Folding it up the same as Al-Sijil folds up books". It's been said, that the word Al-Sijil means book, and the correct meaning that was reported by Ibn Abbas: Al-Sijil means a page in a book and this is what was reported by 'Ali bin Abi Talhah and Al-'Awfi. This was also mentioned by Mujahid, Qatadah and many others. And it's been favored by Ibn Jarir because it is the most accurate and used meaning in the Arabic language and based on the above it proves the meaning of Allah saying "That day when we fold up the sky is the same as rolling up pages in a book as a scroll."

The original text in Arabic for the above translation.

عن ابن عباس قال : يطوي الله السماوات السبع بما فيها من الخليقة والأرضين السبع بما فيها من الخليقة ، يطوي ذلك كله بيمينه ، يكون ذلك كله في يده بمنزلة خردلة . وقوله : (كطي السجل للكتب) ، قيل : المراد بالسجل [الكتاب . وقيل : المراد بالسجل] هاهنا : ملك من الملائكة .

والصحيح عن ابن عبّاس أنّ السّجلّ هيَ الصّحيفة قالَهُ عليّ بن أبي طلْحة والعوْفيّ عنْهُ ونصّ علَى ذلكَ مُجاهد وقتادة وغيْر واحد واخْتارَهُ ابن جرير لأنّهُ المعْرُوف في اللُّغة فعلَى هذَا يكُون معْنى الكَلام يوْم نطْوي السّماء كطيِّ السّجلّ للكِتاب أيْ علَى الكِتاب بمعْنَى المكْتُوب .

⊕ The above evidences are from top Islamic scholars. Mr. Harun is a Turkish man who does not even know how to read and speak Arabic but suddenly he became an authority above the scholars of Islam. Even though his prophet said the opposite of what he claimed, Mr. Harun still went against his prophet's words as if he were saying he's better than Muhammad himself. In the coming hadith, we will see Muhammad explaining what the Qur'an meant to say. Let us read together more evidences from the Qur'an and the hadith.

Qur'an 39:67

"On Judgment day, Allah will seize all of the earth, and the skies will be in His right hand."

This verse again exposes falsehood because it states that all of **the Earth** and **the skies** are going to be seized by Allah's right hand. Nothing will expire or will be destroyed.

I think the best answer Muslims should accept is Muhammad's and Allah's! Let us read how Muhammad's goddebunks Mr. Harun's claim. Please read with me the following verse:

Qur'an 81:1-2

Muhammad H. Shakir's translation

"1 When the sun is covered, 2 And when the stars darkened,"

From Lisan Al-Arab dictionary:

The word "sun" is Kuiret meaning its light collected and

folded-up as folding the Turban and it's a Persian word."

لسان العرب

وكُوِّرَتِ الشمسُ: جُمِعَ ضوءُها ولُفَّ كما تُلَفُّ العمامة، وقيل: معنى كُوِّرَتْ غُوِّرَتْ، وهو بالفارسية﴿ كُورِّبِكِرْ ﴾ وقال مجاهد: كُوِّرَت اضمحلت وذهبت

Mr. Harun quoted "on the Day of Rising the **heavens folded up in His right hand**. Glory be to Him! He is exalted above the partners they ascribe!" (Qur'an 39:67).

If we connect the verses Qur'an 81:1-2 and Qur'an 39:67, how will the light of the sun be covered? By the right hand of Allah.
So what we understand from this are the following:
- ⊕ The sun will get dark but will not be destroyed.
- ⊕ The sun will be darkened because Allah will seize the sun in his right hand as shown in Qur'an 39:67.
- ⊕ The sun darkened, not because it lost its energy but because it's been covered.
- ⊕ The claim that it will be covered by Allah's hand is false according to the hadith below where Muhammad explained exactly what he meant:

Sahih Al-Bukhari (Arabic), Book of the Start of Creation, p. 1171, Hadith 3027

Sahih Al-Bukhari, Book 60, Hadith 326

Sahih Muslim, Book 001, Hadith 0297

Abu Zerr Reported: Once I was with the Messenger in the mosque at the time of sunset. The Messenger of Allah said, "O Abu Zerr! Do you know where the sun goes?" I responded, "Allah and His Messenger know better." The prophet answered, "It goes and travels until it prostrates itself underneath the Throne (of Allah) and takes the permission to rise again, and it is permitted and then until a time comes (end of time) when it is about to prostrate itself but its prostration will not be accepted, and sun will ask (Allah) permission to go on its course, but the sun will not be permitted, but it will be ordered to return where it has come from, and therefore, it will rise in the west". And that is the explanation of the Statement of Allah: "And the sun runs its fixed course (Qur'an 36:38) for a term appointed. That is The Decree of Allah The Exalted in Might, The great."

صحيح البخاري﴾ كتاب بدء الخلق﴾ باب صفة الشمس والقمر

الجزء الثالث :

3027 حدثنا محمد بن يوسف حدثنا سفيان عن الأعمش عن إبراهيم التيمي عن أبيه عن أبي ذر رضي الله عنه قال قال النبي صلى الله عليه وسلم لأبي ذر حين غربت الشمس أتدري أين تذهب قلت الله ورسوله أعلم قال فإنها تذهب حتى تسجد تحت العرش فتستأذن

فيؤذن لها ويوشك أن تسجد فلا يقبل منها وتستأذن فلا يؤذن لها يقال لها ارجعي من حيث جئت فتطلع من مغربها فذلك قوله تعالى
لمستقر لها ذلك تقدير العزيز العليم1171والشمس تجري [ص:]

I would like to make a note about the above hadith. We quoted from the hadith that the sun will go and prostrate itself under the throne of Allah: **"It goes and travels until it prostrates itself underneath the Throne (of Allah) and takes the permission to rise again."**
Now, many of you will not notice the connection between this hadith and other verses in the Qur'an where the god of Islam spoke of the murky water which is stated in the story of Alexander the Great in Qur'an 18:86:

> 86 *Until, while he arrived at the setting-place of the sun, he found it setting in a muddy water spring and found community at that location. We said: Oh Zull-Qarneen! (Alexander the Great) Either penalize or be kind to them.*

Now let us connect the above Qur'an and hadith with the following hadiths so we can have the big picture of Allah's story with regards to the skies, the Earth's creation, and its physical location:
Sahih Al-Bukhari, Book 93, Hadith 514
Sahih Al-Bukhari, Book 54, Hadith 414

> *"...At the same time, as I was with the Prophet, some people from Bani Tamim approached. Therefore, they said: "We ask you what the beginning of this universe was." The Prophet said, "There was Allah and nothing else before Him and His Throne was above the water, and He afterwards created the Heavens and the Earth and wrote everything in the Book..."*

Maybe you already noticed the connection: Allah's throne is above the water ("His Throne was above the water") and the Qur'an says that the sun will set in a murky water while Muhammad says that the sun will go and **prostrate** itself under the throne of Allah. This is based on:

> *Sahih Al-Bukhari, (Arabic) p. 1171, Hadith 3027;*
>
> *Sahih Al-Bukhari, Book 60, Hadith 326*
>
> *Sahih Muslim, Book 001, Hadith 0297*
>
> *Qur'an 18:86*
>
> *Sahih Al-Bukhari, Book 93, Hadith 514*
>
> *Sahih Al-Bukhari, Book 54, Hadith 414*

In very simple words, this means that the sun travels everyday from the East to the West; from point A to point B. And when the sun when arrives to the West, it sets itself straight under the throne of Allah which is above the water. This is why the Qur'an says Alexander the Great found the sun setting in a murky water at the end of the world where Allah stays and his throne located. This certainly brings about a lot of confusion in this religion. How can Allah be in heaven and at the same time be on his throne located above the water? Remember the hadith of Sahih Al-Bukhari, book 93, Hadith 514, claimed that Allah's throne was above the water before the creation of the universe which means that water had to exist before anything else prior to creation. Again, this alone is more contradictory to the hadith itself because he said: "the beginning of this universe was." The Prophet said, "There was Allah and nothing else before Him and <u>His Throne was above the water</u>." There was nothing at all but Allah's throne above the water and that was prior to the creation of the universe. How can he claim there was nothing and the universe was not yet created while at the same time he claimed there was water? I don't think Muhammad himself understood what he was saying.

This coming hadith has a connection to the previous one which we need to use more often.

Sahih Al-Bukhari, Book 60, Hadith 159

Stated by Abu Huraira: Allah's Messenger revealed "The Judgment time will not be demonstrated until the sun rises from the west: and when the people see it, then whoever will be living on the face of the earth will have the belief, but that is the time when believe will do no good to a soul which believe after that if it believed not previously". Chapter Al-An'am (6.158)

Therefore, it's clear that if we accept Mr. Harun's claim, we have to reject Muhammad's words as one of them is false! If you'd ask me which one is false I would say both. One is trying to make himself a prophet with fairy tales and the other is trying to make Muhammad a prophet by making false interpretations of the Qur'an.

- As we saw in the past hadith, the end of time has no Crunch but the sun will come from the west!
- And that again exposes Muhammad as a false prophet. The sun's change of direction makes it appear like it moved from the western side of the earth but that is absolutely false science and foolish. The rotation of the earth in its axis causes us to think that the sun rises from the east and sets in the West, but the fact is that the sun is going nowhere. The seeming movement of the sun is because of the earth's rotation which is what is scientific and true.
- As long as Mr. Harun acknowledges science as true, he better believe science and not his prophet's unreal stories.
- If you look at Mr. Harun's claim, he used the *Big Crunch Theory*. I wonder what he would say if we have scientific proof that this theory is wrong? Would he say that the Qur'an is wrong or that he (Harun) is wrong?
- Let us read together what the Bible says about the end times

and try to figure out if what it claimed thousands of years ago fits with the facts of the universe:

2 Peter 3:9-13 – KJV

⁹ The Lord is not slack concerning his promise, as some men count slackness; but is long suffering to us-ward, not willing that any should perish, but that all should come to repentance.

¹⁰ But the day of the Lord will come as a thief in the night; in the which the heavens shall pass away with a great noise, and the elements shall melt with fervent heat, the earth also and the works that are therein shall be burned up.

¹¹ Seeing then that all these things shall be dissolved, what manner of persons ought ye to be in all holy conversation and godliness,

¹² Looking for and hasting unto the coming of the day of God, wherein the heavens being on fire shall be dissolved, and the elements shall melt with fervent heat?

¹³ Nevertheless we, according to his promise, look for new heavens and a new earth, wherein dwelleth righteousness.

As you see, it's in the Bible. It's saying that all will pass away and that nothing will exist. No heaven or earth. There will be a new heaven and a new earth. Even the Messiah himself said the same thing when in:

Matthew 24:29 - KJV

Immediately after the tribulation of those days shall the sun be darkened, and the moon shall not give her light, and the stars shall fall from heaven, and the powers of the heavens shall be shaken:

Matthew 24:35 - KJV

Heaven and earth shall pass away, but my words shall not pass away.

The Bible also gives us more details in:

Matthew 24:31 - KJV

And he shall send his angels with a great sound of a trumpet, and they shall gather together his elect from the four winds, from one end of heaven to the other.

And you will see the Qur'an copies the Bible scriptures. It's the same in:

> Qur'an 78:18
> *The Day that the Trumpet shall be sound, and ye shall come forth in waves of crowds;*

Muslims' claim

Creation from hot smoke

http://www.miraclesoftheQur'an.com/scientific_04.html
Allah created everything from hot smoke.
End of claim

My answer

Now the Muslims agree that when the earth was finished being created, the universe was nothing but smoke!

The fabrication easy to expose a few pages before we saw the claim of Big Crunch **theory**, or the Sun will expire and he used this verse with his own translation.

If we read carefully what Mr. Harun himself quoted from his Qur'an:

> Qur'an 21:104
> *"That Day, We will fold up heaven like folding up the pages of a book. As We originated the first creation so We will regenerate it. It is a promise binding on Us. That is what We will do."*

The world started by big-bang and will end with big-bang?

- This means in clear words from his god himself, that at the end of the time, Allah will deal with the universe in the same manner when he created the sky. The sky means the space, planets, stars and all other elements in the universe.
- As long Muslims claim that the big-bang is the start of the universe and they claim that Qur'an speak about (the big-bang) that mean the end of the time should be end with big-bang as the Qur'an statements "That Day, We will fold up heaven like folding up the pages of a book. As We originated the first creation so We will regenerate it."

- So folding up the book is the big-bang? I think again Muslims thought we will not read both or connect both and expose the lie.!

- He said: "Let us note that only in the 20th century have scientists discovered that the universe emerged from a hot gas in the form of smoke." Does the verse say that the earth emerged from smoke or that Allah created it in six days? It says earth was created first while the the sky was a smoke as we will read in Qur'an 2:29.

- With that being said, how can Muslims explain the creation of the earth when the universe was not even formed yet nor anything was in existence? And I quote from Mr. Harun, "**He placed firmly embedded mountains on it, towering over it, and blessed it and measured out its nourishment in it, laid out for those** who seek it-all in **_four days_**. **Then He turned to heaven when it was smoke** and said, to it and to the earth, "Come willingly or unwillingly." They both said, "We come willingly." (Qur'an, 41:10-11)"

- **The earth was made in 4 days?** Is that what big-bang says? I do not believe in the big-bang but now Muslims in trouble for accepting it.

- One day for Allah is equivalent of 1000 year of our time, so four days = 4000 years our time, Qur'an 32:5 **"will go up to Him, in one Day, the space whereof is a thousand years of your reckoning"**

- So the Earth was made first with all substance and the Sky was still smoke? But this is against the what science claim, I will quote from a science site:

- "As a scientist, how would you explain how the Earth was created after the Big Bang occurred? Where did animals, plants the human race come from?

- Answer The creation of the universe took place about 15 billion years ago!!! See the Scienceline web site for more on that.

- The EARTH formed the same time the sun formed, about 4.5 billion years ago (4.5 Gyear) the big G stands for giga which means multiple what follows by 1,000,000,000. =1 billion. http://scienceline.ucsb.edu/getkey.php?key=3164

- Is saying that "The *Big Bang* is a theory that **has been proven** with **scientific evidence**" true?

- Does that mean Allah created the earth from GAS? This would mean that the Qur'an is wrong in another verse:

Qur'an 2:29

It is He Who hath created for you all things that are on the *earth; then he turned up, to heaven, and he made it seven heavens, he is all knowing and wise.*

According to this verse, the earth was formed as the only object in this universe before any stars or anything else same as in (Qur'an, 41:10-11). This does not make any sense. I will show you how we can refute Mr. Harun Yahya through his own posts and words. He said, to quote:

"This information given in the Qur'an is in full agreement with the findings of contemporary science. The conclusion that astrophysics has reached today is that the entire universe, together with **the dimensions of matter and time, came into existence as a result of a great explosion that occurred in no time.** This event, known as "The *Big Bang*" proved that the universe was created from nothingness as the result of the explosion of a single point. Modern scientific circles are in agreement that the *Big Bang* is the only rational and provable explanation of the beginning of the universe and of how the universe came into being."
End of quotation.

- If we go back in reading and read the verse posted and translated by Mr Harun in his claim about The Big Crunch theory. He himself said:
  "That Day We will fold up heaven like folding up the pages of a book. As We originated the first creation so We will regenerate it. It is a promise binding on Us. That is what We will do." (Qur'an 21:104).

- This verse indicates that Allah created the heaven as **"like folding up the pages of a book"** and **"As We originated the first creation."** This is again against the *Big Bang* theory because Allah here made it as folding pages, page after page, which means that pages already existed. It's **just about unfolding them, not creating them**, while the *Big Bang* theory claims that space was created simultaneously.

- He is agreeing with the *Big Bang*! He agreed that time and matter did not exist and then things formed based on a big explosion! But this would mean that the earth was formed long before the explosion. Why do I say so?

- Look at the verse and tell me how was the earth able to get any form that fast when everything else was paused? Does the *Big Bang* theory agree that the earth was formed this way or is it the Muslims scientific special education created by Mr. Harun Yahya?

Qur'an 2:29

He it is Who created for you all that is in the earth. Then turned He to the heaven, and fashioned it as seven heavens. And He is knower of all things.

Note this is Muhammad pickthal.

Add to that, the Qur'an says in 41:9:

Say: do you really deny Him Who created the earth in two Days? And make yourselves equal with Him? He is the Lord of two Worlds. (Qur'an 41:9)

And I quote from Mr. Harun the translated verse which he based his argument on:

"He placed firmly embedded mountains on it, towering over it, and blessed it and measured out its nourishment in it, laid out for those who seek it-all in four days. Then He turned to heaven when it was smoke and said, to it and to the earth, "Come willingly or unwillingly." They both said, "We come willingly." (Qur'an, 41:10-11)"

The earth, in creation, was formed in two days, and the verse after that says Allah spent four other days creating the earth's substances. This would mean that the earth was formed billions of years before the sky even had any stars. "**four days**. Then **He turned to heaven when it was smoke**" So the earth was created first and then after it is finished the SKY was a smoke still.

Where did we get the "billions"? Let us see how Mr. Harun shot himself in the foot! Read the coming claim.

Muslims claim

Creation in six days

www.harunyahya.com/miracles_of_the_Qur'an_p1_05.php#3

Your Lord is Allah, who created the heavens and the earth in six days and then settled Himself firmly on the Throne... (Qur'an, 7:54)

When a six-day period of time is calculated according to the relativity of time, it equates to six million million (six trillion) days. That is because universal time flows a million times faster than time on earth. Calculated in terms of years, 6 trillion days equates to approximately 16.427 billion years. This is within the estimated range for the age of the universe.
6,000,000,000,000 days/365.25 = 16.427104723 billion years

End of claim

My answer

Let us quote from Mr. Harun's words: "When a **six-day period** of time is calculated according to the relativity of time." What he is saying is that he made the calculation and that calculation is based on the relativity of time. He came with a number which is 6 trillion days. How he got this number I have no idea. It just proves he is making things up as the following:

> Qur'an 9:36
>
> "The number of months in the sight of Allah is twelve (one year), so ordained by Him the day He created the heavens and the earth"

This means:
Time never changed since Allah (created) the earth.
1. And He even use same lunar calendar used by Muslims today.
2. All created at the same time day, "ordained by Him the day He created the heavens and the earth"

That is more than enough to destroy the fabrication, but for the sake of learning let go for more.

It's very clear that Mr. Harun forgot about his other claim which we did answer in *The Deception of Allah, Volume 1*.
He said in the following chapters and verses about the relativity of time:
> "A day with your Lord is equivalent to a thousand years in the way you count. (Qur'an 22:47)".

> "He directs the whole affair from heaven to earth. Then it will again ascend to Him on a Day whose length is a thousand years by the way you measure. (Qur'an, 32:5)"

> "The angels and the Spirit ascend to Him in a day whose

length is fifty thousand years. (Qur'an, 70:4)"

http://www.miraclesofthequran.com/scientific_32.html

So at that claim it was, ONE day of Allah = 1000 Year but now because he now he come with new fabrication, the Day became equal to 2.666666666666667 billions years????

So as long he agreed that the day of god Allah is equal to 1000 years of our count, let us do the math.

1day for Allah=1000 year
which is exactly the equal day of Allah but we noticed in this claim that Mr. Harun made his god's one day equate to
1 trillion.

Then he claimed that six days is equals to 6 trillion days which means each day for Allah is equal to 1 trillion days.
One day = 1 trillion days

But again, he never thought that we would read both of his claims and exposes his falsehood. Even though we've answered and exposed this false miracle, I would like to share with you more information that shows confusion in Islam and the Muslim's understanding of the words of their god.

I did speak in *The Deception of Allah Volume 1*, pages 241/242:

تفسير Tanwîr al-Miqbâs min Tafsîr Ibn 'Abbâs, Qur'an 41:9

﴿ قُلْ أَئِنَّكُمْ لَتَكْفُرُونَ بِٱلَّذِي خَلَقَ ٱلأَرْضَ فِي يَوْمَيْنِ وَتَجْعَلُونَ لَهُ أَندَاداً ذَلِكَ رَبُّ ٱلْعَالَمِينَ ﴾

"Certain in Him Who created the earth in two Days each day the similar and equal to 1,000 days of the days which you count: Sunday, Monday, etc.,"

Qur'an 17:11 Tafsir of Ibn Kathir

قال تعالى: ﴿ وَكَانَ ٱلإِنْسَانُ عَجُولاً ﴾ وقد ذكر سلمان الفارسي وابن عباس ههنا قصة آدم عليه السلام حين همّ بالنهوض قائماً قبل أن تصل الروح إلى رجليه، وذلك أنه جاءته النفخة من قبل رأسه، فلما وصلت إلى دماغه عطس، فقال: الحمد لله، فقال الله: يرحمك ربك يا آدم. فلما وصلت إلى عينيه فتحهما، فلما سرت إلى أعضائه وجسده، جعل ينظر إليه ويعجبه، فهم بالنهوض قبل أن تصل إلى رجليه فلم يستطع، وقال: يا رب عجل قبل الليل.

And mankind is ever impetuous Salman Al-Farisi and Ibn Abbas referred to the story of Adam, whilst he wanted to get up before his soul arrived at his feet. While his soul was breathed into him, it entered his body starting from his head downwards to his feet. At the same time, as it arrived at his brain, he sneezed, so Adam said, "Al-Hamdu Lil-Lah" praise be to Allah, and Allah responded "May your Lord shower blessing onto you, Adam." while the spirit reached his eyes, he opened them, and when it reached his body main parts and limbs, he started to look at them in amazement, He wanted to get up before it reached his feet, but he could not. He said, "O Lord, hurry up and finish me before night comes."

http://www.qtafsir.com/index.php?option=com_content&task=view&id=2850&Itemid=72

Adam is saying, "finish me before the night comes" (sunset).

- Now this story is good for children.
- How did Adam know Allah's name when he is in the stage of creation?
- How did he know about the sunset or how soon the night would come? When was his first day on earth?
- If it's about billions of years, then what does "finish me before the night comes" mean?

Qur'an 7:54

Tafsir Al-Jalalayn, translation Feras Hamza:

"Surely your Lord is God, Who created the heavens and the earth in six days, of the days of this world, that is to say, in the equivalent thereof, since there was no sun then. Had He willed He could have created them in an instant; but the reason for His not having done so is that He wanted to teach His creatures to be circumspect; then presided upon the Throne,"

As you see for yourself, this is not even our translation or explanation. There was no sun but there were creatures, **"He wanted to teach His creatures to be circumspect"**.

1. "Who created the heavens and the earth in six days, <u>of the days of this world</u>" Qur'an 7:54 Tafsir al-Jalalayn, transl. of Feras Hamza. So, these days are the same as today's, not billions of years!

2. "He wanted to teach His creatures to be circumspect".

How did the trees, the animals and Adam live for billions of years when the sky was in smoke and there was no sun? How many billions of years did Adam live before the sun was created?

The following narration is an approved hadith that gives an account of the creation of the world, referenced from Sahih Muslim, Vol. 4, p. 2150 {Arabic}:

«خَلَقَ اللهُ، (عَزَّ وَجَلَّ)، التُّرْبَةَ يَوْمَ السَّبْتِ، وَخَلَقَ فِيهَا الْجِبَالَ يَوْمَ الْأَحَدِ، وَخَلَقَ الشَّجَرَ يَوْمَ الْاثْنَيْنِ، وَخَلَقَ الْمَكْرُوهَ يَوْمَ الثُّلَاثَاءِ، وَخَلَقَ النُّورَ يَوْمَ الْأَرْبَعَاءِ، وَبَثَّ فِيهَا الدَّوَابَّ يَوْمَ الْخَمِيسِ، وَخَلَقَ آدَمَ، عَلَيْهِ السَّلَامُ، بَعْدَ الْعَصْرِ مِنْ يَوْمِ الْجُمُعَةِ، فِي آخِرِ الْخَلْقِ، فِي آخِرِ سَاعَةٍ مِنْ سَاعَاتِ الْجُمُعَةِ، فِيمَا بَيْنَ الْعَصْرِ إِلَى اللَّيْلِ»

Abu Huraira reported: The Prophet of Allah told me, "Allah created the soil on Saturday, and He created the mountains on Sunday, and He created the trees on Monday, and He created the bad things on Tuesday and He created the light on Wednesday and He created the the walking animals on Thursday and He created Adam on Friday afternoon. He was the last created during the last hour of Friday, between afternoon and night.

This correct hadith is approved in the following hadiths:

الحديث: خلق الله التربة يوم السبت وخلق فيها الجبال يوم الأحد وخلق الشجر يوم الإثنين وخلق المكروه يوم الثلاثاء وخلق النور يوم الأربعاء وبث فيها الدواب يوم الخميس وخلق آدم بعد العصر من يوم الجمعة آخر الخلق من آخر ساعة الجمعة فيما بين العصر إلى الليل] . (صحيح)

Al-Alabany, Vol. 4, Hadith 1833

Book of Al-Mishkat, Hadith 5735

Book of Mukhtasar Al-'Olu Al-Zahbi, Hadith 73

Book of 'Qism Al-Mustfrak, p. 664

http://tafsir.com/default.asp?sid=7&tid=17982

The same story can be found in Tafsir Ibn Kathir, Vol. 7, p. 168, published by 'Tiba publishing company:
http://islamport.com/d/1/tfs/1/27/1244.html

According to the Qur'an, Allah created the earth in six days. However, we just read in the above quote from Sahih Muslim that He began on Saturday and finished the job on Friday, **totaling seven days of creation.** Still, we find the six-day creation of the earth affirmed by numerous verses in the Qur'an, such as Surah 7:54, 10:3, 11:7, 25:59, 32:4, 50:38, and 57:4.

Let's examine the account in:

Qur'an 41:9-12 - Muhammad Pickthall's translation
9 Say (O Muhammad, unto the idolaters): Disbelieve ye verily

in Him Who created the earth in two Days, and ascribe ye unto Him rivals? He (and none else) is the Lord of the Worlds.

10 He placed therein firm hills rising above it, and blessed it and measured therein its sustenance in four Days, alike for (all) who ask;

11 Then turned He to the heaven when it was smoke, and said, unto it and unto the earth: Come both of you, willingly or loth. They said: We come, obedient.

12 Then He ordained them seven heavens in two Days and inspired in each heaven its mandate; and We decked the nether heaven with lamps, and rendered it inviolable. That is the measuring of the Mighty, the Knower.

It tells us that Allah created soil for two (2) days; the trees, water, and mountains for four (4) days; and the skies for two (2) days. If we add the number of days it took Allah to create the earth, we get a **total of eight (8) days** **and not six.** What does that tell us?

The complete account of creation in Surah 41:9-12 clearly contradicts the several verses I mentioned above which says that creation was completed in six days. It also contradicts the hadith even though they somewhat match in the order of creation.

Before we end this topic, Muslims make many claims about the age of the earth, and I heard some of them say that the Qur'an is more accurate than the Bible when it comes to the six-day creation as the Qur'an does not mention the length of these days. The fact is that, as always, Muhammad helps us to expose the Muslims' false science.

Sahih Al-Bukhari, Book 59, Hadith 688

"The Prophet of Allah said, 'The time has gotten its existent looks and shape which it has now, since Allah created the Heavens and the Earth....."

It's so clear from Muhammad's words that the length of time at the period of creation is the same as today's. Moreover, they say that Islam never said that the six days of Allah's creation is the same as today's. As you've read in the above hadith, it's exactly the same. By the way, according to science, days at the beginning of the earth were shorter than today's and they are even getting longer.
See: http://helios.gsfc.nasa.gov/qa_earth.html#earthslow

But on the other hand, Muhammad said, one day for Allah is equal to one thousand years of our reckoning, as we see in:

Qur'an 22:47

"Nevertheless, they ask thee to quicken on the Punishment! However, Allah will not fail in His Promise. Verily, a Day in the sight of your Lord is same as a thousand years of your reckoning."

Therefore, if time never changed, it was at the same shape, as Muhammad said in the above hadith ("The time has gotten its existent looks and shape which it has now, since Allah created the Heavens and the Earth..."), Allah gave them the same names we have and he called them days. This proves more contradictions in Muhammad's words and his god's words. So one of them is telling a lie which ultimately means they are both telling a lie because the first one (Muhammad) told a lie so all that Allah said, is also a lie because it was told by a false witness (Muhammad).

Tafsir of Ibn Kathir

Sahih Muslim, Book 039, Hadith 6707

Abu Haraira Reported that Allah's Messenger (may Allah pray on him), took hold of my hands and said: "Allah, the high-minded and magnificent created the soil on Saturday and He created the mountains on Sunday, and He created the trees on Monday, and He created the things entailing labor on Tuesday and created light on Wednesday and caused the animals to spread on Thursday and created Adam after on Friday afternoon; the final creation at the latest hour of the hours of Friday, which was between afternoon and night.

1) Does the *Big Bang* theory speak about afternoon?
2) Either Muhammad told a lie, or
3) Mr. Harun made up this miracle, and lied. You decide.

As you see for yourself, Mr. Harun created his own dates and numbers:

1. Six days for Allah is 16.427104723 billion years.
2. This means that in two days Allah created the earth as in Qur'an 41:9 states:

   Say: Is it that ye deny Him Allah Who created the earth in two Days?

3. Two days equals to = 2.666666666666667 billions years.
4. Allah needed four more days to create the earth's substances,

83

as Qur'an 41:10 states:

He set on the earth, mountains standing firm, high above it, and bestowed blessings on the earth, and measure on it all things and its substance, in four Days, for those who are in need.

5. Four days + 2 = 6. This means the earth was the only thing created during these 16.427104723 billion years!
6. It's clear that Harun Yahya does not know that the Qur'an has a big mistake when Allah said many times that he created the earth in six days. Chapter 41:9-12 clearly shows that Allah created the earth in eight (8) days. 2 days, earth creation + 4 days, earth's substances + 2 days, sky creation, as seen in Qur'an 41:9-12:

9 Say: Do you deny Him Who created the earth in two Days? And you and take equal Gods to him, he is the Lord of the two worlds.

10 He placed therein on earth mountains standing firm from above it, and He blessed it, and measured on it, its subsistence for its inhabitants in four Days equal by length for all those who ask.

11 After that He rose over towards the heaven when it was smoke, and said, to it and to the earth: move towards both of you by choice or against your choice. They both said, We came with obedience.

12 So He made them as seven skies in two Days, and He assigned to each heaven its duty and command. And We decorated the lower heaven with stars, and provided it with guard. Such is respect of the almighty the Full of Knowledge.

However, one more shot in the head to kill the fabricated science, the Qur'an state with clear words that the Sky was the last to create as we read in:

Qur'an 13:12 Sahih International
"It is Allah who erected the heavens without pillars that you [can] see; THEN He established Himself above the Throne"

Huge Qur'an contradiction

Allah created the Earth first or the Heaven?

1. The first question is why did Mr. Harun in his claim **(Creation in six days)** counts all the chapters addressing creation but he did not count to us chapter 79? Is it because of the contradictions found in chapter 41 with regards to which element Allah created and finished first? And to quote him in these verses (Qur'an 32:4, 10:3, 11:7, 25:59, 57:4, 50:38, and 7:54) *"they mean not only days, but also age, period, moment, term."*

2. In chapter 41, Allah created the earth before the sky as we read from verses 9, 10, 11, and 12. After the earth was created, the sky was still a smoke. And this is pointed out with the word "then" in the verse based on his translation: "He placed firmly embedded mountains on it, towering over it, and blessed it and measured out its nourishment in it, laid out for those who seek it- all in four days. **Then** He turned to heaven when **it was smoke** and said, to it and to the earth, "Come willingly or unwillingly." They both said, "We come willingly." (Qur'an, 41:10-11)"

3. In chapter 79:30, interpretation of Al-Tabari, Vol. 24, p. 208 and Tafsir Ibn Kathir, Vol. 8, p. 316: **"earth was created before the sky"**.

http://www.islamweb.net/newlibrary/display_book.php?flag=1&bk_no=49&surano=79&ayano=30

وقوله : (والأرض بعد ذلك دحاها) فسره بقوله : (أخرج منها ماءها ومرعاها) وقد تقدم في سورة " حم السجدة " أن الأرض خلقت قبل السماء ، ولكن إنما دحيت بعد خلق السماء

The same interpretation can be found in Al-Jalalayn.

> *Qur'an 79:30*
>
> *And after that Allah spread out the earth: He made it flat, for it had been created before the firmament but without having been spread out yet"*

www.altafsir.com

1. Even if we ignore this mistake, there was still no sun, no light, or any other source of light. How then did the created animals and trees of Allah survived on earth for billions of years without light? And what about the oxygen when the sky was still a smoke? Does that mean that the sky was merely composed of fine particles of carbon?

2. In chapter 41:11 it says "**After that He rose over towards the heaven when it was smoke**", so it proves that the earth was already created while the sky was nothing but a smoke which

exposes all the fabrications in Mr. Harun's claims.

Qur'an 9:36

The year of Allah is twelve months from the beginning of the earth and heaven's creation.

One more scientific error to go. If Muslims these days accept the *Big Bang* theory, how then can Mr. Harun reconcile the fact that Allah and his prophet said that a year is made up of 12 months while scientists of the *Big Bang* theory claimed a year used to be only less than 4 months?

> *"Tracing these tiny milliseconds back for 4.5 billion years adds up to a very significant amount of time for a solar day. I have determined that the day/night rotation was 63,000 seconds shorter than the present 86,400 seconds it is today. This would put the Earth's rotation at about 6.5 hours per day/night cycle, when it was created, 4.5 billion years ago. (This is a much faster rate of rotation than the Cassini-Huygens mission (2003 to 2004) determined Saturn's 10.5 hours rotation period to be.)"*

Donald L. Hamilton, author of "*The MIND of Mankind*"
http://novan.com/earth.htm
Reference: Chapter 13, (The Earth's Slowing Rotation) "*The MIND of MANKIND*" - ISBN 09649265-1-2, Published 1996, Suna Press.

As long Muslims accept whatever *Big Bang* scientists say, then they should accept that a day was so short: "This would put the Earth's rotation at about 6.5 hours per day/night cycle," therefore the year was about 4 months only:
the year is about 8765.8127 hours so the year was much shorter 2'317.25 hours and the day was 6.5 hours.
Hours today 24 / 6.5 = 3.692 so the year was less than 4 months to our time today. And this proves Muhammad and his god to be false as we read in the Qur'an

> *Qur'an 9:36 Muhammad H. Shakir's translation*
>
> *Surely the number of months with Allah is twelve months in Allah's ordinance since the day when He created the heavens and the earth, of these four being sacred; that is the right reckoning; therefore, be not unjust to yourselves regarding them, and fight the polytheists all together as they fight you all together; and know that Allah is with those who guard (against evil).*

Sahih Muslim, Book 016, Hadith 4160

Abu Bakr bin Abi Shiba stated that Allah's Messenger said: "Time has completed a cycle and came to its state on the day when Allah created the heavens and the earth. The year is constituted of Twelve months, of which four are sacred"

Muslims claim

The splitting asunder of "The heavens and the earth"

http://miraclesoftheQuran.com/scientific_05.html
Another verse about the creation of the heavens is as follows:

> *Do those who disbelieve not see that the heavens and the earth were sewn together and then We unstitched them and that We made from water every living thing? So, will they not believe? (Qur'an, 21:30)*

The word "ratq" translated as "sewn to" means "mixed in each, blended" in the Arabic vernacular. It is used to refer to two different substances that make up a whole.
End of claim

My answer

Let us take a look at the verse again with this knowledge in mind.

Mr. Harun said, "In the verse, sky and earth are at first subject to the status of ratq. They are separated (fataqa) with one coming out of the other. Intriguingly, when we remember the first moments of the Big Bang, we see that the entire matter of the universe collected at one single point."

Then this is about the Big Bang? Sometimes I ask myself if the claim maker reads his own words.

As long as the Qur'an says that the earth and sky were together, and then separated, this would mean that:

This is about separating, not creating;

- In Mr. Harun's words, the phrase, "we unstitched," is the verb "fataqa" in Arabic and implies that something comes into being by tearing apart or destroying the structure of things that are sewn to one another."
- "Do those who disbelieve not see that the heavens and the earth

were sewn together and then We unstitched them".
- **"that are sewn to one another.** "There was an earth; and There was a sky.
- The unstitching was after their existence as earth and heaven, "and then We **Unstitched them**".

As we see the words, "they are separated (fataqa)" notice that Allah is saying: we separated the earth and the heaven, therefore, there was earth and it was heaven but they were connected and then we separated them from each other.

As we read in Mr. Harun' translation of Qur'an, 21:30

> *"that the heavens and the earth were sewn together and then We unstitched them"*

- The *Big Bang* theory says there was nothing! It doesn't claim that the earth and sky were one and then exploded!
- Those who believe in the *Big Bang* theory claim that the earth is approximately 4.54 billion years old. By the way, I am not saying this is a date that I accept but, as long as the Muslims are accepting the *Big Bang* theory as a fact, they should accept whatever age comes with it. The earth is so young at 4.54 billion years compared to their claim that the universe is 16 billion years old, to quote: "Calculated in terms of years, 6 trillion days equates to approximately 16.427 billion years" I saw in Mr. Harun's website that they claim the universe was created 16 billion years ago. This is proof that the Muslims did not read the book they quoted from. They just picked and chose the cherries they wanted. Actually, this isn't even working for them, because it makes everything very wrong. Why? It's because Allah made the stars (all the stars) long after he created and finished the earth, as we seen in Qur'an 41:9-12.
- It's so clear that they are trying to fool us, when the words are clearly speaking for themselves. All that Allah or Muhammad are saying is that Allah lifted up the sky, as we have seen in the Qur'an 13:2:

> "Allah is He Who raised up the heavens without visible PILLARS that you can see."

This means that the sky was once on top of the earth! Allah then raised the sky up with pillars that we cannot see. It's so clear that what Allah or Muhammad are saying is that Allah raised the sky and by that they were separated from each other. This is surely very false because the earth is inside the sky, not out of it. The earth itself is hanging in the sky (space). I will talk about this verse later in more details in Qur'an 50:1.

When we answered the claim about the universe being created from hot smoke, we read this verse which was posted and translated by Mr.

Harun himself:

> "That Day We will fold up heaven like folding up the pages of
> a book. As We originated the first creation so We will
> regenerate it. It is a promise binding on Us. That is what We
> will do." (Qur'an, 21:104)

So Allah created the earth and the heaven by unfolding something
similar to a book, but we do not see any explosion in the unfolding. If
Allah weren't holding the sky then it would surely fall on us!

Qur'an 22:65

> "Do you not see that Allah has made submissive to you
> whatsoever is in the earth and the ships running in the sea by
> His command? And He withholds the heaven from falling on
> the earth except with His approval most surely Allah is
> forgiving merciful to men."

So, the word "**fataqa**" or "**unstitched them**" means that Allah just lifted
up the sky. No *Big Bang* explosion or even creation of the sky. He just
held it up and kept it from falling on us.

The sky created after the earth

Qur'an 2:29

ثُمَّ

> "Its He Who created for you all that is in the earth. And after
> that ('SUMA) He turned to the heaven, and formed it as
> seven heavens. And He is knowable of all things."

Muslims try to translate the word **'SUMA** ثُمَّ as "simultaneously" which is
an absolute lie because this word exposes huge mistakes in the Qur'an.
See Muslims made video show the true meaning of **'SUMA** ثُمَّ
https://www.youtube.com/watch?v=knFkL7dRo5U
After watching you will understand why I always say never trust a Muslim
speaking about Islam, honesty is missing in Islam.

Qur'an 2:29, Tafsir Al-Jalalayn, transl. Feras Hamza

> "He it is Who created for you all that is in the earth, that is,
> the earth and all that is in it, so that you may benefit from
> and learn lessons from it; then, after creating the earth, He
> turned to, that is, He made His object"

If we go to Qur'an 79:30, Tafsir Al-Jalalayn, transl. of Feras Hamza:

> *"and after that He spread out the earth: He made it flat, for it had been created before the heaven, but without having been spread out;"*

Does the *Big Bang* teach that earth came to existence first and then the stars and galaxy came later in existence?!

That is a clear error in the Qur'an. Also, the earth is not flat!

Muslims' claim

Heavens not supported by pillars

2- God is He who raised the heavens without any pillars...
http://www.quranmiracles.com/2011/03/heavens-not-supported-by-pillars/

My answer

This is a shortsighted claim showing the foolishness of the person's claim. Mr. Harun's statement is supposedly proving that the Bible says that the sky is left it up by columns.! I will quote his claim:

"For instance, in the New American Bible, a picture is drawn to show how the authors of the Bible imagined the world. In that picture, the sky resembles an overturned bowl and is supported by columns (The New American Bible, St Joseph's Medium Size Edition,"

1. He said "show how the authors of the Bible imagined the world." he means God or the translator? If he means God well our God never gave us any drawing, if he means the translator then what this have to do with our bible or God.?

2. There are millions of drawings that represent the art of humans but if you want to prove that the Bible teaches that, then you better show a verse. Since he can't, I will present a very clear verse about what the God of the Bible says about this topic. And since also he quoted from the New American Bible translation, I will give a gift from the same translation to prove how silly his claim is:

Isaiah 40:22 - New American Standard Bible (©1995)
It is He who sits above the circle of the earth, and its inhabitants are like
grasshoppers, Who stretches out the heavens like a curtain And spreads them out
like a tent to dwell in.

The circle of the earth

Imagine thousands of years ago our holy, amazing Book has already revealed to us what took mankind years and many modern tools to discover.

Job 26:7 - KJV
He stretches out the north over empty space;
He hangs the earth on nothing.

For the first time in the history of mankind, a scriptural book reports a scientific fact which was unknown until not long ago! By the way, Muslims have a claim about the expanding universe, but even this one is in the Bible.
If they say that the earth has walls standing on it lifting the sky up, why does the Bible say that the earth **hangs on nothing?** This means there is nothing holding the earth to the sky.

I will now answer his claim about the pillars in the Qur'an.

Muslims try to fool us by posting a translated verse with parts of it taken out. If you look at the post of Mr. Harun about this verse, you will see how he cut short the verse to fit it with his falsification. Read again the verse he quoted:

13:2 God is He who raised the heavens without any pillars...

Can he tell us why he didn't show the rest of the verse when there are just a few words left? He hid it purposely in order for him to fool the readers.

- The verse tells us that the heaven was raised up. Does it mean it was down?
- Are we not inside the space or underneath it?
- It's so clear that this statement in the Qur'an was made based on the belief that the earth is flat.

Qur'an 2:252
".... His Throne wideness is same as skies and the earth, and He has no

weakness in guarding and preserving them intended for He is the strongest the Supreme."

Its so clear that, according to Allah, the earth and the sky are of the same width {Earth width = Sky width} because if his throne is the same width as that of the sky's, would it matter what's in it? The earth would not even equal to a dust in comparison to the size of the galaxy's

If the earth is so insignificantly small and is within the massive space, why does Allah say that the skies and earth have the same size as well as his throne being equal to both?

Qur'an 69:16-17

16 And the sky will split apart for that day it will be breakable.

17 And the angels will be on its sides, and eight of them will, that Day, carry the Throne of, the Lord on top of them.

Ibn Kathir's interpretation

And the angels will be on its sides or borders, the word angels, here is applying to some chosen Angels; meaning the angels will be standing on the sides of the heavens. AL-Rabe` bin Anas said, concerning Allah's testimony.

What is the sky, since it has sides and edges? It's just a roof above the earth.

From Mr. Harun's translation, we read:
"We made the sky a preserved and protected roof yet still they turn away from Our Signs. (Qur'an, 21:32)

This means the earth is equal to the sky by size as a roof must be equal to the size of the house.

Muslims claim

Allah's heavens without pillars

Qur'an 13:2

Allah is He Who raised up the heavens without visible PILLARS that you can see.

اللَّهُ الَّذِي رَفَعَ السَّمَٰوَٰتِ بِغَيْرِ عَمَدٍ تَرَوْنَهَا ثُمَّ اسْتَوَىٰ عَلَى الْعَرْشِ وَسَخَّرَ الشَّمْسَ وَالْقَمَرَ كُلٌّ يَجْرِي لِأَجَلٍ مُّسَمًّى يُدَبِّرُ الْأَمْرَ يُفَصِّلُ الْآيَاتِ لَعَلَّكُم بِلِقَاءِ رَبِّكُمْ تُوقِنُونَ

Notice the Muslim's claim would not show the entire verse. They cut it as this: God is He Who raised up the heavens without PILLARS.

They stopped there so you would not see the rest of the verse. It says clearly that there are pillars, but you can't see them. Since Mr. Harun mentioned the name of Ibn Kathir, let us see what Ibn Kathir said:

والأرض بعد ذلك دحاها) فسره بقوله : (أخرج منها ماءها ومرعاها) وقد تقدم في سورة " حم السجدة " أن الأرض خلقت قبل)
السماء ، ولكن إنما دحيت بعد خلق السماء

Ibn Kathir's explanation

"It's already has been mentioned previously in Surat Ha' Mim Als-Sajdah chapter that the earth was created before the heaven was created, but it was only spread out after the creation of the heaven."

"Between the throne to the ground marching of five hundred years after the A Country marching of five hundred years, and the throne of Allah made of red ruby, was narrated from Ibn Abbas, Mujahid and Hasan, Qatada, that there is pillars but you can't see them."

http://www.qtafsir.com/index.php?option=com_content&task =view&id=1397&Itemid=135

Also, as long he accepts Ibn Abbas, as we have seen in Harun's text, {Ibn Abbas (d. 687 AD), Mujahid (d. 718 AD) and as Ikrima (d. 733 AD) believed in the existence of pillars (mountains) supporting the sky, too}, then check out what Ibn Abbas said and you will surely find it funny. You can read my translation or go to the Muslim's site and see theirs.

And in the Tafsir of Ibn Kathir chapter Qur'an 69:32 which is about inserting a chain of iron in human anus, in the interpretation of Ibn Kathir :"(**If a drop of such a lead - and he pointed to a skull bone - _were sent from the heaven to the earth, and it is a distance of five hundred years travel_, it would reach the earth before sunset.**" you can go **to** www.qtafsir.com to see their translations.

Ibn Abbas' translation

He Allah it is who raised up the skies. He created the heavens and raised them up above the earth without any visible pillars. He says: you see them without support; it is also said, that this means: they have pillars but you cannot see it.

Muslims' translation of Ibn Abbas:

"He has created the heavens without any pillars that you see"

Since he also used Tafsir of Mujahhid, let us get it and see how we can again expose the falsification. Here is the link about it from the Kingdom of Jordan Islamic website.

هـ) مصنف و مدقق]04[تفسير مجاهد / مجاهد بن جبر المخزومي (ت

اللهُ الَّذِي رَفَعَ السَّمُوَاتِ بِغَيْرِ عَمَدٍ تَرَوْنَهَا ثُمَّ اسْتَوَى عَلَى الْعَرْشِ وَسَخَّرَ الشَّمْسَ وَالْقَمَرَ كُلٌّ يَجْرِي لِأَجَلٍ مُسَمًّى يُدَبِّرُ الأَمْرَ يُفَصِّلُ }

{ الآيَاتِ لَعَلَّكُمْ بِلِقَاءِ رَبِّكُمْ تُوقِنُونَ

]2[أخبرنا عبد الرحمن، نا إبراهيم، نا آدم، نا ورقاءُ عن أبي نجيح، عن مجاهد: { الَّذِي رَفَعَ السَّمَاوَاتِ بِغَيْرِ عَمَدٍ تَرَوْنَهَا }]الآية:

أي: بعمد لا ترونها.

I guess Mr. Harun thought that no one would go look up the fabricated falsification inside his book. Actually, this man is greatly exposing the fairytale stories in the Qur'an. Since he accepts the view of Ibn Abbas, I think he has no excuse to reject what Ibn Abbas stated in the following verse.

(My translation) Qur'an 50:1

Ibn Abbas said, that about Allah's quotation (Qaf.): It is a blue mountain around the earth from all directions of worldwide and even the sky it takes its color from this blue mountain; Allah swore by it.
http://quranx.com/Tafsirs/50.1

Some might say there's no way that Muhammad would believe a mountain flying in the sky! The fact is that this is but another fairytale story in the Qur'an.
As you can see, the lie did not live long. Instead of trying to show us a mistake in the Bible, he gave us a fairytale story about a mountain surrounding the earth. To this day, no satellite has ever discovered it! Do you know why it cannot be seen? Muhammad told them it's a blue mountain because when he looked up, he saw a blue color along the horizon and believed that this was a blue mountain that the sky was taking its color from.

That explains the verse Mr. Harun quoted to us about the sky being the same as a dome, as we can see from his translation:

Qur'an 2:22

"It is He Who made the earth a couch for you, and the sky a dome. He sends down water from the sky and by it brings forth fruits for your provision. Do not, then, knowingly make others equal to Allah."

Muhammad thought that there was a mountain surrounding the earth from its sides and was holding up the sky. But there's another verse saying clearly that Allah is the one who holds the sky and keeps it from falling down on us, which is seen in:

Qur'an 22:65
Do you not see that he made for you whatever on the top of the earth for your use, and all ships sail on the sea by His orders? <u>He holds the sky from falling on the earth except by His leave</u>: for Allah is Most Kind and Most Merciful to mankind.

Since Mr. Harun likes Ibn Abbas' interpretation of the Qur'an, we will take references from there.

تفسير *Tanwîr al-Miqbâs Tafsîr Ibn Abbas*
This is the Muslims
Muslims claim
 translations website to show that I am not making things up.

http://www.altafsir.com/

As you can see, Ibn Abbas states that it is Allah who holds the sky from falling down on us, wherein the latter is something that will certainly happen on the Day of Judgment.

This makes things clear that Islam really considers the sky as a physical roof, like a dome, and Allah will make it collapse on us on the Judgment day. Allah even used the word roof, if you remembered reading one of the earlier verses mentioned. Note that this is Mr. Harun's translation.

Qur'an 21:32
"We made the sky a preserved and protected roof yet still they turn away from Our Signs.

Hail come down from mountains in heaven?

"He sendeth down from the heaven mountains wherein is hail," Qur'an24:43 Muhammad Picthal Translation

Ibn Kathir interpretation
 "He sends down from the sky, from mountains in it of ice,
see Muslims site and translation"
Tafsir al-Jalalayn, trans. Feras Hamza
"And He sends down from the heaven out of the mountains (min jibālin: min is extra) that are therein, in the heaven."
altafsir.com

Tafsir Ibn 'Abbas, trans. Mokrane Guezzou

"(He sendeth down from the heaven mountains wherein is hail) He says: He sends down hail from mountains in heaven"

I believe strongly that the Qur'an author was copying his imagination from the old book which is rejected by Christianity it's called the book of **ENOCH, 300 BC Ethiopic editions, whether translated from** Aramaean or Greek, and in some theory it originated of an Aramaic or Syro-Chaldsean.

As an example, in that book two angels came to Enoch and took him up to heaven and there he saw and we quote;

"Enoch Chapter 41;3. There I saw the wooden receptacles out of which the winds became separated, the receptacle of hail, the receptacle of snow, the receptacle of the clouds, and the cloud itself, which continued over the earth before the creation of the world."

and then we find out when Muhammad got his story about the houses of the moon in the Qur'an;

"Enoch chapter 41:1 I beheld also the receptacles of the moon, whence the moons came, whither they proceeded, their glorious return, and how one became more splendid than another."

Qur'an 36:39 "And for the moon We have appointed mansions till she returns like an old wrinkled palm-leaf."

I will give more details about this in my coming book.

Let's go back to the topic about the earth being surrounded by **blue mountains** that are carrying the roof (the sky).
1. He believed that the earth was surrounded by blue mountains which holds the sky up and keep it from falling down on us.
2. Here the sky itself has flying mountains where Allah **store ice on it**.

Reading the coming hadith, you will see how Muhammad explained where the sun is coming from:

Sahih Muslim, Book 004, Hadith 1807

as saying: Do not try to observe prayer when the sun is rising, nor at of its setting time, for it rises between the two horns of Satan.

This is an absolute scientific discovery! Muslims will never make a movie about it! Do not forget the hadith where Muhammad tells the Muslims of the following:

> *Sahih Al-Bukhari, Book 54, Hadith 421*
>
> *"Do you know where the sun goes every day?" He said, "It goes and travels till it arrives and prostrates itself underneath the Throne of Allah and takes the permission from him (Allah) to rise again, and it is permitted*

Have a look at it yourself in the Muslims
Muslims claim
translation's website, which it not really accurate as always, but good enough to prove the point.

I wonder why Muslims do not make a book about this hadith?!

....
Muslims claim

Sub-atomic particles

http://www.miraclesofthequran.com/scientific_36.html
This fact only emerged in the last century, but was revealed in the Qur'an 1,400 years ago:
This verse refers to "atom" and smaller particles still.

My answer

Here is the verse he quoted:

Qur'an 34:3
"He is the Knower of the Unseen, Whom not an atom's weight eludes, either in the heavens or in the earth; nor is there anything smaller or larger than that"

This is not even talking about an atom. The word atom means: the smallest unit of any kind of chemical element.

ذرة
First how its Amazing discovery when the Arab used and made this word before Allah himself or Muhammad use it, if it's the claim is true, then claim the credit must go to the Arab who made this word not to Qur'an

author.

The word **Zarah** means one ant or singular sand, let us read again Mr. Harun's words:
"This verse refers to "atom" and smaller particles still."
Mr. Harun forgot that the verse he posted says this:

> *"an atom's weight eludes, either in the heavens or in the earth; nor is there anything smaller or larger than that which is not in a Clear Book."*

The word **Zarah** has nothing to do with an atom. When the West discovered the atom, we Arabs used that same word because we did not have an equal word for it. All that the verse is saying is that it does not matter how small your work is or how big it is. You are going to see your reward on Judgment day. It has nothing to do with science.

It wasn't meant as a small single object, as we can see in the interpretation of Al-Qur'tubi:

مثقال ذرة أي قدر نملة صغيرة. في السماوات ولا في الأرض ولا أصغر من ذلك ولا أكبر .

He said:

> *"In the weight of Zarah means as a small Ant, nothing bigger or smaller than this ant.*
>
> *Ant = small, nothing, smaller or bigger = all has one size."*

What we understand from this is that it's about one kind or one object of its kind and the ant represents that object. I don't think Muslims will say that the ant is an atom.

To make it clearer from an Islamic translation to the Qur'an, read the following:

Qur'an 10:61, Mohsin Khan's translation
"Neither you (O Muhammad وسلم عليه الله صلى) do any deed nor recite any portion of the Qur'an, - nor you (mankind) do any deed (good or evil) but We are Witness thereof, when you are doing it. And nothing is hidden from your Lord (so much as) the weight of an atom (or small ant) on the earth or in the heaven. Not what is less than that or what is greater than that but is (written) in a Clear Record."

However, if it's true Allah speaking about Atoms and claim to be the smallest he is wrong again, because there Proton and Neutron as an example a lot more smaller than the atom.

"*atom* consists of a tiny nucleus made up of *protons and neutrons,* on the order of 20,000 times *smaller than* the size of the *atom*"

http://hyperphysics.phy-astr.gsu.edu/hbase/chemical/atom.html

----

Muslims claim

Black holes

And I swear by the stars' positions-and that is a mighty oath if you only knew. (Qur'an, 56:75-76) ......
When the stars are extinguished, (Qur'an, 77:8)
[I swear] by Heaven and the Tariq! And what will convey to you what the Tariq is? The Star Piercing [the darkness]! (Qur'an, 86:1-3)

My answer

Let us read the translated verse they chose to make their point.

Qur'an 56:75-76

And I swear by the stars' positions-and that is a mighty oath if you only knew.

In order to understand this verse, we need to read more verses about the stars:

Qur'an 52:49

"And in the night, give Him glory too, and at the setting of the stars"

Qur'an 53:1

"By the star when it descends,"

So stars has positions and they leave their position every morning?
If you remember, this hadith talks about Muhammad asking the Muslims, "Do you know where the sun goes?" His answer can be read here:

Qur'an 36.38

Sahih Al-Bukhari (Arabic), Book the Start of Creation, p. 1171, Hadith 3027

99

Bukhari Book 60, Hadith 326
Sahih Muslim, Book 001, Hadith 0297

Abu Zerr reported: Once I was with the Messenger in the mosque at the time of sunset. The Messenger of Allah said, "O Abu Zerr! Do you know where the sun goes?" I responded, "Allah and His Messenger know better." The prophet answered, "It goes and prostrates underneath and bows down under Allah's Throne; will it ask Allah's authorization to bow down, but he will not accept, then Allah will order it to go and raise back from where it came from, and that is Allah's All-Mighty Statement: 'And the sun runs on its fixed course for a term.

1) As long as the sun rests and sleeps under the throne of Allah, it means that the location of the stars would be the same location as that of the throne of Allah, which is exactly where Allah himself is.
2) In another claim, Harun Yahya said that the seven heavens are the layers of the atmosphere! Why is it then Qur'an is talking about black holes? In their false translation, they posted this: [I swear] by Heaven and the Tariq! And what will convey to you what the Tariq is? The Star Piercing [the darkness]! (Qur'an 86:1-3)" Where did the word "darkness" come from?
3) Let us see what the hadith says about this chapter or verse in the Book of Al-Jame' Le A'hkam Al Qur'an, Vol. 20, p. 3:

Qur'an 86:1-3
Narrated from Ibn Abbas HE said, "The prophet was setting with Abu Talib, then a star came down! And made the ground full of light so Abu Talib got scared and he asked (Muhammad), "What is that?" He, Muhammad, answered, "It's a star being thrown down." And Allah gave him the verse of Al Tariq

1. Is he saying a black hole came down to Muhammad?
2. If not, both of them are telling a lie! A star fell on earth but we're all still alive!

تفسير القرطبي
محمد بن أحمد الأنصاري القرطبي
] سورة الطارق3الجزء العشرون [ص:
ابن عباس قال: " كان رسول الله صلى الله عليه وسلم قاعداً مع أبي طالب، فانحط نجم، فامتلأت الأرض نوراً، ففزع أبو طالب،
} وقال: أي شيء هذا؟ فقال: »هذا نجم رُميَ به، وهو آية من آيات الله« فعجب أبو طالب، ونزل: } وَٱلسَّمَاءِ وَٱلطَّارِقِ

Book of Muhammad Ibn Ahmed Al-Ansari Al-Qur'tubi, Vol. 20, p. 3, chapter of Al Tariq:

And to make it totally clear, Muhammad the prophet of Islam himself will expose this falsified miracle claim by Muslims.

We read in the book of Asbab Al-Nuzul by Al-Wahidi, <u>translation of Mokrane Guezzou, Qur'an 86:2</u>:

(By the heaven and the Morning Star; ah, what will tell thee what the Morning Star is! The piercing Star!) [86:1-3]. This was revealed about Abu Talib. He once went to visit the Prophet, may Allah bless him and give him peace, and the latter offered him bread and milk. As Abu Talib was sitting and eating, a meteor fell, filling everything with fire. Abu Talib was scared. He asked: "What on earth can this be?" The Prophet, Allah bless him and give him peace, said: <u>"This is a meteor that was thrown and it is one of the signs of Allah".</u> Abu Talib was amazed, and so Allah, exalted is He, revealed these verses.

1. So according to Muhammad it's a meteor.
2. But according to Harun Yahia it's a black hole!
3. Now who's telling a lie? Harun or Muhammad?

\-

Muslims' claim

Quasars and the gravitational lens effect

http://www.miraclesofthequran.com/scientific_97.html

\-

My answer

Mr. Harun's translation

{Allah is the light of the heavens and the Earth. The metaphor of His light is that of a niche in which is a lamp, the lamp inside a glass, the glass like a brilliant star, lit from a blessed tree, an olive, neither of the east nor of the west, its oil all but giving off light even if no fire touches it. Light upon light. Allah guides to His light whoever He wills and Allah makes metaphors for mankind and Allah has knowledge of all things. (Surat an-Nur, 35)}

What we understand from this claim about this verse is that Allah is telling us science that no one knows but himself. Is Allah here speaking about **Quasars**? Quoting their words:

"The light referred to in the verse is suggestive, in terms of its brightness, of these celestial bodies known as quasars."

دري - كوكب

The word **Dury** دري means **bright one**. This verse proves that the god of Islam fails to prove himself as God. The word **kawkab** does not mean star. It has always been used in Arabic to mean a **planet**, not a star. I will prove it below.

Why did Muhammad Pickthall translate it once as a star and then translated it another time as a planet?

It's easy to answer. If they translate it as a planet, this would mean that Allah is a making a mistake for planets do not give light. They only reflect light. This would mean that Allah's light is a reflection,

إِذْ قَالَ يُوسُفُ لِأَبِيهِ يَا أَبَتِ إِنِّي رَأَيْتُ أَحَدَ عَشَرَ **كَوْكَبًا** وَالشَّمْسَ وَالْقَمَرَ رَأَيْتُهُمْ لِي سَاجِدِينَ , Yusuf, Qur'an 12:4 سورة يوسف كوكب = كوكبا	12:4: When Joseph said, unto his father: O my father! Lo! I saw in a dream eleven **planets** and the sun and the moon, I saw them prostrating themselves unto me. Muhammad Pickthal Translation
kawkab is translated as **planets**	eleven **planets**
اللَّهُ نُورُ السَّمَاوَاتِ وَالْأَرْضِ ۚ مَثَلُ نُورِهِ كَمِشْكَاةٍ فِيهَا مِصْبَاحٌ ۖ الْمِصْبَاحُ فِي زُجَاجَةٍ ۖ الزُّجَاجَةُ كَأَنَّهَا **كَوْكَبٌ** دُرِّيٌّ Qur'an 24:35	The glass is as it were a shining star Muhammad Pickthal Translation As you see for yourselves, it is the same translator. Once it comes as a star and once it comes as a planet! Why?

not the original which the verse accurately shows. Mainly because I don't want to explain this verse twice, I am going to use it in answering the next claim.

تفسير ابن كثير
إسماعيل بن عمر بن كثير القرشي الدمشقي
دار طيبة
م2002هـ / 1422سنة النشر:
" تفسير القرآن العظيم »» تفسير سورة النور » تفسير قوله تعالى " الله نور السماوات والأرض
قال أبي بن كعب وغير واحد : وهي نظير قلب المؤمن . (الزجاجة كأنها كوكب دري) : قرأ بعضهم بضم الدال من غير همزة ، [59من الدر ، أي : كأنها كوكب من د] ص:
وقرأ آخرون : " دريء " و " دريء " بكسر الدال وضمها مع الهمز ، من الدرء وهو الدفع; وذلك أن النجم إذا رمي به يكون أشد استنارة من سائر الأحوال ، والعرب تسمي ما لا يعرف من الكواكب دراري

From the interpretation of Ibn Kathir, print year 2002, p. 59, chapter of Al-Nur, "Abu Ka'eb said, and many others: the "glass is the same as planet". The word **Dury** ca,e from the word **Dur** [jewelries]. It's a planet made of jewelries "**Dur**". And some others said these are falling stars which were signed while the Arabs however called these <u>unknown planets **Durary**</u>."

"which means pearls, i.e., as if it were a star which is made of pearls (Dur). Others recite of Qur'an it as Dirri'on or Durri'on, **which means reflection (Dir')**,"

دري - كوكب

For the sake of argument, let's say that the words **kawkab dury** mean "brilliant star". The verse would then say, and to Mr. Harun's translation again, "the glass like a brilliant star." Notice the letter "a" as in "<u>a</u> brilliant star." The verse means any shining star, not a specific star at all. Otherwise it would come with the star's name or at least with the word "the" as in "<u>the</u> brilliant star" instead of "a brilliant star." And as I showed you from Ibn Kathir's interpretation, the Arabs called any unknown planet a **dury**.

In some Muslims translation the change the word from Planet to star as they did in www.qtafsir.com

Tanwîr al-Miqbâs min Tafsîr Ibn 'Abbâs (Tafsir Ibn 'Abbas, trans. Mokrane Guezzou)

> "(The similitude of His light) the light of the believers; it is also said that this means: the light of Allah in the heart of the believer (is as a niche wherein is a lamp. The lamp is in a glass) made of gems. (The glass is as it were a shining star) one of the following five planets: Mercury, Jupiter, Venus, Mars and Saturn. All these planets are luminous. ((This lamp is) kindled from a blessed tree)"

At the same time, Allah is saying that he burns like a star. And as Mr. Harun agreed, Allah thinks that stars burn by using olive oil."

From his translation, I quote:
"The metaphor of **His light** is that of a niche in **which is a lamp**, the lamp inside a glass, **the glass like a brilliant star, lit from a blessed tree, an olive,** neither of the east nor of the west, its oil all but giving off light even if no fire touches it." http://www.altafsir.com/

Allah is not self-sufficient

He generates light from " a blessed tree"

103

According to this, Allah says he generates light by burning oil from olive trees provided to the planets or lamp. At the same time, he is saying that the star lights up the same way! Based on this, the brightness of a star results from the olive oil burning. If the Muslims try to say that olive oil was used in those days for lighting, which is why Allah used it as an example, then we should make it clear that he chose to use a wrong example for many reasons.

1) I think the author of the Qur'an was influenced by the Biblical verse about the burning bushes. Read **Exodus 3:1-4:17**.
2) A burning lamp that uses olive oil is not bright at all. It would be very low in light and such a wrong comparison with "**the glass like a brilliant star**" especially with the words "olive oil." To make it clear, what kind of fuel is used for lighting? This leads us to understand how weak the light will be.
3) Since it's about burning and not simply the term "star" as Muslims claim, Allah again is employing a wrong vocabulary. This means Allah will burn out one day just like any other star that will one day die by burning its own source.

Let us read the next claim and see the answer for both.

Muslims claim

Structural differences between the sun, the moon and the stars

http://miraclesoftheQur'an.com/scientific_09.html
We built seven firm layers above you. We installed a blazing lamp. (Qur'an, 78:12-13)
Do you not see how He created seven heavens in layers, and placed the moon as a light in them and made the sun a blazing lamp? (Qur'an, 71:15-16)
with light: self-consuming and burning:
This further emphasis's the miraculous nature of the book of Islam.

My answer

The difference between
The sun and the moon

Qur'an 71:16
"...and made the moon a light (NOOR) and made the sun as a lamp?"

Do the Muslims mean here that Allah knew that the moonlight is a reflected light and the sun is burning?

The fact is, this verse doesn't say anything about a reflecting light. All it says is that we see that the moon has a light and the sun is a lamp. Let's see what word was used in Arabic for the word "light". It's **NOOR** If this word means reflected light, as they claim, this means that Allah's **NOOR** is reflected too for the Qur'an always
says the **NOOR of Allah,** as we can see in the Qur'an.

نور

> *Qur'an 61:8*
>
> *"They wish to extinguish the light (NOOR) of Allah by their mouths but God will Conclude His light, though the disbelievers be averse."*

We go back to Qur'an 24:35

Below is Mr. Harun's translation and I will locate all the words {NOOR} in the verse:

{Allah is the light {Noor} of the heavens and the Earth. The metaphor of His light {Noor} is that of a niche in which is a lamp, the lamp inside a glass, the glass like a brilliant star, lit from a blessed tree, an olive, neither of the east nor of the west, its oil all but giving off light {Noor} even if no fire touches it. Light {Noor} upon light {Noor}. Allah guides to His light {Noor} whoever He wills and Allah makes metaphors for mankind and Allah has knowledge of all things. (Surat an-Noor, 35)}

Therefor Allah is a reflected light because the verse here uses the word *noor*!

What's funny is that it is the exact chapter that the Muslims used to speak about a brilliant star. The same word was used, and now they try to use it as meaning reflection light. Perhaps they never thought that we would remember the previous claim! To prove their lie, I will show you Muhammad's words speaking about the moonlight with details.

> *Sahih Muslim, Book 001, Hadith 0421*
>
> *Sahih Al-Bukhari, Book 54, Hadith 468*
>
> *Abu Huraira recorded The Messenger of Allah I wonder why Muslims do not make a book about this hadith?!*

We quot from the claim the prophet said: *"Seventy thousand individuals would enter Paradise as one crowd and*

105

between them, there would be humans which their faces would be bright like THE MOON."

Muhammad made it clear that even Allah's **NOOR** (light) is the same as that of the moonlight and not the sun. Maybe Muhammad chose the wrong words again!

Sahih Al-Bukhari, Book 72, Hadith 702

Reported by Abu Huraira: I heard Allah's apostle saying, "From among my followers, a group of SEVENTY THOUSAND will enter Paradise without being asked for their current account. Their faces will be shining like the moon."

Allah's *noor*, his *noor*

As you see here, the verse describes Allah's light, *noor*, as (His Light is as a lamp in a niche). This means light, as the word (*noor*), does not mean reflection, because according to this verse, the *noor*, or light, is coming directly from the lamp. This is unless Muslims think that their god borrows his light! (*noor*).

Sahih Al-Bukhari, Book 10, Hadith 547

Reported Jarir bin 'Abdallah: We were there with the Messenger on a full phase of the moon night. He looked at THE MOON and said, "You will definitely see your Lord such as you see this MOON, plus there will be no difficulty in seeing Him."

You can certainly look at the sun but not for a long period of time, otherwise its brightness will blind you. However, Allah's light is the same as the moon's. We can stare at the moon for a long time since its light is just a reflection and nothing more. This shows that once more Muhammad chose the light of his god to be identical with the light of the moon. Maybe Muhammad misrepresented his god again.

Muslims claim

The orbit of the moon

http://www.quranmiracles.com/2011/03/the-orbit-of-the-moon/

The moon orbits earth in 27 days, 7 hours, 43 minutes and 11 seconds. The Arabic word "qamar" meaning **"moon" is used 27 times** in the Qur'an. (The miraculous character of this shall be dealt with in the coming pages.)

My answer

It must be a miracle!

First, if the word moon comes out 27 times, how come it's translated 28 times in the Qur'an? Maybe Mr. Harun, not having knowledge of the Arabic language, doesn't know that the Qur'an uses different words in Arabic such as the word **Qamar**, to identify the moon. If we go to Qur'an 2:189, we will see the word moon in all translations made by Muslims because the Arabic word used there is new moons (**Ahilla**, plural of *Hilāl*).

> *Qur'an 2:189*
>
> *Translations of Yusuf Ali, Muhammad H. Shakir, Muhammad Pickthall and Mohsin Khan*
>
> *"They ask thee concerning the New Moons."*

And that will break Mr. Harun's numbers from 27 to 28.

The fact is, the moon takes 27.3 days to go around the earth. If Allah knew the correct timing of the moon's orbit, which is something that's already been known for thousands of years, why then did he choose the lunar calendar which is 11.5 days shorter than the current calendar?

شهر

It's very obvious that the one who came up with this argument had no idea what the Qur'an is about. This book is based generally on foreign words from other languages specifically Aramaic. The word (Shahr or Shahra) is an Aramaic word used in Arabic which means moon. By today's translation, this word means month. That is the normal understanding for an average person with very limited knowledge in Arabic.

If we take a look at this coming verse, we would find the word Shahr translated as month and that is due to today's standard use of the word. However, the word originally means moon and during Muhammad's time, Arab used the moon to be the basis of their monthly date system just like the Muslims. Both words mean the time by the moon. As an example, instead of saying, "I will pay you in the coming month," I can say, "I will pay you in the coming moon," because the coming moon is the coming month.

Qur'an 9:36
That the number of the months for Allah is twelve months in Allah's book, he created the heavens and the earth.

Based on this, the correct translation would be:
Qur'an 9:36
That the number of the months(moons) for Allah is twelve (moon) in Allah's book, he created the heavens and the earth.

And that makes more sense because the Muslims use the lunar calendar.
If we go to the Arabic Islamic dictionary of Al-qamous Al-Muhee't, or the dictionary of Lisan Al-Arab we will find:
"AL-Shahr mean moon and its named this way because its famous"

This is a direct link to the Islamic dictionaries
www.baheth.info/all.jsp?term=شهر

ابن الأعرابي: يسمى القمر شهرا ؛ لأنه يشهر به ، والجمع أشهر وشهور

Another less-known name is (sahar), related to the Aramaic and Arabic words for moon (sahara and shahr, respectively)
http://jhom.com/topics/moon/hebrew.html

So again, the god of Islam insists that a year is composed of 12 moons appear as the word Shahr.
And that again will break the claim of the word moon which appears in the Qur'an 27 times because the word shahr or moon shows up in the Qur'an 17 times.
So, 27 time as Qamar + 1 time as Ahilla + 17 times as Shahr = 45 times the word moon appears in the Quran.

Muslims' claim

The rotation of the earth around the sun: 365 days

The word "day, "yavm" in Arabic appears 365 times in the Qur'an. It also takes the Earth 365 days to orbit the Sun.

The fact that the word "day" appears 365 times in the Qur'an is very important in terms of its providing information about the earth's orbit hundreds of years ago.
Yaum يوم

My answer

The word "day" appears 365 times in the Qur'an.

It takes the earth 365 days to orbit the sun."

The funny thing is, if this is true and the Muslims agree that the right calendar is 365 days, then why did Allah choose the lunar year which would be wrong since we see them agreeing with science that there's indeed 365 days?!

Also, is it true that the word "day" appears 365 times in the Qur'an?

The actual number of times the word day (يوم) appears in the Arabic Qur'an 478, and the word "day" can be found in this translated version below:

http://www.altafsir.com/Qur'an_Search.asp

1. Just the claim before this one they said Allah said the word moon 27 time and that present the Islamic moon calendar, but now the Islamic month is not the moon month no more its "The Gregorian calendar", also called the Western calendar and the Christian calendar.?
2. The word "yavm" in Mr. Harun's text is very wrong as the Arabic alphabet doesn't have a letter V at all. Also, the word "youm" is not even an Arabic word because it's taken from the Aramaic word "youmu" which means day.
3. The word "day" appears 574 times in 519 verses in Yusuf Ali's translation of the Qur'an.
4. The word "day" appears 532 times in 481 verses in Muhammad H. Shakir' translation of the Qur'an.
5. The word "day" appears 568 times in 513 verses in Muhammad Pickthall's translation of the Qur'an.
6. The word "day" appears 704 times in 579 verses in Mohsin Khan's translation of the Qur'an.

In the Arabic Qur'an, we can find the following phrases and the number of times they are repeated:
The word(s) "يوم" appears 415 verses in the Qur'an

So if Mr. Harun's calculations are correct, that would mean that all other Islamic translations that add the word "day" for more than 200 times is a corruption of the Qur'an. I think Mr. Harun never thought that someone would count after him. And that certainly wouldn't be the Muslims who fund his projects to promote Islam.

The Year for Allah is 12 Months!

Qur'an 9:36

That the number of the months (moons) for Allah is twelve months (moons) in Allah's book, he created the heavens and the earth.

Maybe you do not know this but the 12-month Islamic calendar is a lunar calendar. It's 11.2 days shorter than the correct year with 365.2425 days. The shortened 11.2 days means that in every 3 years, the correct calculation would be 13 months.

shorter days11.2 x 3 = 34.2

Every 3 years, they have to add one more month to obtain the correct year. Therefor Allah's statement that one year is 12- lunar months is incorrect. To explain this in more detail, the month of *Ramadan* is not fixed on a specific date because the month of the lunar calendar lacks 11.2 days every year and the leap year for the lunar year would be 385 days.

Year	Ramadan Month
2000	November, 28
2001	November, 17
2003	November, 6
2004	October, 16
2005	October, 5
2006	September, 24
2007	September, 13
2008	September, 2
2009	August, 22
2010	August 11, 2010
2011	August 01, 2011

2012	August 14, 2012
2013	July 09, 2013
2014	June 28, 2014

1. As we see, the month of *Ramadan* is moving. This year it's in the summer but a few years back it was in the winter season. This is all because the lunar year is drifting and every third year it will turn to a 13-month year if you need the correct dates.

2. The verse states that for Allah, the year had 12 months when he created the earth. I am sure you've seen that many Muslims accept the *Big Bang* theory but the one who accepts this theory should also accept the rest of the claim that a day then have 6 hours. That will make the day change. Therefore, the month and the measurement of the year as well.

3. See Nasa site
   http://spaceplace.nasa.gov/review/dr-marc-earth/earth-rotation.html

4. The Arabs before Muhammad were using the same calendar. Muhammad used the exact same name for each month so how can Allah take a pagan calendar and claim it to be his?

5. As long as the Islamic calendar is wrong, all Islamic events would be on wrong dates.

The birth of Jesus & the birth of Muhammad

Muslims have always questioned Christians about the accurate date of Jesus' birth. They say that Christians celebrate a date which is not even the actual birth of Christ. We as Christians certainly do not celebrate the date but rather celebrate the occasion. To make it simple to understand, no one on the face of the earth celebrates or can even celebrate the date of his exact birth for this reason:

The day you were born will never come back again.
There's no date that is equivalent to that date. There is no accuracy in any calendar to make you celebrate your birthday by hour and second. To make it uncomplicated for you, I think you heard about something called the leap year which occurs once every 4 years in **Gregorian calendar**.
According to the lunar calendar every 3 years. one lunar month is added, so if your age is 36 years according to Lunar Islamic calendar that mean 36 % 3 = 12 which means your correct age would be 37 not 36.
If you were born on January 1st, 2000(**Gregorian calendar**), and you celebrated your 40-year anniversary, it would occur on January 1st, 2040.

You might think it's the same date but in fact, there are about 10 days added to the calendar within the last 40 years. On that ground, if this is what's happening to every individual on earth, this means there is no actual date of birth that is correct. And if this occurs even after using what is called the accurate calendar which is the one we use today, then what will happen with the Muslims when they use a very wrong calendar which is the lunar calendar?

The birth of Muhammad

Muslims question the accuracy of the birth of Jesus. As said previously, we celebrate the occasion of Christ's birth rather than his date of birth. Muslims on the other hand claim to celebrate the birth of Muhammad as a date, not as an occasion. Let us examine together the Muslims Muslims claim
celebration and see if it is accurate or if they are just fooling themselves.

There are different views regarding the date of birth of Muhammad and Muslims do not all agree about it. However, there is one date that is mostly accepted which is Muhammad being born on the 12th Rabi Al Awwal of the Islamic calendar. Ibn Hazm, Alz Zuhri, Ibn Al Qayyim, and Ibn Dihya all claim that Muhammad was born on the **8th Rabi Al Awwal**.

For the Shia Muslims, Muhammad was born on Monday the **17th Rabi Al Awwal**.

And there are many other dates but we will study the date which is accepted by most of the Sunni Muslims.

> *Sahih Muslim, book 006, Hadith 2603, Book 006, Hadith 2606*
>
> *"He was then asked about fasting on Monday, therefore he said: It was the day on which I was born. On which I was nominated with prophet hood, and revelation was sent to me..."*

The Book of Al-kamel Fe Al-Tari'kh
Vol. 1, p. 416
> "Inb Isaq said: the prophet was born on Monday the 12th Rabi Al Awwal (name of Islamic month)."

الكامل في التاريخ عز الدين أبو الحسن علي المعروف بابن الأثير
[الجزء الأول416ص:
قال ابن إسحاق: ولد رسول الله ـ صلى الله عليه وسلم ـ يوم الاثنين لاثنتي عشرة ليلة مضت من ربيع الأول

So if we take a look at the birthday of Muhammad, Monday the 12th Rabi Al Awwal, we will notice how the month of **Rabi Al Awwal** moves around the year. Sometimes, his birthday comes in summer and in other times it comes in the winter season.

12th Rabi Al Awwal	Islamic calendar year	Gregorian calendar year
12th Rabi Al Awwal	1433	Saturday 4 February 2012
12th Rabi Al Awwal	1410	Thursday 12 October 1989
12th Rabi Al Awwal	1353	Sunday 24 June 1934 CE

This proves that Muhammad's birth date is noticeably moving around the year. Therefore, it's a wrong date because of their use of Lunar Calendar which is incorrect.

So why do Muslims complain that our Christmas date is not the real birth date of Christ when the birth date of their prophet is wrong?

Muslims claim

The ozone layer at the poles As the sun rises

http://www.miraclesofthequran.com/scientific_103.html
Until he reached the rising of the sun and found it rising on a people to whom We had not given any shelter from it. (Surat al-Kahf, 90)
The Arabic word "sitran" in verse 90 of Surat al-Kahf means "cover, shelter, curtain or screen." The term "*lam najAAal lahum min dooniha sitran*" describes an environment devoid of any shelter or protection against the Sun. In the light of present-day knowledge, this is suggestive of the ozone layer that protects living things against harmful solar rays.
The area where the ozone layer around the Earth is thinnest, where it protects least against solar radiation, is the poles.1 Scientific research has established a severe thinning of the ozone layer at the North Pole at the moment the Sun rises 2 and this scientific discovery has been described as Sunrise Ozone Destruction (SOD) 3. .....
The Arabic word "matlia" in this verse, meaning the "rising place" of the Sun, may well be a reference to this scientific discovery about the ozone layer.

My answer

First, we need to find out what "**Dhū'l-Qarnayn**" means. It is not a name. It is a description which means "**the man with two horns.**" I believe from my own study that the person who created most of the Qur'an who is Waraqa Ibn Naofal, took that description and used it as if it were a name of a man from the Bible. And he mixed the story with the Syriac Alexander Legend, which is an Egyptian story about the son of their god Ra (the sun god).

However, the Bible spoke about a king with two horns in the following verses:

Daniel 8:15-22 - KJV

"15 And it came to pass, when I, even I Daniel, had seen the vision, and sought for the meaning, then, behold, there stood before me as the appearance of a man.

16 And I heard a man's voice between the banks of Ulai, which called, and said, Gabriel, make this man to understand the vision.

17 So he came near where I stood: and when he came, I was afraid, and fell upon my face: but he said, unto me, Understand, O son of man: for at the time of the end shall be the vision.

18 Now as he was speaking with me, I was in a deep sleep on my face toward the ground: but he touched me, and set me upright.

19 And he said, Behold, I will make thee know what shall be in the last end of the indignation: for at the time appointed the end shall be.

20 The ram which thou sawest having two horns are the kings of Media and Persia.

21 And the rough goat is the king of Grecia: and the great horn that is between his eyes is the first king.

22 Now that being broken, whereas four stood up for it, four kingdoms shall stand up out of the nation, but not in his power."

Notice in here that Islam based itself on Daniel's verses. To give more explanation, we recognize in the book of Daniel that he spoke about the vision which was explained by the angel Gabriel. We see that

Muhammad adopted Daniel's version of events although Muhammad ran to his wife, scared and terrified, because of his intervention with the Jibrel (the Muslim angel Gabriel).

Sahih Al-Bukhari (Book 1, Hadith 3)

"The angel came to him and asked him to read. The messanger replied, "what shall I read?". The Prophet added, "The angel caught me and squeezed me so hard that I could not bear it any more. Then He released me and again asked me to read and I replied, "what shall I read?" Thereupon he caught me again and pressed me a again till I could not handle it any more. Then He released me and again asked me to read but again I replied, "what shall I read?' Thereupon he caught me for the third time and squeezed me, and then released me and said, 'Read in the name of your Lord, who has created (all that exists) has created man from a clot. Read! And your Lord is the Most Generous." (96.1, 96.2, 96.3)"

Muhammad's copying Isaiah 40:5-6:

As we well know, Islam was explained to Muhammad by Jibrel. Muhammad did the same thing with a story taken from the book of Isaiah 40:5-6:

5 And the glory of the LORD shall be revealed, and all flesh shall see it together: for the mouth of the LORD hath spoken it.

6 The voice said, Cry. And he said, What shall I cry? All flesh is grass, and all the goodliness thereof is as the flower of the field:

We did explain this inside Volume 1 of *The Deception of Allah*. He also used the phrase "the man with the two horns" to describe Alexander the Great, as he thought Daniel's prophecy was speaking about Alexander the Great who is called ***Dhū'l-Qarnayn,*** "the man with the two horns."

But for sure that is a wrong understanding of the Bible because the verses spoke about the end times:

Daniel 8:17 - KJV

(...) but he said unto me, Understand, O son of man: for at the time of the end shall be the vision.

The reason I provided you with verses is to inform you, the reader, and make you understand what these verses are about. Mr. Harun, as

115

always, just posts verses and makes stories about them without telling you what the verses are about nor what the background of the story is.

Who is Dhū'l-Qarnayn?

Many Muslims later on found out that it would be bad for Islam to accept that this story is about this king, so they now deny that Dhū'l-Qarnayn is Alexander the Great. This is because the whole world studied the history of this man who was a pagan and also happened to be a bisexual. So it wouldn't make sense that the god of Islam have chosen this man to do *Jihad*, to convert people to Islam and to punish those who didn't.

I will bring you proof in the coming reference, which is called an "authentic" or a "correct" reference, approved by all Muslims.

> *Tafsir Al-Jalalayn, Qur'an 18:83*
>
> *"And they, the Jews, interrogate you concerning Dhū'l-Qarnayn, whose name was Alexander"*

Tafsir Ibn Kathir, Vol. 5, p. 189, print year 2002)

م2002هـ / 1422تفسير ابن كثير سنة النشر :

تفسير القرآن العظيم» تفسير سورة الكهف « تفسير قوله تعالى " ويسألونك عن ذي القرنين قل سأتلو عليكم منه ذكرا "[ص: 189]
نفرًا من الْيَهُود جَاءُوا يَسْأَلُون النَّبِيَّ صَلَّى الله عَلَيْهِ وَسَلَّم عَنْ ذِي الْقَرْنَيْن فَأَخْبَرَهُمْ بِمَا جَاءُوا لَهُ ابْتِدَاء فَكَان فِيمَا أَخْبَرَهُمْ بِهِ أَنَّهُ كَان "
" شَابًّا مِنْ الرُّوم وَأَنَّهُ بَنَى الْإِسْكَنْدَرِيَّة

> *"A group of the Jewish came to the prophet questioning him about Dhū'l-Qarnayn therefore, he said, "he was a young man from the Romans and he built the city of Alexandria."*

> *And in the book of Al Jame' Le A'hkam, Al Qur'an, by Imam Al-Qur'tubi, Beirut, 1992, Vol. 10, P. 420:*

> *from the narration of 'U'qba bin 'Amer that the prophet may Allah pray on him and salute him said, "to men from the people of the book whom they asked him about Dhū'l-Qarnayn, he said, "he was a youth of the Roman then he became the King he marched the arrived to the land of Egypt and he established a city which is called Alexandria, when he is done from it an Angel came to him, raised him up to sky and he told him look down, Dhū'l-Qarnayn said, I see my city only; so the Angel said, to him; this is all the Earth and the black is around it is the sea and it was the wish of Allah to show you the Earth and to make you Sultan on it so march on*

this Earth and teach the ignorant and strength that you knowledgeable(scientist).

حديث عقبة بن عامر أن النبي ـ صلى الله عليه وسلم ـ قال لرجال من أهل الكتاب سألوه عن ذي القرنين فقال : إن أول أمره كان غلاما من الروم فأعطي ملكا فسار حتى أتى أرض مصر فابتنى بها مدينة يقال لها الإسكندرية فلما فرغ أتاه ملك فعرج به فقال له انظر ما تحتك قال أرى مدينتي وحدها لا أرى غيرها فقال له الملك تلك الأرض كلها وهذا السواد الذي تراه محيطا بها هو البحر يريك الأرض وقد جعل لك سلطانا فيها فسر في الأرض فعلم 420وإنما أراد الله ـ تعالى ـ أن وإنما أراد الله ـ تعالى ـ أن [ص :] الجاهل وثبت العالم الحديث . ص:

Based on Muhammad's words above, it's very clear that he considered Alexander the Great as a chosen person and as a messenger of Allah.

1. Allah sent his angel to Alexander the Great.
2. The angel raised Alexander the Great up to heaven.
3. From heaven, Allah made him see all the earth surrounded by the sea, which again means that Muhammad believes that the earth is flat. It would later explain why the Qur'an says that Alexander the Great found the sun setting in murky water.
4. The angel told him that it was Allah's wish (**"it was the wish of Allah"**) to give him authority over the earth so he can go and **teach the ignorant and strengthen them with knowledge.**
5. That means that Alexander the Great is the bisexual messenger of Allah to teach us Islam and morality!

Let's quote the words of the Qur'an as translated by Mr. Harun. I do not agree with it, but let us accept it to show that even when they give false translations, we can prove our point. <u>Mr. Harun quoted:</u>

"Until he reached the rising of the sun and found it rising on a people to whom <u>We had not given any cover from it</u>. (Surat al-Kahf, 90)"

Read what Mr. Harun said, and **I quote:**

"The area where the **ozone layer** around the **Earth is thinnest,** where it protects least against solar radiation,"

The verse says, "we had not given **any** cover from it." It does not say **thin cover.** Allah is speaking about **no cover at all; not a thin cover.** Do you see how easy it is to blow their falsehood?! This short answer is clear. However, it's better to study this chapter because it perfectly confirms that Islam is based on fairytale stories.

The story gets funnier if we recall that this is about where Alexander the Great went.

Mr. Harun said: "The area where the ozone layer around the Earth is thinnest, where it protects least against solar radiation, is the poles."

According to him, the Qur'an speaks about **the poles** so let us examine that.

"Until he reached the rising of the sun and found it rising".

Did **Alexander the Great ever occupy the North Pole?** This is really funny and silly. The fact is that the verse speaks about a very hot location, not cold, and these humans are black African as we see in:

> *Qur'an 18:90 Tafsir al-Jalalayn,*
>
> *Until, when he reached the rising of the sun, the place where it rises, he found it rising on a folk, namely, Negro's African, whom Allah had not provided against the sun a shelter, any form of cover, in the way of clothes or roofing, as their land could not support any structures; they had underground tunnels into which they would go away at the rising of the sun and out of which they would come out when it was at its farther point in the sky.*

trans. Feras Hamza

حتى إذا بلغ مطلع الشمس «موضع طلوعها «وجدها تطلع على قوم» هم الزنج «لم نجعل لهم من دونها» أي الشمس «سترا» من لباس ولا سقف، لأن أرضهم لا تحمل بناء ولهم سروب يغيبون فيها عند طلوع الشمس ويظهرون عند ارتفاعها.

Tafsir Ibn Kathir, Vol. 5, p. 194, print year 2002

(Allah had provided no shelter against the sun.) meaning, they had no buildings or trees to shelter them and shade them from the heat of the sun. 'Qatadah said, "It was spoken of to us that they were in a land where nothing grew, so when the sun rose, they would go into tunnels until it had passed its highest point then they would come out to go about their daily lives and obtain a living."

qtafsir.com

Tafsir Ibn 'Abbas, trans. Mokrane Guezzou

"(Till, when he reached the rising place of the sun, he found it rising on a people for whom We had appointed no helper therefrom) these people had no shelter to protect them from the sun, they had no mountains, trees or clothes. They were naked creatures who were blind to the Truth."

www.altafsir.com

If this is indeed the North Pole (Arctic) region, as per Mr. Harun who is the only Muslim in the world with such claim, how then did Alexander find a nation and the sun's rising place? So he's saying that the sun rises in the North Pole (Arctic) region and then it comes to us?! Also, what nation ever lived there? Muslims, use your brain! If the army of Alexander the Great went to the North Pole (Arctic) region, his army would have been dead long before he could have reached that point.

He established his empire from his homeland Macedonia then went to east going to Syria, Iraq, and Persia (Iran today) and then down south to Egypt and Africa. See this map:

http://www.ancientanatolia.com/historical/alexander_great.htm

The only person who lives there, as far as I know, is Santa Claus!

Read the words carefully. By reading the verse before, it will be understood better. I will post the verse before it, Qur'an 18:89 with verse 90:

Qur'an 18:89-90 Mohsin Khan's translation

[89] Then he followed another way,

[90] Until, when he came to the <u>rising place</u> of the sun, he <u>found it</u> rising on a people for whom We (Allah) had <u>provided no shelter</u> against the sun.

This means:
1. The only problem is the sun's heat; therefore, it wasn't about the pole. At same time if you live in the pole, you will not suffer from the sun's heat but from the intense cold because the sun only appears there in a year for just a short time.
2. For the sake of deception, he did not tell us that this discovery of a new change within the atmosphere is a result of what scientists call global warming and not of something that was there from thousands of years ago during the time of Alexander the Great.
3. It was a road he took that ended where the sun rose.
4. He found where the sun rose on people.
5. They have no covering over themselves as **shelter like houses**.
6. Does this mean that the sun rose from the location where he went?
7. Is that scientific or true?
8. And even Islamic books agreed it's about Africa and its people which we proved from Al-Jalalayn and Ibn Kathir. In a magical way, Africa became the North Pole to the Muslims!
9. Let me make my point clearer. I don't need to go anywhere to

find the rising place of the sun, because the sun rises over every inch of this earth. It's so clear that Muhammad was copying the Syriac/Egyptian legends wherein it says that the sun rises from a known location. Notice what the verse states:

"Until he reached the rising of the sun and (found it rising on a people.)"

It's clear that this location is where these humans have no covering:

- The rising place of the sun.
- The location of these people is the same place, for they live where the sun rises.
- It's a clear scientific error of the Qur'an. The Muslims are trying to cover it with falsification and make it sound as if it's a miracle when it's a disaster!
- To make my point crystal clear, you will later on see that Muhammad spoke about the sun's setting place. This means there are two different locations: one is from where the sun rises and the other is where the sun sits.

As you have seen in the claim, Muslims try to make a fairytale story a scientific miracle!

This is the reason why I named my book *The Deception of Allah*.

According to Allah, there's a setting place of the sun. From where does Muhammad get all of his fairytale bedtime stories?

Qur'an 18:90 حَتَّى إِذَا بَلَغَ مَطْلِعَ الشَّمْسِ وَجَدَهَا تَطْلُعُ عَلَىٰ قَوْمٍ لَّمْ نَجْعَل لَّهُم مِّن دُونِهَا سِتْرًا

> Until he reached the rising of the sun and found it rising on a people to whom We had not given any cover from it.

However, after all what we said, Muhammad the founder of Islam will give the final headshot to this claim

> *I was sitting behind the Messenger of Allahwho was riding a donkey while the sun was setting. He asked me: Do you know where this sets? I replied: Allah and his Apostle know best. He said: It sets in a spring of hot water (Hamiyah). Sunan Abi Dawud 4002*
>
> *Grade: Sahih in chain*

Where is the sun's setting place?

The Tale of Alexander the Great

In the Qur'an, he is called **Zo el Qarnayn**, which means "the man with two horns".

وَيَسْأَلُونَكَ عَنْ ذِي الْقَرْنَيْنِ قُلْ سَأَتْلُو عَلَيْكُم مِنْهُ ذِكْراً83

إِنَّا مَكَّنَّا لَهُ فِي الْأَرْضِ وَآتَيْنَاهُ مِنْ كُلِّ شَيْءٍ سَبَبَا 84

فَأَتْبَعَ سَبَبَا 85

حَتَّى إِذَا بَلَغَ مَغْرِبَ الشَّمْسِ وَجَدَهَا تَغْرُبُ فِي عَيْنٍ حَمِئَةٍ وَوَجَدَ عِندَهَا قَوْماً قُلْنَا يَا ذَا الْقَرْنَيْنِ إِمَّا أَن تُعَذِّبَ وَإِمَّا أَن تَتَّخِذَ فِيهِمْ حُسْناً 86

Qur'an 18:83-86

83 and they ask you (Muhammad) about (Alexander the Great), say, "I will tell you some of it."

84 And We (Allah) made him have control on the earth, and We gave him all kind of power and knowledge over everything.

85 In the way he went through,

86 Until, when he reached where the setting of the sun, he found it set in a spring of muddy water, near it he found a people: We said, to him "O Zo el Qarnayn (Alexander)! We ask you either to punish them, or to treat them with kindness."

1. Here we see Allah is telling the story of Alexander therefore, no mistake is accepted.
2. Allah gave himself the knowledge, as the verse stated. Therefore, there is no way that Alexander was thinking wrongly.
3. Allah is telling us that Alexander found the sun setting in muddy water? Remember, it's not Alexander who is saying that, it's Allah. Therefore, we cannot accuse Alexander for being a fool.
4. The proof that this is an actual location is in the verse itself stating **near it he found** people who live there. Near where? The sun's setting place.
5. If you remember, Muhammad did help us prove earlier that Allah meant an earthly location. Read with me Muhammad's fairytale story and you will know what I am talking about. Muhammad said in:

Sahih Muslim, Book 004, Hadith 1275

As long as the sun has not risen yet; but when the sun rises, stop from prayer, because it rises between the horns of the devil.

Where the devil live? He live on the earth as the Qur'an states:

Qur'an 55:33 Translation of Muhammad Pickthal

"O company of jinn and men, if ye have power to penetrate

121

(all) regions of the heavens and the earth, then penetrate (them)! Ye will never penetrate them save with (Our) sanction.34 Which is it, of the favours of your Lord, that ye deny?35 There will be sent, against you both, heat of fire and flash of brass, and ye will not escape."

And to make it clearer, go to this verse:

Qur'an 76:5 Trasnlation of Mohsen Khan
"And indeed We have adorned the nearest heaven with lamps , and We have made such lamps (as) missiles to drive away the Shayatin (devils), and have prepared for them the torment of the blazing Fire."

Tafsir al-Jalalayn, trans. Feras Hamza
"And verily We have adorned the lowest heaven, the one closest to the earth, with lamps, with stars, and made them missiles against the devils, should they [attempt to] listen by stealth, in which case a meteor of fire detaches itself from the star, just like a brand is taken from a fire, and either kills that jinn or deprives him of his senses: it is not that the star itself is displaced from its position; and We have prepared for them the chastisement of the Blaze, the ignited Fire."

Tafsir Ibn 'Abbas, trans. Mokrane Guezzou
"(And verily We have beatified the world's heaven) the first heaven (with lamps) with stars, (and We have made them) i.e. the stars (missiles for the devils) such that some of them become bewitched, some are killed while others are burnt, (and for them) for the devils (We have prepared) in the Hereafter the doom of flame."

- So, what we understand from this is that the devils are locked up between the ground of the earth and the lowest heaven.

- The devil can't go up to heaven or else Allah will shoot him with a star and kill him.

- So, it says that the sun **"rises between the horns of the devil"** which is on earth zone. And since the sun rises from the north pole according to Mr. Harun, then does that mean Satan lives in the pole? That would mean Santa Claus & Satan are neighbors!

✦ And that location where the sun rises from is where there are people who have no shelter from the sun.

Do you know where the sun goes <u>every day</u>? *He (the prophet) said, "It goes and travels till it arrives and prostrates itself underneath the Throne of Allah and takes the permission from him (Allah) to rise again, and it is permitted* (Sahih Al-Bukhari, Book 54, Hadith 421).

Abu Zerr Reported: Once I was with the Messenger in the mosque at the time of sunset. The Messenger of Allah said, "O Abu Zerr! Do you know where the sun goes?" I responded "Allah and His Messenger know better." The prophet answered, "It goes and prostrates underneath and bows down under Allah's Throne; will it ask Allah to authorize it to bow down, but he will not accept, then Allah will order it to go and rise back from where it came from, and that is Allah's All-Mighty Statement: 'And the sun runs on its fixed course for a term."
Qur'an 36.38, Sahih Al-Bukhari (Arabic), Book the Start of Creation, p. 1171, Hadith 3027; Book 60, Hadith 326.

Remember, the sun goes under the throne of Allah which is already over the water. This is why the sun is going down in the muddy water, to bow down to Allah under his throne, as the verse says in:

Qur'an 18:85-86

[85] In the way he went through.

[86] Until, when he reached where the setting of the sun, he found it set in a spring of muddy water, near it. He found people: We (Allah) said, to him O (Alexander)! We ask you either to punish them, or to treat them with kindness.

Qur'an 11:7

Allah is He who produced the heavens and the earth in six days along with His Throne over the waters.

By making the connection between the hadiths and the verses, you then realize that what Islam teaches is the sun going every night to the end of the earth to bow down to Allah under his throne, in the muddy water.
Now as long we are talking about the sun setting-places and Alexander I have to go deeper to find where Muhammad is getting his story from.

The king Tub'a (King Hassan)

تبعTuba'
This story is coming from the legend of the Arabs through a man named King Hassan. He was known as **Tub'a** تبع and was from Yemen. I am sure some are wondering where all these names are coming from since

you had never heard of them before. At one point of time, these names were very powerful men in their countries and some of them were powerful kings. simply Muhammad wanted to be like them. Let us see who **Tub'a** was and what Muhammad took from him. To do so, we will go to Islamic books so Muslims cannot say we are making up these stories.

First who is Tub'a? The word Tub'a in fact its a title not a name for any king he rules 3 kingdoms in the same time of Saba, Himyar, And Hadramaut.and it was giving for "King Hassan" because he rules the three kingdoms as some historical source,

Tub'a Abu Kariba As'ad, was the Himyarite king of Yemen. He ruled Yemen from 390–420 CE.

Some state that he was from the Jews, but his poet confirms him as a Christian.

The Book of Al-Qur'tubi (collection of Qur'anic laws), print year 1973 (Al Jame' be A'hkam Al Qur'an), p. 421:

[رسول الله - صلى الله عليه وسلم - في عين حمئة ؛ وقال معاوية : هي " 421وقال ابن عباس : (أقرأنيها أبي كما أقرأه [ص: .
حامية " فقال عبد الله بن عمرو بن العاص : فأنا مع أمير المؤمنين ؛ فجعلوا كعبا بينهم حكما وقالوا : يا كعب كيف تجد هذا في
التوراة ؟ فقال : أجدها تغرب في عين سوداء ، فوافق ابن عباس) وقال الشاعر وهو تبع اليماني :
قد كان ذو القرنين قبلي مسلما   ملكا تدين له الملوك وتسجد
بلغ المغارب والمشارق يبتغي   أسباب أمر من حكيم مرشد
فرأى مغيب الشمس عند غروبها   في عين ذي خلب وثأط حرمد

Ibn Abbas said, "my father, Ibn Abbas, read it for me as the prophet Muhammad did." page 421, he said, "it set in muddy water." Moa'aweah said, "it's not muddy, it is hot water." then Ibn Abbas asked (Ka'eb) (this man was Jewish and was forced to convert to Islam), what does it say in your Old Testament, (Ka'eb) said, "in my book the sun sets in muddy water."! So, Ibn Abbas agreed and they accepted the correct word in the Qur'an to be muddy water, not hot water and the poet man (Tub'a) said: "Zo el Qarnayn (Alexander) was before me a Muslim king, a king of who kings obey and bow down to, He reached the end of the west and the end of the east looking for authority by the guide of knowledgeable God, **and he found the sun setting-places in a muddy water.**"

1. Here we notice two things. They are not sure of the correct word in the Qur'an, whether it's hot water or muddy water. I think you would agree with me that the difference of the meaning is huge, yet the Muslims claim Qur'an was preserved! If so, then why are they not sure of the correct word?

2. This poem was told long before Muhammad was even born. Who do you think copied from whom? It's very clear that Muhammad copied the text from King Hassan who was called

Tub'a.

3. King Hassan, as known as Tub'a, was saying in his poem that Alexander the Great was a Muslim and that he had found the sun set in muddy water. Furthermore, notice here that the one who is mentioning the name of Tub'a is the cousin of Muhammad (Ibn Abbas) explaining that the verse is not that strange.

This was the Muslims
Muslims claim
version of the story but if we go deep into the Arab legends, there is a book from Arab Heritage called ("Al-Zerr Salem Al Muhalhel", Vol. 1. This was one of the most powerful tribes of the Arabs and most of them were Christians.

The greatest saga of Hassan the Tub'a

الملحمة الكبرى للتبع حسان
يقول التبع الملك اليماني لهيب النار تشعل في فؤادي
أمير كليب يافارس ربيعه وياحامي النساء يوم الطراد
أريد اليوم أن أعلمك شيئا لتعرف حال أخبار العباد
فموسى كان في الدنيا نبيا له التوراة أعطت للرشاد
وداود النبي قد جاء بعده يبشر بالزبور أهل الفساد
وعيسى ابن مريم جاء ايضا بانجيل الخلاص لكي ينادي
نبي لم يكن في الناس مثله لان الله اختاره يفادي
فكم ميت بكلمته أقامه وسقيم شفاه من الامراض

This is poetry from King Hassan Tub'a, sent to the tribe of Rabi'a, wherein most if not all of them, were Christians.

> The King of Yemen Tub'a said, "A fire in my heart burning O ye the prince (Kleb) the knight of the tribe of Rabi'a O ye who protect the women in the day of war, Today, I will tell you something to inform you about the news of mankind. Moses was a prophet he was in the world with his book of guidance! And David came with the Psalms to help these who have filth! And Jesus the son of Mary brought the Gospel of SALVATION to call a prophet! No one was like him! For God Chose him to be Sacrificed! How many did he raise from death by his words! How many in sick were healed."

Here we see that Tuba, or King Hassan as his real name, is praising Moses and David, but the most important is that **he called Jesus a Savior and as the one who was chosen by God to be sacrificed and that he raised many from death by one word!** It's pretty much Christian.

Also notice that he said, "to call a prophet" which meant that Christ made him a prophet! This "prophet" is doing the same as Muhammad, except with some differences in the way he saw Jesus.

The most important thing we found is where Muhammad got the reproduction story of Alexander the Great. At the same time, we observe some information about the history of some of the false prophets in Arabia before Muhammad, and how they influenced him. Later on, we will talk about a new prophet. His name is Mani.

Things will get more interesting when we read that Tub'a and Muhammad both worshiped the Kaaba! In the book of correct hadith (Musanad Ahmad 37/519), Muhammad said, do not curse Tub'a as he became a Muslim!

(519/37)فقال صلى الله عليه وسلم: (لَا تَسُبُّوا تُبَّعَا ، فَإِنَّهُ قَدْ كَانَ أَسْلَمَ) رواه أحمد في " المسند " (

In the book of AL ROUD AL ANIF الروض الأنف V/1 p71 Ibn Ishaq

وأما تبع فحديثه أقدم من ذلك. يقال كان قبل الإسلام بسبعمائة عام

Now Tub'a had a successor, one of his grandsons (Asa'ad Al Hamiry). Muhammad said that he was the first who dressed the Kaaba in Mecca.

Ibn Ishaq said "he was (Tub'a 700 years before Islam) and that explained his poetry about Christ, so it was most probably that he was in same time of Christ."

وقال رسول الله ـ صلى الله عليه وسلم ـ لا أدري أتبع لعين أم لا وروي عنه ـ صلى الله عليه وسلم ـ أنه قال لا تسبوا تبعا ؛ فإنه كان مؤمنا فإن صح هذا الحديث الأخير فإنما هو بعدما أعلم بحاله ولا ندري : أي التبايعة أراد غير أن في حديث معمر عن همام بن منبه عن أبي هريرة أن رسول الله ـ صلى الله عليه وسلم ـ قال لا تسبوا أسعد الحميري ، فإنه أول من كسا الكعبة

"The Messenger – Allah pray on him – I don't know if he was bad or no, And also he Said don't don't curse Tub'a, He was a true believer,if this is a true hadith the messenger know better and we don't know....,And Abu Huraira said that the Messenger of - Allah pray on him - said to revile don't curse Tub'a he was first to clothed Kaaba."

As you see in here, Tub'a according to Muhammad's story is the first to cover the Kaaba with clothing which means he is not only very wealthy but he is in control.

The fact is that Tub'a was in the 5th Century. Muhammad said, do not curse Tub'a for he was a believer.

On the same page it speaks about one of his successors being the first one to dress the Kaaba. Things get more interesting when Muhammad said, "I am not sure if Tub'a is filthy or not!" If Muhammad is not sure if Tub'a is bad or good, why did Allah count him as one of his messengers in the Qur'an?

Even Allah speaks about Tub'a in his Qur'an

وَأَصْحَابُ الْأَيْكَةِ وَقَوْمُ تُبَّعٍ كُلٌّ كَذَّبَ الرُّسُلَ فَحَقَّ وَعِيدِ

And the Companions of the Wood, and the People of Tub'a;
each one of the two nations rejected the Messengers, and My
warning was truly fulfilled. (Qur'an 50:14).

Tafsir Ibn 'Abbas, trans. Mokrane Guezzou

"(And the dwellers in the wood) the people of Shu'ayb denied Shu'ayb, (and the folk of Tubba') Tubba' was the king of Himyar. His name was As'ad Ibn Malkikarb, and his agnomen was Abu Karb and he was called <u>Tubba'</u> because of the huge number of his followers (atba'); he was also a person who <u>surrendered to Allah</u>: (every one) of these folk (denied their messengers) just as your folk, the Quraysh, denied you, (therefore My threat took effect) and therefore My punishment and torment were enjoined upon them when they denied the messengers.
altafsir.com

You may have some Muslims trying to fool you by saying, "Where did you get that from? This verse means that Tub'a is a prophet of Allah." If you read the verse, you will see the answer there: **each one of the two nations rejected the Messengers**. Allah called this nation after Tub'a's, just as he referred to the Jews as the people of Moses.

> OF the people of Moses there are some who guide and do justice by truth. (Qur'an 7:159)

Also:

> The people of Lot accused their messenger of falsification. (Lot in Islam is a Prophet). (Qur'an 26:160)
>
> ...after the people of Noah. (Qur'an 7:159)
>
> The People of Yunus (Muslim prophet). (Qur'an 10:98)
>
> the People of Hud! (Muslim prophet). (Qur'an 11:69)

"Hey my people! It will Criminalize you to be my enemy, because of your sin, you will suffer a fate similar to that of the people of Noah or of Hud or of Salih, nor are the people of Lot is it not far off from you! (Qur'an 11:89)

In all of these verses, the one that is bad, or accused of being bad, or asked not to do since it's bad, are not the names of these men. Still, all of this is not even enough to convince me that Tub'a is from Islam's prophet-hood. We will go to:

Al-Jalalayn's interpretation

وَ۞أَصْحَابُ الْأَيْكَةِ" الْغَيْضَة قَوْم شُعَيْب "وَقَوْم تُبَّع" هُوَ مَلِك كَانَ بِالْيَمَنِ أَسْلَمَ وَدَعَا قَوْمه إِلَى الْإِسْلَام فَكَذَّبُوهُ "كُلّ" مِنْ الْمَذْكُورِينَ "كَذَّبَ الرُّسُل" كَفُرَيْش "فَحَقَّ وَعِيد" وَجَبَ نُزُولُ الْعَذَاب عَلَى الْجَمِيع فَلَا يَضِيق صَدْرك مِنْ كُفْر قُرَيْش بِك

The people of the wood is the people of prophet (Shoa'eb) and the people of Tub'a who is a king from Yemen who became a Muslim and he called his nation to Islam and they did not believe him (and that makes him a Messenger of Allah).

The important thing to realize is that Muhammad was a copy of men who claimed to be prophets or men of God. He wanted to be like them to the point that he was copying their words and claiming that it was from his god. Just like the poem of Tub'a, which became part of the Qur'an, as I showed you:

Zo el Qarnayn (Alexander the Great) was before me a Muslim king, a king which to him kings obey and bow down to, He reached the end of the west and the end of the east looking for authority by the guide of knowledgeable god, and he found the sun setting-places in a muddy water.

And the amazing discovery is, that the Qur'an which came to existence hundreds of years after Tub'a matches perfectly with the words of this man, in other ways, Muhammad is copying his words of Arabic rap.

Tub'a

And this is one of his statements of his good inspiration.
This book is one of the most famous Arab legends. Al-Zerr Salem was an Arab Christian who was one of the top brave men in the Arab history, same as 'Antra Ibn Shadad. He was also a son of Arab Christians and are both known as the top Arab historical lion hearts.

Note the following Arabic text is the same as it was written in the original book.

The Book of Al-Zerr Salem
Vol. 2, The Greatest Epic Poet

The King of Yemen Tub'a said, "A fire in my heart burning.
يــقـــول الـتـبـع الـمـلـك الـيـمـانـيليهيب الـنـار تشـعـل فـي فـؤادي
O Prince Kuleb you are the knight of Rabi'a (tribe)

Whom is the woman protecting in the day of war?

أمــيــر كــلــيــب يــافــارس ربــيــعــةويــا حــامــي الـنـسـا يــوم الــطــراد

Today, I will tell you something
to inform you about the news of mankind.

اريدالــيــوم ان اعــلــمــك شــيــئـانلـتـعـرف حـــال أخـبـار الـعـبـادي

Moses was a prophet he was in the world with his book of guidance!

فمـوسى كـــان فـــي الـدنيـا نـبـيـالـــه الــتــوراة أعــطــت لـلـرشـاد

And David came with the Psalms to help these who have filth.

وداوود الــنـبـي قـــد جـــاء بــعــدهيـبـشـر بـالـزبـور اهـــل الـفـسـاد

And Isa(Jesus Christ) son of Mary brought the Gospel of Salvation <u>to call
a prophet!</u>

وعيـسى ابـن مـريـم جـاء ايـضـابـانجيل الـخـلاص لـكـي يـنـادي
نـبـي لـم يـكـن فـي الـنـاس مثـلـهلان الله اخــتــاره يــفــادي
فــكــم مــيــت بـكـلـمـتـه اقـامـاومـسـقـوم شـفـاه مــن الـوسـاد

"None comparable to him (Jesus) of the prophet-hood
was chosen by Allah as Savior and.
How many? He (Jesus) by a word from him resurrect from death and sick
ones he heals from the handicap."

....

(Then the poet kept going until it spoke about the Mahdi.)

....

And the Mahdi will appear and fast against him (Dajjal) the(Mahdi) light
will blaze between the people.

ويـظـهـرضـده الــمــهـدي سـريـعـاأويـسـطـع نــوره فـــي الــعـبـاد

....

From here we learn that Muhammad copy the story of Al-
Mahdi from old Arab men:

"Reported Abu Sa'id al Khudri: The Prophet (Allah pray on
him and salute him) said: <u>The Mahdi</u> will be of my offspring,
and will have a broad forehead with long nose. <u>He will fill the
earth will equity and justice as it was filled with injustice and
oppression</u> and he will rule for seven years. (Abu Daoud,
Book 36, Hadith 4272)".

....

And the Mahdi will appear and fast against him (Dajjal) the(Mahdi) light
will blaze between the people.

ويـظـهـرضـده الــمــهـدي سـريـعـاأويـسـطـع نــوره فـــي الــعـبـاد
وبــعــده دابــة تـظـهـر سـريـعـاأفتـفـعـل مـعـجـزات فـــي الــبـلاد

Tub'a said, : And after that a beast will come out fast and will do wounder
on the earth"
"Tub'a said: And after that a beast will come out fast and will do wounder
on the earth."

Qur'an 27:82

"And when the order shall come to pass against them, We

129

shall bring forth for them a beast from the earth that shall I wound them, because people did not believe in Our signs."

ونــار مــن عــدن تـظـهـر وتـسـطـع فتشكـوا الـنـاس مــن هــول النكـاد
وبعده الشمس تظهر من مغيبوتـــزداد الـخـلايـق فـــي الـفـسـاد

وبـــعـــده يـنـغـلـق بـــــاب الـمـراحـموبـــــاب الـشـــر يـفـتـح بـارتـصـاد

"Then after a blazing fire comes out of Eden it will destroy many of the mankind, and afterwords. The sun appears from the west and mankind is full of corruption.
Then the door of mercy will be closed and the door of evil will open."
....

Read with me this hadith and notice how Muhammad is copying his religion from Tub'a's words.

Chapter Al-An'am 6:158
Sahih Al-Bukhari, Book 60, Hadith 159
> Stated by Abu Huraira: Allah's Messenger revealed "The Judgment time will not be demonstrated until the sun rises from the west: and when the people see it, then whoever will be living on the face of the earth will have the belief, but that is the time when belief will do no good to a soul which believing after that if it believed not previously.

ويـاجـوج ومـــــا جـــــوج جمـيـعـأتـحـيـط رجـالـهـم كـــــل الـبـلاد
And Gog and Magog, people swarm from every hill.
....

Qur'an 21:96
> Until the Gog and Magog, people are let through their blockade, and they immediately swarm from every hill.

It's evidently clear that Muhammad copied many of his fairytale stories from **Tub'a** as he used his ways of reciting the Arabic stories.

Sahih Muslim, Book 001, Hadith 0296
Abu Huraira reported that the Messenger of Allah (may Allah pray on him and salute him) explained that: "when three things come true, faith will not benefit anyone but whom he has previously believed, the rising of the sun in its place of setting (the west), the Dajjal (The anti-Christ), and the beast of the earth."

It is certain that Muhammad copied the story of Gog and Magog from Tub'a. And Tub'a got some of his information from the Bible but not all of it. The rest of the text is from his own and others.

Revelation 20:7-10 - KJV

[7] And when the thousand years are expired, Satan shall be loosed out of his prison,

[8] And shall go out to deceive the nations which are in the four quarters of the earth, Gog, and Magog, to gather them together to battle: the number of whom is as the sand of the sea.

[9] And they went up on the breadth of the earth, and compassed the camp of the saints about, and the beloved city: and fire came down from God out of heaven, and devoured them.

[10] And the devil that deceived them was cast into the lake of fire and brimstone, where the beast and the false prophet are, and shall be tormented day and night for ever and ever.

....

Alexander the prophet of Allah

After all of this, the story of Alexander the Great is still finished. Some of you may not know that Alexander was bisexual. This will raise some more questions! How did Allah choose him to be his prophet? Again, some Muslims might say that the Qur'an says he is a prophet based in verse 18:84.

Qur'an 18:84

Allah said, we gave him victory and mean and authority of every kind.

Also, in Qur'an 18:86, Allah is speaking directly to Alexander the Great and states:

Qur'an 18:86

86 Until, while he arrived at the setting-place of the sun, he found it setting in a muddy water spring and found community at that location. We said: O Zo el Qarnayn! (Alexander the Great) Either penalize or be kind to them.

Alexander is executing Allah's orders. He is even closer to Allah than Muhammad was because Muhammad never spoke to Allah. He was always getting his Qur'an verses directly from his favorite angel "pizza delivery boy," Jibreel (Gabriel).

1. The first order was the punishment for those who did wrong. Most of the interpretations of punishment speak about killing them, but some say it's about forcing them to pay.
2. Pay *Jizyah* (penalty for rejecting Allah). If they accept Islam, they are not punished.
3. Be kind to those who do well by becoming a Muslim.
4. This also means that this nation had both Muslims and infidels. As it shows in book of interpretations by:

Al baher Al Muheet/ Abu Haian Islamic year 754

هـ) مصنف ومدقق754تتفسير البحر المحيط/ ابو حيان (ت

وقوله [إما أن تعذب] بالقتل على الكفر { وإما أن تتخذ فيهم حسناً } أي بالحمل على الإيمان والهدى، إما أن تكفر فتعذب، وإما أن تؤمن فتحسن فعبر في التخيير بالمسبب عن السبب.

Tafsir Al Baher Al Muheet/Abu Haian, Islamic year 754

And him saying (Allah) "that either you punish them with Tortures" meaning to kill them for being Kufar (infidels) "or you do good to them" meaning make them accept to believe in Allah, so either call them Kufar and then you have to kill them or they believe and then you will be nice to them.

We can find the same explanation in the book of Majma' AL-Bayian, Vol. 6, p. 940

940 - ص 6مرجمع البيان / ج

The Book of AL-Shirazi, Vol. 12, p.545/549

(549 – 545 - ص (12)للشيرازي / ج

1. Is Alexander the Great a prophet or an angel?

Some Muslims think he was an angel but some interpretations say he was both or an angel. This is the interpretation of Muqatil Ibn Suliman, year 150 Islamic year. He said,:

(هـ)150تفسير مقاتل بن سليمان/ مقاتل بن سليمان (ت

وَيَسْأَلُونَكَ عَن ذِي ٱلْقَرْنَيْنِ } ، يعني الإسكندر قيصر، ويسمى: الملك القابض، على قاف، وهو جبل محيط بالعالم، ذو القرنين، وإنما سمي83علماً يعني ذو القرنين؛ لأنه أتى قرني الشمس المشرق والمغرب { قُلْ سَأَتْلُواْ عَلَيْكُم مِّنْهُ } يا أهل مكة، { ذِكْرًا } [آية:

.[85]، يعني علم أسباب منازل الأرض وطرقها، { فَأُتْبِعَ سَبَبًا } [آية: 84]إِنَّا مَكَّنَّا لَهُ فِي ٱلْأَرْضِ وَآتَيْنَاهُ مِن كُلِّ شَيْءٍ سَبَبًا } [آية: }

حَتَّىٰ إِذَا بَلَغَ مَغْرِبَ ٱلشَّمْسِ وَجَدَهَا تَغْرُبُ فِي عَيْنٍ حَمِئَةٍ } ، يعني حارة سوداء، قال ابن عباس: إذا طلعت الشمس أشد حراً منها } إذا غربت، { وَوَجَدَ عِندَهَا قَوْمًا قُلْنَا يَٰذَا ٱلْقَرْنَيْنِ } ، أوحى الله عز وجل إليه، جاءه جبريل، عليه السلام، فخيره: قلنا: فقال: { إِمَّا أَن يقول: وإما أن تعفو عنهم، كل هذا مما أمره الله عز وجل به وخيره86تُعَذِّبَ وَإِمَّا أَن تَتَّخِذَ فِيهِمْ حُسْنًا } [آية:

Alexander is Czar and he was called the king, the holder, for he held the mountain of Qaf and this mountain is surrounding the world from all sides. And about the name Zo El Qarnayn, he was called this way for he arrived to the two horns of the sun, the west and east, until he found the sun set in a muddy water, meaning hot and black, and so Allah sent him angel Gabriel and he told him either you punish them or you forgive them. These were Allah's orders for him and what he told him.

As we see in this explanation, Alexander is a prophet for sure.

In another interpretation of Al Dor Al Manthor/Al-Soiuty year 911 Islamic calender:

(هـ911ت تفسير الدر المنثور في التفسير بالمأثور/ السيوطي

﴿ وَيَسْأَلُونَكَ عَن ذِي ٱلْقَرْنَيْنِ قُلْ سَأَتْلُواْ عَلَيْكُم مِّنْهُ ذِكْراً ﴾

أخرج ابن أبي حاتم عن السدي قال: قالت اليهود للنبي صلى الله عليه وسلم: " يا محمد، إنما تذكر إبراهيم وموسى وعيسى والنبيين أنك سمعت ذكرهم منّا، فأخبرنا عن نبي لم يذكره الله في التوراة إلا في مكان واحد. قال: ومن هو؟ قالوا: ذو القرنين. قال: ما بلغني عنه شيء. فخرجوا فرحين وقد غلبوا في أنفسهم، فلم يبلغوا باب البيت حتى نزل جبريل بهؤلاء الآيات

A group of Jews came to Muhammad asking him: you told us about many prophets but all are already named in our Book! Can you name for us one prophet that is not in our Book? Then Muhammad said, answering, (ZO EL QARNAYN) and then the Jews left happy. And before arriving to their houses, Gabriel brought the revelation about Zo El Qarnayn!

We need to notice the fact that Muhammad was trapped by the Jews' question. It's very clear that it was a question to expose his falsification. I think they did great when he gave the foolish answer of naming Alexander the Great a prophet.

In the book of Al-Qur'tubi (Al Jame' LE A'hkam Al Qur'an) year 671, Ali (Muhammad's cousin) and his son-in-law said that Alexander the Great was an angel. This is why he said, when he heard a man calling another by the name (Zo El Qarnayn), he (Ali) said, "What's wrong with you? It's enough for you using names of prophets for yourself, but you are using the name of an angel!"

(هـ671ت تفسير الجامع لاحكام القرآن/ القرطبي

وقد روي عن عليّ بن أبي طالب رضي الله تعالى عنه مثل قول عمر؛ سمع رجلاً يدعو يا ذا القرنين، فقال عليّ: أما كفاكم أن إتسميتم بأسماء الأنبياء حتى تسميتم بأسماء الملائكة

I can show many more of these references but at the end, all of them just demonstrate that Muhammad who is himself confused caused a lot of confusion.

The legends of the Arabs and the Persians have no ending because the stories of Alexander are not over yet. After he found out where the sun sat, it was time for him to find where the sun rose.

Qur'an 18:89-90

89 Then he went in other way

90 till, he arrived to the rising place of the sun, he found it rising on a people who I did not provide them with any protection to cover them from the sun.

Book by Al-Qur'tubi

الجامع لأحكام القرآن» سورة الكهف» قوله تعالى ويسألونك عن ذي القرنين قل سأتلو عليكم منه ذكرا
فهذا معنى قوله تعالى: {وَجَدَهَا تَطْلُعُ على قَوْمٍ}. وقد اختلف فيهم؛ فعن وهب بن منبه ما تقدّم، وأنها أمة يقال لها منسك وهي
وقال قتادة: يقال لهما الزنج. وقال الكلبي: هم تارس وهاويل ومنسك؛ حفاة عراة عماة عن 424مقابلة ناسك؛ وقاله مقاتل. ص:
الحق، يتسافدون مثل الكلاب، ويتهارجون تهارج الحمر. وقيل: هم أهل جابلُق، وهم من نسل مؤمني عاد الذين آمنوا بهود، ويقال لهم
بالسريانية مرقيسا. والذين عند مغرب الشمس هم أهل جابرُس؛ ولكل واحدة من المدينتين عشرة آلاف باب،

Al Jame' Le Ah'hkam Al Qur'an, p. 424-425

He found where the sun rose next to people that are Negros and they are naked with no clothes nor shoes, they are filthy and gather like dogs! And they are around each other and they make noises like the Jinn and these who live where the sun raises are called people of JABLQ, they are from the offspring of prophet (HUD), and those who live next where the sun sets are called JABRES, and each of those are two cities (for both are nations), each city has 10,000 doors. About the Almighty saying, "We made no cover over them," which means nothing to cover themselves with when the sun raises, 'Qu'tada said, "they had no cover between them and the sun. They used to live in a place where they cannot build on for the ground was unstable and they hid in tunnels until sunset then they went back to their daily work and farming, which means they have no cover from it [the sun] no cave no house to shelter from it.

Negros, naked with no clothes nor shoes, but Mr. Harun said, this is in the North Pole (Arctic) region?

In the coming part of the story, things will get more complicated and the drama will be more exciting. He will find two nations that are fighting each other, and he will be ordered by Allah and also a request from one of the two nations, to build a dam or a very high wall to prevent them from attacking each other:

Qur'an 18:86-99

86 Until, while he arrived at the setting-place of the sun, he found it setting in a muddy water spring and found a community at that location. We said: O Zo El Qarnayn! (Alexander the Great) Either penalize or be kind to them.

87 He said: As for him who did wrong, we shall punish him, and afterwards he will be delivered back unto his Lord, Who will penalize him with horrible punishments!

88 however, as for him who believes in Allah and did right, and well, We shall give unto him a gentle order.

89 Then he went in a new direction.

Till, when he reached the rising-place of the sun, he found it rising on a people for whom We had appointed no shelter therefrom.

91 thereafter We (Allah) knew all about Zo El Qarnayn! (Alexander the Great).

92 Then he went in a new direction.

Till, when he came between the two mountains, he found upon their hither side a folk that scarce could understand a saying.

94 They said: to you Zo El Qarnayn! (Alexander the Great). The (people of) Gog and Magog are destroying the land. So, may we pay you tribute on a requirement that you build a barrier between us and them?

95 He answered: what Allah already gave me is better, that what you can offer, but help me by your workmen I will set between you and them an embankment.

96 Give me blocks of iron - up to the time that when he had to build up the barrier between the ridges, he said: breathe out - until, when he had manufactured it a fire, he said: Bring me molten copper to pour on it.

97 in addition to (Gog and Magog) never been able destroy it, nor could they pierce (it).

98 he said, (Alexander) this is a mercy of my lord till the time comes and Allah will destroy this wall

99 then we (Allah) will let them attack each other in waves, then the trumpet will be blown.

We will stop here and go over this part of the story. What we understand from this tale is that Alexander traveled between the East (where the sun rises) and the West (where the sun sets). He went all the way to where the sun sets and all the way to where the sun rises. Then he went in another direction, but it doesn't mention where. There he found a people who don't understand nor can't talk (stupid-like). The people asked him to build a dam between them and Gog and Magog. The dam he built was made of iron with melted down copper over it. No one can go over it, for it's very high, and no one can go through it, by making an opening, until Judgment day!

It's time now to expose the mistakes and the falseness. I am sure that all of you might be laughing by now about this Arabic drama movie, where you hear the laughter before the joke!

My questions are:

- ❖ Why does the Qur'an say that the people do not understand and can't talk a word (stupid-like), yet they asked Alexander to build a dam? HOW did they ask him? Did they use sign language?
- ❖ If they are fools, how did they come up with the smart idea to build a dam? How did they know how to make bricks out of iron and copper? We know this is not an easy process!
- ❖ Where did they get all this iron from, to the point that it's high and wide enough to prevent two nations from fighting?
- ❖ Looking closely at the story, we find there are three nations. Not two.
  1. The nation that does not speak, nor understand (stupid-like).
  2. The Gog.
  3. The Magog.

- ❖ If the wall made a barrier between Gog and Magog, on which side of the wall are the poor ones who paid for it to be built? There are just one of two choices:
  - ➢ The Gog or the Magog.
  - ➢ How can they be safe? Let's say the left side was the Gog and the right side of the dam was the Magog. I thought the dam was built to prevent them from fighting each other, and them from attacking the "stupid-like" ones? Now these people will be exposed to one of the two nations, either Gog or Magog!
  - ➢ And if Gog & Magog are from one side in order to

prevent them from coming how long the wall or the dam should be?

> If there are two mountains in the North Pole (Arctic) region and there is a dam between them how come the scientist or the satellites, until now they couldn't find not the mountains and nor dam?

> Notice Gog & Magog are huge nations will cover the earth but yet no one can find them yet!

❖ We also understand that this wall will stand until Judgment day. Where can the two nations, Gog and Magog, be found? To get a better understanding of what and who Gog and Magog are, we will go to the book of:

AL Qurtbi (AL Jame' LE A'hkam AL Qur'an) year 671

الجامع لأحكام القرآن » سورة الكهف » قوله تعالى ثم أتبع سببا حتى إذا بلغ بين السدين427ص:

عبد الله بن مسعود: سألت النبي صلى الله عليه وسلم عن يأجوج ومأجوج، فقال عليه الصلاة والسلام: " يأجوج ومأجوج أمتان كل أمة أربعمائة ألف (أمة) كل أمة لا يعلم عددها إلا الله لا يموت الرجل منهم حتى يولد له ألف ذكر من صلبه كلهم قد حمل السلاح»

قيل: يا رسول الله صفهم لنا. قال: «هم ثلاثة أصناف صنف منهم أمثال الأرْز - شجر بالشام طول الشجرة عشرون ومائة ذراع - وصنف عرضه وطوله سواء نحواً من الذراع وصنف يفترش أذنه ويلتحف بالأخرى لا يمرون بفيل ولا وحش ولا خنزير إلا أكلوه ويأكلون من مات منهم مقدمتهم بالشام وساقتهم بخراسان يشربون أنهار الشرق وبحيرة طبرية فيمنعهم الله من مكة والمدينة وبيت المقدس

Al Qur'tubi (Al Jame' Le A'hkam Al Qur'an), year 671:

Abdulah Ibn Mas'ud: I asked the prophet about Gog and Magog so he said, "May Allah pray on him: Gog and Magog are two nations; each one of them has 400,000 nations and each nation has number of men no one can count, save Allah, and for each one of these men who dies, one thousand more will be born to replace him! From his seeds! And all of them hold his sword." Then we asked the prophet, "Describe them to us." He said, "They are three kinds.

The first kind looks like the Cedar trees from Damascus (by the way, Damascus does not have Cedar trees, we find Cedars in Lebanon) and they are one hundred and twenty arms tall. (120 arms!)

The second nation is one arm high and wide; and the third kind sleep over their left ear and cover themselves with the other one (see how big the ears are!), and they eat whoever dies of themselves, and if they walk by an elephant or beast or a pig, they eat it! And if their front in Damascus their end will be in Iran!! (now they will drink the rivers of the East and the lake of Tiberias." (Al Qur'tubi Al Jame' Le A'hkam Al Qur'an, Vol. 10, p. 426/430, year 671).

137

،وقال على رضي الله تعالى عنه: وصنف منهم في طول شبر، لهم مخالب وأنياب السباع، وتداعي الحمام، وتسافد البهائم
،وآذان عظام إحداها وبرة يشتون فيها، والأخرى جلدة يصيفون فيها

Then Ali, his cousin and his son-in-law said:

"The last kind is one span high they got nails and teeth of lions and sound of doves and they have sex like lions! And one ear is made from bones, they live in it in winter, and the other ear is made from leather and they live in it in summer."

Have you ever heard such crazy imagination? Who and what kind of people is he speaking with? How can they accept these falsifications?

The truth is, most of the Arabs rejected Muhammad's falsification but because they lost the war against him, Muhammad forced them to accept all of his fairytales. Who would dare to say he is making up stories.

Gog and Magog are three kinds.

1. The first group is 120-arm tall. (Where can we find humans like that?)
2. The second group is 1-arm tall. (Where can we find humans like that?)
3. The third kind is they make one ear as their bed and cover themselves with the other. (Where can we find humans like that?) and they are one **span high.!**

الكتب» صحيح مسلم » كتاب الفتن وأشراط الساعة » باب اقتراب الفتن وفتح ردم يأجوج ومأجوج

وحدثنا أبو بكر بن أبي شيبة حدثنا أحمد بن إسحق حدثنا وهيب حدثنا عبد الله بن طاوس عن أبيه عن أبي هريرة عن النبي 2881
صلى الله عليه وسلم قال فتح اليوم من ردم يأجوج ومأجوج مثل هذه وعقد وهيب بيده تسعين

Sahih Muslim

Book 041, Hadiths 6881, 6883, 6885

Abu Huraira reported Allah's Apostle (may Allah pray on him and salute him) said: this day the wall barrier of Gog and Magog has been wide open so much, and Wahaib, in order to explain it, made the symbol of ninety with using his hand.

So, Muhammad was asleep but he suddenly got up and said such a thing!

1. How did Muhammad receive this update in his dream?
2. What is the point of this news or what difference will it make for Muslims or mankind?
3. If the risk was so bad why did we not get to meet Gog and Magog for the last 1400 years, especially after the wall barrier was wide

open?

4. This contradicts the Qur'an's claim that the gate will not open until Judgment day! As the Qur'an said,
Qur'an 18:98

"he (Alexander) said, this is a mercy of my lord till the time comes and Allah will destroy this wall

Was the story of Gog and Magog in this Qur'an only?

The Qur'an of David and the Qur'an of Muhammad.

Many do not know that Islam talks about two Qur'ans:

Sahih Al-Bukhari, Book 60, Hadith 237

Reported by Abu Huraira: The Prophet said, "The recitation of David's Qur'an was made light and easy for David that he used order to have his ridding animal be saddled while he would finish the recitation of the Qur'an before they finish saddling it."

Sahih Al-Bukhari, Arabic (original), Book of Tafsir Al-Qur'an, p. 249, Hadith 4436:

صحيح البخاري» كتاب تفسير القرآن» سورة بني إسرائيل » باب قوله وآتينا داود زبورا

] قوله : باب قوله : وآتينا داود زبور249ب‌باب قوله وآتينا داود زبورا [ص:

حدثني إسحاق بن نصر حدثنا عبد الرزاق عن معمر عن همام بن منبه عن أبي هريرة رضي الله عنه عن النبي صلى الله 4436

عليه وسلم قال خفف على داود القراءة فكان يأمر بدابته لتسرج فكان يقرأ قبل أن يفرغ يعني القرآن

Sahih Al-Bukhari (Arabic), Vol. 3, p. 1256, Hadith 3235

The Prophet said, "was made light the recitation of Qur'an and easy for David that he used order to have his ridding animal be saddled while he would finish the recitation of the Qur'an before they finish saddling it."

صحيح البخاري » كتاب أحاديث الأنبياء » باب قول الله تعالى وآتينا داود زبورا

مسألة: الجزء الثالث

]ص:1256[

حدثنا عبد الله بن محمد حدثنا عبد الرزاق أخبرنا معمر عن همام عن أبي هريرة رضي الله عنه عن النبي صلى الله عليه وسلم 3235

قال خفف على داود عليه السلام القرآن فكان يأمر بدابته فتسرج فيقرأ القرآن قبل أن تسرج دوابه ولا يأكل إلا من عمل يده رواه

موسى بن عقبة عن صفوان عن عطاء بن يسار عن أبي هريرة عن النبي صلى الله عليه وسلم

From the past hadith, we found out that Muhammad was not the first one to be given a book called Qur'an. This will lead us to some extreme important questions:

*   Why the first Qur'an as its called in the hadith above (book of Psalms) didn't mention any of Muhammad's stories, like the story of Gog and Magog.
*   Since the book of David is Qur'an and Muhammad's book is also Qur'an, why then did Allah make the first Qur'an corrupted but he protected the second Qur'an as the Muslims claim?

- The recitation of Qur'an as a rap song is a copy of the the Jews' recitation of the Psalms. This is why Muhammad also called David's Book (The Psalms) the Qur'an. We need then to ask why Muhammad did not call the Book of Isa or the Book of Moses a Qur'an?

The low iq of the prophet and the false prophecy exposed

In the following hadith, we will examine the fiction made by Muhammad and exposed by Muhammad himself to prove him as a false prophet.

صحيح البخاري
محمد بن إسماعيل البخاري الجعفي
دار ابن كثير
م1993هـ / 1414سنة النشر:
صحيح البخاري » كتاب أحاديث الأنبياء » باب قصة يأجوج ومأجوج
مسألة: الجزء الثالث
حدثني إسحاق بن نصر حدثنا أبو أسامة عن الأعمش حدثنا أبو صالح عن أبي سعيد الخدري رضي الله عنه عن النبي صلى 3170
[1222الله عليه وسلم قال قال الله تعالى يا آدم فيقول لبيك وسعديك والخير في يديك فيقول أخرج بعث النار قال وما بعث [ص:
النار قال من كل ألف تسع مائة وتسعة وتسعين فعنده يشيب الصغير وتضع كل ذات حمل حملها وترى الناس سكارى وما هم
بسكارى ولكن عذاب الله شديد قالوا يا رسول الله وأينا ذلك الواحد قال أبشروا فإن منكم رجلا ومن يأجوج ومأجوج ألفا ثم قال والذي
نفسي بيده إني أرجو أن تكونوا ربع أهل الجنة فكبرنا قال أرجو أن تكونوا ثلث أهل الجنة فكبرنا فقال أرجو أن تكونوا نصف أهل
الجنة فكبرنا فقال ما أنتم في الناس إلا كالشعرة السوداء في جلد ثور أبيض أو كشعرة بيضاء في جلد ثور أسود

Sahih Al-Bukhari, Book 55, Hadith 567

Sahih Al-Bukhari, Arabic original text, Book of Prophets, p. 1222, Hadith 3170

"Reported Jarer Ibn Al-'Amash from Abi-Saleh, from Abu Said: The Prophet said, "Allah will say (at the Resurrection Day), 'O Adam.' Adam will respond, up to your request, and you're delighted and all the good is in Your Hand.' Allah will say: 'Bring out the resurrected of the fire.' Adam will say: 'O Allah! What is the resurrected of fire?' Allah will reply: 'From every one thousand, take outside nine hundred and ninety-nine.' At that time children will become white haired headed, every pregnant female will have a miscarriage, and one will see mankind as intoxicated yet they will not be drunken, due to ghastly suffering." The friends of the Prophet enquired "O Allah's Apostle! Whom is that excluded man?" He said, delight; one thousand will be from Gog and Magog, and one man will be from you." The Prophet further said, "By Him in Whose Hands my life is, I hope that you will be quartered upon the people of Paradise." We cheered "Allahu Akbar!" He added, "I hope that you will be one-third of the inhabitants of Paradise." We cheered, "Allahu Akbar!" He said, "I hope that

you will be half of the inhabitants of Paradise." We cheered, "Allahu Akbar!" He further said, "You (the Muslims) are like a black hair in the skin of a white ox or like a tattoo in the skin of a black ox. (i.e. the number of Muslims is very small in comparison with non-Muslims)."

I posted my English translation of the hadith because the Muslims
Muslims claim
translation is extremely incorrect. For that reason, I always provide the readers with the original Arabic text when I see differences between my translations and theirs. However, in either translation, you will find the following:

1. Then he said when the Muslims asked him, 'From every one thousand, take outside nine hundred and ninety-nine.' and then they said to him "O Allah's Apostle! Whom is that excluded man?" He said, "Delight. One thousand will be from Gog and Magog and one man will be from you."
2. But that makes this number: 1000(from Gog) + 1(from Muslims) equals to 1001.
3. But remember, Allah said that 999 would be from Gog and Magog and one from the Muslims which totals to 1000 person.
4. This proves that Muhammad cannot even remember what he said a minute ago, exposing himself as a false prophet.

How many Muslims Muhammad hope
would be in the heaven?

All Muslims will enter hell fire, which is an official order issued by Allah in the Qur'an:

Quran 19:71

"Not even one of you but shall enter hell."

To understand the meaning of this verse we will use Tafsir Al-Jalalayn, translated by Muslims.

"there is not one of you but shall come to it, that is, [but] shall enter Hell. That is an inevitability [already] decreed by your Lord, [something which] He made inevitable and [which] He decreed; He will not waive it." (Qur'an19:71).

See the Muslims
Muslims claim
translation of Tafsir Al-Jalalayn, in the following link:
www.altafsir.com/

Therefore, according to this verse, Muslims will enter hell and each one of them will remain there for a period of time based on their sins committed on earth. It is a must for every Muslim to enter hell with no exceptions.

Therefore, as long as all Muslims will, at the end, go to heaven regardless of the time of their stay in hell prior to being moved into heaven then we should ask these questions:

What is the point of Muhammad saying: **I hope you will be**:
1. One-quarter of heaven
2. One-third of heaven
3. Half of heaven

Why are his hope and numbers coming this way? Maybe you didn't understand yet what I'm trying to say. If all the Muslims will enter heaven, then how do these numbers work?

To analyze this, we need to remember a very important thing. Muhammad is speaking to **Muslim men** and supposedly all Muslim men will enter heaven, but the majority of Muslim women will enter hell fire, as was mentioned in *The Deception of Allah Volume 1*, reference of Sahih Al-Bukhari, Book 6, Hadith 301. Therefore, those men will go to heaven without exception. Therefore, the hope of Muhammad is false and to prove to you that all Muslims are supposed to go to heaven, quoted for you are the following verses and hadiths:

> *"Nay, whoever surrenders himself to Allah and is a worker of good, he will get his wages from his Lord; they shall not have fear, nor shall they sorrow." (Qur'an2:112)*

> *"Lo! Those who say: Our Lord is Allah, so they become people of the straight path, they shall not have fear or sorrow."(Qur'an46: 13)*

> *"However, those who believed in Islam and the righteousness -we do not request from our followers more than they can handle. Such people are the dwellers of Paradise. They will be in it for eternity." (Qur'an7: 42)*

Muslims claim

Please to read all of the Muslims
Muslims claim
claims. Visit this site to see all texts with images.

http://www.harunyahya.com/miracles_of_the_Qur'an_p1_04.php

The layers of the earth & seven-layered sky

http://www.miraclesofthequran.com/scientific_19.html

One item of information about the Earth given in the Qur'an is its
similarity to the seven-layered sky:

My answer

Seven Skies & Seven Earths

The one who made this fabrication forgot he made another claim about
the same verse in another page of his site but after I exposed them in
YouTube they took it off!, however because Muslims copy each other
and they copy Harun Yahya blindly it can be found in many other Islamic
sites like this one http://www.speed-
light.info/miracles_of_quran/seven_heavens.htm
and I quote;

***

> "[Qur'an 41.12] So [Allah] decreed them as seven heavens
> (one above the other) in two days and revealed to each
> heaven its orders. And We [Allah] adorned the lowest heaven
> with lights, and protection. Such is the decree of the Exalted;
> the Knowledgeable.

> According to the Quran, only the lowest heaven has visible
> light. This means that this Dark Matter exists in the six
> Heavens superimposed above the lowest one. Also according
> to the Quran, each of these remaining six Heavens is of a
> different type and each has its own planets like Earth:
> [Qur'an 65.12] Allah is the one who created seven Heavens
> and from Earth like them (of corresponding type); [Allah's]
> command descends among them so that you may know that
> Allah is capable of anything and that Allah knows everything.

> Earth is not a unique planet in Islam. Other planets like Earth
> do exist throughout the other six Heavens. It is just that we

cannot see them nor collide with them but we can detect their gravity."

The end of quotation.
***

I think its clear for you all the dishonesty of Muslims in order to fabricate science in the Qur'an.

- Same verse 65:12 once used to speak about as if it is about atmosphere, and in another claim, it's about galaxies!
- In one claim its speaking about **"Earth is not a unique planet in Islam."** & in the other hand, they made about atmosphere.

Qur'an 65:12

God, who created the seven heavens and of earth a similar number, the Command descends between them so you may know that God knew all things, Capable of everything.

- Do we have SEVEN skies?
- Do we have SEVEN earths?

Where Muhammad this time got his story about the sevens skies & seven earth?
The answer can be found in **The Legends of the Jews**

"Corresponding to the seven heavens, God created seven earths, each separated from the next by five layers. Over the lowest earth, the seventh, called Erez, lie in succession the abyss, the Tohu, the Bohu, a sea, and waters. Then the sixth earth is reached, the Adamah, the scene of the magnificence of God. In the same way, the Adamah is separated from the fifth earth, the Arka, which contains Gehenna, and Sha're Mawet, and Sha're Zalmawet, and Beer Shahat, and Tit ha-Yawen, and Abaddon, and Sheol"

- what is the distance between earth and first sky? The answer in Islamic books; Tfsir Ibn Kathir "It takes five hundred years to walk from the earth to the heavens, and from one end of a heaven to the other, and also from one heaven to the next, and it takes the same length of time to travel from the east to the west, or from the south to the north. Of all this vast world only one-third is inhabited, the other two-thirds being equally divided between water and waste desert land"

- but that is taken from the Legends of the Jews again; "It takes five hundred years to walk from the earth to the heavens, and from one end of a heaven to the other, and also from one heaven to the next, and it takes the same length of time to travel from the east to the west, or from the south to the north. Of all this vast world only one-third is inhabited, the other two-thirds being equally divided between water and waste desert land"

it's so clear the copy paste from legends and Muhammad made it coming as if its from his god Allah.
Let us first see what Muslims say about the seven skies.

One of the miracle claims by Muslims is this:

Layers of heavens

http://www.harunyahya.com/en/Miracles-of-the-Quran/27241/the-layers-of-the-atmosphere

Qur'an 67:3

"He created the seven heavens (skies) in layers. You do not see any imperfection in the creation by the Gracious. Turn your eyes again. Do you see any flaw?

"The different layers of our atmosphere could not have been known at the time of the Prophet. This fact cannot have been established fortuitously. The Qur'an refers to different layers in the atmosphere in perfect accord with each other."
End of quotation.

***

Just to show you the dishonesty of Muslims, allow me to remind you what Allah stated in:

Qur'an 67:5

And We have decorated the lowest heaven with lamps, and made them missiles against the devils and We have prepared for them the punishment of the Blaze.

If the seven heavens (skies) in layers are meant to be the atmosphere:

- Where are the seventy-two "Hoor" women who are waiting for Muslims inside their god Allah's atmosphere? Allah clearly said that he created seven heavens. These are all the heavens and nothing else! Who then created space beyond the atmosphere?

- If all the seven heavens are the seven LAYERS OF the atmosphere, then that would mean stars is in the atmosphere too.
- This would also mean that the confines of the earth are the ground, not the atmosphere, because if we fly inside it, it means we are already inside Allah's heaven.
- On top of that, where does it say in science that the atmosphere contains seven layers?

We get this from NASA:
Earth's atmosphere: the atmosphere. It reaches over 560 kilometers (348 miles).

Troposphere *The troposphere starts at the Earth's surface and extends 8 to 14.5 kilometers high (5 to 9 miles).*

Stratosphere *The stratosphere starts just above the troposphere and extends to 50 kilometers (31 miles) high.*

Mesosphere *The mesosphere starts just above the stratosphere and extends to 85 kilometers (53 miles) high.*

Thermosphere

The thermosphere starts just above the mesosphere and extends to 600 kilometers (372 miles) high

It's so clear that Muslims counted the layers of the atmosphere and they made it seven! Sure! Why not? We can lie for the sake of Allah! Right?

We now have to consider the other part of the verse:
Qur'an 65:12

God, who created the seven skies and of earth identical number,

It sounds like Muhammad is copying numbers from other books and ancient stories. Seven skies, seven seas, seven dwarfs... Where can we find the seven earths? **Are there seven continents?**

The definition of a continent is: *one of several large land masses on earth.* They are part of the earth. They can't each be an earth by itself. If we dry out all the water, they're all separated by appearance but in fact moving as one large landmasses over the hot magma. Let us take a look at how Muslims see the verse in their explanation.

تفسير Tafsir Ibn Kathir

{ اللَّهُ الَّذِي خَلَقَ سَبْعَ سَمَاوَاتٍ وَمِنَ الْأَرْضِ مِثْلَهُنَّ يَتَنَزَّلُ الْأَمْرُ بَيْنَهُنَّ لِتَعْلَمُواْ أَنَّ اللَّهَ عَلَى كُلِّ شَيْءٍ قَدِيرٌ }
{ وَأَنَّ اللَّهَ قَدْ أَحَاطَ بِكُلِّ شَيْءٍ عِلْماً }

"God created the seven heavens." The interpretation means that Noah said to his people: "Did you see how God created the seven heavens one above another?" He also said, "seven heavens and earths and deeds" as well as "and of the earths as a female." of equal numbers There are seven earths and the distance between each them is **five hundred years**. Ibn Mas'ud and others also said the same thing. "

In Ibn Kathir's interpretation, there are 7 earths inside our earth and the distance between each one of them is 500 years. I am not sure if 500 years is the distance with the speed of a camel, or a horse, or a donkey, but for sure I don't need 500 years with walking speed to go the distance between the two poles of the earth.

As you see in Ibn Abbas' explanation, who has received all of his information from his cousin Muhammad, he said the following:

> Allah Who created seven heavens one on top of each other like a dome, and of the earth a same number, seven earths which are flat.
>
> *Again, this is taken from The Legends of the Jews as we read;*
>
> *"Thus, one earth rises above the other, from the first to the seventh, and over the seventh earth the heavens are vaulted, from the first to the seventh, the last of them attached to the arm of God. The seven heavens form a unity, the seven kinds of earth form a unity, and the heavens and the earth together also form a unity."*

There are seven earths and they are all flat! This means there must be six other earths just like ours! Allah should know that the word *continent* already existed in the Arabic language. If Allah meant to use this word, he should have used it! Also, if the Qur'an says that Allah created seven earths and seven skies, this would mean that the number of planets in universe is only seven as with earth being one of it!

If the seven earths mean seven continents, this would be a scientific mistake, for the oceans may separate them, but they're all part of one earth. On top of that, science tells us that earth used to be one huge continent. They were not created as seven, but as one. Although Allah said he created seven earths, this would mean that they were seven earths created right from the beginning of his creation. This is not the case for the continents. In fact, what science says today is that there used to be one continent but due to the movement of the magma, the one continent became many.

Sahih Muslim
Book 010, Number 3925; see also Numbers 3920-3924

Allah's Messenger said: He who takes over even a piece of land would be made to have on around his neck seven earths.

Let us see from where the Qur'an got the number of seven earths. If you search for old writings of **the planets** in early Greek astronomy, and I'm talking about thousands of years before Islam even existed, you will find they counted seven planets that could be seen with the naked eye: Mercury, Venus, Mars, Jupiter, Saturn, the Sun and the Moon. These all are from Greek Mythology.

Greek Mythology connected gods to astronomy; therefore, the planets were ascribed to deities. Each one had a job and a name. Notice they considered the sun as a planet too, which totaled the seven:

Saturn: *Kronos*　　　Sun: *Phoebus*
Jupiter: *Zeus, Jove*　Mercury: *Hermes*
Mars: *Ares*　　　　Moon: *Selene*
Venus: Inanna, Aphrodite, Ishtar, Isis, Lucifer

Sahih Al-Bukhari, Vol. 4, Book 54, Number 417
See also Numbers 418, 420; Volume 3, Book 43, Numbers 632-634
> *Reported by Muhammad bin Ibrahim bin Al-Hadith: From Abu Salama bin 'Abd-Al-Rahman which had an argument with some people on a division of land, and therefore, he went to 'Aisha and said, to her regarding it. She said, "O Abu Salamah, avoid the land, for Allah's Apostle revealed, 'Any human being, that seizes even a span of land unfairly his neck shall be surrounded with it down seven earths.'"*

As a result, Muhammad was most likely copying the words he had heard in his own community, but he must have been very confused about them because in his words, as we saw in the hadith, he thought there were seven earths in the earth, "**shall be surrounded with it down seven earths.'"**

Notice here what Allah is saying:

Qur'an 65:12

God, who created the seven heavens and of the earth a same number, the Command descends between them so you may know that God knew all things, capable of everything.

It says he will descend between them. The word *"them"* goes for both the seven heavens and seven earths. The word "command" is about the angels, as it states in:

Qur'an 70:4

(The Angels and the Spirit ascend unto Him in a Day the measure whereof is fifty thousand years,) who rule the seven heavens and seven earths for Allah,

Add to that, the Qur'an clearly said many times that Allah created one earth as we see in:

Qur'an 3:190

In the creation of the heavens and the earth and the alternation of night and day are signs for men of understanding.

Notice here that it says heavens and earth.

Why is he talking about seven now? Simply because he is referring to the planets around the earth including the seven skies. It's very clear that he meant the seven planets which were known thousands of years before Muhammad that could be seen with the naked eye.

English translation of Sahih Al-Bukhari

Book 21, Hadith 246:

Muhammad said, "Our Lord, the great, comes every night down to the lowest Heaven to us by the last third period of the night, calling, 'anyone in attendance to call upon Me, so that I may answer to his intercession? Is there any attendance anyone to ask Me, so that I may grant him what he is asking me for? Is there anyone struggling for My forgiveness, so that I may forgive him?'"

After reading this hadith, if the seven heavens (skies) in layers are meant to be the atmosphere, then this means:

- Allah lives in the thermosphere (the top of atmosphere).
- Allah comes down to the lowest heaven; therefore, does Allah live and move between the layers of the atmosphere?
- When Muhammad went to his god in heaven, he did not leave earth! He was in the atmosphere where he found seven gates and gardens and big trees and four rivers, including the Nile River and the Euphrates. See *the Deception of Allah Volume 1*, Hadith translation, Sahih Al-Bukhari, Book 58, Hadith 226.

How do Muslims explain this hadith to us?

Sahih Al-Bukhari, Book 93, Hadith 578

Allah's Messenger said, "There are angels coming to you in a cycle at night, and others during the day, and they all (the angels) gather at the time of 'Asr (afternoon) and Fajr prayer (morning prayer). Then the angels who have stayed with you overnight ascend to Allah (Allah's Heaven), and He questions them, although he impeccably apprehends their affairs. 'In what state have you left, my slaves?' They say, 'When we left them, they were praying and when we approached them, they were praying.'"

- And they all (the angels) gather at the time of 'Asr (afternoon) and Fajr prayer (morning prayer).
- This means the earth has one time of Fajer prayer.
- There are only two shifts for the angels: day and night, in a 24-hour cycle.
- This means the earth has one time zone. This is why there is one for the afternoon prayer, and one for the morning prayer.
- All angels gather in one location to do the morning prayer and the afternoon prayer for there is always one-time zone.
- This is false and it proves that the angels go through the seven skies. They go up and down facing one direction at the top of the flat earth which means all angels have one time zone only.
- All of this proves that Muhammad is telling a falsification.

Muslims claim

The expanding earth

http://www.miraclesofthequran.com/scientific_98.html

My answer

This claim is not even worth the time to answer as it's going to be answered when we speak about the flat earth in the Qur'an. Yes, that is exactly what Muhammad said. We will see that when we answer the topic of the flat earth.

Read these Biblical verses:

Job 26:7 - KJV

He stretcheth out the north over the empty place, and hangeth the earth upon nothing.

Isaiah 40:22 - KJV

It is he that sitteth upon the circle of the earth, and the inhabitants thereof are as grasshoppers; that stretcheth out the heavens as a curtain, and spreadeth them out as a tent to dwell in:

This verse alone shows three scientific facts.
1. It is he that sitteth upon the circle of the earth
2. that stretcheth out the heavens, and
3. spreadeth them out as a tent.

Muslims claim

The earth disgorges its charges

http://www.miraclesofthequran.com/scientific_24.html

When the earth is convulsed with its quaking and the earth then disgorges its charges and man asks, "What is wrong with it?", on that Day it will impart all its news. (Qur'an, 99:1-4)

The word "zilzal" in Arabic means earthquake, or tremors, and the word "athqalaha" means "charges, heavy burdens." When one considers the above verses in the light of the first meaning, it can be seen that reference is being made to an important scientific fact about earthquakes.

My answer

Muslims think they can blind us by blending foolishness with science. What scientists say has nothing to do with what the Qur'an said. Let us expose the falsification:

Qur'an 99:1-8

[1] *When the earth is trembled with its last-minute earthquake.*

2 And when the earth sends out its loads.

3 And man will say: "What is the wrong with it?"

4 That Day it (earth) will reveal its news.

5 For its Lord will have given her (earth) inspiration.

6 That Day (Judgment day) mankind will move on in disordered groups that they may be disclosed their records (bad and good deeds).

7 therefore, whosoever does good equal to the weight of Sand atoms. He shall see it.

8 And whosoever does evil equal to the weight of Sand atoms shall see it.

Sand atoms

Here, the Qur'an speaks about Judgment day and not about the present day which can be found in all Islamic interpretations.
Earth will tell its news. It's not about anything that they are saying but about the sin of mankind.

Qur'an 99:4

That Day it (earth) will reveal its news." The load of the earth is the news of mankind.

Tanwîr al-Miqbâs min Tafsîr Ibn 'Abbâs

That day the earth is shaken and it will relate its recorders, the earth will inform its news about good and evil that were done on its outside face.

a. For sure, the earth will not *talk* of the news. It's about the sins of mankind: bad, good, and deeds.
b. Qur'an 99:5: "For its Lord will have given her (the earth) inspiration." Is the earth inspired by Allah a metal?
c. What is the metal in this verse of the Qur'an? All that the Qur'an is speaking about is **something** that many who live in earthquake-prone areas already know. You can even read that Mecca itself is under a big earthquake threat. (A swarm of thousands of earthquakes that struck the corner of Saudi Arabia). http://www.msnbc.msn.com/id/39380701/

My comment to Muslims is that it's so embarrassing to make up stories and to create miracles from nothing.

Muslims claim

The ratio of the sea to the land

http://www.miraclesofthequran.com/mathematical_17.html

My answer

I will show you why we cannot trust numbers given by Muslims. Never ever.

According to them, the word *land* appears **13 times in the entire Qur'an**! If you can, please go to the Saudi government's website. It's in English. Search for the word "land". It will appear **273 times** in the Qur'an!

http://Qur'an.al-islam.com/Search/AdvSrch.asp?Lang=eng

If you search for the word *land* in **Arabic أرض on** searchtruth.com, it will come as this:
The Arabic word(s) "Ared" or in Eng as "land" appears in **461 verses** in the Qur'an. Depend of the translation.

- In Mohsin Khan's translation, the word *land* appears 136 times.
- In Yusuf Ali's translation, it appears 108 times.
- In Muhammad H. Shakir's translation, it appears 124 times.
- In Muhammad Pickthall's translation, it appears 125 times.
- The reason that the total count of land word is not same when you search for it Arabic "Ared" or in english as "Land" because its the same word some time is used as "EARTH", and some time as "LAND" but both are one word in Arabic, and translators use either word in their translation.
- The word earth as example appear 423 time(s) in Yusuf Ali translation.

So did Mr. Harun come up with the number 13?
According to Muslims, they've counted the word 13 times only!

If we search in Arabic the word "*land*" (أرض), which is the correct way to search, not using translations, it will give the best accurate number to **appear 461 times in 440 verses** as shown in the search result.

<u>What about the word "sea"</u> its pronounced as " Ba'her بحر"

According to the Muslim claim

The word(s) "بحر" appears in 38 verse(s) in the Qur'an

If we search for the word "land and sea" in English:
- In Yusuf Ali's translation, the word "sea" appears 27 times in 27 verses in the Qur'an.
- In Muhammad H. Shakir's translation, the word "sea" appears 38 time but its a wrong translation he 'Shakir" he translated as an example many words as see when its not as we read here:

"Until when he reached the place where the sun set, he found it going down into a black sea, and found by it a people. We said: O Zulqarnain! either give them a chastisement or do them   a   benefit. (Qur'an18:86)

- as we read in the translation of Yusuf Ali the word sea disappears:

"Until, when he reached the setting of the sun, he found it set in a spring of <u>murky water</u>: Near it he found a People: We said: "O Zul-qarnain! (thou hast authority,) either to punish them, or to treat them with kindness."

- but the truth is there is no word sea in that verse.

Muslims claim

The star Sirius

http://www.harunyahya.com/miracles_of_the_Qur'an_p1_05.php#9
The star Sirius appears in Surat an-Najm (meaning "star"). The double stars that comprise Sirius approach each other with their axes in a bow-shape once every 49.9 years. This astronomical phenomenon is indicated in the verses Surat an-Najm 9 and 49.

My answer

I was laughing my head off when I read this! This is the answer for this joke:

- The Qur'an never called that star Sirius. It's called Al Sh'ara.

- If we assume that it's the same one, what does this verse "**He was two bow-lengths away or even closer**" have to do with it? Does it mean that the star was a few feet away from Muhammad? Or "**The stars in Sirius system follow a course toward one another in the shape of a bow**."
- The Qur'an is calling the star a *He*?
- The star, Sirius, came to earth?!
- Sirius was a few feet away from Muhammad and neither he nor the earth was burned or destroyed?!
- This is amazing! If this star was to get close to the earth, it would be swallowed up by that huge star. Just note that there is Sirius **A** and **B**: Sirius A has a mass of around 2.1 times than that of the sun.

Qur'an 53:8-10 Muhammad H. Shakir's translation

8 Then he drew near, then he bowed

9 So he was the measure of two bows or closer still.

10 And He revealed to His servant what He revealed.

This verse (Surat an-Najm, 9) is simply referring to Gabriel, as Muslims claim he brought down the revelation to Muhammad and not the star! But it's not Gabriel, it was Allah and I did speak about that when we spoke about **Muhammad's hallucination.**

Sahih Al-Bukhari, Book 54, Hadith 455
Arabic Sahih Al-Bukhari, Book of Tafsir Al-Qur'an, Surat Al-Najem, Vol. 4, p. 1841, Hadith 4576

> *Reported by Abu Ishaq-Al-Shaibani: I asked Zerr bin Hubaish concerning the Statement of Allah in Qur'an 53.9-10: "And was at a distance of but two bow-lengths. or nearer; So He conveyed The Inspiration to His slave. On that, Zerr said, "Ibn Mas'ud informed us that the Prophet had seen Gabriel having 600 wings."*

What Muslims try to cover by giving false translations of Qur'an 53:10 **"He did convey The Inspiration to His slave."**

So the one who was conveyed to with the inspiration is Muhammad, his slave. Therefore, it must be Allah as no Muslim would accept that Muhammad is Gabriel's slave but Allah's slave.

Reading more verses, we can see that Muhammad, during his trip to Allah's heaven, saw Allah's tree and the person referred to as *"he"* in verses 8, 9, and 10 is, as I've said, the angel Gabriel. Referenced in Ibn

Kathir's interpretation:

Qur'an 53:11-16

11 *his heart never felt it's a lie, what is seeing?*

12 *What! Do you then fight against with him as to what he saw?*

13 *And he saw him once more again.*

14 *At the furthest away lote-tree;*

15 *Near which is the heaven home garden.*

16 *while that whatever covers covered the lote-tree;*

If it is the star Sirius, how is it getting closer to the tree? I hope Allah is not having a Christmas tree up there otherwise Muhammad will make a *Fatwa* on his head!

> And Gabriel approached Muhammad as he fell to the ground until it was between him and Muhammad, peace be upon him, just around nearer by half a bow length Maeda said, Mujahid, Qatada.

أَيْ فَاقْتَرَبَ جِبْرِيل إِلَى مُحَمَّد لَمَّا هَبَط عَلَيْهِ إِلَى الْأَرْض حَتَّى كَانَ بَيْنه وَبَيْن مُحَمَّد صَلَّى الله عَلَيْهِ وَسَلَّم قَاب قَوْسَيْنِ أَيْ بِقَدْرِهِمَا إِذَا مُدّا قَالَهُ مُجَاهِد وَقَتَادَة

You can see it in the Muslims
Muslims claim
site for yourselves:
http://tafsir.com/default.asp?sid=53&tid=50905

Does this mean that Allah OR Gabriel is a star now? This would mean that Muhammad is also a star for the verse is speaking about two things getting closer to each other. Muhammad and Allah. As I proved, it is Gabriel as Muslims' claim it is!

Muslims claim

Gender and the 23rd chromosome pair

> The words "man" (رجال) and "woman" (نساء) both appear 23 times in the Qur'an.

> The 23rd chromosome is the main element that determines an individual's gender.

My answer

One more lie to go. "Man" comes in the Qur'an 73 times in 66 verses.

Please note that this search was done in the Arabic language for accuracy.

"Woman" comes in the Qur'an 59 times in 53 verses.

http://Qur'an.al-islam.com (Saudi government's site)

This next claim is really funny!

Muslims claim
> *The Returning Sky & The Formation of Rain & The Proportion of Rain*

Mr. Harun Yahya's claim

The returning sky

http://www.harunyahya.com/miracles_of_the_Qur'an_p1_04.php#2

The verse 11 of Surat at-Tariq in the Qur'an, refers to the "returning" function of the sky.

[I swear] by Heaven which returns. (Qur'an, 86:11)

> *The word "rajaai" interpreted as "return" in Qur'an translations has meanings of "sending back" or "returning". As it's known, the atmosphere surrounding the earth consists of many layers. Each layer serves an important purpose for the benefit of life on earth. Research has revealed that these layers have the function of turning the materials or rays they are exposed to back into space or back down to the earth. Now let us examine, employing a few fitting examples, this "returning" function of the layers encircling the earth.*

The formation of rain

In one verse, this formation is described in this way:

"It is God Who sends the winds which stir up clouds which He spreads about the sky however He wills. He forms them into dark clumps and you see the rain come pouring out from the middle of them. When He makes it fall on those of His slaves He wills, they rejoice." (Qur'an, 30:48)

The proportion of rain

http://www.miraclesofthequran.com/scientific_43.html

My answer

The Muslim's claim (Harun Yahya) is:

"{The verse 11 of Sura Tarik in the Qur'an refers to the "returning" function of the sky.

"By Heaven with its cyclical systems."

Cyclical in Qur'an 86:11

This word interpreted as "cyclical" in Qur'an translations also has the meanings of "sending back" or "returning".

My answer to this is that it's not talking about any system. Even the words *cyclical systems* do not exist in the chapter. To prove that Mr. Harun is making up a false translation, we need to look at all the Muslims Muslims claim
translations. Not even one of them is as Mr. Harun said it. On top of that, the word رجع "**RAJE'**" **means cloud, not return**, as we see in the book of:

Al Jame' Le A'hkam AL Qur'an /AL TABRI, Vol. 24, p. 360, print year 2002

"He said, Al Raje' is the word that means *the cloud*. It's a name of the cloud, or the water, and does not mean return."

From the Arabic dictionary *Lisan Al Arab*, we find the meaning:
According to the hadith in the attack of AL RAJE', and it's a weak water, Abu 'Obida said, (Al Raje' is the water for the Arab), and according to Al Azhari, he said, even they call the

thunder as Raje'.

(ت 310هـ)تفسير جامع البيان في تفسير القرآن/ الطبري (ت)
حدثنا ابن حميد، قال: ثنا مِهران، قال: ثنا سفيان، عن خصيف، عن عكرمة، عن ابن عباس. {وَالسَّماءِ ذاتِ الرَّجْع } قال: السحاب
فيه المطر

Isn't it strange that Allah does not straightforwardly say what he means to say? Because of this, Muslims play with words making it a sort of game maybe? If Allah wants to speak about the cycle of rain, can't he use clear words and say it as it is?

As you have seen in Qur'an 86:11, you can also see in Qur'an 43:11, which is:

Qur'an 43:11

"It is He who sends down water in due measure from the sky by which We bring a dead land alive. That is how you too will be restricted."

The fact is that we will see the real meaning about what these verses mean again when we explain Qur'an 21:104.

1. This verse is about Resurrection Day and how Allah will resurrect humans through a rain that will come down from under this throne. This rain will be <u>sperm</u>; the same sperm as any man's. We will read Book of Al Qur'tubi, p. 435, in the interpretation of chapter 21:104.

2.

" تفسير الطبري» تفسير سورة فاطر» القول في تأويل قوله تعالى " والله الذي أرسل الرياح فتثير سحابا فسقناه إلى بلد ميت
[: ذكر من قال ذلك443ص:]

حدثنا ابن بشار قال: ثنا عبد الرحمن قال: ثنا سفيان ، عن سلمة بن كهيل قال : ثنا أبو الزعراء ، عن عبد الله قال : يكون بين
النفختين ما شاء الله أن يكون ، فليس من بني آدم إلا وفي الأرض منه شيء قال : فيرسل الله ماء من تحت العرش ، منيا كمني الرجل
، فتنبت أجسادهم ولحمانهم من ذلك ، كما تنبت الأرض من الثرى ، ثم قرأ (والله الذي أرسل الرياح فتثير سحابا فسقناه إلى بلد ميت
...) إلى قوله (كذلك النشور) قال : ثم يقوم ملك بالصور بين السماء والأرض ، فينفخ فيه فتنطلق كل نفس إلى جسدها فتدخل فيه

I will summarize this long explanation by what is important to us.

Al-Tabari said, that Allah will send from under his throne water, which is a sperm, the same as the sperm of man, and when it falls down on the dead human, he will raise from the dead, as the rain raises or gives life to the dead land, and their bodies will grow as as plant. (Al-Tabari, Vol. 20, p. 443).

As we know, the Qur'an even claims that Allah sends down hail from mountains located inside the sky!

Qur'an 24:43, Muhammad Pickthall's translation

Hast thou not seen how Allah wafteth the clouds, then gathereth them, then maketh them layers, and thou seest the rain come forth from between them; He sendeth down from the heaven mountains wherein is hail, and smiteth therewith whom He will, and averteth it from whom He will. The flashing of His lightning all but snatcheth away the sight.

English translation of its meanings by Royal Aal al-Bayt Institute for Islamic thought:
In most of the English translations that Muslims have, they add **clouds like mountains**. The fact is that it's a lie. In Muhammad Pickthall's translation was found the most honest translation with regards to this verse. It clearly says that Allah sends down hail from mountains up in the heaven, and uses it to punish the ones he does not like!

Allah knows about the cycle of rain, but he does not know where the hail comes from! This is clear evidence that Allah does not know what the formation of the rain is. Anyone who does not know how hail is formed and thinks it's coming from mountains in heaven will certainly not know how it is formed.

On top of that, about the verse we read about the wind leading the cloud, is it really a secret that no one knows? How funny! Not only this, the Bible gives us clear details about it, as in:

Psalm 135:7 - KJV

He causes the vapors to ascend from the ends of the earth;

He makes lightning for the rain;

He brings the wind out of His treasuries.

Jeremiah 10:13 - KJV

When He utters His voice,
There is a multitude of waters in the heavens:

"And He causes the vapors to ascend from the ends of the earth.

He makes lightning for the rain,

He brings the wind out of His treasuries."

Job 36:27-29 - KJV

For He draws up drops of water,

Which distill as rain from the mist,

Which the clouds drop down

And pour abundantly on man.

Indeed, can anyone understand the spreading of clouds,

The thunder from His canopy?

1 Kings 18:44 - KJV

[44] *And it came to pass at the seventh time, that he said, Behold, there ariseth a little cloud out of the sea, like a man's hand. And he said, Go up, say unto Ahab, Prepare thy chariot, and get thee down that the rain stop thee not.*

Can someone claim a discovery for something already known long before his claim? Not only this, where can we find the Qur'an saying that rain comes from the sea? Nowhere! It's non-existent.

Concerning *the Proportion of Rain*, Muslims claim that Allah sends down the rain in measure and that this is approved by science.

Qur'an 43:11

"It is He who sends down water in due measure from the sky by which We bring a dead land alive. That is how you too will be restricted."

This is something that Muhammad copied as it was written in the Bible thousands of years before the Qur'an existed. We see it in:

Job 28:25 - KJV

To establish a weight for the wind, and apportion the waters by measure.

1. This means, if this is what Muslims claim, that they stole it, or Muhammad did from out of a book!
2. By the way, we do not see Christians or Jews making a big deal about an amazing scientific fact about the weight of winds or the measurement of water or rain!
3. Do you know why we don't? Simply because it's not really a big deal. As an example, the first person who informed us about gravity was a mathematician and physicist by the name of Sir Isaac Newton three hundred years ago. Does this mean that he was God simply because he knew something we didn't?

4. It's the foolishness of a man that makes him do such a thing and think this way. If a man can find out about this, can't Satan do that as well?

Muslims claim

The genetic code of the bee

"Surat an-Nahl, meaning "Bee," is the 16th Surah. The bee has 16 chromosomes."

My answer

The fact this is not true at all bee does not have 16 chromosomes, we can read more from this science site
http://www.glenn-apiaries.com/principles.html
from there we quote "Bees have a different number of chromosomes. Females, workers and queens have 32, 16 are contributed by the queen's eggs and 16 come from the drone's sperm."

Muslims claim

The seas not mingling with one another

http://www.miraclesofthequran.com/scientific_50.html

One of the properties of seas that has only recently been discovered is related in a verse of the Qur'an as follows:

"He has let loose the two seas, converging together, with a barrier between them they do not break through."

(The Qur'an, 55:19-20)

Mr. Harun always distorts the meaning of his god's book, trying to fool those who do not speak Arabic, and I can prove that again and again.

Qur'an 55:19-22

19 *The Prairie of two seas, meeting together:*

20 *Between them is a Barrier which they can't pass:*

21 *Then which of the favors of your Lord will ye deny?*

22 *Out of them comes Pearls and Coral*

These are the verses in Arabic as they are. We can go read all the Islamic translations, any of your choice, and you will notice by thinking deeply that the verses are not about water mixing in the same sea!

Here's how I can prove it:

- In verse 20 we read: ***"Between them is a Barrier which they can not pass."*** So, what is between them? A barrier they **CANNOT** pass. Is that the case for the salt water and the fresh water? Absolutely not because they will mix afterwards.

1. The word **Barzakh برزخ** means **land barrier.** To prove this, we will read the Islamic interpretations of the same verse from Ibn Kathir. I hope Muslims will not tell me now that Ibn Kathir is a Christian scholar or that he doesn't know Arabic! This is the Muslims
Muslims claim
translation site of IBN Kathir.

{ وَقَدْ اخْتَارَ ابْنُ جَرِير } قَوْلُه تَعَالَى" وَهُوَ الَّذِي مَرَجَ الْبَحْرَيْنِ هَذَا عَذْب فُرَات وَهَذَا مِلْح أُجَاج وَجَعَلَ بَيْنهمَا بَرْزَخًا وَحِجْرًا مَحْجُورًا "
هَهُنَا أَنَّ الْمُرَاد بِالْبَحْرَيْنِ:

{"He prevents them from meeting by placing a Land as barrier He placed it between them to separate them and Allah saying: "The two seas, one is salty and the other is fresh and salty waters, the former coming from running rivers and}

- In the Islamic English version of Ibn Kathir, they try not to post the entire text. I understand why because it will show the ignorance of Muslims and Islam. Here's the link:
www.tafsir.com/default.asp?sid=55&tid=51616

1. As we see, it's talking about **two seas** and not one. (55:19: ***The Prairie of two seas, meeting together:***)
1. It's not about salt water and fresh not mixing together in one sea!
- Here is another verse in the Qur'an. As we read in, Al-Furqan, Qur'an 25:53 states the same thing:

٥٠ وَهُوَ الَّذِي مَرَجَ الْبَحْرَيْنِ هَذَا عَذْب فُرَات وَهَذَا مِلْح أُجَاج وَجَعَلَ بَيْنهُمَا بَرْزَخًا وَحِجْرًا مَحْجُورًا

Al-Furqan, Qur'an 25:53

it's he who let the two seas free one moving, one is fresh and one is salty and bitter, and he made between them an unbreakable barrier.

Please see the Muslims link www.qtafsir.com

NOTICE **"an unbreakable barrier."** So, there is no way of mixing them ever. But this is not what scientists say about salt water and fresh water. They mix but it takes time.

برزخ **(a barrier) is dry land**, as you will see in Ibn Kathir, and even in their own translation.

1. Anyone who speaks Arabic knows that **barzakh** is a stretch of land that is between two waters, regardless whether salt or fresh. One example is the Isthmus of Suez Canal in Egypt.

We can find the same in

An-Naml, Qur'an 27:61

and has set a barrier between the two seas.

- The question is this: Why do they lie?

Muslims claim

Darkness in the seas and internal waves

http://www.miraclesofthequran.com/scientific_51.html

Muslim claim is in Qur'an, 24:40

....

My answer

أَوْ كَظُلُمَاتٍ فِي بَحْرٍ لُجِّيٍّ يَغْشَاهُ مَوْجٌ مِّن فَوْقِهِ مَوْجٌ مِّن فَوْقِهِ سَحَابٌ ۚ ظُلُمَاتٌ بَعْضُهَا فَوْقَ بَعْضٍ إِذَا أَخْرَجَ يَدَهُ لَمْ يَكَدْ يَرَاهَا ۗ وَمَن لَّمْ يَجْعَلِ اللَّهُ لَهُ نُورًا فَمَا لَهُ مِن نُّورٍ

This is one of the funny scientific miracles because everyone knows that the deeper you go in water, the darker it will be. This is why I think it's a silly claim. Furthermore, the darkness of the seas can be found in books written long before Islam. We even find examples in the Bible.

- If we take a look at all the Muslim's translations, they add the word <u>deep</u> sea. Question: where does the verse mention the word "deep"?
- In the deep sea, it's impossible to see anything because its totally dark but the verse said: **"he is almost unable to see it"**, it does not say you can't see but it say **almost** and there is a huge difference.
- If you read carefully, you will see that the darkness is not in the sea. Rather, the sea is covered on a stormy day, cloud-like layers and massive.
- It's about stormy day and if a man put his hand he **will not almost able** to see it, how can the man be in the deep sea any way, Muhammad was talking in time when people can max go few meters down.!

164

- The verse speaks of the light of God and the darkness of the heart of the disbelievers, copying a Bible verse as we read in:
Jude 1:13

Raging waves of the sea, foaming out their own shame; wandering stars, to whom is reserved the blackness of darkness forever.

If the verse is speaking about the deep sea, as Muslims claim, it's speaking about a few miles down in the sea. What is the dark cloud for? Is the deep sea going to be affected? I'm sure it will not. It says, "when he holds out his hand (the man), he is almost unable to see it..." If it's about a man in the deep sea, where there's practically no light, why does Qur'an 24:40 says that he is <u>almost</u> unable to see? Almost means he sees it, but with weak vision.

2 Samuel 22:12 - KJV

And he made darkness pavilions round about him, dark waters, and thick clouds of the skies.

1. What about the Internal Waves? Arabs have always called the Atlantic بحر الظلمات (the sea of darkness), and this is long before Muhammad was even born.

2. Where in the verse does it say *Internal Waves*? To understand what internal wave mean watch this video

   https://www.youtube.com/watch?v=x7GXLJQ2Zn0

3. The Qur'an is speaking in a clear way about the surface of the sea. In the translation of the Muslims, they do not show the word لج . "*LEJ*" which means the roar of the ocean and its waves, because it is silent in the deep.

4. The meaning of the word is very easy to find:
We can go to the Arabic dictionaries (Lisan AL Arab) and find the word there as *high noise.* وسمعت لَجَّة الناس، بالفتح، أي أصواتهم وصخبهم؛ (I heard the lojah of people. Meaning, I heard their noise or Hustle.)

http://baheth.info/all.jsp?term=لجي#0

ولُجُّ البحر: عُرْضُه؛ قال: ولُجُّ البحر الماءُ الكثير الذي لا يُرَى طرَفاه، وذكر ابن الأثير في هذه الترجمة: وفي الحديث: من ركب البحر إذا الْتَجَّ فقد بَرِئَتْ منه الذّمَّةُ أَي تَلاطَمَتْ أَمواجُه؛ والتَّجَّ الأَمرُ إذا عَظُمَ واخْتَلَطَ

5. **When we say LAJ the sea it means it's an endless width sea with a lot of water and its borders cannot be seen.** The hadith says that, the one who is sailing and the "Laj" sea, meaning it

has high waves and became very huge and stormy.

6. It's so clear that the one who does not have a dollar looks for a penny. This is the case of Muslims.
7. Plus, we all know (at least most of us) that the deeper you go in the water, the darker it gets. You can't even see a few feet down.

....
Muslims claim

The point of departure of our odyssey & the big bang

http://www.quranmiracles.com/2011/08/the-point-of-departure-of-our-odyssey/

Qur'an 21:30
"Have not those who disbelieve, that the heavens and the earth were sewn together and made from water every living thing not then believe?"

My answer

First, I would like to apologist, we are like repeating our self again, because we answered the claim about the Big-Bang before but we got answer here again.

It's so clear that Muhammad is making up a story basing his falsification by using Biblical Scriptures. And as always, when a thief tries to cover his theft, he had to make some changes:

Genesis 1:6 - KJV

And God said, Let there be a firmament in the midst of the waters, and let it divide the waters from the waters.

And that shows in Muhammad's words as we see in the following hadiths:

- Sahih Al-Bukhari, Book 93, Hadith 514, and
- Sahih Al-Bukhari, Book 54, Hadith 414

"...At the same time, as I was with the Prophet, some people from Bani Tamim approached. Therefore, they said: "We ask you what the beginning of this universe was." The Prophet said, "There was Allah and nothing else before Him and His Throne was above the water, and He afterwards created the Heavens and the Earth and wrote everything in the Book..."

Genesis 1:2 - KJV

And the earth was without form, and void; and darkness was upon the face of the deep. And the Spirit of God moved upon the face of the waters.

Book of Fath Ul-Ari, Sahih Al-Bukhari, Book of The Beginning of Creation, p. 334, print year 1952.

There was nothing but Allah, no water or throne or anything else, and his throne was over the water, meaning that he first created the water then he created the throne over the water. The meaning of this is that he created the water first then he created the throne, then he created the pen. And he said to the pen, write everything being! Then he created the sky and the earth.

This hadith clearly emphasized that the things Allah first created <u>by order</u> were:
- Water
- Throne
- Then the pen
- The earth
- The heaven

So, does the *Big Bang* theory accept Allah's idea of creation? Sure, it does not. Therefore, according to Mr. Harun, Muhammad was wrong. As long as Mr. Harun accepted the *Big Bang* to be a fact, then he needs to accept that his prophet telling a lie is also a fact.

Is that what the *Big Bang* theory is about? Let us read from the NASA:
"The Big Bang model is a broadly theory for the origin and evolution of our universe. It postulates that 12 to 14 billion years ago, the portion of the universe we can see today was only a few millimeters across. It has since expanded from this hot dense state into the vast and much cooler cosmos we currently inhabit. We can see remnants of this hot dense matter as the now very cold cosmic microwave background radiation which still pervades the universe and is visible to microwave detectors as a uniform glow across the entire sky."

Look here at the manipulation of facts. The verse clearly says "...heavens and the earth were closed together and then We parted them."

Qur'an 21:30

> *Have not those who disbelieve, that the heavens and the earth were sewn together and made from water every living thing not then believe?*

This is my answer.

♦ The *Big Bang* is a theory, not a fact. Why are they talking as though it's a fact when many scientists don't accept it, and there's no proof of it?

♦ It's a primeval explosion. Did Allah speak about an explosion that created everything at once or was it a 6-day creation?

♦ One day for Allah is Equal to <u>1000 years of our counts</u> Qur'an 22:47 Yusuf Ali translation

> *"47 Yet they ask thee to hasten on the Punishment! But Allah will not fail in His Promise. Verily a Day in the sight of thy Lord is like a thousand years of your reckoning"*

This is a copy from the Bible.
Psalm 90:4 (KJV)

> *"For a thousand years in thy sight are but as yesterday when it is past, and as a watch in the night."*

> *2 Peter 3:8 (KJV)*

> *"8 But, beloved, be not ignorant of this one thing, that one day is with the Lord as a thousand years, and a thousand years as one day."*

So, if one day for Allah is 1000 years in our present-day count then that will end with 6000 years in most Qur'an verses and 8000 years in other Qur'an verses. So where is the Big Bang?

• The verse speaks about two things – the earth and heaven were initially bounded together and then were separated. This means that the first thing that existed was the earth. The *Big Bang* theory doesn't approve of two or even three things to have first existed, but it was one matter that became the universe today, as I have showed you from NASA: (*the portion of the universe we can see today was only a few millimeters across. It has since expanded from this hot dense state into the vast and much cooler cosmos we currently inhabit*).

• Do Muslims accept that the earth, as we can see today, is only a portion of the universe that is <u>only a few millimeters across?</u>

• This means Allah lied to us when he said in:

Qur'an 25:59

> *Who created the heavens and the earth in six days and then he (Allah) rose over the Throne the merciful, ask the expert!*

Were the 6 days of Allah meaning "postulates 12 to 14 billion of years?" We will see more answers in this verse:

Qur'an 41:9

Say, ye really deny Him Who created the earth in two days, and ascribe ye unto Him rivals' worlds, that is the lord of the world.

Let us see what Muhammad's cousin, Ibn Abbas has to say in the following verse:

تفسير Tanwîr al-Miqbâs min Tafsîr Ibn 'Abbâs

{ قُلْ أَئِنَّكُمْ لَتَكْفُرُونَ بِالَّذِي خَلَقَ ٱلْأَرْضَ فِي يَوْمَيْنِ وَتَجْعَلُونَ لَهُ أَندَاداً ذَلِكَ رَبُّ ٱلْعَالَمِينَ }

Say to them O Muhammad: you Disbelieve, O people of Mecca by (Him Who created the earth in two Days) each day equals to 1,000 days of the days of the earth: Sunday, Monday.

see the Muslim site translation yourself

www.altafsir.com

Notice in here Allah's days start at Sunday. His day-off is Saturday, not Friday!

What we see in here are 2 days equating to: *Who created the earth in two Days.* Each day is equivalent to 1,000 days. Is that what the *Big Bang* says or does it *postulates that 12 to 14 billion of years*?

Now I will let Muhammad himself get the fabrication of science exposed for he names the days of Creation as our days today and even he mentioned the word afternoon as we read:

Allah, the Exalted and Glorious, created the clay on Saturday and He created the mountains on Sunday and He created the trees on Monday and He created the things entailing labor on Tuesday and created light on Wednesday and He caused the animals to spread on Thursday and created Adam (peace be upon him) after 'Asr on Friday; the last creation at the last hour of the hours of Friday, i. e. between afternoon and night.

Sahih Muslim 2789

Muslims claim

169

We are created out of nothing

> *[2:117]*
> *Originator of the heavens and the earth, and if He decrees a thing He says to it Be! and it is.*

My answer

The funny thing is that this is a miracle when a second ago they were telling us about the *Big Bang*. NASA: **"the portion of the universe we can see today <u>was only a few millimeters across</u>."** Accordingly, the *Big Bang Theory dose not* says that out of nothing, the universe existed. Anyway, let us take a look at the verse.

He decrees a thing, He but says to it 'BE', and it is.

I challenge all the Muslims in the world to show me one verse where Allah created something, anything, by saying "BE" and it was? The only verse in the Qur'an talking about such creation is this one:

Qur'an 3:59

The similitude of Jesus before Allah is as Adam, He created him from dust, then said, to him, Be, and he was.

This verse proves to us that Allah contradicted himself again. He said, "Be" and it will be. This is how he made Adam. ("*He created him from dust, then said, "to him, 'Be', and he was.*") But in another verse Allah says:

Qur'an 17:11

And that man prays for evil the same for good, and the man has no patience (very hasty).

Tafsir Ibn Kathir

(And man is ever hasty) It was reported Salman AL FARISY (the Persian), Ibn Abbas here is the story of Adam, peace be upon him, while they are promoting in place before it reaches the Spirit to his feet, and before it arrived to his head, when the spirit reached his brain he sneezed, he said, praise be to Allah! Allah answered, "Have mercy Lord, O Adam," When the spirit arrived his eyes were opened when the spirit spread on his body he tried to move before the spirit reached to his feet, but he could not, he (Adam) said, "Allah, hurry up before the

sunset."

Allah never did create anything by saying **be and it was.** The only thing he mentions in the Qur'an is Adam's creation, and as you see, he did not create him by saying a single word as Adam was asking Allah to finish him up before the night falls!

One more verse to clear it all:

Qur'an 32:7

Who perfected everything He created, and began the creation of man from clay;

This means there are three steps in for creation:
- He first created the dust;
- He made a clay figure; and
- He breathed into it.

Qur'an 3:59

The similarity of Jesus to Allah is the same as Adam's. He created him from dust, then said to him: Be, and he was.

This is another mistake in the Qur'an, for Jesus is not in the likeness of Adam as the Qur'an states, Adam was made from clay. Was Jesus too? No. It's a contradiction in the Qur'an itself because the Qur'an confirms he was not created for he is the Word of God, and the Word of God in Islam, is not a creation. Please read the Qur'anic verse below to show you the contradiction:

Qur'an 3:45

When the angels said, 'O Mary, God gives you good news of a Word from Him, whose name is the Messiah, Jesus, son of Mary, honored he will be in this world, and the afterlife, he be from those brought close to Allah.

According to the Qur'an Jesus is the Word of God. A Muslim might say: "Well, the verse says he is a word of God, not his word. There is a huge difference." Then my answer would be: "Great! I have the answer for this!"

In Yousef Ali's translation, we see this:
Qur'an 4:171

O People of the Book! Commit no excesses in your religion: Nor say of God aught but the truth. Christ Jesus the son of

Mary was (no more than) an apostle of God, and His Word, which He bestowed on Mary, and a spirit proceeding from Him: so believe in God and His apostles. Say not "Trinity": desist: it will be better for you: for God is one God: Glory be to Him: (far exalted is He) above having a son. To Him belong all things in the heavens and on earth. And enough is God as a Disposer of affairs.

As we see in here, there are three important keys about Jesus:
- Jesus is an apostle of God.
- Jesus *is* His Word, which Allah bestowed on Mary, and
- A spirit proceeding from Him.

He (Jesus) the man (the apostle) is *the* **Word** of God, **not *a* word**. This means Jesus must be God because the Word of God is:
- Holy, as Qur'an says about Jesus in 19:19: "gift of holy son."
- Eternal, for he is alive & never die according to Islam! All Muslim believe in this as stated in:

Qur'an 3:55

"When Allah said: "O Jesus! I will take thee and raise thee to Myself and clear thee of those who blaspheme; I will make those who follow thee superior above those who reject faith, until the Day of Resurrection, then all shall come back unto me, and I will judge between you of the issues which you all disagree."

- Perfect.
- Unique, as he is the only one who is born from the Word of God, not from a man.

If we take the number one point "holy," we will see that the Qur'an calls only for one person to be holy and it's not Muhammad for the Qur'an clearly states that Muhammad is a sinful man. Do you know who it is? The Holy one is Jesus as we will see in Yusuf Ali's translation. My translation would be the same.

Qur'an 19:19

He said, (Allah's spirit), I am only a messenger from your Lord, to give to you the gift of a holy son.

Is Muhammad a holy son?

To conclude the subject about Allah saying "Be, and it will be," we have found that this is very false. Allah made Adam in 3 steps; first he **had to**

create the dust then **make a man figure out of clay**, and **then he breathed into the figure**.

So, if the Qur'an says Jesus was created the same way Adam was, this is an error in the Qur'an proving the Qur'an to be false again.

It's the same way that the God of the Christians created Adam. If our God created Adam the exact same way, it does not mean that He does not create more important and massive creations in size or nature.

However, we can find that the God of the Christians is the only One who said, *be and it was.*

Genesis 1:3 - KJV

And God said, Let there be light: and there was light.

Genesis 1:6 - KJV

And God said, let there be a firmament in the midst of the waters, and let it divide the waters from the waters.

Genesis 1:9 - KJV

And God said, Let the waters under the heaven be gathered together unto one place, and let the dry land appear: and it was so.

Genesis 1:11 - KJV

And God said, Let the earth bring forth grass, the herb yielding seed, and the fruit tree yielding fruit after his kind, whose seed is in itself, upon the earth: and it was so.

I think this is more than enough. If this is a miracle, it's not in their book; it's in the Bible of the Christians and of the Jews.

Let me ask a big question. It's very simple. Does Allah know *what* he created first?

Muslims claim

The miracle of iron

http://www.miraclesofthequran.com/scientific_30.html
Iron is one of the elements highlighted in the Qur'an. In Surat al-Hadid, meaning Iron, we are informed:

And We also sent down iron in which there lies great force and which has many uses for mankind. (Qur'an 57:25)

My answer

As always, it's a long article talking about science, trying to fool us by mixing things up. The target here is <u>deception</u>, Here's the verse they posted:

Qur'an 57:25

And We also sent down iron in which there lies great force and which has many uses for mankind.

You may not be able to see how they cut the verse. Do you know how and why the cut was purposely made? What would Mr. Harun lose if he had posted few more words of the verse? He would lose the opportunity to deceive, and then Islam would not be about science anymore!

Qur'an 57:25

We sent our apostles with Clear evidence and sent down with them the Book and the Balance of justice, to guide men for practicing Justice; and We sent down Iron, as a kind of material of mighty war, as well as many benefits for mankind,

Maybe now you see why he covered that part of the verse!

and sent down with them the Book	and We sent down Iron
sent down with them	and We sent down Iron

In Arabic when we use the word *and*, which sounds like **WA**, this **and** present is the same kind of sending down, between the first and the one after. Note here this:

and sent down with them the Book	and	We sent down Iron
Did Allah send prophets from the sky and books with them?	If this is true then the other sending must be about...	Physical sending
Send down first	and	Send down after

This is of extreme importance to understand the verse, because the verse is not talking about something physically being sent down. It's speaking about what Allah, the god of Muslims, gave to mankind. As you see here, Allah sent the iron for killing first, as a gift to mankind!

Just for the sake of argument, let us assume that the Muslims claim that the Qur'an is speaking of sending *physically*. This would mean that Allah got it wrong again! How?

Let us read some of the claim again:

"**5 million** years ago. Iron-60 is a radioactive isotope of iron, formed in supernova explosions, which decays with a half-life of 1.5 million years. An enhanced presence of this isotope in a geologic layer indicates the recent nucleosynthesis of elements nearby in space and their subsequent transport to the earth (perhaps as part of dust grains).40

This is something that happened 5 million years ago! But it says Allah sent the prophets and books, and then he sent the iron.

Qur'an 57:25

We sent our apostles with Clear evidence and sent down with them the Book and the Balance of justice, to guide men for practicing Justice; and We sent down Iron, as kind of material of mighty war, as well as many benefits for mankind,

First	Second
and sent down with them the Book	and We sent down Iron
Allah send iron	benefits for mankind
So mankind was existing before the iron, as the verse itself shows as the Qur'an gave it in order	And iron sent to us

Qur'an 7:26

يَا بَنِي آدَمَ قَدْ أَنزَلْنَا عَلَيْكُمْ لِبَاسًا يُوَارِي سَوْآتِكُمْ وَرِيشًا ۖ وَلِبَاسُ التَّقْوَىٰ ذَٰلِكَ خَيْرٌ ۚ ذَٰلِكَ مِنْ آيَاتِ اللَّهِ لَعَلَّهُمْ يَذَّكَّرُونَ

(سورة الأعراف, Al-Araf, Qur'an 7:26:

Oh, off springs of Adam we sent down upon your clothes to cover the awful of yourselves and feathering, as cloth of modesty that is for your finest and your benefit as a manifestation from Allah maybe you would remember.

Is it true that Allah sent down **clothes** to us from the sky, as well as

featherings?

For sure the Muslims will say, "Oh, this is metaphorical." It's going to be funny to say, that right? Let's say that one day a Japanese scientist named **Yama I do Lie Yama** found underwear or some clothes falling down from the sky out of space five million years ago. Then it would not be metaphorical anymore. This is just the Muslims
Muslims claim
game of deception. We move on.

What about Geometrical Values of The Arabic Alphabet

The word "hadid", which means "iron", appears in the Qur'an in many chapters, as we see in:
The iron in chapters of the Qur'an in order.
(سورة الحج , Al-Hajj, Chapter 22, Verse 21)
(سورة سبأ , Saba, Chapter 34, Verse 10)
(سورة ق , Qaf, Chapter 50, Verse 22)
(سورة الحديد , Al-Hadid, Chapter 57, Verse 25)

- ◆ Did Allah give the Qur'an its orders or numbers? The answer is no. The fact is that the first chapter of the Qur'an is chapter 96. It was done by the **Khalifa Uthman** who had ordered many men to collect the Qur'an and give it numbers as found in the Bible. None of these numbers and divisions of the Qur'an verses and chapters are from Allah as all Muslims would agree with.
- ◆ The real number of the chapter is 94 as send by revelation order but because Muslims played with their book in today Qur'an its 57.

Chapter real # 94	Al-Hadid	Today Qur'an # 57

- ◆ In the Qur'an translated by Yusuf Ali, in the commentary to his translation, (chapter 80:13) print year 1934, vol. 13: "At the time this Sura (80:13) was revealed, there were perhaps only about 42 or 45 Suras in the hands of the Muslims." This means that <u>chapter 80</u> should've been <u>chapter 41</u> as the proper order.

Tafsir Al-Qur'an by Ibn Kathir, Vol. 1, p. 48, says:
I heard Suleyman saying: "why did you place in the beginning of the Qur'an when the Chapter of the Cow (chapter 2 in today's Qur'an) and Al 'Imran (chapter 3 in today's Qur'an) when in fact there are more than EIGHTY

chapters before it?"

سمعت سليمان بن بلال يقول: سئل ربيعة : لم قدمت البقرة وآل عمران ، وقد نزل قبلهما بضع وثمانون سورة ؟

http://www.islamweb.net/newlibrary/display_book.php?flag=1&bk_no=49&ID=5

♦ Reading this following hadith will give more proof:

"Reported by Abdullah Ibn Abi Mas'ud, he said: The Chapters of Bani Israel, Al-Kahf, Mariyam, Taha and Al-Anbiya are from the very first old chapters which I learned by heart, and they are my first possessions." (Sahih Al-Bukhari, Book 60, Hadith 263).

This means the first chapters of the Qur'an are:

Chapter name	Quran today	Quran of Muhammad
Bani Israel	Can't be found	Can't be found
Al-'Alaq	Chapter # 96	Chapter # 1
Al-Kahf	Chapter # 18	Chapter # 69
Taha	Chapter # 20	Chapter # 45
Al-Anbiya	Chapter # 21	Chapter # 73

So, if we count chapter of *Al-'Alaq* as chap. 1, *Al-Kahf* is chap. 2, Mariyam is chap. 3, Al-Anbiya is chap. 4, this changes all the numbers of the Qur'an as it exists today.

"Reported by 'Aisha: The beginning of the Divine Inspiration to Allah was the chapter of Al-'Alaq Chapter 96." (Sahih Al-Bukhari, Book 87, Hadith 111، Book 60, Hadith 479).

1. Now by connecting the last hadith of Sahih Al-Bukhari, book 60, Hadith 263 and what we found in Tafsir Al-Qur'an by Ibn Kathir, Vol. 1 p. 48, Muslims agreed that "more than **EIGHTY** chapters came before it" **and** were before the Chapter of the Cow and Al 'Imran. This means that all numbers in today's Qur'an have nothing to do with the way it was brought down from the false god Allah. Rather, it was how Uthman's men created his own Qur'an.

The word "hadid" which means iron, existed before the Qur'an and was used by the Arabs thousands of years before Islam. That being said, this means that the first Arab man who named the iron, **AL HADID, MUST BE GOD** because he chose the name and as we can see its geometrical values in the Arabic alphabet is it equals to the iron. At the same time, the number 57 equals to the iron, not iron alone.

Arabic today AL = The
A =1 , L = 30

Iron = حديد

ح 'H	د D	ي Y	د D
8	4	10	4

Iron = **Hadid**: 8+4+10+4=26; added to the value if
The = **AL**: 31+26=57.
Concerning the chapter number being **57**, what will we do with the other three chapters where the word iron appears? Notice that the first-time iron appears in the Qur'an is in Al-Hajj, Chapter 22, Verse 21.

1.   Al-Hadid chapter is 57 but the verse is 25?
(Qur'an, 57:25), but Mr. Harun said, *"The numerological value of the word "hadid" alone is 26. And 26 is the atomic number of iron."* so why didn't Allah make the chapter number perfect with the scientific number by making it 57:26 if it's meant to be a scientific proof and not of luck made by Uthman not by Allah?
All these chapter numbers were not made by neither Allah or Muhammad. It was Uthman. You cannot give credit to Allah nor to Muhammad, as it shows in the book of Imam Al-Suyuti, book Al-Itqan fii 'Olum al Qur'an, p. 96.

Qur'an 55:35

There will be sent against you both, smokeless glows of fire and molten copper, and you will not be able to shelter yourselves.

Why did copper appear in Qur'an 55:35 and not at the same time that iron was mentioned? Shouldn't had Allah listed the word copper in Qur'an 29 to fit it with science?

Same goes for Gold atomic number *is 79, it appears in chapter 3:14, the word gold(Zhb) equal to 710 as numerological alphabets number. So why only the iron was scientifically correct as Muslims claim.?*

This is funny. Suddenly the verse is talking about fighting cancer! The fact is, the verse is speaking about the use of iron as a tool for killing humans in war, not saving life-threatening illness, which means it's totally the opposite.

Qur'an 57:25

We sent our apostles with Clear evidence <u>and sent down with them the Book</u> and the Balance of justice, to guide men for practicing Justice; <u>and We sent down Iron, as a kind of material of mighty war,</u> as well as many benefits for mankind,

- Allah just said in that verse, *"We sent down Iron, as a kind of material of mighty war.*" It's amazing how Muslims flip the meaning of their own book, from being an iron sent for killing into an iron that fights cancer.

- If the reference they gave about destroying cancer cells is true, why do millions of people still face death every year because of cancer?

- In the Qur'an of Ibn Mas'ud, The Hadid chapter is 56! In his Qur'an, the Al Fatiha chapter and two more chapters do not exist.

Let's go to the book of the Imam Al Qur'tubi:

Al-Jame' Le A'hkam Al-Qur'an Vol. 20, p. 225

Ibn Mas'ud dropped the Al Fatiha chapter from his book, he even dropped two more chapters from the Qur'an claiming that these are prayers made by the prophet and not from Allah, but the prophet used to use them as his own way to seek refuge in Allah. The two are called Al Mo'wazten المعوذتين سورة الناس), Al-Falaq, chapter 113, verse 1) and (سورة الفلق Al-Nas, chapter 114, verse 1)

إن المعوذتين كان يقال لهما المقشقشتان؛ أي تبرئان من النفاق. وقد تقدم. وزعم ابن مسعود أنهما دعاء تعوذ به،
الجامع لأحكام القرآن» تفسير سورة الفلق الجزء العشرون ص:225
فإسقاط فاتحة الكتاب

وعَنْ عَبْدِ الرَّحْمَنِ بْنِ يَزِيدَ قَالَ كَانَ عَبْدُ اللهِ يَحُكُّ الْمُعَوِّذَتَيْنِ مِنْ مَصَاحِفِهِ، وَيَقُولُ: إِنَّهُمَا لَيْسَتَا مِنْ كِتَابِ اللهِ -تَبَارَكَ وَتَعَالَى

Anyway, we do not know the first Arab man that translated or made the word iron in Arabic but it has already been used for thousands of years.

Since Mr. Harun used the Geometrical Values of The Arabic Alphabet, we will use the same letters to solve some secrets in the Qur'an.

Is the Qur'an the only words of Allah?

We just proved to you that the Qur'an is not what Muslims claim it to be as being the preserved word of God. Certainly, the Islamic references showed that it was not well preserved.

Now it's time to prove to you that Islam cannot be trusted to be from God even if the Qur'an was preserved, as Muslims like to claim. Having said that, in case you don't know, Islam is not based on the Qur'an alone but is also based on the Sunnah. The Sunnah is whatever Muhammad said and what the Muslims practiced according to his orders.

Qur'an 4:59

O ye who believe! Obey Allah, and obey the Messenger, and those charged with authority among you. If ye argue in

anything between yourselves, consult it to Allah and His Messenger, if ye do believe in Allah and the Last Day: That is best understanding.

Qur'an 3:32

Say: "Obey Allah and His Messenger: However, if they turn back, Allah loves not those who reject Islam.

Qur'an 59:7, Yusuf Ali's translation

What Allah has bestowed on His Messenger (and taken away) from the people of the townships - belongs to Allah - to His Messenger and to kindred and orphans, the needy and the wayfarer; in order that it may not (merely) make a circuit between the wealthy among you. So take what the Messenger assigns to you, and deny yourselves that which he withholds from you. And fear Allah; for Allah is strict in Punishment.

I think all of us heard the Muslims say plenty of times that there are many hadiths that are weak or invalid. However, they do not accept as Muslims those who don't believe in both the Qur'an and the Sunnah. But as we see, the Sunnah is not preserved.

You can visit any Islamic website you want made by Muslims. You will see that all these Islamic websites agree that there are many hadiths that said and reported about the prophet of Islam which are not true. Then how can Muslims always say that Islam is based on both **Qur'an and Sunnah when the second part of Islam is not preserved.** Also, how do Muslims decide as to which hadith is true and which one is false? You will actually notice that what is true for some, is false for other Muslims. Also, most things these days do not even go by the rules which were established in the last 1400 years according to the hadiths as to what is accurate and not. These rules prove the failure of Islam as it never been able to make Muslims agree on one story regarding their prophet Muhammad. The other failure is in the modern era, because Muslims today are rejecting anything that will make Islam look like a false religion. As an example, the most accurate books for Muslims regarding the hadiths are called the "*sahih*" books. Sahih means correct, therefore, "correct books." Examples of these Islamic books are those of Sahih Al-Bukhari and Sahih Muslim.

Although these books are supposed to be accurate since the last 1400 years, not all Muslims agree about their accuracy. Some Muslims from the same sect and religious group accept the same books but individuals have different opinions about what is right and what is wrong, what is false and what is true. As long as this religion has no infallible book that all Muslims would agree about, especially with the hadiths, Islam then is impossible to understand and practice because nothing is unanimously approved by the teachers of this religion.

Geometrical Values proving who is Christ from the Qur'an

This is good news and will prove a lot of things about the Qur'an.

First, what is the Geometrical Values of The Arabic Alphabet? Simply put, every letter has an equal number used for coding the words and was used so for many reasons. It was copied from the Aramaic and the Hebrews.

It can be used to make short words or lines and to make secret words that no one could understand except for the very well educated. I am sure many of you have heard about the codes of the Bible.

In the coming image, you can see each letter and its equal number. I have added English letters so you can see what these letters are. Figure # 1:

Letter	أ = a	ب = b	ج = j	د = d	ه = h	و = w	ز = z	ح = h	ط = t	ي = k
	1	2	3	4	5	6	7	8	9	10
Letter	ك = K	ل = L	م = m	ن = n	س = s	ع = '	ف = f	ص = s	ق = q	ر = r
Value	20	30	40	50	60	70	80	90	100	200
Letter	ش = sh	ت = t	ث = th'	خ = kh	ذ = z	ض = da	ظ = z	غ = gh		
Value	300	400	500	600	700	800	900	1000		

In the Qur'an, there are letters at the beginning of some chapters and Muslims agree that no one knows what they mean except for Allah!

That does not make any sense at all. Why would Allah say something just to confuse? The Qur'an says in many chapters that Allah explained his book in details, which is a contradiction to Qur'an 3:7. It says, no one knows a big part of what the Qur'an means.

181

Qur'an 7:52 Muhammad Pickthall's translation

"Verily We have brought them a Scripture Which We expounded with knowledge, a guidance and a mercy for a people who believe."

These letters are (A + L + R).

As I've said, not even one Muslim knows what they mean or why they are at the beginning of these verses!

Soon we will find out what they mean. As I've said previously, each letter is equal to a number as seen in Figure #1. This means that these letters, added together, represents a total amount.

A+ L+ R = 1 + 30 + 200 = **231**

What does these 231 means? As I've also said, these are codes and were made to be used this way. Then what does the 231 in the code mean? Take a look with me to find out.

A   L   R here three letters found in the beginning at chapters 10,11,12,14,15

A	L	R	Total
1	30	200	231

The equal numbers of this Arabic sentences are 231 الأب و الأبن اله واحد:

The son and the father are one God!

This is the Qur'an's own code! I think this is an amazing discovery!

We are not done yet. Someone might say. "I can make words or sentences that fit with these numbers." Is it true? Yes, sure I can. It's not a big deal. You just have to relate the sentences to religion and fit them with the fixed letters and fixed code!

Should we see what the coming code is? Please, remember these numbers to know where they come from.

These letters were mentioned in the Qur'an for five times as shown in Figure #1. Why was it for five times? Do you think it's just by chance? I don't think so.

Remember, this is the equal number of one verse as: (A L R)
A+ L+ R = 1 + 30 + 200 = 231. Let us try this. A L R appears in Qur'an 5 times. This means:

A L R = 231 x 5 = 1155

What does this new number mean now?

الكلمة صار جسدا وحل بيننا ورأينا مجده لوحيده من الأب = 1155

What does this Arabic sentence mean? Read with me.

John 1:14

14 *And the Word became flesh and dwelt among us, and we beheld His glory, the glory as of the only begotten of the Father,*

A L R appear in the Qur'an 5 times, which means:

A L R = 231 x 5 = 1155 = John 1:14

{It's equal to the words you see below, not the entire verse.}

John 1:14 - KJV

And the Word became flesh and dwelt among us, and we beheld His glory, the glory as of the only begotten of the Father,

This is enough to prove to us a lot of things.

These codes are there for a reason: to deliver a secret message for those who know the language of coding in order for them to warn mankind about the cult of Islam.

If we go to Qur'an 19:1, there is a big secret there. First of all, you should know that chapter 19 has the name of **Mary, the mother of Christ.** Its first letters are Kaf, Ha, Ya, 'Ain, and Sad. These really are not letters. They are about how the letters are pronounced. Let's see what these letters equal to using the alphabet code.

ص	ع	ي	ه	ك
90	70	10	5	20

SS	'A	Y	H	K

K + H + Y + 'A + SS = 195

20 + 5 + 10 + 70 + 90 = 195

Now, what does 195 means?

We have to look at this in the Biblical coding of Arabic to see what these numbers equal to. In doing so, we will find this:

K + H + Y + 'A + S = 195 = " المسيح الهي " = Christ is my God!!!

Is this not amazing? Now remember the location of this verse is so important, and the meaning makes a lot more sense. Why?

1. It's in the first verse of the chapter of Mary (Maryam).
2. What is important about Maryam?
3. The mother of Christ.
4. The Christ, the "Messiah."

And of this lead us to this, this is first verse of the chapter of Maryam which teaching us about Christ, it come worth a code Muslims has no idea whatsoever it does mean, and then we find it fit with perfection with Arabic coding, to prove that Christ is God?
Who put this code in the Qur'an and why?

There are two theories

> *1st theory - The monk, Buhira, Muhammad's biggest help after Waraqa Ibn Naofal died, wanted to repent to God and fix his crime of helping create Islam. Therefore, he gave Muhammad these words (coded letters). Muhammad had no idea what they meant, as for most of the Qur'an, he just recited what the monk gave him. By doing so, Buhira gave the code, telling those who knew the code and how it worked, that Muhammad was a false prophet. At the same time, he was repenting to Christ by posting this code about Him; that he is Lord! I am more inclined to accept this theory than the second one.*

2nd theory - Waraqa Ibn Naofal was copying Scriptures from Christian Aramaic and Arabic books. He gave Muhammad what he was copying, though he did not know what they meant.

Waraqa was an educated man and spoke more than two languages. It really doesn't make sense that he didn't know what they meant but we really can't be sure.

In the book of Sahih Al-Bukhari, book 87, Hadith 111, we read the following:

> Khadija then took Muhammad to her cousin Waraqa Ibn Naofal, son of Asad son of 'Abdul 'Uzza son of Qusai. Waraqa was the son of her uncle, who was converted to Christianity before Islam used to write the Arabic writings and used to write the Gospels in Arabic as much as Allah wished him to write.

The last hadith raises a question in my mind and I can't help but ask. Was Waraqa writing a gospel from the supposed corrupted Gospel? As long as this Gospel and I mean the one was Waraqa writing is accepted by Muslims
Muslims claim
, where it is? And why didn't Muhammad and Allah preserve what was already in Muhammad and Waraqa's hands?!

If you read the story, you will see that it was Waraqa who announced to Muhammad that what he'd seen in the cave was an angel (or was it the devil?). Maybe you need to take note that the one Muslims call Gabriel the angel, never said to Muhammad: "I am the angel Gabriel!" It was Waraqa who informed Muhammad of his name! Please read the following hadith:

In the book of Sahih Al-Bukhari, book 87, Hadith 111, we read the following:

> Khadija said, to him (Waraqa), "Oh my cousin! Please listen to the story of your nephew". Waraqa answered, "Oh my nephew! Tell me What did you see?" The Prophet reported to him whatever he had seen. Then Waraqa said, "This is the same angel Gabriel (Jibreel), the angel who delivered the secrets whom Allah had sent to Moses."

- Note here that Muhammad is the prophet, but he was the last person to know he'd become one!
- Waraqa who have never even seen this angel before already knew his name. He was sure it was Gabriel!
- Why didn't the angel tell Muhammad who he was?
- Have you ever heard of a prophet that the cousin of his wife was the one to tell him, "You are a prophet," but he

didn't know it yet?!

Waraqa said, "Tell me *what* did you *see*?" Muhammad's wife didn't tell Waraqa anything about what Muhammad saw. She just told Waraqa to hear Muhammad's story!

Waraqa Ibn Naofal, The Maker of Islam

To prove how important Waraqa Ibn Naofal was in the creation of Islam and that he was the one who made Muhammad a prophet, we will look at the same hadith. When Waraqa Ibn Naofal died, Muhammad tried to commit suicide.

ما جئت به إلا عودي وإن يدركني يومك أنصرك نصرا مؤزرا ثم لم ينشب ورقة أن توفي وفتر الوحي فترة حتى حزن النبي صلى الله عليه وسلم فيما بلغنا حزنا غدا منه مرارا كي يتردى من رءوس شواهق الجبال فكلما أوفى بذروة جبل لكي يلقي منه نفسه تبدى له جبريل فقال يا محمد إنك رسول الله حقا فيسكن لذلك جأشه وتقر نفسه فيرجع فإذا طالت عليه فترة الوحي غدا لمثل ذلك فإذا أوفى بذروة جبل تبدى له جبريل فقال له مثل ذلك قال ابن عباس فالق الإصباح ضوء الشمس بالنهار وضوء القمر بالليل

In the Book of Sahih Al-Buhttp://coper/khari, book of Ta'abeer, Vol. 6, Hadith p. 2561, 2562

In the English translation, we see this story in Book of Sahih Al-Bukhari, Book 87, Hadith 111

> "Waraqa died and the Divine Inspiration also stopped for a while, and the Prophet became so sad, as we have heard, that he tried uncountable times to throw himself from the top of high mountains.

Notice here: Waraqa died = Qur'an stopped coming to Muhammad!

But if Waraqa died, who did provided Muhammad with more chapters in his Qur'an? The answer to that is very easy because from the same hadith we can read and record the following:

> "Waraqa Ibn Naofal's bin Asad's bin 'Abd Al-'Uzza bin Qusai. Waraqa was the son of her father's brother, who during the Pre-Islamic period, became a Christian and used to write the Arabic writings and used to write the Gospels (Christian doctrines) in Arabic as much as Allah wished him to write."

As we would notice, Waraqa Ibn Naofal was writing down the Gospel of what is considered to be the true Scriptures of which he had. He was even writing the Gospel by the inspiration of Allah, *"He used to write the Arabic writings and used to write of the Gospels (Christian doctrines) in Arabic as much **as Allah wished him to write**."*

And you notice in here again that he is doing this as Allah wished for him to do. Therefore, it must be 100% approved Scriptures by Muslims about Muhammad. This means when this person has gone away, he left behind a gospel which is the gospel of **Waraqa Ibn Naofal's, and that I believe strongly what is called the Qur'an today.**

Based on this scenario, when Waraqa Ibn Naofal's passed away, Muhammad got so sad for he can no longer provide more chapters for the Qur'an. But some might say that even if Waraqa Ibn Naofal left the gospel behind with Muhammad, he cannot read and write which makes this book useless.

The fact Qur'an says nowhere that Muhammad can't write and read. What the Muslims use to prove this claim is the word 'Umi أمي . But the meaning of this word is totally different from what the Muslims claims to be, and we are going to prove that with all the evidence we need from the Qur'an itself.

Was Muhammad an illiterate man & a monotheistic man?

The word **'Umi** mentioned many times in the Qur'an means: the ones who <u>does not know the Scriptures</u>, not someone who does not know how to write nor read. We are going to prove that in the following:

وَمِنْهُمْ أُمِّيُّونَ لَا يَعْلَمُونَ الْكِتَابَ إِلَّا أَمَانِيَّ وَإِنْ هُمْ إِلَّا يَظُنُّونَ

(سورة البقرة , Al-Baqara, Qur'an 2:78)

> 78 And there are among them illiterates أميون ['Umeuna], who know not the Book, but (see therein their own) desires, and they do nothing but conjecture. (Qur'an 2:78), Yusuf Ali translation

'Umeuna] أميون is the plural of the word **'Umi**. The Qur'an calls them such a name because they have no knowledge of the Book, which is the Scriptures of God. It's important to note that the Qur'an calls the Christians and the Jews "People of the Book" as at that time, there was no way to believe that Christians and Jews did not know how to write and read. They are called "People of the Book" because they have knowledge about the Scriptures of God.

Qur'an 3:20, Yusuf Ali's translation

"So, if they dispute with thee, say: "I have submitted My whole self to Allah and so have those who follow me." And say to the People of the Book and to those who are unlearned: "Do ye (also) submit yourselves?" If they do, they are in right guidance, but if they turn back, Thy duty is to convey the Message; and in Allah's sight are (all) His servants.

The word **'Umeuna** أميون translated and taught in most of the Qur'anic translations comes as illiterate. As we read in the above verse, there are two kinds of people: Those called the "People of the book" and the others who are the "unlearned." So it's very clear that the word illiterate is referred to the individuals who do not know the Scriptures. This is why the Christians and the Jews were not described as illiterate and Muhammad was called an illiterate as he was considered not to know God's Scriptures.

Muslims altogether say that Muhammad was a believer in God even prior to becoming a prophet and that he was not illiterate about God but a follower of Abraham's faith. However, the Qur'an proves the opposite:

(سورة الشورى , Ash-Shura, Qur'an 42:52)

> *"And thus have We, by Our Command, sent inspiration to thee: thou knewest not (before) what was Revelation, and what was Faith; but We have made the (Qur'an) a Light, wherewith We guide such of Our servants as We will; and verily thou dost guide (men) to the Straight Way,"* *(Translation of Yusuf Ali).*

When Muslims tell us that Muhammad was a believer in Ibrahim (Abraham), it is nothing but deceptions and falsification. Not only did Muhammad not know what the Revelation was, but he also never knew about faith. For sure, the verse is speaking about Muhammad being faithless and faith is meaningless for him. So how can Muslims claim that he was a believer when the Qur'an states he was not? What the Qur'anic verse speaks about is that Muhammad was an illiterate man as he had no faith and had no knowledge of the Scriptures, which are the inspiration of God. He was at a stage of ignorance. Therefore, it's not about knowing how to write and read.

At the same time, Muhammad came from a pagan family and that made him an ignorant from the ignorant, which means an illiterate from the illiterate, as he and his own people also did not know the Scriptures of God.

In the following hadith, we will see Muhammad stating in his own clear words that his father is in the hell fire:

Sahih Muslim, Book 001, Hadith 0398

> *"Anas stated Verily, an individual said: Messenger of Allah, where is my father? He said: He is in the Fire. When he turned away, the Prophet called him and said: Verily, my father and your father are in the Fire."*

It's also the same with regards to his mother; she is in hell fire as she was pagan:

Sahih Muslim, Book 004, Hadith 2129

"Abu 'Huraira stated Allah's Messenger, (may Allah pray on him and salute him) as saying: I requested permission to petition forgiveness for my mother, but He (Allah) did not grant it to me. I sought permission from Him to visit her grave, and He granted me permission."

In a different chapter of the Qur'an, we see it saying that Muhammad was <u>an illiterate sent to the illiterate</u>. That was the description for him and his family as they were disbelievers and illiterate about God.

هُوَ الَّذِي بَعَثَ فِي الْأُمِّيِّينَ رَسُولًا مِنْهُمْ يَتْلُو عَلَيْهِمْ آيَاتِهِ وَيُزَكِّيهِمْ وَيُعَلِّمُهُمُ الْكِتَابَ وَالْحِكْمَةَ وَإِن كَانُوا مِن قَبْلُ لَفِي ضَلَالٍ مُّبِينٍ ٥
(سورة الجمعة , Al-Jumua, Qur'an 62:2)

Qur'an 62:2

"It is He (Allah) Who has sent among the Unlettered an apostle from among themselves, to recite to them His Signs, to cleanse them, and to instruct them in Scripture and Wisdom, although they had been, before, in plain deception."

After reading this verse, if Muhammad was for a moment an illiterate sent to the illiterate, it would mean that he could not had been sent to those who knew how to write and read as it would cause Islam a big problem; because then, Muhammad would not be a prophet to the entire world except to those who can't write and read. To say that Muhammad was illiterate is really a foolish thing to say. Therefore, all these references prove to us that Muhammad was not an illiterate man but rather a person who well knew how to write and read. The word illiterate in the Qur'an is used to describe him as a person who did not know God prior to becoming a prophet. The same with his parents and his family. He was not from the pagan sent to the pagan, and verse 62:2 actually presents another mistake in the Qur'an. <u>As long as the Qur'an agrees that Muhammad was a prophet from the illiterate to the illiterate, it means he could not have been claimed a prophet to the Christians and the Jews as the Qur'an never described them as illiterate but as the</u> **"People of the Book"**.

In the following verse, we read:

Qur'an 25:5, Mohsin Khan's translation

"And they say: "Tales of the ancients, which he has written down: and they are dictated to him morning and afternoon." Say: "It (this Qur'an) has been sent down by Him (Allah) (the Real Lord of the heavens and earth) Who knows the secret of the heavens and the earth. Truly, He is Oft-Forgiving, Most Merciful."

Why were people accusing him of writing down stories? As they were from his own people, they knew pretty much if he was illiterate or not. **"Tales of the ancients, which <u>he has written down</u>: and they are dictated to him morning and afternoon."**

And the evidences altogether will explain to us why Allah said that in the chapter given to Muhammad when he was in the cave. It was the first chapter supposedly revealed to Muhammad as the story of Islam which can now be found in the Qur'an:

Qur'an 96:1-5, Muhammad H. Shakir's translation

1 Read in the name of your Lord Who created

2 He created man from a clot.

3 Read and your Lord is Most Honorable,

4 Who taught (to write) with the pen

5 Taught man what he knew not.

As you see in here, <u>the first word</u> that was given to Muhammad as an order from Allah was "**Read**". So, if Muhammad did not know how to read, it meant that the god of Islam was an ignorant god as he was not informed that Muhammad was an illiterate man, as Muslims claim.

Some Muslims might say that the word "**read**" means to recite or to proclaim. If that is the case, it means that the entire chapter of the Qur'an was fabricated, because,
1) The word **recites** mean repeat aloud or declaim (a poem or passage) from memory before an audience.
2) But if this is the first time ever Muhammad heard his first words of his god how he can declaim (a poem or passage) from memory? Did Allah used the wrong Arabic word?
3) Why in the world a grown man in his 40's would not have been able to recite or to repeat what the supposed angel ordered him to?
4) The claims Muslims make about Muhammad being illiterate were mostly based from this verse in which Muhammad replied to the angel commanding him to read: "I cannot read." The fact is that the verse does not say: "I cannot read," it says in Arabic: "**Ma 'Ana Be Qare'**" which means "**What should I read**" rather than "I cannot

read". Arabic is a very rich language and there's no need to use the word "read" when it comes to reciting or repeating words or phrases.

At the same time, if the word "read" is about reciting, it would then be problematic for Muhammad because the meaning of the word "recite" is about saying what's already been memorized in the mind. As long as "read" was the first word Allah spoke to Muhammad, how then can he recite something he's never heard or learned before? Therefore, if the word meant "recite," then it would've meant that Muhammad was saying what was memorized in his head rather than what the angel ordered him.

From the Muslims
Muslims claim
exact words, here is their translation from the following hadith:

Sahih Al-Bukhari, Book 87, Hadith 111

(...) till suddenly the Truth descended upon him while he was in the cave of Hira. The angel came to him and asked him to read. The Prophet replied, "I do not know how to read." (The Prophet added), "The angel caught me (forcefully) and pressed me so hard that I could not bear it anymore. He then released me and again asked me to read, and I replied, "I do not know how to read," whereupon he caught me again and pressed me a second time till I could not bear it anymore. He then released me and asked me again to read, but again I replied, "I do not know how to read (or, what shall I read?)"

Please visit this following link if you want to read the entire translation made by Muslims.
http://www.searchtruth.com/book_display.php?book=87&translator=1&start=0&number=111#111

Notice here with me: Muhammad himself is saying in the Muslims
Muslims claim
translation: "*again I replied, "I do not know how to read (or, what shall I read?)*"."

You can tell how confused the Muslims are because they translate the meaning into two different meanings, not just one.

1. one is coming as "I do not know how to read"
2. the other comes as "what shall I read?"

For sure both sentences are totally different and don't have the same meaning. Based on what I've provided you, it must be "**what shall I read**" especially if you also noticed that He (the angel) gave Muhammad an order as one word (read). The angel came to him inside the cave and asked him to read. The Prophet replied, "I do not know how to read (or, what shall I read?)." So why is it that an adult can't recite a word, even just a single word, which is "read"? It's very clear that Muhammad was rather asking him "**what shall I read**" because the angel did not give him any text to read. That again proves that this story was purely fabricated using and choosing the wrong words, wrong orders, and the wrong reactions.

Now we need to go back to Qur'an chapter 96:4-5

4 Who taught (to write) with the pen

5 Taught man what he knew not.

In verses four and five, Allah is stating that he taught him by the pen. Notice that Allah talking about a knowledge of scripture which is taught by the pen. This means that Allah always spoke to people using their pen and he inspired them and they write down what he said. That is specifically made for the prophet of God and this was specifically was meant for Muhammad. **So, if Allah taught his prophets only by the pen** as this verse states and Muhammad spent his life unable to read and write this means Muhammad must be a false prophet and this verse must be a false statement coming from false god Allah.

With all the evidences, we can understand that Muhammad was a person who, in fact, knew how to write and read. After the death of Waraqa Ibn Naofal, he tried to commit suicide several times. Because Muhammad was now in trouble, how was he going to bring and make new verses for the Qur'an when it was Waraqa making them and providing them? The hadith clearly states that Waraqa used to write as much as Allah wished him to. He wrote the gospel in Arabic. Waraqa Ibn Naofal had left behind a book he spent his life working on. He was a very old man and this means that he started writing the book when he was still in good health and it is almost finished when he died. Therefore, Muhammad got a book in his hand and he knew how to read and write and had the opportunity to proclaim himself prophet of God.

Muhammad attempted suicide many times?

Six Reasons People Attempt Suicide

- o **They're depressed**.
- o **They're psychotic**.
- o **They're impulsive**.
- o **They're crying out for help**.

- o **They have a philosophical desire to die.**

- o **They've made a mistake.**

So, what was the case of Muhammad?

Sahih Al Bukhari, Book 87, Hadith 111

"And every time the prophet climbed on top of a mountain trying to throw himself down from the top of it, Jibreel would appear in front of him and say, "O Muhammad! You are truly Allah's Apostle in truth." Whereupon then the prophet would calm down and become quiet and would return back. And whenever the period of the coming of the inspiration used to become long without coming, he would do the same as he did before (attempting Suicide), but when he used to reach the top of a mountain, Jibreel would again appear before him and tell him the same words he'd said before."

In this story, we find that Muhammad is not a stable man. We also learn important things about Islam in that time and about the most important figure in Islam: Muhammad.

"climbed on top of a mountain trying to throw himself down."

1. To do such a thing, you need to think about it for a long time before you decide to kill yourself.
2. Why did Muhammad choose to die in such a way?
3. Why didn't the angel Gabriel appear to Muhammad before he'd begin climbing a mountain?
4. The angel appeared to Muhammad many times in order to stop him! Each time Muhammad, would go back home only to attempt throwing himself off a mountain again.
5. Why did Muhammad do this many times? Wasn't the first time enough for the angel to tell him not to?
6. Why did Muhammad try to kill himself after Waraqa's death?
7. Why did the Qur'an stop coming to Muhammad right after Waraqa's death?
8. The Qur'an: "the inspiration used to become long without coming." Why?
9. Why was Allah doing that to Muhammad?
10. Why didn't the angel solve Muhammad's problem of not receiving the inspiration, which made him want to kill himself?
11. Every time Muhammad changed his mind about killing himself

was when the angel, Gabriel, told him, "**O Muhammad! You are truly Allah's Apostle**".

12. Is it possible that Muhammad was not sure that he was a prophet of God? And the angel he saw was fake?

13. The fact is that Muhammad had a problem accepting himself as a prophet, which the Qur'an explains:

Qur'an 10:94

If you are in doubt of what we sent down to you, ask the people of who read the Book before you (the Christians and Jews).

● If Muhammad himself wasn't certain of him seeing or speaking to an angel and receiving the book of God, then who could be sure?

● According to scientific studies, most suicide attempts are directly associated with mental health problem.

● Was Muhammad suffering from mental health problems? We will find out more later on.

Muhammad suffering from mental health problems

I showed you that Muhammad attempted to kill himself several times but it does not prove that he was suffering from mental problems. We need more proof.

Muhammad had the strangest story!

● Muhammad's first wife, Khadija, was about 27 years older than him while he was in his 18th year. Some Muslims claim he was 25 at that time.

● What made him marry a woman older than his mother? It can be for two reasons. Khadija was rich and he was working for her. The reasons are:

● Money

● Muhammad was an orphan and he was looking for a mother and Khadija was the one who could address that.

He got two in one. Muhammad received messages not only from God but even from Satan! (see the satanic verses in Qur'an 22:52) That makes him:

● He is Satan's messenger and God's messenger at the same time!

● Muhammad had bad sexual problems affecting his life.

- In fact, he is the only prophet who spoke of how powerful his private part was.
- { أُعْطِيتُ قُوَّةَ أَرْبَعِينَ فِي الْبَطْشِ وَالْجِمَاعِ } He is the only prophet whose god sent him a dish of faith & wisdom via the angel Gabriel. After he got the dish, he received the sexual power of 40 men!

Here's the link to type in for: Fateh Al-Bari fe Sharh, Sahih Al-Bukhari, p. 450 (arabic):

> **"The prophet of Allah used to say that I was among those who have little strength for intercourse. Then Allah sent me a pot with cooked meat. After I ate from it, I found strength any time I wanted to do the work."Ibn Sa'd, Kitab Tabaqat Al-Kubra, Vol. 8, p. 200.**

وكان نبينا صلى الله عليه وسلم يطوف على إحدى عشرة امرأة له في الساعة الواحدة

Sahih Muslim, Book of Eman, Vol. 3, p. 282, print yr 1966

"The prophet of Islam used to do his 11 wives in an hour."

Sahih Al-Bukhari, Book 5, Hadith 268

" ص105 - 265 كان النبي قال أنس بن مالك حدثنا قتادة عن أبي حدثني معاذ بن هشام قال حدثنا محمد بن بشار قال حدثنا
صلى الله عليه وسلم يدور على نسائه في الساعة الواحدة من الليل والنهار وهن إحدى عشرة قال قلت لأنس أوكان يطيقه قال كنا
نتحدث أنه أعطي قوة ثلاثين

Sahih Al-Bukhari, Book 5, Hadith 268

Reported Qatada: Anas bin Malik previously mentioned The Prophet used to visits all his eleven wives in a round, in one night, and they were." I questioned Anas, "Had the Prophet the strength for it?" Anas responded "We used to say that the Prophet was given the strength of thirty men."

"Narrated Anas bin Malik: The Prophet used to go do all his wives in one night (to have intercourse), and at that time he had nine wives. (Sahih AL-bukhari Book 62, Hadith 142)

even Muhammad's stories about other prophets is about sexual-intercourse power as we read in this coming story:

Narrated Abu Huraira: The Prophet said, "Solomon son of David said, 'Tonight I will have sexual-intercourse with seventy ladies each of whom will conceive a child who will be a mujahid fighting for for the sake of Allah.' His companion said, 'If Allah will.' But Solomon did not say so; therefore, none of those women got pregnant except one who gave birth to a half child." The Prophet further said, "If the Prophet Solomon had said it (i.e. 'If Allah will') he would have begotten children who would have fought in Allah's Cause." Shuaib and Ibn Abi Az-Zinad said, "Ninety (women) is more correct (than seventy)." (Sahih Al-Bukhari Book 55, Hadith

635)

- That been said it explaining to us the way Muhammad think, powerful prophet must be powerful in bed! Who in the word will believe that any man can have sex with ninety women in one night? That mean Solomon had 90 ejaculations in 8 hours = one ejaculation every 5 minutes for 8 hours none stop!
- That makes this angel, Jibreel, the same who delivered to Muhammad the Book of God and gave the sexual enhancement material!
- He is the only prophet whose god sent a chapter about his penis. See Qur'an, chapter 108.
- The only prophet who spoke about miracles of which no witnesses had seen but him!
- The only prophet who doesn't have time for the poor and kicks the blind out of his house because he was busy dealing with rich people! See Qur'an, chapter 80.
- The only prophet who married a 5-year-old child (6 years old in the Islamic lunar calendar = 5 years in our calendar).
- The only prophet who taught to a nation, while according to Muslims
  Muslims claim
  claims, he didn't know how to read or write.
- The only prophet who never spoke to his god in his book!
- The only prophet who chose to change his name by himself. Not by God, like Jacob. In case you do not remember, the real name of Muhammad was **Qathem (look it up in Vol. 1)**.

Later, we will talk about these things in more detail.
....

Insert in him a chain in the anus

by scaring them with low IQ "Intelligence Quotient" stories

Qur'an 69:32

30 "seize him, and tie him,

31 "And burn ye him in the Blazing Fire.

32 inserts in him a chain, whereof the length is seventy cubits!

33 because he does not believe in Allah Most High."

If we read these verses together based on the Islamic translation of the Qur'an, we will notice that we would have a hard time to find the true translation of those verses. As an example, in Yusuf Ali's translation, reading "**insert in him a chain**" comes as "**make him march in a chain**" which is absolutely false and a way to deceive in order to cover up an extreme foolishness.

Of all the Muslims
~~Muslims claim~~
translations, I only found one honest translation of this verse, by Muhammad Pickthall: "[32] **And then insert him in a chain whereof the length is seventy cubits**".

The reason I'm showing you the Muslims
~~Muslims claim~~
translations are because someone might say it does not say that. It is a lie and the best way to prove it if we can is from Muslim translations Going back to the Qur'an, we need to go and find out what exactly this verse means based on the understanding of the scholars of Islam. Those Islamic scholars are approved by all the Muslims.

Let us read together the interpretation of one of the biggest scholars of Islam:

> *Tanwîr al-Miqbâs min Tafsîr Ibn 'Abbâs*
> *Insert in him (Allah ordering the angels) the chain in his anus and extract it from his mouth, and of what remains of the chain length turn it around his neck, and its width is seventy cubits. It is also said to mean: 70 fathoms.*

The best way to know Muhammad is to read his words as if you are someone studying psychology & human behavior science.

1. That being said, everything Muhammad told his followers was as if it came from his god. It was meant to make Islam "attractive," such as promising them plenty of women for sex, owning 70,000 boys as servants, having a river of honey, a river of milk and a river of wine.

2. But what if all these attractive promises did not work, meaning even after Muhammad would tell them what they would receive, they would still not obey him? He would need to find a way to assure obedience by terrifying those who think about not obeying. As an example, Muhammad told Muslims that they are going to be tortured even in their grave, which means that the torture process begins the second a

197

human being dies, not on Judgment Day. Later on, we will speak about the story of the punishment in the grave and analyze it.

3. For now, think about this chapter where Allah will insert to an individual's anus such a huge chain which is extremely hot to the point it makes a mountain melt in contact with it, as we read in the interpretation of:

Tafsir al-Tustari, Vol. 2, p. 178

{ثُمَّ فِي سِلْسِلَةٍ ذَرْعُهَا سَبْعُونَ ذِرَاعاً فَاسْلُكُوهُ}

And bind him in a chain seventy cubits long. Each cubit is equivalent to seventy fathoms and each fathom is longer than the distance between Kufa (in Iraq) and Mecca. If you were to put one of its joints on the top of a mountain, the mountain would melt, just as lead melts.

How big this chain would be?

From Ibn Kathir book we quote; "Every ring of it will be equal to the entire amount of iron found in this world.'... (Then fasten him) "It will be entered into his buttocks and pulled out of his mouth. Then they will be arranged on this (chain) just like locusts are arranged on a stick that is being roasted."

If you ever watched a horror movie, I don't think the director's imagination would reach Muhammad's level. His imagination leads us to serious questions:

-   I can understand that God is going to punish people for not being good but we cannot understand God ordering his angels to play with somebody's anus.
-   If an individual is 5 to 6 feet tall, what is the point of using a chain that's 70 times longer than the distance between the two cities of Kufa & Mecca, which is equal to: 1,930 kilometers x 70 = 135,100 km or 83,947 miles?
-   The ring is so big to the point each ring of the chain will be "Every **ring of it will be equal to the entire amount of iron found in this world**" ... how big this anus is to take such a ring?
-   If Muhammad claimed that it is what his god Allah said, it can't be logical due to the size of a man and the size of the chain which can cross USA many times around, as the distance between New York and California is less than 3,000 miles which also means this chain is almost 3 times the distance between

California and New York. If such claim is not enough to prove that the god of Islam is just making up a lie then I am not sure what kind of proof you need to recognize how big the lie is.

- As if it is not enough that Allah will insert a chain inside your anus, this chain is hot enough to melt a mountain! This means that the anus of a disbeliever, his entire body and mouth, will not melt but the mountain will?

Ask no questions or we will kill you

All of us think that questions are allowed and essential with regards to faith. For me, the best way of educating is to provide answers to questions. In Islam's case, it's the opposite. It's forbidden to ask questions especially when they might make Islam look embarrassing or to prove that the founder of Islam, the scholars, and leaders of Islam have no answer to them.

As long as they have no answers to it, they have to find distractions to stop those questions which make people maybe think seriously about Islam being a false religion that can't provide answers.

The coming story is about the most famously smart and just man in the history of Islam. According to Muslims, the caliph 'Umar Ibn Al-Khattab came in right after the prophet of Islam. It is about when the caliph heard that a man called a question about the Qur'an's allegorical verses which no Muslim dared to give an answer for.

In the explanation book of Jame' of A'hkam Al-Qur'an by Imam Al-Qur'tubi, Vol. 4, p. 14:

> *Reported by Ishmael son of Isaac, the judge had been told by Suleyman son of 'Harb from 'Hamad son of Yazied son of 'Hazm from Suleyman son of Yasar: that there was a man whose name is Subi'q son 'Asal* صبيغ بن عسل*. He came to the city of Medina and asked questions about allegorical Qur'an and the news reached out to 'Umar the caliph. The caliph then ordered to bring him and had prepared sticks of branches out of a palm tree. Then 'Umar asked him: who are you? The man replied, I am the slave of Allah, Subi'q. 'Umar said, and I am the slave of Allah, 'Umar. So 'Umar stood up and beat him on his head and made a cut on his head and continued beating him until blood covered his face. Then the man Subi'q said, "enough the ruler of believers, all the*

questions in my head are gone".

What we learn from this story is that torture was the way of practice by Muhammad and then practiced by Muslims who followed. It is the only way to silence individuals, even believers, who asked questions just to learn the cause. Questions are embarrassing and Muslims cannot tolerate them as they have no

الجامع لأحكام القرآن » سورة آل عمران » قوله تعالى هو الذي أنزل عليك الكتاب منه آيات محكمات هن أم الكتاب
الجزء الرابع ص14

حدثنا إسماعيل بن إسحاق القاضي أنبأنا سليمان بن حرب عن حماد بن زيد عن يزيد بن حازم عن سليمان بن يسار أن صبيغ بن عسل قدم المدينة فجعل يسأل عن متشابه القرآن وعن أشياء ، فبلغ ذلك عمر ـ رضي الله عنه ـ فبعث إليه عمر فأحضره وقد أعد له عراجين من عراجين النخل . فلما حضر قال له عمر : من أنت ؟ قال : أنا عبد الله صبيغ . فقال عمر ـ رضي الله عنه ـ : وأنا عبد الله عمر ، ثم قام إليه فضرب رأسه بعرجون فشجه ، ثم تابع ضربه حتى سال دمه على وجهه ، فقال : حسبك يا أمير المؤمنين فقد والله ذهب ما كنت أجد في رأسي

answers for them.

When reading that the caliph ordered to have this man brought to him, you would probably think that 'Umar wished to educate him, as he was one of the best companions of the prophet. Supposedly, Muhammad's companions had more knowledge than the others.

- The caliph 'Umar did not ask the man anything about any of his questions.
- 'Umar did not ask him what he would like to know and what is causing him to be confused.
- 'Umar started beating him severely until he made him bleed and blood covered his face. That was how bad that act of violence was.
- If caliph 'Umar is portrayed as the most just man in the history of Islam, then what would an unjust man really do?
- Ask any Muslim who is best described to be the man of justice in the history of Islam. The answer will be instant: 'Umar the caliph. Now, imagine putting into practice 'Umar's ways of justice **into our schools, in the streets, inside our Courts of law**. And if anyone asks a question about Islam or even tries to question Islam, the fair practice would be to beat the individual until he/she repents and no questions would ever be asked again...as Subi'q told 'Umar he had no more questions left to ask in his mind!

And that is not a a mistake of 'Umar but its an order from Allah as we read in;

Qur'an 5:101-102

"O ye who believe! Ask not questions about things which, if made plain to you, may cause you trouble. But if ye ask about things when the Qur'an is being revealed, they will be made plain to you, Allah will forgive those: for Allah is Oft-forgiving, Most Forbearing.102 Some people before you did ask such questions, and on that account lost their faith."

Who is the worst criminal among the Muslims?

Book of Tafsir Al-Qur'an by Ibn Kathir p. 123.

"The prophet of Allah said: 'The worst criminal among the Muslims is he who asks if a matter is unlawful or not, and it becomes unlawful because of his asking about it.' It is recorded in the Sahih that the Messenger of Allah said, (Leave me as I have left you, those before you were destroyed because of many questions and disputing with their Prophets.) An authentic Hadith also states."

We noticed together here the following things:

1. There is a big risk if you Ask question.
2. Why I am not only a criminal but I am the worst for asking Muhammad, can we eat pork? And later Allah made it unlawful so where is the crime?
3. Muhammad fear questions because it might expose his falsehood.

Which did Allah create and finish first? Earth or Heaven?

If Allah is a true god, he should not be confused. Even a child would answer correctly after we teach him. We will see a very clear contradiction and a huge mistake in Qur'an 41:9.

Qur'an 41:9

Say: Do you really disbelieve in the One who created the earth in two days, and ascribe to Him partners? That is the Lord of the two Worlds.

Muslims believe there are two worlds. One for mankind and the other for the Jinn's.

Qur'an 41:10-12

10 And made it firm mountains from above it and blessed it and measure therein its sustenance in four days whether to ask

11 Then He turned to heaven when it was smoke, and said, to the heaven and the earth: come to me voluntarily or involuntarily.

12 So he made them seven heavens in two Days and inspired in each heaven its mandate and adorned the lower heaven with lamps, and to preserve the estimation of the knower, the respected.

Let's look at Qur'an 79:28:

Qur'an 79:28-32

28 He raised and made it level,

29 and darkened its night, and he brought forth the day;

30 and after that He made the earth wide and flat;

31 from it (meaning the earth. This is a contradiction, as many verses say the water came from the sky)

He has ejected its waters and its pasture,

32 and has fixed on it the mountains.

The mistake in here is so clear.

1. In verses 41:9 and 79:28, Allah created the earth first.
2. In 41:10, 11 and 12, he finished the earth and then went to heaven and made it seven heavens.
3. But in 79:29, 30, 31 and 32, he made and finished the earth, mountains, trees and water after the sky.
4. The Qur'an itself says, "if this book is not from god, you will find in it many contradictions".

Qur'an 4:82

If this book is not from god you will find in it many contradictions.

I think Allah shot himself in the foot!

Uthman's Misstructuring of the Qur'an

In the Qur'an of Ibn Mas'ud, he said that Al Fatiha is not from the Qur'an, but rather a prayer Muhammad used to say. This is why it's not included inside Ibn Mas'ud's Qur'an.

The first revelation Muhammad allegedly received from Allah via the angel Jibrel (Gabriel) is Sura # 96. If it was the first revelation to Muhammad from Allah, then this Sura should be Sura # 1. The question is, why is it Sura # 96, and not Sura # 1?

Muslims claim that the Qur'an is not corrupted and no one changed it. However, since Allah wanted Sura # 96 to be the first Sura, we need to ask which Muslim has the right to change the location of the verse to Sura # 96?

What happened was Uthman Ibn Affan, the one who collected the Qur'an after Muhammad's death, placed this verse as Sura # 96. It's interesting to note that the name of this book isn't even named after Muhammad; it really shouldn't even be named Qur'an. We generally call it Qur'an but since Uthman the caliph, after Muhammad specified how the Qur'an would be structured, he rendered the Qur'an technically in name **Mushaf of Uthman**.

The Qur'an has 114 chapters. After examining how Sura 96:**1** [Muhammad's first revelation] was interjected into a later Sura instead of being at the beginning of the Qur'an, it demonstrates from early on how Muslims played with Allah's word, and it continues to this day.

In Sura 1:1, Allah is talking to himself. Why is he saying "**In the name of Allah**"? Remember that Allah has 99 names, but Allah is the most used name. Looking at Sura 1:5, Allah is saying, "**Thee do we worship and Thine aid we seek.**" This means that Allah is worshiping Allah and seeking his own help. Remember, the Qur'an is supposed to be the direct words of Allah.

Muslims claim this is a prayer. However, Allah gives no indication that this is how to pray. It is Allah saying the words directly. When people asked Jesus how to pray, He showed them how. There are many passages in the Qur'an where Allah directs Muhammad to recite by saying: "**Say,**" but in Sura 1:5 it's exclusively Allah speaking. At this point Allah is not revealing anything to Muhammad. If a Muslim says that this is Muhammad praying, it means that the Qur'an is from Muhammad, not Allah.

Again, looking at the Qur'an, the fact that Uthman put it together and Muslims don't seem to know how he did it shows that Allah is speaking to himself.

The Beginning of this Universe

The Pen

Qur'an 96:1-4

1 Read in the name of your lord who create,

2 made human from a clot of blood,

3 it's your lord the giver,

4 who taught the human by the pen

Another mistake is in Sura 96:4 regarding the use of the pen. How did Allah teach through the use of the pen? Muhammad did not know how to write or read, according to the Muslims
Muslims claim
claims!

Apparently, the pen was one of Allah's first creations.

Sahih Al-Bukhari, Vol. 9, Book 93, 514

So, we ask you what the beginning of this universe was. The Prophet said, "There was Allah and nothing else before Him and His Throne was over the water and He then created the Heavens and The Earth and wrote everything in the Book."

First, the prophet said that in the beginning of times, there was Allah and nothing before him, yet Muhammad went on saying that Allah's <u>Throne</u> was over the <u>water</u>. How can he say there was nothing before Allah and yet his throne was over the water?

As we see, Muhammad was contradicting himself due to the fact that **a)** there was a throne; and **b)** there was water.
Moreover, the verse shows that that water existed before heaven and earth, which were said to be the first things created.

- The first thing that Allah created was a pen, but he ordered it to write on what? Doesn't he first need to create something to be written in or on?
- Then the pen wrote everything in a book.
- How did it do that? What book is Muhammad referring to? Allah has a book next to him but no one can read that book since it's

only made for Allah. So, the question is...

- Why is Allah writing things for himself? Does he suffer from memory loss?
- This brings us back to the question, why was Allah teaching himself through the pen?
- Remember, according to Muslims
  Muslims claim
  claims, Muhammad could neither write nor read.

Allah Swears by a fruit, vegetable, planet, himself and a pen!

Ibn Abbas 95:1

And from the interpretation of Ibn Abbas, he said in regards to the interpretation of Allah's saying (by the fig and the olive): Allah swears by the fig,

Usually when people swear, they swear by something that is greater than them. A person doesn't swear by a chicken, a cockroach, a rat, or a cat. One doesn't swear by the zucchini, onion, or carrot because it isn't something that a normal person would do.

In the above verse we've read, Allah swears by the olive and the fig. What was Allah's point in swearing by the olive and the fig? If someone swears, he/she is trying to make a point.

God should not swear by his own creation because he can destroy it and create it again if he so chooses. Maybe Muhammad was hungry? This verse really demonstrates a characteristic of Muhammad. He was noted as always wanting to eat off the bounty of the lands he violently conquered or never set foot on.

The verse Ibn Abbas wrote seems more like lyrics of a rap song rather then the words of a prophet. Perhaps Muhammad was preoccupied with hunger rather than revelation. Muslims have a very difficult time explaining this verse. One can only wonder, if Muhammad lived today, would he swear by the iPod or by another type of fruit such as a banana. Muhammad is showing a god, who supposedly created the universe, swearing by fruits and vegetables.

Are our lives represented by the fig tree? Hardly. If this verse gave a word such as bread, that may have an entirely different intrinsic meaning. Still, using bread wouldn't make sense but it would be more readily accepted as a form of common necessity for life, even metaphorically. What does the fig have to do with Allah swearing? What has this even taught us about Allah?

Many, many times the confusion of Muslims comes out when they try to piece together the context of what Allah is trying to say. Allah seems a bit odd in the fact that he swears by a fig, an olive and many other things too. For example:

Qur'an 16:63

By Allah, we verily sent messengers unto all nations before thee, but the devil made their works seem to be good to them and at the end they will be punished.

Allah swears by Allah in Qur'an 16:63. The mistake in this verse is clear. Allah is swearing by the fig and olive and at the same time swearing by himself. He is making himself equal with the fig and olive, because these three, by Allah's standard, are the greatest. If a Muslim was to go to court, he or (no-she) should be given one of three options, either to swear by the holy fig, holy olive, or Allah. The clerics should not say they cannot do that because if it's good enough and holy enough for Allah to swear by, isn't it good enough for his followers?

Ibn Abbas 68:1

Ibn Abbas said, regarding this verse, Allah is saying "nun", (pronounced like "noon"). It means he swears by the nun and the pen. And he said, that nun is a whale. His name is Lewash. He carries the earths on its back while in water and under, the bull, the name of the bull is Bahamot, there is a rock, and under the rock, over there is sand, and no one knows what is under the sand, but Allah. And from under there are 4000 cracks were 4000 springs of water come out. It is also said, that; that nun one of Allah's names coming from Al Rahman al-Rahman (the mercy); and it is as well as said, that nun is an inkwell. Then Allah swears by the (by the pen) Allah swore by the pen. And this pen is made of light, and its height is equal to the distance between sky and earth. It is with this pen that Allah wrote everything in the protected and Guarded Tablet. It is also said, that the pen is one of the angels by whom Allah swears by.

Muslims claim that Allah is swearing by *Nun* (a whale). In Arabic, *nun* is only the letter "N", not a word. Technically Allah is swearing by a letter, not a whale, as the Muslim author would have us believe.

The narrator of this verse seems to be struggling to determine who and what *Nun* is. At the beginning, it is determined *Nun* is the letter "N", then the verse goes on to say *Nun* is a whale (who's name is not specifically known), then a bull (who's name is not specifically known), then Allah. If *Nun* is one of the names of Allah, then Muhammad lied when he said, that Allah had only ninety-nine names. The name *Nun* would make it one hundred names, yet it is not listed as one of Allah's names. It is very difficult even for scholars and any Muslim to understand this verse, or to resolve the mysteries in the confusing Qur'an. It seems Allah gave a confusing message. Why is Allah saying things no one can understand?

Now if we take a deeper look, we will find the following points in this verse:

1. Muslims are confused of what Allah meant.
2. On one time, *nun* comes as a whale, another it might be Allah himself, and then once it's a pen.
3. What is the point of this oath when Allah never told them what he meant by *nun*? No one knows what the word even means! However, it's so clear that Muhammad, himself, did not know. Otherwise, Muslims would not be left in confusion with its meaning. They just repeat what the Qur'an makers said.
4. We know that there are two guys who were partners in this Qur'an making: Waraqa Ibn Naofal and the monk Buhira.

Qur'an 68:1 continues with Allah swearing by the pen. Why would Allah need to swear by the pen?

> This pen is made of light and its height is equal to the distance heaven and earth.

DOES size matter? This is one huge pen. The verse goes on to give many explanations of the pen. Allah allegedly wrote down things on a guarded tablet. Would Allah forget things if he hadn't written them down because of his short memory?

Now the pen changes into an angel? Allah now swears by an angel. Could it be the angel was made of ink and Allah squeezed the angel and wrote with it? Muhammad had a talent for telling fairytale stories. Children would even laugh at these stories. What can anyone learn from this? It just says Allah swore by a pen.

Qur'an 53:1

[1] By the Star when it sets,

Why does Allah swear by the star? What does it mean "by the star"? These are questions left unanswered by Muslims.

Previously we have noted Allah swearing by:

- ★ the fig;
- ★ the olive;
- ★ a whale;
- ★ and men.
- ★ Swearing by himself; and
- ★ by a star.
- ★ In other verses, Allah swears by:
- ★ the sky;
- ★ the pen;
- ★ the setting places of the stars.

Qur'an 56:75

Nay, I swear by the setting-places of the stars

In Qur'an 53:1, Allah swears by the location of the star but in Qur'an 56:75, he says he doesn't swear by the location of the stars. Muhammad says Allah simultaneously accepts and denies swearing by the stars. There is a lot of confusion created by Muhammad's god. God speaks to us to teach us, not to confuse us by vague words that we can't understand the meaning of.

Another mistake is that Qur'an 56:75 speaks about stars having a setting place. Do stars have a setting place? Is this some Islamic scientific discovery never shared with the rest of the world?

Tafsir Al-Jalalayn, Qur'an 56:76

Surely if you knew how great is my oath, swearing by the setting of the stars, it is a tremendous oath, if you only knew, if you were people of high knowledge, you would know how great is this oath.

<u>Why is this a tremendous oath for Allah?</u> What makes it so tremendous? What is the magnitude of this oath?

This verse also assumes that the reader is not knowledgeable or unable to understand it. Who would be the one to understand this verse? Neither Jalalayn nor any other scholar gave an explanation for this verse. This is another verse that gives us nothing, yet many Muslims just recite it without knowing what they are repeating. This can only be from Satan because it lacks substance of knowledge.

Qur'an, Sura 3:7 says no one can understand the Qur'an. Yet the scholars say they believe what it says even if they don't understand the verses. What's the point of making a book and saying it's from God when no one will be able to understand it or explain it? If a crazy person speaks and no one is able to understand him or her, it will not make sense.

Qur'an 3:7

That he sent down to you from the verses of the book are entirely clear, they are the basic teaching of the book, and other verses are confusing and not clear will be to as for those who in their hearts and follow the deviation from the similarity in order to sedition, but no one knows its true meanings except Allah, and those who are strong in knowledge say we accept, and we believe (but still the knowledgeable ones don't know they are called knowledgeable for saying we accept).

If Allah is saying in a lot of verses of the Qur'an that no one knows what they mean or what they're meant to be, why did he send it to us? What for? The fact is the verse says clearly that these verses are made to deceive. I ask the following questions:

- Why is Allah doing Satan's job by deceiving me?
- Why is he sending unclear verses that will even create division among Muslims when all of them are supposed to love Allah?
- What is the benefit of that? Is Allah playing with the human race as if we were his toys?
- Isn't this really a hateful thing to do from someone who claims to be god? If God does that, what is Satan for?
- As long as no one knows what these verses mean, save Allah, was Muhammad himself confused about them?

If we take a deeper look, we will see that this verse proves my point about Muhammad, just copying what he doesn't understand. This verse is made to protect *him* from questions that he can't answer because he has no knowledge of what Waraqa Ibn Naofal and Buhira the monk are telling him. He is just a messenger, which is clearly shown in:

Qur'an 5:101

Ask not questions about Qur'an, about things that look ugly for you and bad in it.

Qur'an 5:102

For people of former generations asked the same questions and they caused them to lose their faith.

What was the purpose of these two verses?

> ➤ Do not ask, because he (Muhammad) had no answers.
> ➤ Asking these questions is forbidden.
> ➤ Whoever asks will be punished because it leads to being a *kafir* or an infidel (non-believer of Islam).
> ➤ If he/she asks, he/she will most surely leave Islam.

Who do the angels really serve?

Do they belong to Allah or to Elohim?

Many of us have read the names of the angels but don't really know what they mean. Besides Michael and Gabriel, which are found in the Scripture, the following angels' names are not mentioned in the Biblical scriptures. They are: Raphaiel, Selaphiel, Jegudiel, Barachiel, and Jeremiel.

These names can be found in the *apocrypha*, which is a collection of books that are not accepted as Holy Biblical scriptures. Instead, the apocrypha contain stories that are not confirmed as factual. The names of the angels end in "el" which means "of God." The angels' names mentioned here clearly indicate to whom they are attached to.

You may even notice that the word angel, even in English, ends with "El". The word angel means *a messenger of God* (El). "El" is a Hebrew word associated with Elohim אֱלֹהִים which is the plural name of "El".

EL vs AL

In Hebrew, we can find the use of the word EL all over the old and new testament, however the word EL appear in the new Hebrew, and it was AL = God in the ancient Hebrew as example:

New Hebrew	Ancient Hebrew
Ezekiel EL = God	EzekAL AL=God
Israel	IshraAL
Michael	MichaAL
Gabriel	GabriAL

However how Quran use such a word?
The angels named in the Qur'an are:

- ⊕ *Jibrel*: The angel responsible for revealing the Qur'an to Muhammad,
- ⊕ *Michael*: Archangel of mercy who is responsible for bringing rain and thunder to earth,
- ⊕ *Israfel*: The angel responsible for signaling the coming of Judgment Day by blowing a horn and sending out the Blast of Truth,
- ⊕ *Azrael*: The angel of death.

As in Quran	EL = GOD
Israel	Isra**EL**
Jibrel	Jibr **EL**
Michael	Micha **EL**
Israfel	Israf **EL**
Azrael	Azra **EL**

"El" is found at the end of each one of these names and as noted above, "El" means "of God" as found in Gabriel and Michael, which are angels mentioned in the Bible.

Allah has 99 names and none of those 99 names mentioned include "**El**".

Since the name of God is "El" and all these angels belong to God or "El", this puts Allah in a rather bad situation. As long as these angels mentioned in the Qur'an belong to God whose name is "El", it means that Jibrel, who allegedly brought the revelation of the Qur'an to Muhammad, is not the angel of Allah. That makes me wonder about the source of Muhammad's revelations being very suspicious under examination.

Muhammad heard the story about the biblical angel Gabriel who brought a message to Mary when he announced to her that she will be blessed by God and conceive a son and he will be named Yahshua.

Luke 1:26 - KJV

And in the sixth month the angel Gabriel was sent from God unto a city of Galilee, named Nazareth,

The only reason the angels' names appear in the Qur'an is because Muhammad copied them from the Bible or from know either from the bible Scripture or Catholic, Orthodox Church Tradition, and put them in his book. Muhammad had no idea what the angels' names meant, yet used them in his book anyway. Muhammad had also no idea that they were the angels of the God of the Jews and of the Christians. We can definitely see that the angels don't belong to Muhammad's god and that once again, Muhammad shows himself being a thief.

Allah claimed to be the God of Moses and other prophets, written in the Scriptures. Their names have nothing to do with Muslims simply because Muhammad stole this information and put it in his book.

It doesn't matter how smart someone thinks he is or how big of a liar he is. The thief will always make a mistake and reveal his deception.

Later on, Islamic scholars noticed the connection between "El" and the God of the Jews and the Christians. By then, it was too late to add "El" to the list of Allah's 99 names. Names of which Muhammad himself counted and therefore, the scholars could not add any more to it.

Qur'an 2:40

O Children of IsraEL, remember My favor upon you.

The word Israel means to strive, to overcome, then rule with **EL,** God's people will rule with Him.

The Arabic version of this verse is claiming that Israel means; the children of Jacob. This verse references Jacob's name to mean slave of Allah, according to Muhammad. Therefore, Muslims claim Israel ultimately means "slave of Allah" and "El" means Allah. If "El" is one of the names of Allah, why is it not in the Qur'an as one of his 99 names?

The author of this Qur'anic verse knew that "El" meant the God of Jacob, the God of the people of Israel. "El" is the real God, not Allah, and this is why "El" is not part of the 99 names of Allah, nor it is included in the Qur'an. Allah's 99 names are only in Arabic. If the Qur'an is for all places and times, how can it only be in Arabic? Why doesn't Allah's message contain all languages? The God of the universe is not limited to one language; however, it seems Allah is. Muslims claim Abraham's son, Ishmael, was an Arab. This is false as well. The angels' names in the Qur'an, Jibrel and others that end in "El", expose the author of the Qur'an as deceptive.

Look at the name of Ishmael, let us look at this name carefully in Arabic **ES-MA-El = Ishmael** the meaning of Ishmael is "**God listens.**" Again,

Allah did not make the right choice, because these names belong to the God, EL.

Since I mentioned the name of Ishmael, I would like to ask those who teach in our churches where they got the information that Ishmael was an Arab? It's shameful that many church leaders repeat these words their entire life and never questioned themselves about the source of this information. Let me break it down for you.

The Arabs existed way before the birth of Ishmael. Therefore, how would that make Ishmael the father of the Arabs? Sadly, at the same time, our church teachers keep teaching false information about Muslims being the sons of Ishmael. How crazy and how wrong that is. The fact is that Muslims have nothing to do with Ishmael. If we look at the Muslims, they are not even 3% of are Arab, Muslims only claim this to give Muhammad genuine rights that he is from Abraham in order to claim that he was from a prophet's family and thus, had the right to be one too. As if it's a family business and not God's choice. Even that is against the Qur'an.

Qur'an 29:27

And we gave Abraham, Isaac and Jacob, and ordained from his offspring the Prophet-hood and Revelation, and We granted him his reward in this life; and he was in the life after death of the companion of the Righteous.

As you can see, the Qur'an clearly says that the prophet-hood is only from Isaac and Jacob. Did Allah forget Ishmael? It's so clear that it was a mistake from the one who made the Qur'an.

Allah's anatomy confusion on Judgment Day

The following verse talks about those who come with failure to Allah on Judgment Day. They will give their record in a certain way.

Qur'an 69:25, Yusuf Ali's translation

But he will be given in his left hand his Record and say, I wish I never had it.

And he that will be given in his left hand, will say: "Ah! I wish that my Record had not been given to me!"

This is saying that the person uttering these words seems to be filled with sorrow for what he did but the point is he will be given his record in his left hand.

Qur'an 84:10

"But he who will be given his Record behind his back,"

Qur'an 84:10 says the record will be given from behind his back. Which one is it really? It can't be both the left hand and behind the back. The left hand isn't located on a person's back. Here we have another mistake in the Qur'an to add to the long list of mistakes.

Sahih Muslim, Book 019, Hadith 4309

"It is reported on the authority of Abu Sa'id that the Messenger of Allah said: On the Day of Judgment there will be a fixed flag in his back in the buttocks of every human being guilty of the violation of faith."

We notice in here that Allah is doing the following:

The flag will be fixed inside every individual's buttocks.

But that is going to lead to a very important question.

In another chapter of the Qur'an, we observe that Allah divides the believers from the disbelievers by making the believers white and the disbelievers black, as we read in Qur'an;

Qur'an 3:106, Mohsin Khan's translation

106 On the Day (i.e. the Day of Resurrection) when some faces will become white and some faces will become black; as for those whose faces will become black (to them will be said,): "Did you reject Faith after accepting it? Then taste the torment (in Hell) for rejecting Faith."

It's very clear that Allah is confused about how he will differentiate believers from disbelievers. It is not enough for him to make all the bad ones turn black, which is a very clear sign of racism, proving that Allah is a very hateful person towards black people as he considers that his enemies, all of them, should be black. Therefore, being black is a punishment for those he hates. But if Allah had already made some people black, what is the need for a flag to be fixed inside the buttocks?

In the Bible, the Lord Jesus Christ will separate the bad ones from the good ones without using tags or color or flags. The real God does not need to do such a thing.

But that's not all. We also notice right away the savage language used in the Qur'an and the hadiths about describing how Allah will recognize the bad people from the good ones.

Let us now go and read the Bible from King James version:

"He shall separate them one from another"

> *Matthew 25 - KJV:*
>
> *31 When the Son of man shall come in his glory, and all the holy angels with him, then shall he sit upon the throne of his glory: 32And before him shall be gathered all nations: and he shall separate them one from another, as a shepherd divideth his sheep from the goats: 33And he shall set the sheep on his right hand, but the goats on the left.*
>
> *34 Then shall the King say unto them on his right hand, Come, ye blessed of my Father, inherit the kingdom prepared for you from the foundation of the world: 35 For I was an hungred, and ye gave me meat: I was thirsty, and ye gave me drink: I was a stranger, and ye took me in: 36 Naked, and ye clothed me: I was sick, and ye visited me: I was in prison, and ye came unto me. 37 Then shall the righteous answer him, saying, Lord, when saw we thee an hungred, and fed thee? or thirsty, and gave thee drink? 38 When saw we thee a stranger, and took thee in? or naked, and clothed thee? 39 Or when saw we thee sick, or in prison, and came unto thee? 40 And the King shall answer and say unto them, Verily I say unto you, Inasmuch as ye have done it unto one of the least of these my brethren, ye have done it unto me.*
>
> *41 Then shall he say also unto them on the left hand, depart from me, ye cursed, into everlasting fire, prepared for the devil and his angels: 42 For I was an hungred, and ye gave me no meat: I was thirsty, and ye gave me no drink: 43 I was a stranger, and ye took me not in: naked, and ye clothed me not: sick, and in prison, and ye visited me not. 44 Then shall they also answer him, saying, Lord, when saw we thee an hungred, or athirst, or a stranger, or naked, or sick, or in prison, and did not minister unto thee? 45 Then shall he answer them, saying, Verily I say unto you, inasmuch as ye did it not to one of the least of these, ye did it not to me. 46 And*

these shall go away into everlasting punishment: but the righteous into life eternal.

***

People of the Cave fairytale or Science

The Chapter called Al-Kahf, which means cave.

This story is about a group of men who want to worship Allah. A majority of the men are Christians; however, the Muslims are confused as to whether they are Christians or not. Perhaps the group of men wanted to share Jesus Christ with the Muslims?!

> *Qur'an 18:10-12*
>
> *10 When the young men of the cave said, Lord, give us mercy from Thee, and furnish us with your guidelines,*
>
> *11 we covered their ears, and we made them sleep for long and many years*
>
> *12 Then We resurrected them, to examine which of the two parties were best at calculating of how many years they were asleep.*

First, Qur'an 18:10 talks about the youth or the young people. Supposedly, Allah made them fall asleep for a number of years. It is mentioned that they slept for 300 years.

> *Who is doing the counting and had knowledge about the youths, when the youths told no one where they went?*
>
> *Who are the two parties if everyone who lived at their time was dead by the time they woke up?*
>
> *The verse says, "we raised them." (Resurrection. This word (bath بَعَثْنَاهُمْ) can be used for raising the dead but doesn't the verse say they were asleep?*
>
> *On top of all this, who are these young men and what can we learn from the story? Nothing! It's just foolish talk!*

> *Qur'an 18:22*
>
> *"They said, three and their dog the fourth, and sixth would say five and their dog, they say, seven and their dog Say My Lord knows best what to teach them a little but there is no*

doubt and he knew of their real number."

The drama here is that there's a fight over how many there are. The answer from Allah is: "Only Allah knows". Huh? Why don't you tell us, Allah? What is even the point to all of this? Maybe it's because that someone has nothing to say so he creates dumb stories?

***

Allah & Animal Planet

Is Allah using wrong words again or his Arabic not good? Or is it a scientific error?

Mistranslation of "Yemshi" and "Dab" as creep

Qur'an 24:45

And Allah has created every animal from water, some of them walking on their stomachs and some of them walking on two legs, and others walk on four. Allah creates what He wills for Allah has power over all things.

This verse is saying that Allah created every animal from water and some of them walk on their bellies.

The Arabic language used for this verse is much different than the English translated version. The Arabic version of this verse is as follows.

The word used in Arabic is **"Yemshi"**, which in English means "walk". When the narrator translated this verse into English, knowing that no snake or any animal that crawls on its belly can walk, he translated **"Yemshi"** يمشي as **"creep"**. The word creep is erroneously translated from this Arabic word. Creep in Arabic is **"Yezhav"** يزحف . Walking only applies to humans and animals with feet to walk with. Animals that move in their bellies have no feet to walk with so **"Yemshi" erroneously applied to the Arabic verse.**

"Daba" دب
The word "**Daba**" means "everything that walks on the earth by hitting the ground with his feet "lifting and setting down each foot in turn, never having both feet off the ground at once. This could be any living creature that walks on earth, human or animal. "**Dab**" is derived from the word meaning "He hits the ground with his feet". Usually "Daba" is mentioned when donkeys are talked about amongst Arabs. It is not normally used to refer to human beings.

The English definition of "Daba" according to http://dictionary.sakhr.com/ (Islamic site is an animal or beast. The Arabic definition defines "Daba" as "everything that walks on the ground". This cannot refer to anything that creeps.

Examples of animals that walk on legs whether living on land or in the sea are: Crabs, centipedes, and ants, to name a few.
"Yadub" يدب
Aron Yhiya said that "Dab" means every living thing. This is in fact false and intentionally misleading on his part. The question is why don't Muslims give an accurate translation in here? Why would someone change the meaning of his god's words?

The answer is:

1) To cover Allah's mistake in saying in very plain Arabic that snakes walk. Arabic is a strong language and in no way, would be used for the word yamshi يمشي concerning a snake.
2) This is additional proof of the weak expression in language in the Qur'an showing the opposite of what they say about how strong the Arabic is in this book, when it's full of Arabic mistakes, which will lead to scientific mistakes.

I am not yet done with this verse. There are other mistakes following in this next verse.

How many legs *creators* has?

Qur'an 24:45

And Allah has created every animal from water, some of them walking on their stomachs and some of them walking on two legs, and others walk on four, Allah creates what He wills for Allah has power over all things.

We already spoke about animals walking on their bellies but what about the 3 kinds of walking that Allah said:

- walk on belly;
- with two legs; and
- with four legs.

Is that really true that there are 3 kinds of animals or creatures and the way they walk? Then what about:

1) Centipedes have between 15 or 17 pairs of legs (30

or 34 legs)
2) Pill bugs (7 pairs of walking legs) = 14 legs
3) Crabs have 10 legs
4) Spiders have 8 legs
5) Insects have 6 legs
6) Starfishes have 5 legs

By: Trevor Stokes, LiveScience Contributor
Published: 11/14/2012 09:44 AM EST on LiveScience
The world's leggiest creature on record is even more bizarre than its **750 wiggling limbs attest**, according to new research.

It's very clear how wrong Allah is about the number of legs that are used by those who walk over the earth.

***

The Beasts The Ring & The Stick

Since Muslims like to explain to us the science written in their book, then let us take a look at this story and see if the Qur'an is a valid scientific book that provides facts or if it's a fiction book.

"The Lord of The Ring"

That is not a name of a fiction movie that is from the Quran!

> *Qur'an 38:34*
>
> *And We did test Solomon: We placed on his throne a (his dead body), but he did turn to Us in true loyalty.*

If we go to the book of Ibn Kathir and observe the Muslims
Muslims claim
English translation, the meaning will be different from the original Arabic text. Below, is my English translation of the original Arabic text. That being said, the Muslims
Muslims claim
English translation is nothing more than a fabrication.

> *Tafsir Ibn Kathir, print year 2002, vol. 7, p. 68 to 71.*
>
> *Reported by Ibn Abbas, may Allah bless him, he said, "And we did taste Solomon: We placed on his throne (his dead body), but he did turn to us in true loyalty." Solomon wanted to go to*

the bathroom so he gave his ring to his wife Al Jaradah, and she was one of the most beloved wives of his, then Satan came to her in the image of Solomon and said to her: "give me my ring" so she gave it to him, so he wore the ring, therefore, he became in control and in charge of mankind and jinn's, then prophet Solomon came out of the bathroom and he asked his wife to give him back his ring, she said: "I gave it to Solomon" then he said: "I am Solomon!" She said: "you're a liar, you are not Solomon". Afterwards, each time Solomon went out he said "I am Solomon" and all the people said to him: "you are not Solomon, you're a liar".

At this point, even kids were throwing rocks and stones at him on the streets.

And then Solomon noticed that this is something that happened from Allah, the high the magnificent. Then Satan became the ruler of mankind, until Allah wanted Solomon to go back as the King of his kingdom, so Allah put in the heart of the people the rejection of the Satan [the false Solomon], so that people did send a group to question the wives of Solomon, and they asked them (the wives) if there is anything Solomon behave upsetting you?

They said: "yes, he is having intercourse with us while we have our menstruation and he never did this to us before. Therefore, Satan noticed that people realized that he wasn't the real Solomon, so they wrote a paper that has magic written on it, and they buried the paper under the throne of Solomon, and it activated the magic and it read the magic to the people. Therefore, Solomon (the false one) started acting as an infidel. (Page 69) And by the act of magic Solomon overcame the people, therefore, the people announced him as an infidel and they kept doing this until Satan [the false Solomon] sent his ring to be thrown in the sea, then the fish swallowed the ring. And the real Solomon used to work [after he lost his kingdom ship authority] as a Porter and he was paid for that, then a man came to him and said: "how much do you charge me for carrying this fish load?"

Solomon said: "I will take one of these fishes". The man agreed, when they arrived to the door of the house of that man he gave Solomon the fish which had the ring inside it, as wages as they agreed.

So, Solomon took the fish and opened its stomach and found the ring, so when he wore the ring the mankind and Jinn's *became under his command and control(again), and he became again a king as the old days, therefore, Satan ran away to an island far in the sea so Solomon sent asking for him to come.*

And Satan was a giant jinni, so they could not get him until one day they came to him and found him asleep, so they jumped on him and poured on him lead, if you try to move in the house the lead move with him.

Then Ibn Abbas continued saying: so, they tied him up and took him to Solomon. Therefore, Solomon ordered them to make a bed for him made from marble and sculpture of room inside it and they jailed Satan inside that marble room then they sealed the door with cooper and threw it in the deep sea, and this is what Allah meant in the verse "And We did taste Solomon: We placed on his throne a (his dead body), but he did turn to Us in true loyalty. (Qur'an 38:34)

Same story can be found of the book of Fateh Al-Qadir of Al-Riwaiah & Driah V1 p1265/1267

The Arabic Text of Ibn kathir for **Qur'an 38:34** تفسير ابن كثير

إسماعيل بن عمر بن كثير القرشي الدمشقي

مسألة: الجزء السابع

م2002هـ / 1422سنة النشر:

حدثنا علي بن الحسين حدثنا محمد بن العلاء وعثمان بن أبي شيبة وعلي بن محمد قالوا : حدثنا أبو معاوية أخبرنا الأعمش عن المنهال بن عمرو عن سعيد بن جبير عن ابن عباس [رضي الله عنهما] (وألقينا على كرسيه جسدا ثم أناب) قال : أراد سليمان أن يدخل الخلاء فأعطى الجرادة خاتمه ـ وكانت الجرادة امرأته وكانت أحب نسائه إليه ـ فجاء الشيطان في صورة سليمان فقال لها : هاتي خاتمي . فأعطته إياه . فلما لبسه دانت له الإنس والجن والشياطين فلما خرج سليمان من الخلاء قال لها : هاتي خاتمي . قالت : قد أعطيته سليمان . قال : أنا سليمان . قالت : كذبت لست سليمان فجعل لا يأتي أحدا يقول له : " أنا سليمان " ، إلا كذبة حتى جعل الصبيان يرمونه بالحجارة . فلما رأى ذلك عرف أنه من أمر الله ـ عز وجل ـ قال : وقام الشيطان يحكم بين الناس فلما أراد الله أن يرد على سليمان سلطانه ألقى في قلوب الناس انكار ذلك الشيطان . قال : فأرسلوا إلى نساء سليمان فقالوا لهن : أتنكرن من سليمان شيئا ؟ قلن : نعم إنه يأتينا ونحن حيض وما كان يأتينا قبل ذلك . فلما رأى الشيطان أنه قد فطن له ظن أن أمره قد انقطع فكتبوا كتبا [بهذا كان يظهر سليمان على 69فيها سحر وكفر ، فدفنوه تحت كرسي سليمان ثم أثاروها وقرءوها على الناس . وقالوا : [ص: الناس [ويغلبهم] فأكفر الناس سليمان ـ عليه السلام ـ فلم يزالوا يكفرونه بعث ذلك الشيطان بالخاتم فطرحه في البحر فتلقته سمكة فأخذته . وكان سليمان يحمل على شط البحر بالأجر فجاء رجل فاشترى سمكا فيه تلك السمكة التي في بطنها الخاتم فدعا سليمان فقال : تحمل لي هذا السمك ؟ فقال : نعم . قال : بكم ؟ قال بسمكة من هذا السمك . قال : فحمل سليمان ـ عليه السلام ـ السمك ثم انطلق به إلى منزله فلما انتهى الرجل إلى بابه أعطاه تلك السمكة التي في بطنها الخاتم فأخذها سليمان فشق بطنها ، فإذا الخاتم في جوفها فأخذه فلبسه . قال : فلما لبسه دانت له الجن والإنس والشياطين وعاد إلى حاله في البحر وهرب الشيطان حتى دخل جزيرة من جزائر البحر فأرسل سليمان في طلبه وكان شيطانا مريدا فجعلوا يطلبونه ولا يقدرون عليه حتى وجدوه يوما نائما فجاءوا به إلى سليمان ، من رصاص فاستيقظ فوثب فجعل لا يثب في مكان من البيت إلا انماط معه الرصاص قال : فأخذوه فأوثقوه وجاءوا به إلى سليمان ، فأمر به فنقر له تخت من رخام ثم أدخل في جوفه ثم أمر به سد بالنحاس ثم طرح في البحر فذلك قوله : (ولقد فتنا سليمان وألقينا على كرسيه جسدا ثم أناب) قال : يعني الشيطان الذي كان سلط عليه .

And not strange for me, that I couldn't find this story in Ibn Kathir english translation, because the translator he do not like you to read these stories ever.

Let us analyze this story:

✓ Who gave Solomon his ring?
✓ Its magical ring?
✓ Satan took the shape of Solomon, came to his wife and told her to give him the ring, and she did. The real Solomon then went to her asking for his ring, and she said: "you are not Solomon". The question I have in mind is how can Satan clone Solomon? He is Allah who cloned Jesus before as in Qur'an 4:157.?
✓ It's very clear that Solomon couldn't enter the bathroom with his ring on his finger.
  1. Why He can't?
  2. The ring will get wet?
  3. His ring is electronic?
  4. His Ring is holy, can't be taken to bathroom?

♦ He knew that his authority was in this ring. So how then did he trust, even his wife, to hold the kingdom's authority in her hands as anyone who wears this ring will become the King?

♦ Since Satan wore the ring, it's only logical that he didn't need to take the image of Solomon, as the power is held in the ring, not in someone's image. The story says that whoever wears the ring takes control of mankind and Jinn's.

♦ This leads us to another lie in the story, which all of us understand to be a fairytale story. As long as the control comes by the power of this ring, how come Satan could not control the people who later on found out he was "clone" Solomon and start doing action by placing magic under his throne and later even forced him to throw the ring into the sea.

♦ And how foolish was this Satan when he knew that all the powers were held in this ring but still, he threw it out the sea.

♦ Solomon was able to get his kingdom from the fish who swallowed the ring. Now, when this fish swallowed the ring, why did it not become ruler of mankind and jinn's?

♦ How come Allah did not give those kinds of rings to anyone else and especially to Muhammad is the out of them?

♦ This is a futile ring and its maker is not better as he made it in a way that anyone who wore it had control over the world.

....

Qur'an never said that the earth was fully covered with water?

The Flood of the Bible

Some Muslims claim that the flood did not cover the entire earth, they claim its scientifically false. But yet its same ben thought in their own book but as always, the Muslims are the last one to read what is even written in their own book.

Today we hear how scientist warn about "Global Warming" and they claim it will cause a global flooding to cover the earth.
So it can happened now but it cannot happened before?

Let us now show the Muslims what our book say & refute them about their claim, regarding global flood is missioned only in the bible-scripture, not in the Qur'an, which mean the flood never cover all the earth according to the Qur'an.

in Genesis 7:18-19 says the opposite:

> "And the waters prevailed, and were increased greatly upon the earth; and the ark went upon the face of the waters. And the waters prevailed exceedingly upon the earth; and all the high hills, that were under the whole heaven, were covered."

This is evidence of the whole earth being covered with water. Even Genesis gives clear language about the earth's complete coverage of water.

> Genesis 7:19-20 - KJV
>
> "And the waters prevailed exceedingly upon the earth; and all the high hills, that were under the whole heaven, were covered. Fifteen cubits upward (milemaelah) did the waters prevail; and the mountains were covered."

To make the point short and clear, the Bible says clearly that the earth was totally covered by water.

Muslims go on to ask what was left over from the flood. All over the earth there are signs of the effects of the flood, even on mountains. Science shows that the whole earth faced extreme conditions at one time. Even their god Allah supports the fact that there was indeed a flood.

> Qur'an 11:42
>
> And the boat was Floating over amid waves like mountains, and called Noah and his son who was in isolation, my son ride with us, not with the infidels!

> Qur'an 11:43
>
> He said, (Noah's son) I will go and ride to the high mountains. (Noah answered) He said, no protection today from Allah

223

except who Allah has mercy upon, and the wave parted them and he was from those who were drowned.

In here I will show how false the Muslims
Muslims claim
claim is when they say the Qur'an never said that the earth was covered in water. By the way, in these verses I am not proving a mistake in the Qur'an, but a lie and false statements made by Muslims when saying that what the Bible states about the earth being covered in water is a mistake while even modern science agrees with the Bible. If you read with me these verses you will see that the waves were like mountains and were so high! Was Allah exaggerating or was it real?

If Allah exaggerated, it means he lied. If we read the verse after, we'll see that the son of Noah went to the top of the mountains and the Qur'an states with no doubt that he was with those who drowned. This means that the flood must have covered the top of the mountains. That makes the Qur'an saying the exact same thing as the Bible. The fact is that the Bible says water was fifteen cubits upward. When Muslims make false claims, I sometimes wonder if they even read their own book!

Qur'an 11:42

And the boat was floating over amid waves like mountains, and called Noah and his son, who was in isolation, my son ride with us, not with the infidels!

وَهِيَ تَجْرِي بِهِمْ فِي مَوْجٍ كَالْجِبَالِ وَنَادَى نُوحٌ ابْنَهُ وَكَانَ فِي مَعْزِلٍ يَا بُنَيَّ ارْكَبْ مَعَنَا وَلَا تَكُنْ مَعَ

Let us see what Ibn Kathir's interpretation says about this verse.

وَقَوْلُهُ " وَهِيَ تَجْرِي بِهِمْ فِي مَوْجٍ كَالْجِبَالِ" أَيْ السَّفِينَة سَائِرَة بِهِمْ عَلَى وَجْه الْمَاء الَّذِي قَدْ طَبَّقَ جَمِيع الْأَرْض حَتَّى طَفَتْ عَلَى رُءُوس الْجِبَال وَارْتَفَعَ عَلَيْهَا بِخَمْسَة عَشَر ذِرَاعًا وَقِيلَ بِثَمَانِينَ مِيلًا وَهَذِهِ السَّفِينَة جَارِيَة عَلَى وَجْه الْمَاء

And Allah saying, "They are making them in waves like mountains" any ship moving with them on the face of the water that has been applied to all the earth until washed ashore on the top of the mountains rose by fifteen cubits, and some said, it was eighty miles on top of the mountains.

They lie even when they copy the exact same thing from the Bible! To read the story from Muslims English site click her

***

The Flat Earth

> Qur'an 51:48
>
> *And the earth, We spread it we made it as a carpet, what excellent spreaders we are!*

> Tafsir Al-Jalalayn

{ وَآلأَرْض فَرَشْنَاهَا فَنِعْمَ ٱلْمَاهِدُونَ }

وَالأَرْض فَرَشْنَاهَا" مَهَّدْنَاهَا "فَنِعْمَ الْمَاهِدُونَ" نَحْنُ"

> *"And the earth, We stretched it out like a bed, and We made it flat. What extraordinary spreaders then. We are."*

Maybe someone will say that it's really not clear that the earth is flat in this verse. Then let us read more proof.

> Qur'an 79:30
>
> *And after that He spread out the earth and made it flat;*

As we know, all these are Islamic translations. The fact is that the word in Arabic for "**dahaaha**" دحاها means **flat**. This is why Tafsir Al-Jalalayn used the word flat as you will see:

تغسير Tafsir Al-Jalalayn

{ ولأرض بَعْدَ ذَلِكَ دَحَاهَا }

> *In addition to then after that He stretched out the earth: He made it flat, on behalf of Allah had created the earth before the heaven, but without having been spread out yet;*

I've heard many opinions from Muslims in regards to the word **dahaaha**. Some say it means to be an ostrich egg, which is ridiculous and a big lie! This is from the book of Al Tabari. He explains how the word dahaaha is used when relating to that bird:

He said, it says the ostrich nest (**Adaha** means it's flat) for it's flat and after that he is quoting a poet to prove his point. What the Muslims did was make the word about the egg, when it's about the

وَيُقَال لِعُشْ النَّعَامَة أَدْحَى ; لِأَنَّهُ مَبْسُوط عَلَى وَجْه الأَرْض
. وَقَال أُمَيَّة بْن أَبِي الصَّلْت: وَبَثَّ الْخَلْق فِيهَا إِذْ دَحَاهَا
فَهُمْ قُطَّانهَا حَتَّى التَّنَادِي وَأَنْشَد الْمُبَرِّد : دَحَاهَا فَلَمَّا رَآهَا اسْتَوَتْ
عَلَى الْمَاء أَرْسَى عَلَيْهَا الْجِبَالًا وَقِيلَ: دَحَاهَا سَوَّاهَا

flat nest of an ostrich, but in their false debate they say Allah said, the

earth is the same as an ostrich egg. The fact is, it's about the nest not the egg, because it's flat. You can see the reference in the government of Jordan website. Copy the text into the Google translator.
Read it from the King of Jordan Islamic site altafsir.com

(He Made it Flat)

Maybe some still don't accept all of this. Let's read more verses from the Qur'an.

Qur'an 15:19

And the earth We have spread out (like a Rug, and placed on it firm mountains, and caused vegetation to grow with balance.

Tafsir Al-Jalalayn

{ والأرض مَدَدْنَاهَا وَأَلْقَيْنَا فِيهَا رَوَاسِيَ وَأَنبَتْنَا فِيهَا مِن كُلّ شَيْءٍ مَّوْزُونٍ }

Plus, the earth We have stretched it out, spread it flat, and threw on it firm mountains, to fix the earth from moving, and we made everything grow in balance.

Qur'an 50:7

In addition to the earth, We have stretched it out, and threw on it firm mountains, and established on it pairs of every kind to grow on it.

تفسير Tanwîr al-Miqbâs min Tafsîr Ibn 'Abbâs

{ وَآلأَرْضَ مَدَدْنَاهَا وَأَلْقَيْنَا فِيهَا رَوَاسِيَ وَأَنبَتْنَا فِيهَا مِن كُلّ زَوْج بَهِيج }

In addition to the earth had We spread out over water, and threw firm mountains so the earth does not move.

Qur'an 71:19

And Allah has made the earth flat for you,

وَٱاللَّهُ جَعَلَ لَكُمُ الأَرْضَ بِسَاطًا

You can go to this link to see the Muslim translation for yourself: www.altafsir.com

In this verse, the word flat comes as it is, even in the Muslims

226

Muslims claim
translation. They will not be able to hide it anymore.

تفسير Tafsir Al-Jalalayn

{ وَٱللَّهُ جَعَلَ لَكُمُ ٱلْأَرْضَ بِسَاطاً }

And God has made it the earth flat, for you.

There is thousands of TV programs from Islamic countries earth is flat
and the sun move in top of it from east west every day.
Watch youtube; search "earth is falt quran"

We have to remember something that is so important. The Muslims were
ordered to pray in the direction of Mecca. Then we have to ask:

a) How can they pray in the direction of Mecca if they live in USA or
   Australia? The only way is maybe to put your head in the
   bathroom seat and your legs up! Doesn't Allah know that the
   earth is not flat?
b) If Allah knows that the earth is not flat, how will the Muslims pray
   five times a day if they live in Alaska or the North Pole, when
   nights can go for a few months? We know these prayers are
   measured according to the movement of the sun. They are: near
   dawn (**fajr**), just after the sun's noon (**dhohr**), in the afternoon
   (**asr**), just after sunset (**maghreb**) and around nightfall (**isha'a**).
c) However, the Qur'an only calls for three prayers. This is one of
   the mistakes of the Qur'an where Allah called for only three
   prayers, but Muhammad called for five. As in:

Qur'an 11:114

*And establish daily prayers at the two ends of the day and at
the approaches of the night.*

*But still, how am I going to pray at the approach of the night
in the North Pole? Will, I wait 3 months to do my daily
prayer?*

In the deception of Allah, vol.1, p. 271, we quoted this following hadith:
English translation of Sahih Al-Bukhari, Book 21, Hadith # 246:

Muhammad said, "Our Lord, the great, <u>comes every night
down to the lowest Heaven to us at the last third period of
the night</u>, calling, 'anyone in attendance to call upon Me, so
that I may answer to his intercession? Is there any
attendance anyone to ask Me, so that I may grant him what
he is asking me for? Is there anyone struggling for My
forgiveness, so that I may forgive him?'"

Reading this hadith carefully will lead us to a very clear understanding about Allah's science regarding the geology of the earth:

- Allah comes down once every night.
- He comes at the last third of the night.
- This means there is one last third part of the night on this earth.
- To make it easier to understand, the third part of the night is 3 o'clock in the morning, it means Allah comes down only once a day at 3 in the morning but the earth has many time zones and the same hour is going to be repeated in many locations around the globe.

The angels get together at the time of the Dawn and afternoon prayers.

Sahih Al-Bukhari, Book 10, Hadith # 530

Reported by Abu Huraira: Allah's messenger said, "Angels come to you in sequence by night and day, and all of them get together at the time of the Dawn and Afternoon prayers. Those who have passed the night with you (the shift of Angels, who spend the night with you) ascend to Allah, even though he knows everything about you, Then Allah inquires "In what condition did you leave my slaves?" The angels answer "When we left them, they were praying and when we arrived, they were praying"

Here we go again! Muhammad is explaining to us without knowing how he is exposing the science of his god. From the above hadith, we understand:

- Angels of Allah have 24 hours in a day.
- All the angels meet together twice a day: at dawn and in the afternoon.
- And as long all of them meet together amongst all the angels of Allah, they all have the same time zones.
- There are two shifts of angels during the cycle of the day and the night.

Conclusion: the earth must be flat with one time zone according to Muhammad and his god Allah.

Muslims claim

The earth's gravitational force

http://www.miraclesofthequran.com/scientific_95.html

Did we not make the earth a receptacle? (Surat al-Mursalat77: 25)

My answer

These claims blow my mind and are often silly. You really don't know how silly they are until you learn Arabic. The verse has nothing to do with gravity, contrary to what they claim. It's simply about the earth being our grave. Nothing more. This is why they only posted the verse they liked and not the one right after. The word "**kifatan**," is a dish, or a container, where humans are buried.

> *Surat al-Mursalat 77: 25*
>
> *Did we not make the earth a receptacle?*

> *Qur'an 77:26*
>
> *for the dead and the living one,*

This is why Mr. Harun did not post the verse that followed the one he'd posted since everything is about deception.
Why he do not quote one veres before and after? Because if he do then we will find out his falsification:

> *Qur'an 77*
>
> *"16. Did We not destroy the ancients people, 17. So shall We make later generations to follow them? 18. Thus do We deal with the criminals. 19. Woe that Day to the deniers,20. Did We not create you from a despised water21. Then We placed it in a place of strong hold, 22. For a known period),23. So We did measure, and We are the best to measure. 24. Woe that Day to the deniers!) (25. Have We not made the earth Kifat (a receptacle)) 26. For the living and the dead,27. And have placed therein fixed towers, and have given you Furat water, 28. Woe that Day to the deniers!"*

Since Mr. Harun likes Ibn Abbas' interpretation of the Qur'an, then maybe he can explain why Ibn Abass stated, "**we made the earth a receptacle place where they will be contained in**". You can read the translation for yourself from the Muslims

Muslims claim
 website.
Or we can read from "Kifat means a place of shelter." Mujahid said, "It keep the dead ones so that nothing is seen of it." Al-Sh-Sha`bi said, "Its interior is for your dead and its surface is for your living." Ibn Kathir

----

Muslims claim

The use of electricity

http://www.miraclesofthequran.com/predictions_11.html

And We made a fount of molten copper flow out for him. (Qur'an, 34:12)

> *One of Allah's great blessings to Prophet Sulayman (as) was "a fount of molten copper." This can be understood in several senses. By the use of melted copper, it may be referring to the existence, at his time, of an advanced technology that employed electricity.*

My Answer

First of all, what does all of this have to do with electricity? Does the word *electric* appear anywhere? All the verse is saying is that Allah gave him a lot of wealth, to the point copper was running like a river, when money was copper!

The big question is this: why did they cut off the verse? Would it be because they don't want us to know about the *Flying Carpet* **written in that verse?** I thought they were trying to prove that the prophecies about amazing technology was in the Qur'an? Let's read about this fairytale in the Qur'an since we are already here.
Let us make a little deep study of one of most fictions stories in the Qur'an. We will go over:
- Islam against making statues.
- Idols worshipping.
- Solomon dead standing for one year.
- The flying carpet.

Flying Carpet Ride!

Qur'an 34:12

وَلِسُلَيْمَانَ الرِّيحَ غُدُوُّهَا شَهْرٌ وَرَوَاحُهَا شَهْرٌ وَأَسَلْنَا لَهُ عَيْنَ الْقِطْرِ وَمِنَ الْجِنِّ مَن يَعْمَلُ بَيْنَ يَدَيْهِ بِإِذْنِ رَبِّهِ وَمَن يَزِغْ مِنْهُمْ عَنْ أَمْرِنَا نُذِقْهُ مِنْ عَذَابِ السَّعِيرِ

Qur'an 34:12

Plus, unto Solomon We subjected the wind. Its morning journey was a month's journey, and its nightfall was a month's journey. And We made a fount of flowing copper to follow for him. And of the Jinn's they were working for him by the leave of his Lord. And such of them tried to break Our command, We would make them taste the chastisement of the flame.

What we understand from this verse, which they try to hide from us, is how the Qur'an is filled with legends.

4. Solomon is flying by using the wind, which is a flying carpet. I will prove this by showing Qur'an 21:31 later.
5. This wind flies him at high speed. What normally is one month travel now only taking him few hours of his morning!
6. It's saying a morning journey which should have been one month of travel.
7. It must have been a really high-speed flying carpet.
8. I'm just wondering how the one who speaks about electricity, airplanes and computers believes in flying carpets and jinn slaves!
9. The jinn's worked for Solomon as slaves!
10. If they try to disobey him, Allah will burn them with blazing fire!

The fact is that it was taken from a legend of the Jews, as we read:

The Legend of The Jews BY LOUIS GINZBERG
LESSONS IN HUMILITY

"Great and powerful as Solomon was, and wise and just, still occasions were not lacking to bring home to him the truth that the wisest and mightiest of mortals may not indulge in pride and arrogance. Solomon had a precious piece of tapestry, sixty miles square, on which he flew through the air so swiftly that he could eat breakfast in Damascus and supper

in Media. To carry out his orders he had at his beck and call Asaph ben Berechiah among men, Ramirat among demons, the lion among beasts, and the eagle among birds. Once it happened that pride possessed Solomon while he was sailing through the air on his carpet, and he said: "There is none like unto me in the world, upon whom God has bestowed sagacity, wisdom, intelligence, and knowledge, besides making me the ruler of the world." The same instant the air stirred, and forty thousand men dropped from the magic carpet. The king ordered the wind to cease from blowing, with the word: "Return!" Whereupon the wind: "If thou wilt return to God, and subdue thy pride, I, too, will return." The king realized his transgression"

Solomon master of the jinn's

The word Genies, or AL-Jinn as its in the Qur'an is Romanized, and mostly earliest tales in it came from India and Persia, like 'The Thousand Nights' or later the Arabic copy called "1,001 night" which consists of legends dating back to 2400 BC, featuring all kinds of mythological creatures.
first take a note Jinn's in the Qur'an are not same as demons in the bible-scripture. Its made from smoke and fire and it can take the shape of anything, just to make it clear Satan himself is from the Jinn's.

> *Qur'an 50:18*
>
> *"Behold! We said to the angels, "Bow down to Adam": They bowed down except Iblis. He was one of the Jinn's"*

> *Qur'an 55:15*
>
> *"And He created Jinn's from fire free of smoke:"*

Jinn are creators and Allah made from fire (it is not demons) send them Muslim Jinny prophets too from their own kind:

> *Qur'an 5:130*
>
> *"O you assembly of jinn and mankind! "Did not there come to you Messengers from amongst you, reciting unto you My Verses and warning you of the meeting of this Day of yours?" They will say: "We bear witness against ourselves." It was the life of this world that tempted them. And they will bear witness against themselves that they were not believers."*

Satan is on of the Jinn's and he has kids! As we read
> Qur'an 18:50

> *"Behold! We said to the angels, "Bow down to Adam": They bowed down except Iblis. He was one of the Jinn's, and he broke the Command of his Lord. Will ye then take him and his progeny as protectors rather than Me? And they are enemies to you! Evil would be the exchange for the wrong-doers!"*

Allah will burn Jinn's in fire but it's made from fire!

There is Jinn's Muslims and infidels, and the infidels of the jinn will be burned in hell fire:

> *Qur'an 7:38 He(Allah) will say: "Enter and join the company of the peoples who passed away before you - men and jinn's, - into the Fire." Every time a new people enters, it curses its sister-people (that get in hell before them),*

> *Qur'an 7:12*

> *(Allah) said: "What prevented you (Satan) from bowing down when I commanded thee?" He said: "I am better than he: Thou didst create me from fire, while him Thou didst create of mud"*

Qur'an 55:15
> *"And He created the jinn from a smokeless flame of fire."*

> *Qur'an: 15:27*

> *"And the Jinn race, We had created before, from the fire of a scorching wind."*

Devils (Jinn's) work for Solomon!

It is very interesting to find out That the king Solomon he had many employees, and the best of them is devil!
But what is the job exactly they do?
- Diving.
- Building.
- Fighting
- And some of them in Jail!

Qur'an 38:37

"And also, the Shayatin (devils) from the jinn (including) every kind of builder and diver,"

The funny thing that each time I read Ibn Kathir or other translations made by Muslims, I find 90% of the original text disappear in their translation so they take off every nonsense story to make Islam look better, and that why I say do not ever trust their words.

From Book of Ibn Kathir V.4 p.73 we read (Arabic)

"And also, the Shayaten, {from every kind of builder and diver,} means, from them (the Jinn's) were some whom he used to build high rooms, images, statues, and other difficult tasks which humans were unable to do. And there was another group, who dived into the sea recovering pearls, jewels and other precious things which cannot be found anywhere else, and some of them (the Jinn's) was cuffs and chained for disobeying or he refuse to work, or he did it wrong or for aggression."

وقوله : (والشياطين كل بناء وغواص) أي : منهم من هو مستعمل في الأبنية الهائلة من محاريب **وتماثيل** وجفان كالجواب وقدور راسيات إلى غير ذلك من الأعمال الشاقة التي لا يقدر عليها البشر وطائفة غواصون في البحار يستخرجون مما فيها من اللآلئ والجواهر والأشياء النفيسة التي لا توجد إلا فيها (وآخرين مقرنين في الأصفاد) أي : موثقون في الأغلال والأكبال ممن قد تمرد وعصى وامتنع من العمل وأبى أو قد أساء في صنيعه واعتدى .] ص: 74[

The text above is as it is in Arabic, and you will notice that Muslims in their false translated book of Ibn Kathir took the word "statues" out of their translation.

The devils build statues for Solomon?

The reason they hide this from the story because its contradiction of everything Muhammad claim regarding destroying Statues, but the surprising most is how even they fabricated the Qur'an translations in order to hide this big contradiction, they can hide it from you but from me, for very simple reason, I do not need translated Qur'an, Arabic is my first Language so this fabrication is against the ones who can't read their books in Arabic. Let us now go to the Qur'an and show more of dishonesty.

However I found only one translation was more honest about this issue.

Muhammad Picthal translation

Qur'an 34:13

They made for him what he willed: synagogues and statues, basins like wells and boilers built into the ground. Give thanks, O House of David! Few of My bondmen are thankful.

- Solomon is a Muslim prophet according to the Qur'an so how his God allowed him to make Statues?

- Statues for who?

- For what reason?

- These statues must be so huge to the point humans are unable to make the like of it.

- So Allah is not the God of Abrahamic faith.

- There is no reason for god of islam to allow such a thing, and logic its nothing but a contradiction to Yusuf Ali translation.

Qur'an 22:33

"Lawful to you (for food in Pilgrimage) are cattle, except those mentioned to you (as exception): but shun the abomination of idols, and shun the word that is false,"

Army of Solomon

Now when speak about an Army of king we will not imagine that the army have birds.

Like imagine we introduce colonel rooster to you as an officer of the King Solomon Army!

Yusuf Ali Qur'an 27:15

And before Solomon were marshalled his hosts, - of Jinn's and men and birds, and they were all kept in order and ranks.

This Army was so unique in every mean, according to

Tafsir al-Qurtubi *V.3 p.156 ;*

'Regarding Allah saying "And before Solomon were marshalled his hosts, - of Jinn's and men and birds, and they were all kept in order and" it ben said that Solomon peace be upon him; It is said: his Army it was a hundred leagues camping in a hundred: Twenty-five of the Jinn's, and twenty-five mankind, and twenty-five of the bird, and twenty-five of the monster, and had a thousand house of made as bottles placed on the wood where three hundred women, for sex and, seven hundred army brigade'

235

وحشر لسليمان " حشر " جمع والحشر الجمع ومنه قوله عز وجل : وحشرناهم فلم نغادر منهم أحدا واختلف الناس في مقدار جند :
سليمان عليه السلام ؛ فيقال : كان معسكره مائة فرسخ في مائة : خمسة وعشرون للجن ، وخمسة وعشرون للإنس ، وخمسة
وعشرون للطير ، وخمسة وعشرون للوحش ، وكان له ألف بيت من قوارير على الخشب فيها ثلاثمائة منكوحة وسبعمائة سرية

Leagues (The league was used in Ancient Rome, defined as 1.5 Roman miles)

- The size of the army is 100 X 100 = 25,000 mi.^{2} Leagues. That equal to 5 time the size of country like Lebanon.

- 25% as first line of his army is from Jinn's, that means 6,250 mi.^{2} the size of army of Jinn's.

- 25% of his army are from birds, which equal 6,250 mi.^{2} the size of army as birds.

- Is we saying each bird will take one foot space maximum, that means his birds army was about 3,300,0000 million birds!

- But how Solomon order his birds? (his Army), the answer in the Qur'an 27:16 "And Solomon inherited David. He said, "O people, we have been taught the language of birds, and we have been given from all things. Indeed, this is evident bounty."

- but what kind of birds his army was made of? The Qur'an speak of one kind of birds only as we read in Qur'an 27:20 "And he took attendance of the birds and said, "Why do I not see the hoopoe - or is he among the absent?"

- If you are a bird you better not to lie to Solomon or he will behead you! and before he does that he will take your Feathers one by one! Qur'an 27:21 "I will surely Torture him with a severe torment, or slaughter him, unless he brings me a clear reason."

- The hoopoe has two jobs according to Muslims interpretation, he was a minster of irrigation, and to find women to Solomon due to his sharp vision.

- Note Allah thought Solomon the language of birds only but yet Solomon understand the language of Ants? as we see in Qur'an:

Qur'an 26:19 Pickthall trans:

"And (Solomon) smiled, laughing at her speech (the ant), and said: My Lord, arouse me to be thankful for Thy favour wherewith Thou hast favoured me and my parents, and to do good that shall be pleasing unto Thee, and include me in (the number of) Thy righteous slaves."

http://morethinking.com/2014/06/11/how-ants-communicate/

In case you do not know Ants are deaf and mute they communicate by chemical and vibration, so its clear scientific error in the Qur'an.

The Wisdom of Solomon

Al-Bidaia Wa Al-Nihaya By Imam Ibn Kathir V 5 p. 358; or in Tafsir Ibn Kathir V 3 p. 188

"Thus, the story reported by Hafiz Abu al-Qasim Ibn'asakir in translation "Solomon peace be upon him" of his history, reported by El Hassan bin Sufian, Safwan Bin Saleh, from Waleed ibn Muslim, Said ibn Bishr, for Qatada, the Mujahid, Ibn Abbas - he recalled a lengthy summary of the story - that a woman very beautiful woman in the time of the children of Israel, four Israeli leaders wanted to sleep with her, but she refused them all, so they planed among themselves against her, so they reported her and witnessed against her to David, peace be upon him, that she had sexual-intercourse with a dog, so he (David), ordered he punishment by stoning. When he was on the evening of that day, Solomon sat and met with some young youth, and four of them dressed same as the four accusers, and another dressed as women, and testified that that she enabled the dog to have sexual-intercourse with her, Solomon said: separate them. He said to the first of them: What color was the dog? He said: black. Then he order him to be isolated, and summoned the other one and asks him about his color, he said: red. The other said: white with black mix. The other said: white. Therefore he ordered to kill them, what Solomon did reported David, summoned the four men, he asked them each alone about the color that dog, But they gave different color each, so he David order to kill them."

What this is story teach is something Amazing;

❖ David was a fool he almost stoned the woman without *questioning* the legitimacy of the accusers.
❖ Solomon the kid is more wise than the Father.
❖ Women in the time of Solomon used to be accused of having sex with dogs?
❖ Where Muhammad get his stories from, if none of this ever reported in the bible-scripture.?

Never has there lived a man privileged, like Solomon, to make the

أن امرأة حسناء في زمان بني إسرائيل ، راودها عن نفسها أربعة من رؤسائهم ، فامتنعت على كل منهم ، فاتفقوا فيما بينهم عليها ، فشهدوا عليها عند داود ، عليه السلام ، أنها مكنت من نفسها كلبا لها ، قد عودته ذلك منها ، فأمر برجمها . فلما كان عشية ذلك اليوم ، جلس سليمان ، واجتمع معه ولدان مثله ، فانتصب حاكما وتزيا أربعة منهم بزي أولئك ، وآخر بزي المرأة ، وشهدوا عليها بأنها مكنت من نفسها كلبا ، فقال سليمان : فرقوا بينهم . فقال لأولهم : ما كان لون الكلب؟ فقال : أسود . فعزله ، واستدعى الآخر فسأله عن لونه ، فقال : أحمر . وقال الآخر : أغبش . وقال الآخر : أبيض . فأمر بقتلهم ، فحكي ذلك لداود ، فاستدعى من فوره بأولئك الأربعة358[، فسألهم متفرقين عن لون ذلك الكلب ، فاختلفوا عليه ، فأمر بقتلهم . [ص:

Jinn's amenable to his will

(Qur'an 34:12 And of the jinn's they were working for him by the leave of his Lord. And such of them as try to brake Our command, we would make them taste the chastisement of the Blaze).

THE LEGENDS OF THE JEWS VOLUME IV
BIBLE TIMES AND CHARACTERS
by
BY LOUIS GINZBERG

Part 3
http://www.fullbooks.com/THE-LEGENDS-OF-THE-JEWS-VOLUME-IV-BIBLE3.html

God endowed him with the ability to turn the vicious power of demons into a power working to the advantage of men. He invented formulas of incantation by which diseases were alleviated, and others by which demons were exorcised so that they were banished forever. As his personal attendants, he had spirits and demons whom he could send hither and thither on the instant. He could grow tropical plants in Palestine, because his ministering spirits secured water for him from India.

As the spirits were subservient to him, so also the animals. He had an eagle upon whose back he was transported to the desert and back again in one day, to build there the city called Tadmor in the Bible This city must not be confounded with the later Syrian city of Palmyra, also called Tadmor. It was situated near the "mountains of darkness," the trysting-place of the spirits and demons. Thither the eagle would carry Solomon in the twinkling of an eye, (as you see from here Muhammad got the flying carpet) and Solomon would drop a paper inscribed with a verse among the spirits, to ward off evil from himself. Then the eagle would reconnoiter the mountains of darkness, until he had spied out the spot in which the fallen angels 'Azza and 'Azzael lie chained with iron fetters a spot which no one, not even a bird, may visit. When the eagle found the place, he would take Solomon under his left wing, and fly to the two angels. Through the power of the ring having the Holy Name graven upon it, which Solomon put into the eagle's mouth, 'Azza and 'Azzael were forced to reveal the heavenly mysteries to the king. After reading all of this, we know where Muhammad got the flying carpet story from. The coming claim will lead us to more information about the flying carpet.

Muslims claim

Modern means of transport

http://www.miraclesofthequran.com/predictions_07.html

> *And horses, mules, and donkeys both to ride and for adornment. And He creates other things you do not know. (Qur'an, 16:8)*

End of the claim

My answer

The first verse is about donkeys and horses and it says he (Allah) created other things you do not know. What does this have to do with airplanes? Is Allah the one who made airplanes?!

The verse after (Qur'an 36:41-42) is about Noah and how he was saved from the flood. What does this have to do with airplanes? It's mind blowing how they fabricate stories.

More details are to come with regards to these false claims by answering the next claim.

Muslims claim

Plane technology

http://www.miraclesofthequran.com/predictions_08.html

> *And to Sulayman We gave the fiercely blowing wind, speeding at his command toward the land that We had blessed. And We had full knowledge of everything. (Qur'an, 21:81)*

My answer

So, is this about airplanes or a flying carpet?

The fact is that this is one of those fairytale stories of the Qur'an about a flying carpet being given to Solomon. I will explain this in detail and show how Islam only fits for cartoon movies.

My word to Muslims: you are really doing a great job exposing this fairytale book and its stories because it makes us search and read!

The Flying Carpet

Qur'an 21:81

And to Solomon We subjected the wind, blowing strongly, under his command toward the land which We blessed, And We are of all things Knowing.

Interpretation of Ibn Kathir

وَقَوْلُه " وَلِسُلَيْمَانَ الرِّيحَ عَاصِفَة " أَيْ وَسَخَّرْنَا لِسُلَيْمَانَ الرِّيحَ الْعَاصِفَة " تَجْرِي بِأَمْرِه إِلَى الْأَرْض الَّتِي بَارَكْنَا فِيهَا " يَعْنِي أَرْض الشَّام " وَكُنَّا بِكُلِّ شَيْءٍ عَالِمِينَ " وَذَلِك أَنَّهُ كَانَ لَهُ بِسَاط مِنْ خَشَب يُوضَع عَلَيْهِ كُلّ مَا يُحْتَاج إِلَيْهِ مِنْ أُمُور الْمَمْلَكَة وَالْخَيْل وَالْجِمَال وَالْخِيَام وَالْجُنْد ثُمَّ يَأْمُر الرِّيح أَنْ تَحْمِله فَتَدْخُل تَحْته ثُمَّ تَحْمِله وَتَرْفَعه وَتَسِير بِه وَتُظِلّه الطَّيْر تَقِيه الْحَرّ إِلَى حَيْثُ يَشَاء مِنْ الْأَرْض فَيَنْزِل وَتُوضَع آلَاته وَحَشَمه قَالَ اللَّه تَعَالَى " فَسَخَّرْنَا لَهُ الرِّيح تَجْرِي بِأَمْرِه رُخَاء حَيْثُ أَصَابَ " وَقَالَ تَعَالَى " غُدُوّهَا شَهْر وَرَوَاحهَا شَهْر " قَالَ اِبْن أَبِي حَاتِم ذُكِرَ عَنْ سُفْيَان بْن عُيَيْنَة عَنْ أَبِي سِنَان عَنْ سَعِيد بْن جُبَيْر قَالَ كَانَ يُوضَع لِسُلَيْمَان سِتُمِائَة أَلْف كُرْسِيّ فَيَجْلِس مِمَّا يَلِيه مُؤْمِنُو الْإِنْس ثُمَّ يَجْلِس مِنْ وَرَائِهِمْ مُؤْمِنُو الْجِنّ ثُمَّ يَأْمُر الطَّيْر فَتُظِلّهُمْ ثُمَّ يَأْمُر الرِّيح فَتَحْمِلهُمْ" صَلَّى اللَّه عَلَيْهِ وَسَلَّم

"We gave him a mat, a carpet made of wood, the wind blows for him strongly and under his command to the land which we blessed meaning great Syria, and he would place all the equipment of his kingdom on top of it like horses, camels, tents and troops, then he commands the wind to carry it, and the wind goes underneath the carpet and it carries him and goes high with him and the brides will fly on the top of him to keep him in the shades and protect him from the heat, until he arrives to wherever he wants to go, and Ibn Jaber said, that the carpet Solomon had 600,000 chairs on it. And to the first line of chairs, human believers sit on, then jinn believers,"

وَقَالَ عَبْد اللَّه اِبْن عُبَيْد بْن عُمَيْر كَانَ سُلَيْمَان يَأْمُر الرِّيح فَتَجْتَمِع كَالطَّوْد الْعَظِيم فَتَجْتَمِع كَالْجَبَل ثُمَّ يَأْمُر بِفِرَاشِه فَيُوضَع عَلَى أَعْلَى مَكَان مِنْهَا ثُمَّ يَدْعُو بِفَرَس مِنْ ذَوَات الْأَجْنِحَة فَتَرْتَفِع فَتَصْعَد عَلَى فِرَاشِه ثُمَّ يَأْمُر الرِّيح فَتَرْتَفِع بِه كُلّ شَرَف دُون السَّمَاء وَهُوَ مُطَأْطِئ رَأْسه مَا يَلْتَفِت يَمِينًا وَلَا شِمَالًا تَعْظِيمًا لِلَّه

And Abdulah said, Solomon used to order the wind and it used to gather itself as huge as a mountain and he orders his bed and it will be placed and on the upper top of it, then he calls horses that have wings and they raise him with his bed until

he reaches the high sky with all honors and he doesn't turn his face left or right for showing respect to Allah!

Solomon speaks the language of birds only but yet he understands Ants too?

> *Qur'an 27:16*
>
> *And Solomon inherited David's. He said, (Solomon), "O you people! We have been taught the language of birds, and on us Allah has bestowed some of all things: this is the gift of Allah.*

> *Qur'an 27:17*
>
> *And before Solomon, were mobilized his hosts, of jinn and men and birds, and they were organized in ranks.*

Solomon spoke the language of birds! Why? What for? Did he want to convert them to Islam? Is this just one more fairytale story? When Solomon speaks to a chicken, does he make a voice of one? For sure he does! They don't speak his language so he speaks theirs! How many languages do birds have?!

The fact is that Muhammad took all of this from {The Legends of The Jews.}

The queen of Sheba

> *"Solomon, it must be remembered, bore rule not only over men, but also over the beasts of the field, the birds of the air, demons, spirits, and the specters of the night. He knew the language of all of them and they understood his language.*
>
> *When Solomon was of good cheer by reason of wine, he summoned the beasts of the field, the birds of the air, the creeping reptiles, the shades, the spectres, and the ghosts, to perform their dances before the kings, his neighbors, whom he invited to witness his power and greatness. The king's scribes called the animals and the spirits by name, one by one, and they all assembled of their own accord, without fetters or bonds, with no human hand to guide them."*

(Source: Louis Ginzberg, Legends of the Jews, [The Jewish Publication Society of America, Philadelphia, 1909], Vol. IV, Chapter V: Solomon)

Qur'an 27:20-21

20 And he did search for the hoopoe, how come I cannot find him!

21 I will punish him and torture or butcher him, if he did not give a good reason for his nonattendance.

"On one occasion the hoopoe was missed from among the birds. He could not be found anywhere. The king, full of wrath, ordered him to be produced and chastised for his tardiness. The hoopoe appeared and said:

"O lord, king of the world, incline thine ear and hearken to my words. Three months have gone by since I began to take counsel with myself and resolve upon a course of action. I have eaten no food and drunk no water, in order to fly about in the whole world and see whether there is a domain anywhere which is not subject to my lord the king. and I found a city, the city of Kitor, in the East. Dust is more valuable than gold there, and silver is like the mud of the streets. Its trees are from the beginning of all time, and they suck up water that flows from the Garden of Eden. The city is crowded with men. On their heads, they wear garlands wreathed in Paradise. They know not how to fight, nor how to shoot with bow and arrow. Their ruler is a woman, she is called the Queen of Sheba. If, now, it please thee, O lord and king, I shall gird my loins like a hero, and journey to the city of Kitor in the land of Sheba. Its kings I shall fetter with chains and its rulers with iron bands, and bring them all before my lord the king, the hoopoe's speech pleased the king." (Source: Louis Ginzberg, Legends of the Jews, [The Jewish Publication Society of America, Philadelphia, 1909], Vol. IV, Chapter V: Solomon)

Look at how Muhammad copied the story into Qur'an 27:22:

Qur'an 27:22-29

22 But he did not stay far long, and he said: I have found out about things from Sheba with sure tidings.

23 I found a woman ruling over them, and she hath been given from all things, and she has a mighty throne.

24 I found her and her people worshiping the sun instead of Allah; and Satan maketh their works as good to themselves, and depart them from the truth;

25 So that they don't worship Allah, who brings the hiding from the sky and the earth, who knows what you hide and you knowledgeable of,

26 Allah; there is no god but Him, the Lord of the great Throne.

27 He said, (Solomon), We will see whether you (hoopoe) speakest truth or you are one of the liars.

28 Go with this my letter and throw it down unto them; then stay away and see what they will do as return,

29 She said, (The Queen of Sheba): to one of her noble helpers there hath been thrown unto me a noble letter.

Let us continue reading and you will see how the Qur'an is identical with the legend of the Jews.

The clerks of his land were summoned, and they wrote a letter and bound it to the hoopoe's wing. The bird rose skyward, uttered his cry, and flew away, followed by all the other birds.

And they came to Kitor in the land of Sheba. It was morning, and the queen had gone forth to pay worship to the sun. Suddenly the birds darkened his light. The queen raised her hand, and rent her garment, and was sore astonished. Then the hoopoe alighted near her. Seeing that a letter was tied to his wing, she lost it and read it. And what was written in the letter? "From me, King Solomon! Peace be with thee, peace with the nobles of thy realm! Know that God has appointed me king over the beasts of the field, the birds of the air, the demons, the spirits, and the spectres. All the kings of the East and the West come to bring me greetings. If thou wilt come and salute me, I shall show thee great honor, more than to any of the kings that attend me. But if thou wilt not pay homage to me, I shall send out kings, legions, and riders against thee. Thou askest, who are these kings, legions, and riders of King Solomon? The beasts of the field are my kings, the birds my riders, the demons, spirit, and shades of the night my legions. The demons will throttle you in your beds at night, while the beasts will slay you in the field, and the birds will consume your flesh."

(Source: Louis Ginzberg, Legends of the Jews, [The Jewish Publication Society of America, Philadelphia, 1909], Vol. IV, Chapter V: Solomon)

We find that the story told in the Bible says the total opposite. It's the Queen of Sheba who heard of Solomon and she came to visit him. No birds had any involvement in the story.

> *2 Chronicles 9:1 - KJV*
>
> *And when the queen of Sheba heard of the fame of Solomon, she came to prove Solomon with hard questions at Jerusalem, with a very great company, and camels that bare spices, and gold in abundance, and precious stones: and when she was come to Solomon, she communed with him of all that was in her heart.*

- Every kind of bird has their own language. Can you imagine how many languages of birds Solomon had learned from Allah!
- The *Legends of the Jews* is a false source. The maker of the Qur'an took other nations' fairytale stories and then make it as his god's words.
- There is an army of birds and Jinn's and they have ranks!
- After all of this, how can someone in the year 2012 believe in any of these stories? What is even the point of it?
- Why is Allah giving Solomon all of this amazing power over humans and Jinn's, a flying carpet, birds, and money, when Solomon doesn't fit as a servant of Muhammad? As Islam claims, Muhammad is the greatest!
- Add to all of this, the Muslim Solomon did not even leave a book of what he did! What was he able to accomplish?
- No book.
- No teaching.
- Not even one sentence in the Qur'an tells us about something Solomon was like. What's the purpose of all these fairytale stories? Why didn't Allah tell us about the wisdom of this man?
- Why can't the Qur'an focus in a topic and put the story of Solomon in one chapter? We can see it in many chapters, like 21:81, 34:12 and 38:36. All of them are just repeating over and over the same story.
- Does this god love to say words for nothing?

As the Lord said, in
> *Matthew 6:7 - KJV*
>
> *But when ye pray, use not vain repetitions, as the heathen do: for they think that they shall be heard for their much speaking.*

As long as reciting the Qur'an is a prayer from Muslims by repeating

Allah's words, therefore what's the point of saying the same words over and over again?

Muslims claim

The army-ant in technology

http://www.miraclesofthequran.com/predictions_13.html

My answer

The Talking Ant!

So according to the claim the Qur'an speaks about "Latest Developments in Miniature Technology: Army-Ant Robots"
Let me quote the words of Mr. Harun, but please do not laugh!

"...the fact that Prophet Sulayman (as) **could hear the ants talking** among themselves..."

Now we have no problem explaining to anyone that it's about **hearing the ant talk**! Please remember this for later, because this is very important; especially when we find out that ants are deaf, and of course, cannot speak.

Before I present you the story, I have one question. What does all of this have to do with an "Army-Ant Robot?" It's every Muslim's fantasy that everything should be written in their Qur'an. I hope that soon we will get a claim about finding a Disney Mickey Mouse cartoon inside their book.

Even more funny, why are Muslims using an army of ants when Allah (or Muhammad) did not use it?

> *Qur'an 27:18-19*
> *18 Till he (Solomon) arrived to the ant's valley, and an ant said to the other ants, "Hide in your houses before Solomon's army smashes you with their feet without knowing,"*
> *19 So he smiled, amused at its speech.*

1. The first funny thing in this verse is that this valley can only be

found in Syria! Where is it?

2. Does it mean that Solomon only found ants in his way in that place? Aren't there ants all over the earth?
3. Does it mean that this was the state of the ants and Solomon was crossing their borders?!
4. Solomon can listen to all insects talk? This would make any man go crazy due to the remarkable number of insects.
5. A simpler question to ask first is, do ants talk?
6. Question: How do ants communicate in an organized, complex colony? Answer: Ants use pheromones (chemical signals), physical touch, and sometimes the vibration of their bodies to send messages about food, enemies, and the nest.

You can visit this link and read what the professionals say about the communication of ants:
we did provide before a video above for how ants communicate but you can read more;

http://www.sciencedirect.com/science/article/pii/S0960982206018343
Pheromones

"By releasing chemical signals, called pheromones, ants guide each other's in their colony to directions of food sources, or warn them of any danger.

Sound
"Using a variety of methods, such as clicking their mandibles or knocking their heads against solid objects, ants can produce squeaks and grating noises that are sometimes even audible to humans. Nearby ants will get the message, which is often one of alarm, by detecting the sound vibrations."

We see big mistakes in the verse.

1. Ants are 100% deaf.
2. They communicate by chemical signals and sometimes by vibration but not by talking.
3. Did Solomon have to vibrate with them? Does he have their chemical signals?
4. The Qur'an 27:19 reads: Thus, he smiled, **amused at its speech**. Speech...even when ants are deaf?
5. Were Solomon and the ants clicking their mandibles or knocking their heads against each other?

It's clearly a mistake and a fairytale story made to impress these Arabs. The fact is, we might find out how Muhammad got these funny stories from Jewish legends, which are filled with fairytale stories. Many are about Solomon, as follows:

On one occasion, he strayed into the valley of the ants in the course of his wanderings. **He heard one ant order all the others to withdraw, to avoid being crushed by the armies of Solomon.** The king halted and summoned the ant that had spoken. She told him that she was the queen of the ants, and she gave her reasons for the order of withdrawal. Solomon wanted to put a question to the ant queen, but she refused to answer unless the king took her up and placed her on his hand. He acquiesced, and then he put his question:

(Source: Louis Ginzberg, Legends of the Jews, [The Jewish Publication Society of America, Philadelphia, 1909], Vol. IV, Chapter V: Solomon)

and that is exactly what The Qur'an said;
> Qur'an 27:18-19
>
> *18 Till he (Solomon) arrived to the ant's valley, and an ant said to the other ants, "Hide in your houses before Solomon's army smashes you with their feet without knowing,"19 So he smiled, amused at its speech.*

Solomon Was Standing for One Year After His Death

I wish I can keep going with more of funny stories good for kids but its endless so this is the last one will be in this book about Solomon fairytale stories.

Should I say; Once upon a time, there was a King who ruled a great and glorious nation he has a flying horse, and flying carpet can take 600,000 chairs, and he can move all his war equipment on it!

He has Jinn's work for him, to dive and bring him gold and jewelry, from the deep sea, once he went to bath room and the Satan come to his wife after he clone the look of Solomon!

He the Satan told her to give the ring back to him as if he is Solomon the King, He wore it, and then he became the king.

I think I better stop here or you guys might sleep and go back to old day when grandma was telling us same kinds of stories.

I am really amazed about the great imagination of the story make to come with such a story.

But what I couldn't believe, that someone will put in a "holy book" a story of a man dies standing and stay standing for one year after his death!

> Qur'an 34:14 Yusuf Ali trans.

"Then, when We decreed (Solomon's) death, nothing showed them his death except a little worm of the earth, which kept (slowly) gnawing away at his staff: so when he fell down, the Jinn's saw plainly that if they had known the unseen, they would not have tarried in the humiliating Penalty (of their Task)."

So the story is simple he Solomon died standing and had his staff(stick) with him at the moment he died, so because of that he was standing for a year after, and no one notice that he is dead, including his wives, Jinn's, minsters, solders, even his children's, till the worm ate his staff and he fall to ground floor?

The interpretation can be found in all Islamic books as, Tafsir Al-Qur'anAL-'Azem by Ibn Kathir V.6 p

Tanwîr al-Miqbâs min Tafsîr Ibn 'Abbâs

(And when We decreed death for Solomon, Solomon died and remained standing in his retreat for one year (nothing showed his death) the death of Solomon a woodworm (worm gnawed away his staff) and it is said: his short stick. when Solomon fell to the ground, the jinn and human beings saw clearly that they do not know the unseen, they would not have continued in their subservience serving Solomon after his death. People thought before this that the jinn knew the unseen but when they saw this they discover that they did not.

what we learn from this is the flowing:

✓ Allah made Solomon die standing.

✓ His stick was the reason not to fall down, because when the worm ate it(the stick) he fall to the ground.

✓ Is it possible that some one stays standing for a year just because he is holding a stick?

✓ And wasn't noticeable eventually to his wives, children's, officers, minsters or even the Jinn's?

✓ If I hold a stick on my hand it might help me to balance, it's not what keeps me standing, especially when it's only one stick, so the body itself is standing on both feet not because of the stick I am holding

✓ According to the interpreter, Allah wanted to show man kind that the Jinn's do not know the unseen, but the fact this is it has nothing to do with the unseen, because they can see him in-front of them, same time if he falls down after one year or one day it will not change anything because a man who does not breath, talk, move, blink, he must be cold as a dead body, its very easy to recognize that man is a dead man.

✓ No one even did try to talk to him for one year? If you enter a room and there is a person there you know, and he don't respond to your words and he do not move don't we try to figure out what is wrong with him?

✓ It's not a secret that after death all kind of God creations go throw a new stage, and in less than 48 hours dead body will smell so bad, after approximately two to three days bacteria are active and the body is swollen with gases and accompanying odors.

"Decomposition in the air is twice as fast as when the body is under water and four times as fast as underground."

http://www.memorialpages.co.uk/articles/decomposition.php

but yet Muslims claim their book is the book of science not fairytales!

\---

Muslims claim

Atomic energy and fission

> *Allah splits the seed and kernel. He brings forth the living from the dead, and produces the dead out of the living. That is Allah, so how are you misguided? (Qur'an, 6:95)*

The terms "seed" (al-habb) and "kernel" (an-nawa) in the above verse may indicate the splitting of the atom.

\---

My answer

I wasn't going to answer this for it's actually too silly, but I will do it. Look at how they turn something very simple to be about ATOMIC ENERGY! What does this verse have to do with any of that? Honestly, this is insanity. All the verse is saying is:

    1) Allah makes the seeds split and gives forth food to us.
    2) Same as he made the dead alive, for the seeds look dead, but they're not.
    3) Notice how the Muslims use the word *may*. What does *may* mean? Either it's saying that or it's not. They know

they are making up something false so we have to live with maybe and may! **"...verse *may* indicate the splitting of the atom."**

4) Maybe the Bible is speaking about Atomic Energy as we see in this verse:

Genesis 1:11 - KJV

And God said, Let the earth bring forth grass, the herb yielding seed, and the fruit tree yielding fruit after his kind, whose seed is in itself, upon the earth: and it was so.

Genesis 1:12 - KJV

And the earth brought forth grass, and herb yielding seed after his kind, and the tree yielding fruit, whose seed was in itself, after his kind: and God saw that it was good.

Honestly, I think it's a silly claim.

Muslims claim

Bone loss in old age

http://www.miraclesofthequran.com/scientific_105.html

> *"And said, 'My Lord, my bones have gone frail and my head is crowned with white, but in calling on You, My Lord, I have never been disappointed'."*
>
> *(Surah Maryam, 4)*

The Arabic word "**wahana**" in verse 4 of Surah Maryam means "relaxed, weakened or insufficient." The use of this word in the context of aging and changes taking place in the bones is most wise. Bone scanning performed taking detailed measurements using modern technology makes it possible to image the disease known to the medical world as "osteoporosis," or bone loss.

Bearing in mind that x-rays were only discovered in the 1890s,

----

My answer

- It's not a secret that humans know they get weaker as they get older.
- On top of that, Muslims miss the point that it's not Allah talking there! It was Zachariah. Does that make Zachariah God?
- The Bible is saying the same but we do not say it's an amazing science.

> *Psalms 3:10 - KJV*
>
> *For my life is spent with grief, and my years with sighing: my strength faileth because of mine iniquity, and my bones are consumed.*

Muslims claim

A red rose in the sky: the rosette nebula

http://www.miraclesoftheQur'an.com/scientific_106.html

> *When the Heaven shall be cleft asunder, and become rose red, like stained leather. (Surat ar-Rahman, 37)*

The Arabic expression translated above as "become rose red, like stained leather" is "verdeten ke eddihani." This term compares an image appearing in the sky to a red rose. This description bears a close similarity to red celestial bodies with a plicate appearance, especially the "Rosette Nebula."

My answer

I don't think Muslims read their own words. If this claim is true it means that the Qur'an is false. Do you know why? Read again the verse given by Mr. Harun:

"When the Heaven shall be cleft asunder, and become rose red, like stained leather. (Surat ar-Rahman, 37).

Actually, the Qur'an speaks about the cloud turning into red, not stars and gas or stars. That is explained inside Ibn Kathir

Qur'an 25: 25

A day when the heaven with the clouds will be rented asunder and the angels will be sent down, by his order

(Allah).

This verse speaks about Judgment Day, which means it is something that will occur **only on Judgment Day**. Quoted from the interpretation of Ibn Kathir:

> This demonstrates the measure of the terrors of the Mighty Day of Resurrection.

And you can read it yourself from the Muslims translations and website in the following link:

www.qtafsir.com/index.php?option=com_content&task=view&id=1517&It emid=111

But in his article, he spoke about **Nebula** which already exists. From his words, we quote "Nebula is the name given to cloud-like masses of gas in space. **Before they become nebulae, they are stars,**"

We quote from the NASA

Cat's Eye Nebula

Three thousand light-years away, the Cat's Eye Nebula, a dying star throws off shells of glowing gas. This image from the Hubble Space Telescope reveals the nebula to be one of the most complex planetary nebulae known. In fact, the features seen in the Cat's Eye are so complex that astronomers suspect the bright central object may actually be a binary star system. The term planetary nebula is misleading; although these objects may appear round and planet-like in small telescopes, high resolution images reveal them to be stars surrounded by cocoons of gas blown off in the late stages of stellar evolution."

To see more of images or articles about it visit this site please.
http://search.nasa.gov/search/search.jsp?nasaInclude=Nebula

From the Bible we quote the following in regards to Judgment Day:
Acts 2:20 - KJV

The sun shall be turned into darkness, and the moon into blood, before the great and notable day of the Lord come:"

Muslims claim

The solidity of the atom and electron orbits

http://www.miraclesoftheQur'an.com/scientific_107.html

> *"You will see the mountains you reckoned to be solid going past like clouds – the handwork of Allah Who gives to everything its solidity. He is aware of what you do." (Surat an-Naml, 88)*

The above verse **may be** a reference to the strength of the atom,

The verse **may also** be indicating the clouds of electrons around atomic nuclei, whose movement is likened to "mountains... going past like clouds."

My answer

First of all, I think Muhammad copying the book of Revelation.
Revelation 6:14

> *"The sky was split apart like a scroll when it is rolled up, and every mountain and island were moved out of their places."*

however again and again we quote from the Muslims "The above verse **maybe ... and may also**"????

تحسب

The word **Ta'hsab** means "you think" in the present tense, which means when you look at it you see it as if it is fixed but the fact is that it's moving. And actually, the one who made the claim forgot that he made different claim using the same verse from the same chapter. We will quote his own words, please keep this in mind.
"In one verse, we are informed that mountains are not motionless as they seem, **but are in constant motion**."

> *Surat an-Naml, chap. 88*
>
> *"You will see the mountains you reckoned to be solid going past like clouds – the handwork of Allah Who gives to everything its solidity. He is aware of what you do."*

Let us read the end of his claim again.

"It is impossible to understand the structure of the atom and establish this cloud-like appearance of electrons without such high-tech devices as electron microscopes."

All that can be understood from this verse is that mountains will pass like a cloud! Imagine someone telling you that the tree will pass like the clouds and then he tries to convince you that it's about the atom? How and where is the connection? The mountain is a word for one object which is extreme huge so what this has to do with atoms?

1. Look again at the claim and read it. You will see that it's based on {**The verse maybe, The verse may also**}. How can somebody try to present us scientific facts based on "**may be**" and "**may also**"?
2. Just because I do not like to repeat myself, I will show some verses in the Qur'an explaining exactly what this verse is talking about in the next claim. They have used the same verse for another claim too. I will save these verses to show you the full picture of the story.
3. I would like you to keep in mind the coming line, for I will need it to expose Mr. Harun with his own words.

   "if a vase is shattered, only the atoms that make it up remain solid."

4. The only thing we need to do is read the verse prior to this one in order to realize it's about Judgment Day, not something that's happening right now which proves the falseness of the claim. *Qur'an 27:87*

   And on the day [Judgment Day] when the trumpet shall be blown and scared is going to be whoever is in the skies or on the earth, except whom as Allah pleases, and all shall come with humble.

Which you might notice is something stolen from the Bible:
Matthew 24:31

And he shall send his angels with a great sound of a trumpet, and they shall gather together his elect from the four winds, from one end of heaven to the other."

5. The verse is speaking about Judgment Day and Allah, as Muhammad stated: "you think these mountains will stay? But they will move cloud-like," which means nothing will stay in Judgment Day. All of a sudden, it's about "The rapid movement of electrons."

We read **Ibn Kathir**'s interpretation which you can read yourself by

following this link in the Muslims
Muslims claim
website.

> *Interpretation of Ibn Kathir, Qur'an 27:88*
>
> *They look like to you as if they are fixed, and as if they will stand as they are, but they will pass away as the passing away of the clouds, which means they will move away from their locations."*

www.qtafsir.com/index.php?option=com_content&task=view&id=2220&It
emid=83

The same is mentioned in:

> *Qur'an 52:9-10*
>
> *"On the Day [Judgment Day] when the firmament trembles with a dreadful shaking, and the mountains will move away as it's walking."*
>
> *Qur'an 18:47*
>
> *"And when the Day [Judgment Day] We shall cause the mountains to pass away, and you will see the earth as a flattened with no cover."*

One verse two translations, both made by Mr. Harun.

If someone translates the same verse, using different words in each translation, I see nothing wrong with it as long as they both give the same meaning. At the end, a translation is meant to give the most accurate meaning not the exact text. However, in this case, we will see that Mr. Harun intentionally played with the same translation. Let us compare both.

When he talked about the atom and electron orbits he gave us the following translation which you can read here:
http://www.miraclesoftheQur'an.com/scientific_107.html

1st Translation

> *"You will see the mountains you reckoned to be solid going past like clouds – the handwork of Allah Who gives to everything its solidity. He is aware of what you do." (Surat an-Naml 27, 88)*

But it's a claim about the movement of mountains. The translation

changed and again you can read it yourself from his website:
http://www.miraclesofthequran.com/scientific_26.html

> 2nd Translation
>
> *"You see the mountains you reckoned to be solid going past like clouds." (Qur'an, 27:88)*

The regular reader might not necessarily notice the important difference. In the 1st translation, Mr. Harun used **"You will"**. In the 2nd translation, he purposely took out the word **will.**

The difference is enormous. The reason he used "you will see" (1st translation) is because he wanted to make it sound like a discovery that will happen in the future; but in his claim concerning the movement of the earth, he wanted it to be as Allah presenting scientific facts about the movement of the earth as well as the movement of the mountain. Later on, we will prove his claim to also be false and incorrect.

> *Job 14:18 - KJV*
>
> *But the mountain falls and crumbles away,*
>
> *and the rock is removed from its place;*

Here we go, we have the same verse which Muhammad stole from the Bible. We just don't see any Christians or Jews linking this verse to electrons and atoms. Right! These things only happen in Islam.

> *II Peter 3:10-13 - KJV*
>
> *10 But the day of the Lord will come as a thief in the night; in the which the heavens shall pass away with a great noise, and the elements shall melt with fervent heat, the earth also and the works that are therein shall be burned up.*
>
> *11 Seeing then that all these things shall be dissolved, what manner of persons ought ye to be in all holy conversation and godliness,*
>
> *12 Looking for and hasting unto the coming of the day of God, wherein the heavens being on fire shall be dissolved, and the elements shall melt with fervent heat?*
>
> *13 Nevertheless we, according to his promise, look for new heavens and a new earth, wherein dwelleth righteousness.*

If you look carefully at the last two verses, it will be clearer as to where Muhammad was getting his story. The fact is that after things got at the point of melting because of extreme heat, the earth will burn up and will be nothing but dust in the space. Notice that the believers in Christ get "*a new heaven and a new earth*".

I will show you that Mr. Harun is not honest in his claims by not being consistent with his own words. Maybe he forgot what he posted on his site, or maybe it's a group of liars working there, not just one!

Read with me the coming claim and you will see their contradictions.

Muslims claim

The function of mountains

http://www.harunyahya.com/en/Miracles-of-the-Quran/27329/the-function-of-mountains
The Qur'an draws attention to a very important geological function of mountains:

> *We placed firmly embedded mountains on the earth, so it would not move under them... (Qur'an, 21:31)*

The verse states that mountains perform the function of preventing shocks in the Earth. This fact was not known by anyone at the time the Qur'an was revealed. It was, in fact, brought to light only recently, as a result of the findings of modern geological research.

My answer

What we have from this long page is that the mountains are stopping the earth from moving in another way and that mountains have roots!

If you read the last verse that Mr. Harun stated, it said:

> *Qur'an 31:10*
>
> *"He cast firmly embedded mountains on the earth so that it would not move under you..."*

Notice the words there are **embedded mountains.** This does not mean at all what they are trying to say that the mountains, in the Qur'an, are not part of the earth, its embedded so the mountain's root extends down through the earth.

This is a deceptive game Muslims always play to fool the readers and make them confused by mixing the Qur'an with science. They take the Qur'an's errors, as in this verse, and make them appear like a scientific discovery when it's false and a huge mistake. Honestly, I do enjoy defeating falsification so let's do it together.

1. First, since the Muslims translated this word, we will go to the English dictionaries and see what "embed" means and understand why Muslims chose it as a perfect meaning for the Arabic word. We find this:

Embed is to fix into a surrounding mass: to embed stones in cement. Or to fix something firmly into a substance.

Here's the link:
http://dictionary.cambridge.org/dictionary/british/embed
http://dictionary.reference.com/browse/embed

2. This means that Muslims have agreed that the mountains are not part of the Earth. They are embedded in! This is proof that everything they claim is a lie. The fact is, we have very clear evidence that will prove the false claim from the Qur'an. I will use Mr. Harun's translation and his own words so that no one will say they do not agree with my translation. His quote:

"In other verses, this role of the mountains is pointed out by a comparison with **"pegs"**:
Have We not made the earth as a bed and the mountains its pegs? (Qur'an 78:6-7)"

3. The answer is right there in front of our eyes! Allah is saying that the earth is like a bed and that mountains are embedded and fixed down by nails or pegs. Did the Muslims think before posting their claim?

"Mountains *emerge* as a result of the movements and collisions of massive plates forming the earth's crust. When two plates collide, the stronger one slides under the other, the one on the top bends and forms heights and mountains. The layer beneath proceeds under the ground and makes a deep extension downward. Consequently, as stated earlier, mountains have a portion stretching downwards, as large as their visible parts on the Earth."

4. Then this means they are formed from the inside of the earth to the outside of the earth. Not from outside to the inside, as portrayed by the word **pegs**!
5. Even the mountains have been sent down from the sky as we

see in chapter 35 of the Qur'an:

أَلَمْ تَرَ أَنَّ اللَّهَ أَنْزَلَ مِنَ السَّمَاءِ مَاءً فَأَخْرَجْنَا بِهِ ثَمَرَاتٍ مُخْتَلِفًا أَلْوَانُهَا ۚ وَمِنَ الْجِبَالِ جُدَدٌ بِيضٌ وَحُمْرٌ مُخْتَلِفٌ أَلْوَانُهَا وَغَرَابِيبُ سُودٌ

سورة فاطر , Fatir, Qur'an 35:27 :

> *"We send down from the sky rain from fruits come out and mountains from it tracts white, black, red and others in color and strange black."*

The Muslims, through their translation, will try to make it as if it's not about mountains coming from the sky. However, we have strong proof stating otherwise as Allah himself (Muhammad) agreed that hail comes from mountains located up in the sky.

We need to go to other verses that show how things come from the sky, including mountains.

Where does hail comes from, according to the Qur'an?

In Muhammad Pickthall's translation:

> *Qur'an 24:43*
>
> *"He sendeth down from the heaven mountains wherein is hail."*

My translation:

> *Qur'an 24:43*
>
> *"Have you not seen how God drives the clouds, subsequently composes them, after that constructs them up, whereat you see the rain flowing from the midst of them? And He sends down from the heaven out of the mountains that is therein hail, and smites with it whom He will and turns it apart from whom He will. The brilliance of its lightning would almost take away the eyes."*

ألم تر أن الله يزجي سحابا ثم يؤلف بينه ثم يجعله ركاما فترى الودق يخرج من خلاله وينزل من السماء من جبال فيها من برد فيصيب به من يشاء ويصرفه عن من يشاء يكاد سنا برقه يذهب بالأبصار

It says that hail originates from mountains in the sky, and it's used by Allah as a punishment, not as part of a weather act or behavior.

English translation of its meanings
Royal Aal al-Bayt Institute for Islamic Thought

In most translations Muslims have in English, they added "clouds like mountains." What a lie! The Qur'an clearly says that Allah sends hail from mountains up in heaven and uses it to punish the ones he doesn't like!

> *Tafsir Al Jalalayn*
>
> *And He sends down from the heaven out of the mountains that are therein*

It's just one more mistake. Proof that the Qur'an cannot be from God. But where Muhammad got his story from about hail stored on heaven? Again, we find this in **(The Legends of the Jews, Volume One, Louis Ginzberg)** "The sixth heaven is an ucanny spot; there originate most of the trials and visitations ordained for the earth and its inhabitants. **Snow lies heaped up there and hail;** there are lofts full of noxious dew, magazines stocked with storms, and cellars holding reserves of smoke. Doors of fire separate these celestial chambers..."

Muslims claim

The movement of mountains

http://www.miraclesofthequran.com/scientific_26.html
In one verse, we are informed that mountains are not motionless as they seem, but are in constant motion.

> *You see the mountains you reckoned to be solid going past like clouds. (Qur'an 27:88)*

My answer

Look with me at the name of the title of the claim:

"The movement of mountains"

If we go to a past claim, we can see that they said it's about the electrical structure of the atom!

Read with me here how it's about the constant motion of a physically existent mountain. Look at the translation, which does not fit with any Islamic texts and you will read "**going past**." Is that going to come to pass in the future or is it about something happening right now? From Mr. Harun's words, we read the following:

"In one verse, we are informed that mountains are not motionless as they seem, but are in constant motion."

It's about all the mountains moving, not the electrical structure of the atom as he tried to make it look like in his last claim. I will show you the correct translation of the verse compared to Mr. Harun's.
If you remember we showed you how Mr. Harun has two translations for the same verses.
Mr. Harun's translation:
http://www.miraclesofthequran.com/scientific_26.html

> *"You see the mountains you reckoned to be solid going past like clouds. (Qur'an 27:88)*

> *http://www.miraclesofthequran.com/scientific_107.html this one was about "the solidity of the atom and electron orbits"*

> *"You will see the mountains you reckoned to be solid going past like clouds. (Qur'an 27:88)*

Because he wanted in the first claim to make it look its about now, and in other claim, it's about the future discovery as if its prophecy, that is clear proof of dishonesty pulse it shows that there is no limitation of dishonesty, to the point the fabricators are willing to add word to their god words just to make you believe it's science.

If we post one verse to Muslims will say you are taking out of contacts, but yet they have no problem to do so if its going to serve converting others to Islam.
So, the question why he did not quote the verse before it?

> *My translation: Qur'an 27:88*

> *"and you think that the mountains are firmly fixed but they will pass like the clouds."*

You may go, and see any other Islamic translations, you shall notice that Mr. Harun's translations are always false.
Just as I said before, it's something that will be on Judgment Day, I can prove it very easily. Just read the verse before it;

Qur'an 27:87-88 Yusuf Ali translation

"And the Day that the Trumpet will be sounded - then will be smitten with terror those who are in the heavens, and those who are on earth, except such as Allah will please (to exempt): and all shall come to His (Presence) as beings conscious of their lowliness. 88 Thou seest the mountains and thinkest them firmly fixed: but they shall pass away as the clouds pass away: (such is) the artistry of Allah, who disposes of all things in perfect order: for he is well acquainted with all that ye do."

Tafsir Ibn Abbas

To you Muhammad when the first trumpet blows all the hills that look solid to you, they will fly like a cloud.

Tanwîr al-Miqbâs min Tafsîr Ibn 'Abbâs

We can find the same in the following verses:

Qur'an 70:8-9

8 The day when the sky will melt and become as molten copper

9 And the mountains become as wool,

Qur'an 56:1-5

1 When the time of the event cometh

2 Then will no (soul) entertain falsehood concerning its coming.

3 many people will be as low; many will be exalting others;

4 When the earth shall be shaken hard,

5 And the mountains shall be crumbled to ashes,

As you see, Muhammad is just copying again. Compare these to Biblical scriptures:

Job 14:18 - KJV

But the mountain falls and crumbles away, and the rock is removed from its place;

Luke 21:11 - KJV

And great earthquakes shall be in divers places, and famines, and pestilences; and fearful sights and great signs shall there be from heaven.

II Peter 3:10-13 - KJV

10 But the day of the Lord will come as a thief in the night; in the which the heavens shall pass away with a great noise, and the elements shall melt with fervent heat, the earth also and the works that are therein shall be burned up.

11 Seeing then that all these things shall be dissolved, what manner of persons ought ye to be in all holy conversation and godliness,

12 Looking for and hasting unto the coming of the day of God, wherein the heavens being on fire shall be dissolved, and the elements shall melt with fervent heat?

13 Nevertheless we, according to his promise, look for new heavens and a new earth, wherein dwelleth righteousness.

Judgment Day in the Bible and Qur'an

Bible – King James Version	Qur'an
II Peter 3 [12] Looking for and hasting unto the coming of the day of God, wherein the heavens being on fire shall be dissolved, and the **elements shall melt** with fervent heat?	70:8 The day when the sky **will melt become as molten copper** 70:9 And the mountains become as wool,
Matthew 24:31 And he shall send his angels with a great **sound of a trumpet**, and they shall gather together his elect from the four winds, from one end of heaven to the other.	Qur'an 56:2, 6:73, 18:99, 20:102, 23:101, 27:87, 36:51, 39:68, 50:20 ,69:13, 74:8, 78:18 **trumpet blow** on Judgment Day
Isaiah 29:5 5 Moreover the multitude of thy strangers shall be like small dust, and the multitude of the terrible ones shall be as chaff that passeth away: yea, it shall be at an **instant suddenly**.	6:31 when the hour comes upon them all of a sudden 6:47 when punishment of Allah **come suddenly** 7:187, same in 12:107, and in 16:77
Isaiah 29:6 Thou shalt be visited of the LORD of hosts with thunder, and with **earthquake**, and great noise, with storm and tempest, and the flame of devouring fire.	22:1 the **earthquake** of earth (in the Judgment day) is a great thing 91:1 when the earth shaken, and gives out its **earthquake**
Matthew 24:36 But of that day and hour knoweth no man, no, not the angels of heaven, but my Father only.	33:63 and they asking you the day and the hour, say only Allah knows the hour.

Job 14:18 But the **mountain falls and crumbles away**, and the rock is removed from its place;	56:5 And the **mountains shall be crumbled to ashes,**
Revelation 1:7 **Behold, he cometh with clouds**; and every eye shall see him, and they also which pierced him: and all kindreds of the earth shall wail because of him. Even so, Amen. Matthew 24:30 And then shall appear the sign of the Son of man in heaven: and then shall all the tribes of the earth mourn, and they shall see the Son of man coming in the clouds of heaven with power and great glory.	2:210 **do they look till Allah comes to them in canopies of clouds,** with his angels
Ezekiel 7:19 They shall cast their silver in the streets, and their gold shall be removed: their silver and **their gold shall not be able to deliver them in the day of the wrath** of the LORD: they shall not satisfy their souls, neither fill their bowels: because it is the stumblingblock of their iniquity.	26:88 **The day when no money or offspring will benefit them**.
Matthew 25:31 When **the Son of man shall come** in his glory, **and all the holy angels with him**, then shall he sit upon the throne of his glory:	89:22 And thy **Lord will come, with His angels**, rank after rank,
Revelation 14:18 And another angel came out from the altar, which had power over fire; **and cried with a loud**	50:41 And listen for that Day **when the Caller he will be calling out** from a place quite near,

cry to him that had the sharp sickle, saying, Thrust in thy sharp sickle, and gather the clusters of the vine of the earth; for her grapes are fully ripe.	50:42 The Day when **they will hear a mighty Blast** in truth: that will be the Day of Resurrection.
Matthew 13:41 The Son of man shall send forth his angels, **and they shall gather out of his kingdom all things that offend, and them which do iniquity;**	50:44 The Day when the Earth will be rent asunder, from mankind hurrying out: **that will be a gathering together, that is so easy for Us.**
(No Intercession) Matthew 25:12 But he answered and said, Verily I say unto you, I know you not.	31:33 a Day when no father can avail aught for his son, nor a son avail aught for his father
Matthew 24:19 And woe unto them that are with child, and to them that give suck in those days! Mark 13:17 But woe to them that are with child, and to them that give suck in those days! Luke 21:23 But woe unto them that are with child, and to them that give suck, in those days! for there shall be great distress in the land, and wrath upon this people.	22:2 The Day ye shall see it, every mother giving suck shall forget her suckling to her child, and every pregnant female shall drop her embryo, and mankind as if they are drunken, yet not drunk: but the punishment of Allah is sever.
Mark 13:12 Now the brother shall betray the brother to death, and the father the son; and children shall rise up against their parents, and shall cause them to be put to death.	80:33 Then when the second blowing of the Trumpet start, 80:34 That Day shall a man flee from his brother, 80:35 And from his mother and his father, 80:36 And from his wife and his children. 80:37 Every one will have enough to forget about others

There are many more verses, but I think the point is clear that Muhammad was copying and making up his own book. Remember, Muslims might say it's normal to have many similar things because the Bible is from Allah. It's only true if it's word by word. Someone might ask if copying word by word would be stealing Christ's words.

Let me explain it in another way. If Muslims claim we corrupted the Bible, what is the corruption about? That Jesus is God? Great! A verse describing hell has nothing to do with Jesus, unless the verse itself speaks about Jesus. Therefore, why would Christians change the way hell is? This is why I am saying that if the Qur'an is from God, it should match the Bible's description of hell word by word. What Muhammad was doing here is trying to change the look and the words so he could claim these words to be his. Any thief will paint a stolen car.

Human Biology

Qur'an and Biology

Muslims made many claims about Allah's science. We can prove all of them to be false and a lie. As an example, they claimed:

1. Man was created from dust and water
2. Semen is a compound
3. Creation from a quintessence and child's sex
4. Hanging on the wall of uterus
5. Chewed lump of flesh
6. Bone formation and clothing of bones with flesh
7. Creation in three darkness
8. Identity on finger tips

All of these are supposedly in their claims as amazing scientific discoveries about how Allah knows. According to them, scientists have only found out today what the Qur'an has already said 1400 years ago. Is it true?

Muslim claim

267

The identity in the fingerprint

http://www.harunyahya.com/miracles_of_the_Qur'an_p1_08.php#8

Everyone, including identical twins, has a unique fingerprint. In other words, people's identities are coded at their fingertips. This coding system may also be compared to the barcode system that is used today.

While it is stated in the Qur'an that it is easy for Allah to bring man back to life after death, peoples' fingerprints are particularly emphasized:

> *Yes, We are able to put together in perfect order the very tips of his fingers. (Qur'an, 75:4)*

My answer

The Identity in the Fingerprint

Muslims claim that Allah mentioned the fingerprint in the Qur'an, as in:

> *Qur'an 75:4*
>
> *"Yes, We are able to put together in perfect order the very tips of his fingers."*

We should always ask ourselves a very simple question: why do they always post for us one verse out of the whole chapter? Usually if you read for Muslims a verse from the Qur'an they would say to you: "you're taking it out of its context, read the whole thing!" Let us then do as they request and expose the falsehood of the fingerprint ID scientific discovery in the Qur'an.

أَيَحْسَبُ الْإِنسَانُ أَلَّن نَجْمَعَ عِظَامَهُ

Qur'an 75:3

Does man think we cannot gather his bones?

بل قَادِرِينَ عَلَى أَن نُّسَوِّيَ بَنَانَهُ

Qur'an 75:4

Yes, for sure we can put together his finger.

It's obviously so clear that the verse is speaking about Allah at **Resurrection Day** and **not when we are alive**, for he will put together our bones, even the smallest ones because it's known how small finger bones are. It has nothing to do with fingerprints as these Muslims claim. Go to the Al-Jalalayn's explanation: click here

This is their own Islamic website and their own scholar saying clearly that it's about putting back the bones together, and the finger print is nothing but falsehood.

Muslim claim

Pregnancy and birth

http://www.miraclesofthequran.com/scientific_62.html

> *Curse man for his ingratitude! From what thing did He create him? From a drop of sperm, He created him and proportioned him. Then He eases the way for him. (Qur'an, 80:17-20)*

My answer

Please feel free to read the whole claim from the link mentioned above. He is simply saying that scientists discovered fluid which comprises sacs, which will enlarge the mouth of the womb and that will ease the delivery for women.

However, what does this have to do with the coming verse? There is a very simple method about reading, just try to understand what the words are saying. If you read the verse with me you will notice that the verse says it will **ease the way for him** not **for her**. I think that even a blind person could see it.

> *Qur'an 80:20*
> *"Then He eases the way for him."*

> *Now we can read any interpretation like Ibn Kathir's:*
> *"Ibn Abbas said: Then He made his coming out of his mother's belly easy for him.".*

Or, we can read other scholars' interpretations which all say the same thing: Allah eases the way for him. A person might not realize the difference as the interpretation speaks about the effortless in giving birth for him when coming out of the belly. The difference is very important.

Imagine someone saying "it was so easy for Osama bin Laden to kill 3000 Americans." Does it mean it was easy for the 3000 Americans to die and to burn alive? Surely not! This is a foolish statement to say.

This is really funny! Mr. Harun posted a verse about Mary in pain when she was giving birth. Then he goes on saying that the Qur'an says that Allah made it easy!

http://us1.harunyahya.com/Detail/T/7EZU2FZ0164/productld/8190/marya m_and_the_birth_of_jesus

I will quote Mr. Harun's words, and notice in here how bad it is for a woman to deliver a child. But because this claim is made for a different issue, it was about that Allah a lot to eases Mary delivery. It was not about the fluid in the womb but rather about the effortless at giving birth by a stream of water and by shaking the palm tree.

Quote from Mr. Harun:
> "Allah fully supported Maryam throughout her pregnancy. It is very difficult for a woman to give birth, a potentially life-threatening experience, all alone, without medical equipment or a midwife's assistance. Nevertheless, Maryam overcame all of these difficulties by placing her complete trust in Allah."

As you notice, women giving birth is not easy anymore for Mr. Harun and suddenly it became like a horror movie because now the target is different.

> The pains of labor drove her to the trunk of a date-palm. She said, "Oh if only I had died before this time and was something discarded and forgotten!"
>
> A voice called out to her from under her, "Do not grieve! Your Lord has placed a small stream at your feet. Shake the trunk of the palm towards you and fresh, ripe dates will drop down onto you." (Surah Maryam, 23-25)

> "Then He eases the way for him." (Qur'an, 80:20)

It is very well known that half a million of women and babies die every year during labor. The following is **from the authority for health within the United Nations**.

Q: Why do so many women still die in pregnancy or childbirth?

Question and answer archives
Submit a question

A: Every minute, at least one woman dies from complications related to pregnancy or childbirth – that means 529,000 women a year.

http://www.who.int/features/qa/12/en/index.html

Trying to fabricate things does not help Allah. Rather, it raises questions to why Muslims try hard to create these claims out of simple words "we ease his way."

It's clear that they repeat whatever they've been told, but think no one else will go search for the information. And since we spoke about human birth, we have to speak about death.

that will lead us to coming claim;

http://www.harunyahya.com/en/Makaleler/8190/Maryam-and-the-birth-of-Jesus

Allah advised Maryam to eat ripened dates to give birth easy!

Mr. Harun Said; "**Eat Dates:**
Allah advised Maryam to eat freshly ripened dates. Today, such dates are considered to be food and medicine. Scientists now know that dates contain more than ten substances considered essential for the human body's well-being and continuing health."
"**Modern medical findings suggest that dates benefit women who are almost ready to give birth.** Doctors now advise pregnant women to take fructose-containing foods on their due dates, for such foods provide energy used by the weakened body to revitalize itself, have a trigger effect on the milk hormones and thus help the woman's body produce milk, and also increase the volume of that milk.
This information reveals some of the wisdom inherent in Allah's advice to Maryam."

Now honestly when I read Muslims science claims in the Qur'an I feel sad for them, at the same time it makes me angry, because I always I ask my self if these are people who love God, why do they to try make us believe in their god by making up lies?

If we read together the Qur'an shall notice easy the deception in the above claim.

- First Mary already gave birth, and then after the delivery, she heard a voice from her underneath, telling her not to worry your lord provided you a spring of water underneath, and she have the palm tree above her to eat from.
- The dates are good for giving birth this is true but the woman need to start eating at least one month before her date of delivery. We quote **"Women who ate dates daily during their ninth months** were less likely than non-date eaters to need medication to start labor or to help it keep progressing, a new study published in the *Journal of Obstetrics and Gynecology* found. They were also more dilated upon arrival at the hospital and labored seven hours less." click here to read more http://www.fitpregnancy.com/pregnancy/labor-delivery/three-surprising-tips-easier-labor
- Did he say **"Allah's advice to Maryam"**? That is the most idiotic claim I ever heard from a Muslim, because the one is talking in the verse was talking from underneath her, Mary is on the top of Allah? from his translation I quote "**A voice called out to her from under her**"
- Therefor this is can't be Allah then who? The fact the absurd thing about the Qur'an, that until now no Muslim able to give an answer who was it because Qur'an is meant to be the book of confusion, the Pearson or the voice was talking from underneath of Mary, some say it was Jesus, others said its Jibrel, but this is the first time ever I see a Muslim announce its Allah.
- The logic says, it's Jesus because she is giving birth and as Qur'an proclaimed that Jesus spoke when right after his birth, as in **Qur'an 19:29 "Then she pointed to him. They said: "How can we talk to one who is a child in the cradle?"**
- To show you how confused Muslims are about it let read this translation of Muhsin Khan, Qur'an 19:24 "Then [the babe 'Iesa (Jesus) or Jibrael (Gabriel)] cried unto her from below her, saying: "Grieve not! Your Lord has provided a water stream under you;"
- From Ibn Kathir we quote, (Then cried unto her from below her,) "This is referring to 'Isa bin Maryam." moreover, 'Abd Alur-Razaq narrated from Ma`mar that Qatadah said that Al-Hasan said, "This is referring to her (Mary)son (`Isa)." This is also one of the two opinions reported from Sa`eed bin Jubayr -- that it was her son, 'Isa, speaking.
- So, she was told after Jesus birth not before it to eat dates
- But the only person among a billion Muslim who said its Allah speaking from underneath is Harun Yahya, just to serve his fabricated scientific miracles.
- How can a woman shake the trunk of palm tree?
- Allah must be talking about Samson. Not even twenty strong men

can shake the trunk of a date-palm tree.

As long as we are talking about women giving birth then we need to talk about things nobody knows except Allah. Muhammad said in the hadith of the book of Sahih Al-Bukhari:

Sahih Al-Bukhari, Book 2, Hadith # 47
Sahih Al-Bukhari, Book 60, Hadith # 300
> *"Five things which nobody knows with the exclusion of Allah. The Prophet then counted the knowledge of the Hour is with Allah (alone). He sends down the rain, and knows what is in the wombs."(Qur'an 31:34).*

In this hadith, we have two things combined together, we have:

> *"34 it is Allah only who has the knowledge of the hour, and when He sends down rain, and He Who knows what is in the wombs. Nor does anyone know what it is that he will earn on the morrow: Nor does anyone know in what land he is to die. Allah is all knowledgeable was of all things." (Qur'an 31:34)*

So, what we understand from both hadiths and the Qur'an is the following:

- Only Allah knows what's inside a woman's womb, which basically means that the only thing he knows is the sex of the child: girl or boy. It also means that Allah is an ultrasound machine, which is found today in every birth clinic. Since no one knows what is inside women's wombs except Allah, we have no other choice except to announce that the ultrasound machine is the God of Islam.
- No one knows what is going to its going to rain except Allah. By this we know how the weather news station gets its weather forecast – whether it will rain or snow. Allah must be providing them the information.

***

Since we are talking about giving birth, maybe we should talk about death in Islam.

Death in Islam is a person in the shape of a ram

Qur'an 19.39
Sahih Al-Bukhari, Book 60, hadith 254

It narrated by Abu said, Al-Khudri: Allah's Messenger said, "On the Day of Resurrection, Death will be brought forward to you in the shape of a black and white ram. Afterwards, a shout-maker will shout 'O people of Paradise!' Therefore, they will extend their necks and look around carefully. The caller will say, 'Do you know who this is?' They will say, 'Yes, we do. This is Death.' along after that, all of them will have seen it. Afterwards, it will be broadcasted again, 'Oh people of Hell!' They will extend their necks and look around carefully. The caller will say, 'Do you know who this is?' They will say, 'Yes, we do. This is Death.' And after then, all of them will have seen it. Afterwards, that ram will be slain, and the caller will say, 'Oh people of Paradise! Immortality for all of you and no death, Oh people of Hell! Immortality for you and no death.' Then the Prophet, recounted and admonished them of the Day of suffering when the time came, while for now they are in a state of carelessness (i.e. the humans worldwide), and they do not believe.'

- According to the story, Death is a person.
- Then Allah will kill this person [Mr. Death]
- Do you Know how you can kill Death?
- The purpose of killing Death is to make us live forever.
- When in fact, death is the non-existence of LIFE and nothing more. I think this is very pure science of Islam.
- Same as darkness, you do not need to create it, its already exist just eliminate the light and darkness will be there.

Muslims claim

The sequence in development of human organs

www.miraclesoftheQur'an.com/scientific_63.html
It is He Who has created hearing, sight and minds for you. What little thanks you show! (Qur'an, 23:78)

Allah brought you out of your mothers' wombs knowing nothing at all, and gave you hearing, sight and minds so that perhaps you would show thanks. (Qur'an, 16:78)

Say: "What do you think? If Allah took away your hearing and your sight and sealed up your hearts, what god is there, other than Allah, who could give them back to you?". (Qur'an, 6:46)

We created man from a mingled drop to test him, and We made him hearing and seeing. (Qur'an, 76:2)

The above verses refer to a number of senses given to human beings by Allah. These are always referred in a specific order in the Qur'an: hearing, sight, feeling and understanding.

My answer

Again, Muhammad is affected by the Bible.

Exodus 4:11

And the LORD said, unto him, Who hath made man's mouth? or who maketh the dumb, or deaf, or the seeing, or the blind? have not I the LORD"

1 John 1:1- ESV

1 That which was from the beginning, which we have heard, which we have seen with our eyes, which we have looked upon, and our hands have handled, of the Word of life;

However, I want to remind you that in the coming few pages we are going to refute all the claims regarding the human creation, without the need to mention the titles, one by one, as mentioned by Mr. Harun. If one of them is wrong the rest will be wrong. At the same time, what we will provide from the Qur'an and the words of Muhammad himself are all connected because all of them speak about one topic, which is about human creation. It starts from the stage of the sperm to the stage of complete embryo including what determines the gender of the baby, according to Islam.

Mr. Harun said, and we quote:

"These are always referred in a specific order in the Qur'an: hearing, sight, feeling and understanding".

This is absolutely false and we will show him examples from where

275

seeing comes before hearing;

> *(Qur'an 90:8-9)*
>
> *"Have We not made for him two eyes? (9) And a tongue and two lips?"*

In order to use the tongue or lips hearing is a must so its about hearing, and hearing is coming afterwards of eyes.

> *Qur'an 18:101 Shih International*
>
> *"Those whose eyes had been within a cover [removed] from My remembrance, and they were not able to hear."*

Qur'an 32:12 where seeing comes before hearing; Qur'an 22:46 where understanding comes before hearing and seeing.

In some verses heart (understanding) comes before hearing or seeing.

> *(Qur'an 16:108)*
>
> *"They are those upon whose hearts(understanding), hearing (ears) and sight (eyes) Allah has set a seal. And they are the unaware."*
>
> *(Qur'an 17:86)*
>
> *'And We have placed over their hearts covers, lest they understand it, and in their ears deafness'*
>
> *(Qur'an 22:46)*
>
> *Do they not travel through the land, so that their hearts may therefore, learn comprehension, and their ears may therefore, learn to hear? Sincerely, it is not their eyes that are blind, but their hearts, which are in their chests.*

As you see in this verse, a lot teaches about science according to Muslims because remember, they're the ones who made these verses about science. It is no longer about them being metaphorical. Therefore, according to Allah's science, we would understand from this verse the following:

1. Understanding is in the heart not in the brain.
2. Ears and Eyes came after understanding.
3. Therefore, according to Mr. Harun' logic, Allah is very wrong because this is not the correct order according to his claim.

In the Middle East, there is a street expression that goes like this: "the water to expose the false diver". Mr. Harun himself chose this verse for us claiming that it speaks about the stages of creation of the embryo. From his translation, we quote:

"It is He Who has created hearing, sight and minds for you. What little thanks you show!" (Qur'an, 23:78)

The verse has nothing to do with science, its speaking of Allah favor upon man kind that is all, they are desperate for a miracle because their proclaimed prophet never had any.

If you read the verse carefully, Allah is saying that someone calling him He, created hearing. He did not say created Ears, seeing not Eyes; and to make it simple for you, the Muslims in here speak about which organs started to develop first, which means in this stage there is no hearing, there is seeing and no duty or job or function to do. This is how Muslims make miracles out of nothing. But based on the claim we understand, the order of the creation was this:
1. Ears.
2. Eyes.
3. Brain.

This is absolutely false because the brain starts to develop before the ears and eyes, as we will show you, but for the sake of argument, if we assume that in the above verses, the stages of creation is accurate, this means Allah always spoke about our human organs by the stages of creation, then the Qur'an has a problem where in the following chapter we read:

Qur'an 2:7

"Allah hath set a seal on their hearts and on their hearing, and on their eyes, is a veil; great is the penalty they (incur)." Yusuf Ali Translation.

According to this verse, the stages are:
1. Heart.
2. Hearing.
3. Eyes.

Qur'an 46:26

"and we gave them and empowered them, and had assigned them with (1) ears and (2) eyes and (3) hearts; but their ears and eyes and hearts did not help them since they denied the revelations of Allah; and what they used to mock surrounding them."

According to this verse, the stages are:
♦   Ears.

♦ Eyes.
♦ Heart.

But according to science this is absolutely false because the heart is one of the first organs in the embryo to develop and the heart starts to beat about 16 or 18 days after the conception, which is the **fifth week** of pregnancy. The heart begins to pump fluid and in the same week, which is the fifth, the brain starts to also develop. The ears and eyes develop between the **sixth and seventh week**, which of course means after the heart has been created...and these all makes the Qur'an a very bad reference.

Surely, I am not a doctor and I don't claim to be one. But with the help of the Internet, you can get all the answers you seek. To be certain that I am giving you a very accurate information, please search the information yourself. Search for this article written in the American government's website:
"U.S. Department of Health and Human Services, Fetal development".
Or U.S. National Library of Medicine
http://www.nlm.nih.gov/medlineplus/ency/article/002398.htm

Since I'm speaking about this topic, let me then expose a contradiction in the Qur'an and a hadith regarding the stage of development of the embryo. The Qur'an, and the Hadith says in another verse, as we will read:

مسند أحمد ـ مُسْنَدُ الْمُكَثِّرِينَ مِنَ الصَّحَابَةِ ـ إن النطفة تكون في الرحم أربعين يوما على حالها لا تغير

حَدَّثَنَا هُشَيْمٌ أَنْبَأَنَا عَلِيُّ بْنُ زَيْدٍ قَالَ سَمِعْتُ أَبَا عُبَيْدَةَ بْنَ عَبْدِ اللهِ يُحَدِّثُ قَالَ قَالَ عَبْدُ اللهِ قَالَ رَسُولُ اللهِ صَلَّى اللهُ عَلَيْهِ وَسَلَّمَ إِنَّ 3543 النُّطْفَةَ تَكُونُ فِي الرَّحِمِ أَرْبَعِينَ يَوْمًا عَلَى حَالِهَا لَا تَغَيَّرُ فَإِذَا مَضَتِ الْأَرْبَعُونَ صَارَتْ عَلَقَةً ثُمَّ مُضْغَةً كَذَلِكَ ثُمَّ عِظَامًا كَذَلِكَ فَإِذَا أَرَادَ ـ أَشَقِيٌّ أَمْ سَعِيدٌ أَقَصِيرٌ أَمْ طَوِيلٌ أَنَاقِصٌ 375 اللهُ أَنْ يُسَوِّيَ خَلْقَهُ بَعَثَ إِلَيْهَا مَلَكًا فَيَقُولُ الْمَلَكُ الَّذِي يَلِيهِ أَيْ رَبِّ أَذَكَرٌ أَمْ أُنْثَى «ـ ص أَمْ زَائِدٌ قُوتُهُ وَأَجَلُهُ أَصَحِيحٌ أَمْ سَقِيمٌ قَالَ فَيَكْتُبُ ذَلِكَ كُلَّهُ فَقَالَ رَجُلٌ مِنَ الْقَوْمِ فَفِيمَ الْعَمَلُ إِذَنْ وَقَدْ فُرِغَ مِنْ هَذَا كُلِّهِ قَالَ اعْمَلُوا فَكُلٌّ سَيُوَجَّهُ لِمَا خُلِقَ لَهُ

Book of Musnad Ahmad/Musnad AL-Mukthren, p. 375, Hadith # 3543:

The prophet said, the sperm will stay in the women's womb for forty days, as sperm without any changes at all, when the forty days are over it will turn into a blood clot, then it will change into a piece of flesh, after that into the fetus, afterwards, Allah will send his angel, therefore, the angel will say: "O Lord, male or female? Happy or sad? Short or tall? Weak or strong? Healthy or sick? As a result, it would be written for him all of this in his destiny." Then a man said, "Why do we do good deeds?" The prophet responded, "Your work, it would be instructed by Allah!!!"

The same story is referenced in:
Sahih Muslim, Book 033, Hadith # 6392
Sahih Muslim, Book 033, Hadith # 6395

But before we continue where Muhammad got this story from again it's in
(**The Legends of the Jews V.1**) as we read:

> *"When a woman has conceived, the Angel of the Night,
> Lailah, carries the sperm before God, and God decrees what
> manner of human being shall become of it--whether it shall
> be male or female, strong or weak, rich or poor, beautiful or
> ugly, long or short, fat or thin, and what all its other qualities
> shall be."*

Sahih Muslim, Book 033, Hadith # 6391

*The prophet said, the sperm will stay in the women's womb
for forty days as sperm.*

Sahih Muslim Book 033, Hadith 6390
Sahih Al-Bukhari, Book 55, Hadith 549
According to Abdullah (bin Masud) that the Messenger of Allah regarding
your creation Allah will. Brings together the constituents of one of you for
**(1) forty days in his mother's belly in the form of blood, and then (2)
it will become a blood clot in another period of forty days. (3) Then
it will become a piece of flesh and forty days later** Allah will send an
angel to it with instructions concerning four things, so the angel writes his
livelihood, and his death, his deeds, his fortune and misfortune.

صحيح البخاري ـ كِتَاب الْقَدَر ـ إن أحدكم يجمع في بطن أمه أربعين يوما ثم علقة مثل ذلك ثم يكون مضغة مثل ذلك
حَدَّثَنَا سُلَيْمَانُ بْنُ حَرْبٍ حَدَّثَنَا حَمَّادُ بْنُ أَبِي بَكْرِ بْنِ أَبِي بَكْرٍ عَنْ أَنَسِ بْنِ مَالِكٍ رَضِيَ اللَّهُ عَنْهُ عَنِ النَّبِيِّ صَلَّى اللَّهُ 6222
عَلَيْهِ وَسَلَّمَ قَالَ وَكَّلَ اللَّهُ بِالرَّحِمِ مَلَكًا فَيَقُولُ أَيْ رَبِّ نُطْفَةٌ أَيْ رَبِّ عَلَقَةٌ أَيْ رَبِّ مُضْغَةٌ فَإِذَا أَرَادَ اللَّهُ أَنْ يَقْضِيَ خَلْقَهَا قَالَ أَيْ رَبِّ أَذَكَرٌ
أَمْ أُنْثَى أَشَقِيٌّ أَمْ سَعِيدٌ فَمَا الرِّزْقُ فَمَا الْأَجَلُ فَيُكْتَبُ كَذَلِكَ فِي بَطْنِ

Sahih Al-Bukhari, Book of AL-Qader hadith, 6222 (Arabic)

> *The Messenger said, Allah commits an angel to be responsible
> for the uterus, and the angel says, 'O Lord, it is sperm! O Lord,
> it is at this point a clot! O Lord, it is right now a piece of flesh.'
> And after that, if Allah wishes to finish its creation, the angel
> inquires 'O Lord, a male or a female? Miserable and wicked
> deeds or joyful? How much will his provisions be? What will
> his age be?' Subsequently all that is written while the being is
> still in the mother's uterus. (Sahih Al-Bukhari, Book 77,*

Hadith 594)

صحيح البخاري ـ كِتَاب بَدْءِ الْخَلْقِ ـ فأتيت بطست من ذهب ملئ حكمة وإيمانا فشق من النحر إلى مراق البطن ثم غسل البطن بماء زمزم

3036 حَدَّثَنَا الْحَسَنُ بْنُ الرَّبِيعِ حَدَّثَنَا أَبُو الْأَحْوَصِ عَنْ الْأَعْمَشِ عَنْ زَيْدِ بْنِ وَهْبٍ قَالَ عَبْدُ اللَّهِ حَدَّثَنَا رَسُولُ اللَّهِ صَلَّى اللَّهُ عَلَيْهِ وَسَلَّمَ ص ـ «‏ إِنَّ أَحَدَكُمْ يُجْمَعُ خَلْقُهُ فِي بَطْنِ أُمِّهِ أَرْبَعِينَ يَوْمًا ثُمَّ يَكُونُ عَلَقَةً مِثْلَ ذَلِكَ ثُمَّ يَكُونُ مُضْغَةً 1175 وَهُوَ الصَّادِقُ الْمَصْدُوقُ قَالَ إِنَّ مِثْلَ ذَلِكَ ثُمَّ يَبْعَثُ اللَّهُ مَلَكًا فَيُؤْمَرُ بِأَرْبَعِ كَلِمَاتٍ وَيُقَالُ لَهُ اكْتُبْ عَمَلَهُ وَرِزْقَهُ وَأَجَلَهُ وَشَقِيٌّ أَوْ سَعِيدٌ ثُمَّ يُنْفَخُ فِيهِ الرُّوحُ فَإِنَّ الرَّجُلَ مِنْكُمْ لَيَعْمَلُ حَتَّى مَا يَكُونُ بَيْنَهُ وَبَيْنَ الْجَنَّةِ إِلَّا ذِرَاعٌ فَيَسْبِقُ عَلَيْهِ كِتَابُهُ فَيَعْمَلُ بِعَمَلِ أَهْلِ النَّارِ وَيَعْمَلُ حَتَّى مَا يَكُونُ بَيْنَهُ وَبَيْنَ النَّارِ إِلَّا ذِرَاعٌ فَيَسْبِقُ عَلَيْهِ الْكِتَابُ فَيَعْمَلُ بِعَمَلِ أَهْلِ الْجَنَّةِ

Allah's Messenger said: "About the issue of your creation, each one of you are placed in the womb of his mother (as a sperm) for the first forty days, and after that he comes to be a clot, and then you will be a clot for the coming forty days, and after that you will be transformed to a piece of meat for another forty days. Afterwards Allah sends an angel, and he will be ordered by four words, to write, four destinies; he writes his (the baby's) deeds, time of his death, means of his subsistence and whether he will be miserable (infidel) or blessed in a religious meaning. Afterwards, it will be breathed the soul into his body. So, a man will do the deeds of people of heaven and only the distance of an arm is between him and the heaven, then what has been written by the angel supersedes, and so he starts doing deeds of the people of hell fire and enters hell fire. Identical a person may do deeds and work of hell fire subsequently the deeds which are written to him by the angels will be in command to surpass, so he will change to do the work of the people of paradise, so he enters paradise.

This means, as Muhammad is saying, that:

1. "The prophet said, the sperm will stay in the women's womb for forty days as sperm without any change at all." Is that what science teaches? A sperm cannot live for more than 5-7 days max. Not forty as Muhammad claimed.
2. Science proves that by the third week, the embryo has already developed all the organs' system. But for Muhammad there is still only sperm.
3. It becomes a blood clot in another forty-day period.
4. Forty days later, it becomes a piece of flesh.

To learn more, visit the Indiana University's website or just search this title: **"Human Reproduction and Development"**.

Now Mr. Harun and all the other Muslims use the name of Dr. Keith

Moore who wrote a paper, not a book, about some verses in the Qur'an dated year 1986 which is more than 26 years ago. What's funny is that Dr. Moore never converted to Islam. He made that paper upon request because he was invited to Saudi Arabia at that time.

We need to remember that what was science 30 years ago is nothing compared to what science is today. At that time, doctors had no computers, and all of us know that computers revolutionized science.

We will use the hadiths above. It will give us a big hand in exposing the false claim and the Qur'an's error.

This entire claim is based on this:

That paper is published in the Journal of the Islamic medical, which is found in this link:
http://jima.imana.org/article/view/8693/18_1-15-17

And after reading it carefully I found out that Dr. Keith Moore was a victim of a false translation of the Qur'an. From his article, we quote:
"This statement is a from sura 23:14 the word "Alaca" refers to a leech or bloodsucker. This is an appropriate description of the human embry".

As an example, regarding the translation of Qur'an 23:14, they translated to him the word "**Aalaqa**" as *leech or bloodsucker* in order for him to be misled by the word's meaning. Dr. Moore was speaking maybe with honesty based on what the Muslims told him, because he himself does not know Arabic. You can go and read all the Islamic translation for this verse and you will see not even one of them translated the word "**Aalaqa**" as *leech or bloodsucker*. Now ask yourself if this is truly the real meaning of the word. Why do all the Muslims
Muslims claim translation never comes with such translation? All the translations come either as a **clot or congealed blood**, but you will not find one of them using the word leech or bloodsucker and that is for a very simple reason: it is an absolute lie. You can check it out yourself with any of the following translators: Yusuf Ali, Muhammad H. Shakir, Muhammad Pickthall, Mohsin Khan.

Accordingly, based on the false translation, Dr. Moore made this paper. I think he made this paper when he was eating his breakfast because chapter 23:14 says that the sperm transforms into blood. Even with the fussy translation he was given with which says that the sperm transforms into a leech and that each according to his paper is the woman's egg, then how in the world can he accept that?

{"Then we made out the chewed lump bones, and they closed

the bones in flesh". The continuation of Surah 23:14 indicates that out of the chewed lump stage, bones and muscles form. This is in accordance with embryological development. First the bones form as cartilage models and then the muscles (flesh) the global around them from the somatic mesoderm. "Then we developed out of it another creature".

The next par of surah 23:14 implies that the bones and muscles result in the formation of another creature. This mirror affair to the humanlike embryo that forms by the end of the eighth week."}

It's very clear that Dr. Moore has a very wrong understanding of what the Qur'an stated. The Qur'an did not say that bones and flesh are created altogether simultaneously because of what he called as "**cartilage models" is not considered bones.** Yet in the Qur'an, the words are so clear that he made from the clot a chewed lump and that lump transformed into bones. As the hadith showed us, the timeline for these stages is 40 days each which is a total of 120 days. This means the baby is created and ready to get out from his mother's womb in four months.

And this is why Muhammad forbade women from leaving their houses during a period of 3 months, after divorcing. The reason is because Muhammad thought these women might have a baby in a stage of creation. He thought that if they got remarried and had sexual intercourse before the end of the 3-month period, the new husband's sperm would mix with the sperm of the old husband. Then, no one would know who fathered the baby. Referenced in:

Qur'an 2:228

Divorced women should keep themselves away from any sexual relationships during three (monthly) menstrual cycles, and it is not lawful for them to hide that which Allah hath created in their wombs if they are believers in Allah and the Last Day.

Since Allah is the one who asked these women to wait for three months, it proves that the Muslims
Muslims claim
 god has a better understanding of women's menstrual cycle. If you ask any Muslim what is the point for a woman to wait for three months before she can remarry, the answer will be to know who the father of the baby is and to be certain that she is not pregnant from the previous husband. But scientifically, how many menstrual cycles does it take for women to know if they are pregnant? It's a basic knowledge that if a woman misses her menstrual cycle, it is an evident sign of pregnancy. Therefore, what is the

need for three menstrual cycles? Nothing at all! It only displays the ignorance of the person who made the verse.

Questions

What does "**chewed**" mean? From dictionary.com's English dictionary, we find the meaning:

> *to crush, damage, injure, etc., as if by chewing (often followed by up): The faulty paper feeder chewed the letters up.*

Take note that it is not my translation of the word "**chewed**". It was written the paper of Dr. Moore as it was given to him by the Muslims. So, don't come to me and tell me it's the wrong word. I am using the article of which Muslims are so proud about.

Is a woman's egg not even mentioned in the Qur'an can be called or considered a chewed lump? The answer is negative as a chewed lump is a piece of meat that's been chewed, which means destroyed; when in reality the egg of the women is not destroyed, it is the opposite. It's the start of creation of a human being's body.

To learn more, visit the Indiana University's website; or just search this title: "**Human Reproduction and Development**".

This will lead to a big problem for the Muslims. Since they accept the words of Dr. Moore as a reference, they have to agree with him in this. This means, Dr. Moore even agrees that there is nothing about forming bones first, because he never said that. At the same time, he said Mesoderm is going to make mesenchymal cells. Then these cells will make muscles, and can make bones.

This is another big problem for the Muslims. Since they accept the words of Dr. Moore as a reference, they have to agree with him that sperm is not turning into blood and it's not the blood that is making flesh and bones but the Mesoderm!

ثُمَّ خَلَقْنَا النُّطْفَةَ عَلَقَةً فَخَلَقْنَا الْعَلَقَةَ مُضْغَةً فَخَلَقْنَا الْمُضْغَةَ عِظَامًا فَكَسَوْنَا الْعِظَامَ لَحْمًا ثُمَّ أَنْشَأْنَاهُ خَلْقًا آخَرَ ۚ فَتَبَارَكَ اللَّهُ أَحْسَنُ الْخَالِقِينَ
(سورة المؤمنون , Al-Mumenoon, Qur'an 23:14)

> We made the sperm into a clot, and the clot into congealed blood, and we made the congealed blood into bones, and we dressed the bones with flesh.

This means we have:

Sperm-drop —Into→ Congealed-blood —Into→ Chewed Lump —Into→ Bones

Does science agree that sperm turns into a clot?

"And the clot into congealed blood" equals dead blood! Then dead blood makes a baby?

I advise Dr. Moore to carefully study Muslims translations and be aware of the deception of Allah.

The sperm of the man (Nu'tfah)
http://www.miraclesoftheQur'an.com/scientific_57.html

I read long pages of articles and I could not find one thing in that article that had to do anything with Islam or the Qur'an. You can visit the link yourself and see what I'm talking about. This is exactly what Muslims do: they try to convince you that science matches perfectly with the verses of the Qur'an. It is simply nothing but a joke. Anyway, what we provided as evidence is enough to destroy the Qur'an regarding any claims that the it speaks of about the creation of human being. There was nothing more information to share for the sake of education so you can defeat their claims by your own.

A woman's egg is fertilized by one sperm
or a drop of sperm

> *Qur'an 56:57-59*
>
> *57It is We Who have created you: why will ye not accept the Truth?*
>
> *58Do you not see your sperm-drop?*
>
> *59Is it you who creates, or are we the Creators?*

Muslims try to convince us that the verse speaking about one sperm or semen is scientifically proven to be true that only one sperm will fertilize the egg.

> *Qur'an 75:36-37*
>
> *36Does man thinks he is made without orders?*
>
> *37Was he not a drop of sperm that was spilled?*

Some Muslims do admit it is a single sperm that fertilizes the egg, but in the Sura (a sura is a chapter) it says: **drop of semen**. A drop of human male semen contains on average about 200 plus million sperms.

Qur'an 75:37, Yusuf Ali's translation
Was he not a drop of sperm emitted (in lowly form)?

Let us see what the word "**Nu'tfah**" means in the Islamic dictionary. Lisan AL Arab dictionary has called (**Nu'tfah**) as little water.

وروي عن النبي، صلى الله عليه وسلم، أنه قال: لا يزالُ الإسلامُ يزيد وأهله ويَنْقُصُ الشِّرك وأهله حتى يسير الراكب بين النُّطْفتين لا
يخشى إلا جوراً؛ أراد بالنطفتين بحر المشرق وبحر المغرب، فأما بحر المشرق فإنه ينقطع عند نواحي البصرة، وأما بحر المغرب
فمُنْقَطَعُه عند القُلزم؛ وقال بعضهم: أراد بالنطفتين ماء الفُرات وماء البحر

> *"Reported from the Prophet Muhammad that he said: There is still Islam and it grows by its family, and decreases "Shirk" (means paganism) and his family, so he as the passenger will travel between Alntftin (meaning two nu'tfah or between two sperms) not afraid but the bad; wanted Alntftin Sea, the East and the sea, of the West, he meant sea of Iraq and sea of Rome. Some said, it's the Euphrates and the sea"*

As we see the word **Nu'tfah** can be a little water or even a sea. Either way, it can't be what science says.

Another example of the error of the Muslims
Muslims claim
claim, one drop of water is not one part of the water. It is many particles of the structure of waters that complete its make-up. Let's look at the definition of drop in the following Tafsir.

Tanwîr al-Miqbâs min Tafsîr Ibn Abbâs- 75:37
Was he not Abu Jahl, who was made from a drop of fluid?

This Tafsir emphasizes "drops" not drop. The Oxford dictionary defines drop as a small round pear-shaped portion of liquid. A drop has many parts, not just ONE part.

Al-Jalalayn 75:37
Was he not! Indeed, he was a drop of SPERM

The Muslims claim that we are made from sperm. However, observable science shows that the sperm ONLY fertilizes the ovum (egg of the female) and dies shortly after the fertilization process. EVEN IN HERE we have one more mistake, not a science. No man was created from a sperm-drop. I will accept it metaphorically, but as science, it's purely a mistake. As long as the Muslims made it about science, we cannot consider it as a metaphorical word.

The author of this book is not making a scientific claim here. He is only stating that this is a false claim of the Muslim community.

The gender of the baby

> Mr. Harun's translation: "Does man reckon he will be left uncontrolled [without purpose]? Was he not once a drop of ejected semen?" (Qur'an, 75:36-37)

Muslims attempt at explaining how the gender of the baby is determined.

> Qur'an 53:45-46
> 45 That He created you in pairs male and female,
> 46 From a spilled sperm-drop.

In verse 45 you might notice that there is a scientific mistake saying that God created things in pairs, which means males and females from everything that have supposedly been created by Allah. It's very clear that Allah did not know anything about bacteria, which is actually the major population of this earth. We are now about 7 billion humans but in the case of bacteria, there are trillions of trillions, all over the earth living in water, ice, air, and even inside our body. Actually, our life itself would be impossible without them and it is very obvious that Allah did not know that bacteria do not have gender and that they do not reproduce themselves by sexual-intercourse. I gave the bacteria as an example and you can search yourself and find many other species living on earth which are one-cell creatures with no gender. Someone might say that the verse above about Allah speaking to mankind is not talking about every kind of creation. This is true if the Qur'an had not said this verse:

> Qur'an 36:36

> Praise be to Allah, Who created in pairs all things that the earth manufactures, as well as yourself and other things of which they have no knowledge of.

Child Resemblance to who orgasms first?

How does a child resemble his father or mother?

Since Muslims are opening the pages of science and claim that their prophet teaches nothing wrong, let us read together and find out how Muhammad understood the reasons for a child to resemble his mother or his father.

In the interpretation of A'hkam AL Qur'an Vol. 4, p. 80, by Ibn {Al-'arabi Qur'an 42: 49 {the Almighty said:

> "To Allah the kingdom of the heavens and the earth. He creates what he wills, he grants females to whom he wills, and he grants males to whom he wills." (Usama Dakdok translation), as the prophet said: if the man has orgasm first before the women the baby will be a boy, if the women has orgasm first the baby will be a girl.}

the same can be found in Sahih al-Bukhari 3938, Book 63, Hadith 164, English (Vol. 5, Book 58, Hadith 275)

> "As for the child, if the man's discharge before the woman's discharge, the child attracts the similarity to the man, and if the woman's discharge proceeds the man's, then the child attracts the similarity to the woman."

مسألة: الجزء الرابع80أحكام القرآن لابن العربي]ص:[
سورة الشورى فيها ثمان آيات « الآية الثامنة قوله تعالى لله ملك السموات والأرض يخلق ما يشاء
الآية الثامنة قوله تعالى : } لله ملك السموات والأرض يخلق ما يشاء يهب لمن يشاء إناثا ويهب لمن يشاء الذكور أو يزوجهم ذكرانا
وإناثا ويجعل من يشاء عقيما إنه عليم قدير {
كما قال النبي صلى الله عليه وسلم: } إذا سبق ماء الرجل ماء المرأة أذكرا ، وإذا سبق ماء المرأة ماء الرجل أنثا {

The interpretation of Ibn Kathir, Vol. 2, p. 75, print year 2002, Qur'an 3:93

A group of Jewish taking the prophet, and he said, to him we have five questions for you Abu Qasim (Qasim is Muhammad's nickname. Abu Quasim means "Father of Qasim"), if you give us the correct answers that prove you to be a prophet, we will follow you. The prophet said: May Allah be my witness on you, as Allah requested upon the children of Israel quoting from (Qur'an 12:66), he said, give me your questions. They said, (the Jews): what is the sign of the prophet hood? He (Muhammad) said: "his eyes are asleep but his heart never." The Jews said: tell us what causes the pregnant women to deliver male or female? He (Muhammad) said: "the water of the man and the woman met together, therefore, if the man has orgasm first the baby would be a boy, and if the women has orgasm first, the baby would be a female." The Jews said: tell us what Israel forbade upon himself? He (Muhammad) said: "he was ill by Sciatica, therefore, he found that only milk would fit with him which is etc. etc.

"Ibn Kathir said: created by Imam Ahmad, he meant the camel's so he forbade eating it." The Jews answered; you said,

the truth, and they continued asking what is the thunder? He (Muhammad) said: "he is one of the angels in charge of the clouds by his hand or in his hand a fire-belt he beats the cloud with it, and he drives the cloud in whatever direction Allah orders him to drive it to." The Jews said: what is That sound we hear? He (Muhammad) said: "it is his voice" (he meant the thunder sound is the voice of the angel). The Jews said: "you're telling the truth, there is one question left if you answer it will follow thee, every prophet has an angel to him deliver news, so tell us who is your angel who delivers the news to you?" He (Muhammad) said: "Jibrel (Gabriel)."

م2002هـ / 1422] تفسير ابن كثير سنة النشر: 75[الجزء الثاني]ص:

طريق أخرى : قال أحمد : حدثنا أبو أحمد الزبيري حدثنا عبد الله بن الوليد العجلي ، عن بكير بن شهاب ، عن سعيد بن جبير ، عن ابن عباس قال : أقبلت يهود على رسول الله صلى الله عليه وسلم ، فقالوا : يا أبا القاسم ، نسألك عن خمسة أشياء ، فإن أنبأتنا بهن [. قال : " هاتوا " 66عرفنا أنك نبي واتبعناك ، فأخذ عليهم ما أخذ إسرائيل على بنيه إذ قال : (الله على ما نقول وكيل) [يوسف : قالوا : أخبرنا عن علامة النبي ؟ قال : " تنام عيناه ولا ينام قلبه " . قالوا : أخبرنا كيف تؤنث المرأة وكيف تذكر ؟ قال : " يلتقي الماءان ، فإذا علا ماء الرجل ماء المرأة أذكرت ، وإذا علا ماء المرأة ماء الرجل آنثت . قالوا : أخبرنا ما حرم إسرائيل على نفسه ، قال : " كان يشتكي عرق النسا ، فلم يجد شيئا يلائمه إلا ألبان كذا وكذا ـ قال أحمد : قال بعضهم : يعني الإبل ـ فحرم لحومها " . قالوا : صدقت . قالوا : أخبرنا ما هذا الرعد ؟ قال : " ملك من ملائكة الله موكل بالسحاب بيده ، أو في يده ـ مخراق من نار ينزجر به السحاب ، يسوقه حيث أمره الله عز وجل " . قالوا : فما هذا الصوت الذي يسمع ؟ قال : " صوته " . قالوا : صدقت ، إنما بقيت واحدة ، وهي التي نتابعك إن أخبرتنا بها ، فإنه ليس من نبي إلا له ملك يأتيه بالخبر ، فأخبرنا من صاحبك ؟ قال : " جبريل عليه السلام "

You can read the Muslims
Muslims claim
 translation's website yourself where 90% of the story is gone. This is why I'm posting the original text in Arabic as it is.
http://www.theholybook.org/content/view/6705/2/

(Sahih Al-Bukhari, Book 60, Hadith # 7)

"And if a man discharges his water first before the woman, then the child resembles him; and if a woman discharges her water first before the man, then the child resembles her."

In this coming hadith Muhammad was asked this Question by some Jews;

"The Book of Menstruation, Chapter: Women are obliged to perform washing if they emit fluid "Anas b. Malik reported that the mother of Sulaim, that she asked the Messenger of Allah about a woman who sees in a dream what a man sees (sexual dreams). The Messenger of Allah answered her saying:

In case a woman sees that, she must take a bath. Mother of Sulaim said: I was shy on account of that and said: Does it happen? Upon this the Messenger of Allah said: Yes (it does happen), otherwise how can (a born child) resemble her? The Man's discharge (i. e. sperm) is thick and white and the discharge of woman is thin and yellow; so the resemblance comes from the one whose will be above or the one who had cum first prevail or dominate."

وَهَلْ يَكُونُ هَذَا فَقَالَ نَبِيُّ اللهِ صلى الله عليه وسلم " نَعَمْ فَمِنْ أَيْنَ يَكُونُ الشَّبَهُ إِنَّ مَاءَ الرَّجُلِ غَلِيظٌ أَبْيَضُ وَمَاءَ الْمَرْأَةِ رَقِيقٌ أَصْفَرُ فَمِنْ أَيِّهِمَا عَلاَ أَوْ سَبَقَ يَكُونُ مِنْهُ الشَّبَهُ "

In the Muslims translation, they provide false translation for this hadith as we read "Man's discharge (i. e. sperm) is thick and white and the discharge of woman is thin and yellow; so, the resemblance comes from the one whose genes prevail or dominate"
http://sunnah.com/muslim/3/32
But they forgot to match the false translation with other hadith books report the same hadith like Sunan Ibn Majah & Sahih Al-Bukhari which exposed their lies, as we read about the some Jews asking Muhammad this question;

"Why does a child resemble its father, and why does it resemble its maternal uncle" Allah's Apostle said, "Gabriel has just right now told me of their answers." ... If a man has sexual intercourse with his wife and gets discharge first, the child will resemble the father, and if the woman gets discharge first, the child will resemble her."

Bukhari Vol. 5, Book 58, Hadith 275

http://sunnah.com/bukhari/63/164

""O Messenger of Allah, does that really happen?" He said: "Yes, the water of the man is thick and white and the water of a woman is thin and yellow. Whichever of them comes first or predominates, the child will resemble (that parent)."

Book of Sunan Ibn Majah Vol. 1, Book 1, Hadith 601

For sure this is a falsification science proving to use one more that Muhammad is making things up and he claim that his answers come from God by the Angel Gabriel, so it's not his own answer but Allah answer as we noted in the hadith **"Gabriel has just right now told me**

of their answers."

From the above story, which came from Muhammad's mouth, we learn the following:
1. If you want to know why you look like your father, Muhammad has the answer: your father had orgasm first. Is it not amazing! Thanks to Muhammad, you can find out which of your parents had orgasm first!
2. All of us know that women can get pregnant without having any orgasm. Even doctors today are able to use sperm and fertilize the egg out of the body of the woman and still make it possible for the child to resemble his mother.
3. This hadith proves to us again that Muhammad considered the reason of women to be pregnant is her water, "sexual fluid," and that appears in Qur'an 86:6-7.
4. Don't forget! Muhammad explained in a scientific way what is the thunderbolt. According to him, an angel leads from place to place and the fire is his fire-belt, which he uses to lead the cloud as Allah wishes him to lead. This is an amazing science and by the way the same story about the thunder can be found in the Qur'an 13:13
   "And the thunder praises with his praise, and the angels, for fear of him. And he sends his thunderbolts, so he smites with it whom he will while they dispute concerning Allah." (Usama Dakdok translation)
5. Israel (Jacob) was ill by Sciatica, and his medication is camel milk? So this is why he forbade the slaughtering of the camel meat so no one kills it!

Allah made the Rats from the Jews!

What's funny is that in another hadith Muhammad said that Jews do not drink camel milk and proof is that rats are made of a group of Jews! Sahih Al-Bukhari, Book 54, hadith 524:

It is reported by Abu Huraira: The Prophet said, "A clan of children of Israel was lost. No person knows what they acted upon. However, I do not see them except that they were cursed (by Allah) and transfigured into rats, because if you put the milk of a she-camel in front of a rat, it will not drink it, but if you put in front of it the milk of a sheep, it will drink it." I told this to Ka'eb who asked me, "Did you hear this from the Prophet?" I said, "Yes." Ka'ebe asked me the same question several times; I said, to Ka'eb "Do I read the Torah? (i.e. I tell you this from the Prophet.)"

From the hadith above we learn;

- Rats are jews.
- If you ever killed a rat, I have bad news for you, you just killed a Jew and IDF will go after you!
- But they are orthodox Jews, they keep the law word by word and their food has to be kosher.
- Even after Allah transformed them into Rats but still they live as Jews, and eat only kosher food!
- That mean they keep the Sabbath, so rats do not go to work in Saturday?
- Do they have a synagogue in the underworld?
- Do not forget Allah said in Qur'an that he made Jews Pigs and Monkeys, and by adding this hadith we can add Rats too, to the chain of transformation.

Qur'an 5:60

"those whom He Allah has cursed and with whom He became angry and made of them monkeys, and pigs"

Qur'an 2:65

"And indeed, you knew those amongst you (the Jews) who transgressed in the matter of the Sabbath (keeping the Sabbath). We said to them: "Be you monkeys, sservile and tacky."

Why Allah made them Pigs and Monkeys? They did fishing in Saturday! Must be true story!

I wonder why Muslims don't make any articles about these hadiths. I think the answer is very well known and that is they know their prophet speaks foolishly. Best to hide the things he's said.

Sperm of Women & Sperm of men
You might not believe what I'm going to show you in the coming study. It's basic science that women do not have sperm. Allah however, doesn't necessarily agree with this science.

In Qur'an 86:6. He is created from a water gushing forth, 7. Proceeding from between the backbone and the ribs.

As we see it is so clear: sperm is coming from the back bone of men and the ribs of woman. But do women have sperm? Well Allah is saying that, so science must be wrong? and since when is men's sperm coming from bones?

From Ibn Kathir we read: "(Proceeding from between the backbone and the ribs.) meaning, the backbone (or loins) of the man and the ribs of the woman, which is referring to her chest."

Allah sent down 8 pairs of animals

Qur'an 39:6

It is He that created you from one soul: and he made a like of it from itself, and He sent you down eight pairs of animals "An'aam" in pairs, He created you, in the belly of your mothers, in creation after creation, in three veils of darkness.

Again, where Muhammad got his information about animals created in pairs its from The Legends of The Jews V1

"The Divine resolution to bestow a companion on Adam met the wishes of man, who had been overcome by a feeling of isolation when the animals came to him in pairs to be named...... Before the flood the number of unclean animals had been greater than the number of the clean. Afterward the ratio was reversed, because while seven pairs of clean animals were preserved in the ark, but two pairs of the unclean were preserved."

So, in the Legends of the Jews is 9 pairs of animal and I believe Muhammad made it eight to cover the copy.

The funny thing in here is that Muslims made many videos, articles and even books, but they never explained how Allah sent down eight pairs of animals. Is that because they knew it was false? I wonder, if we truly only had eight pairs of animals, how much would the Muslims be speaking about it? But because they know it's false, they simply sleep on it. Also, as long as the eight are in pairs, male and female, the eight would now turn into four. Do we only have four?

From Ibn Kathir's interpretation we read:

"And it is Allah who has sent to you cattle's in eight pairs." He (Allah) meant, He has created for mankind from among the cattle's, eight pairs. These are the ones that are mentioned in Surat Al-An'aam, eight kinds of them, which are a pair of

sheep's, a pair of goats, a pair of camels and a pair of oxen."

If you go to the English dictionary, you will find out that the word **cattle** not only those four kinds of animals, between all kinds of animals which live in groups, including donkeys, horses, swine, and many others and even a human being.

And it is the same in Arabic except that the word is used in the Qur'an as **An'aam**, which means in all kind of animals. And notice that Muslims did not make any article about this verse, because they cannot play with it much.

Conclusion:
- The word "**An'aam**" animals, means all kinds of animals, with no exceptions. By science there are six basic groups of animals: Invertebrates, Amphibians, Fishes, Reptiles, Mammals, and Birds. This would mean that Allah is wrong again if the Muslims are counting four kinds as eight, like two camels, two cows, two lambs and two goats. This means all other animals are not Allah's creation, because he is clearly saying eight kinds! Muslims might mostly defend the Qur'an by saying *eight* has a metaphorical meaning. So, the entire verse speaks of science except for the number here? How funny! It's a very clear mistake.
- To say that there are only 4 kinds of animals, as eight pairs, sent down from Allah is false.
- Let's see about the creation of the baby in the mother's womb!
- Do we really come from the mother's womb? I will let this one go because they will say it's metaphorical as always. Then let's go to the three darkness of Creation.
- I will see what Muhammad himself explains in this verse. He will help me expose the falsification!

As always, when you go to Ibn Kathir's interpretation in Arabic, you find that it has no match whatsoever with its English translation.

This is the link as an example of the English translation: www.qtafsir.com which doesn't even hold 10% of Ibn Kathir's original Arabic text. This is what Ibn Kathir, Vol. 7, p. 86 said, about the following verse in the Arabic book:

"and he made you in your mother's belly, creation after creation" that means he created you and your mother's belly, each of you were as sperm, then he became a clot, then he became a chewed lump, and then he would be created as flesh then bones and nerves, so Allah breathed into him then

became a new creation, and He is saying "in three darkness's"
He Allah meant; that darkness of the womb, the darkness of
the placenta which is membrane of production, and the
darkness of the belly."

وقوله: (يخلقكم في بطون أمهاتكم خلقا من بعد خلق) أي : قدركم في بطون أمهاتكم (خلقا من بعد خلق) أي : يكون أحدكم أولا
نطفة ، ثم يكون علقة ، ثم يكون مضغة ، ثم يخلق فيكون لحما وعظما وعصبا وعروقا ، وينفخ فيه الروح فيصير خلقا آخر ، ( )
[14فتبارك الله أحسن الخالقين)] المؤمنون :
وقوله: (في ظلمات ثلاث) يعني : ظلمة الرحم ، وظلمة المشيمة ـ التي هي كالغشاوة والوقاية على الولد ـ وظلمة البطن

Sahih Muslim Book 033, Hadith 6390

According to Abdullah (bin Masud) that the Messenger of
Allah regarding your creation Allah will. It brings together
the components of one of you for 1) forty days in his mother's
belly in the form of blood, and after that 2) it will become a
blood clot intended for another period of forty days. 3) Then it
will become a piece of flesh. In addition to forty days later,
Allah sends an angel to it with orders concerning four things,
so the angel writes his livelihood, and his death, his deeds, his
fortune and misfortune.

The Period of Pregnancy in Islam

In chapter 13:8, by the interpretation of Al-Qurtbi, Vol. 9, p. 251, the
scholars disagree about the maximum duration of pregnancy.

Reported from Ibn Gurij from Gamila Bint Sa'ed, from Aisha,
she said: "the maximum lenght of pregnancy is two years, the
same as the change of shadow of spindle (age of spindle
before it broke). Narrated by Al-drqani and Gamilah Bint
Sa'ed, the sister of 'Ubid Ibn Sa'ed, and narrated by Laith Ibn
Sa'ed, that the maximum length of pregnancy is three years.
And from the Imam Al-Shafie the maximum is four years, and
narrated by Imam Malik the most famous one, it's five years,
and even there is no limitation to how many years a woman
can be pregnant, even if it is more than ten years, and
according to Al Zuhri,said it is six to seven years.

Now notice with me how Muslims are confused about their book,
including those who lived in Muhammad's days. This goes even to
scholars who present the majority of the population on earth today such
as Imam Malik and Imam Al-Shafie.

For your reference, an "Imam" is a Muslim leader and a scholar. An
Imam is qualified to teach and give orders according to the book of
Muhammad.

From the interpretation of the Imam AL-Qur'tubi (AL Jame' LE-A'hkam AL-Qur'an) year 671 of Islamic year, he said, women can be pregnant according to **Al-Shafi'e, during 4 years.** According to **Malik, 5 years.** He also said that if a woman's pregnancy is more than 4 years, it might be up to 10 years! Also, in a third story, AL-Zouhry said, it might be up to 7 years. Abu 'Omar and other of the prophet's companions said, it's 7 years and Shafi'e said that the length of it is 4 years.

وعن الشافعي أربع سنين؛ وروي عن مالك في إحدى روايتيه، والمشهور عنه خمس سنين؛ وروي عنه لا حدّ له، ولو زاد على العشرة الأعوام؛ وهي الرواية الثالثة عنه. وعن الزّهري ست وسبع. قال أبو عمر: ومن الصحابة من يجعله إلى سبع؛ والشافعي: مُدّةٌ الغاية منها أربع سنين

As you see in this book, written 700 years after Muhammad, the Muslims are still accepting such teachings. All of this was intended to cover Muhammad's birth. His grandfather accepted Muhammad as a grandson by the same method. They cannot delete it and stay away from it. For sure Muslims will say these scholars are wrong but the fact is, it's the Qur'an that's stating these as we see in Qur'an 13:8. What these scholars are doing is just giving an interpretation to what Allah is saying. After all, isn't it what interpretation means?

> *Qur'an 13:8*
>
> *It's Allah, who knows what every womb will bear, and what wombs give in shorter or longer time or even exceed. Every single thing for Allah has the proportion.*

As you see here, Allah is not sure about the duration of pregnancies and he can't even explain how some are short and some exceed the allotted time!

We have some big names that maybe you guys didn't notice in the interpretation. Al-Shafi'l and Maliki present the majority of the Muslims in the world.

In this same page from Imam Al-Qur'tubi (AL Jame' LE-A'hkam AL-Qur'an) interpretation of Qur'an 13:8, we see this hadith:

> *"Oh, Abu Yahaya, please Prophet, pray for this woman. She has been pregnant for four years and is in a bad situation." So, Malik got angry and said, "What's wrong with these people? Don't they see we are prophets?!" Then he read and prayed saying, "Allah, if this woman has gas let it go? If she has a child, let her give birth." Afterwards the prophet came and said to that man (whose wife is pregnant for four years), "Go to your wife (she is giving birth)." And before the prophet*

left the mosque, the man came back with his new born son on his shoulder, and he was 4 years old and has curly hair and growing teeth and his umbilical cord is cut off.

إذ جاءه رجل فقال: يا أبا يحيى أدع لامرأة حبلى منذ أربع سنين قد أصبحت في كرب شديد؛ فغضب مالك وأطبق المصحف ثم قال: ما يرى هؤلاء القوم إلا أنا أنبياء! ثم قرأ، ثم دعا، ثم قال: اللهم هذه المرأة إن كان في بطنها ريح فأخرجه عنها الساعة، وإن كان في بطنها جارية فأبدلها (بها) غلاماً، فإنك تَمحُو ما تشاء وتُثُبِت، وعندك أمّ الكتاب، ورفع مالك يده، ورفع الناس أيديهم، وجاء الرسول إلى الرجل فقال: أدرك أمرأتك، فذهب الرجل؛ فما حطّ مالك يده حتى طلع الرجل من باب المسجد على رقبته غلام جَعْد قَطَطَ أبن أربع سنين، قد استوت أسنانه، ما قُطِعت سراره؛

In the interpretation of Qur'an 46:15 by Abu Baker AL-Razi, he said, Abu Ali Bin Sina (a big time, very knowledgeable Muslim scholar) Abu'l 'Ali al-Husayn b. 'Abd Allah Ibn Sina. Muslims are very proud about him as a physician and Ibn Sina's philosophy. This is the funniest thing about the corrupted Arab history. They call him an Arab scientist when he was not even born in any Arab land, nor is he an Arab.

Now let me show you that not everything you see on the internet or on TV is true. See if Ibn Sina is a great Persian physician! Let us see if Muslims will be proud after reading this:

أبو علي بن سينا: في الفصل السادس من المقالة التاسعة من عنوان الشفاء، بلغني من حيث وثقت" به بكل الثقة، أن امرأة وضعت بعد الرابع من سني الحمل ولداً قد نبتت أسنانه وعاش
"(هـ606تفسير مفاتيح الغيب، التفسير الكبير/ الرازي (ت

In the book of Tafsir Mafateh AL-Ghaeeb by the very knowledgeable Muslim scientist Abu Baker AL-Razi (look what the two of the biggest names of Islamic science say):

"Abu Ali Bin Sina in his chapter six in the ninth article named AL-Shifa' (healing), I have been informed with trust the knowledgeable results that a woman gave birth after four years of pregnancy and the boy's teeth were growing, and he lives"

He even said that the baby will be completed in full. The prophet said, he will be done (created) as a baby in 40 days in his mother womb. This is their bigtime scientist and they say his book was great education for all of Europe!

This is why Muhammad ordered Muslim women, whose husbands were missing, to not remarry until four years had passed, as we see in this hadith of 'Omar the Khalifa (King):

Malik's Muwatta. Book 29, Hadith 29.19.52
"The woman, which her husband is missing, has to wait for four years, before she can marry again.

In another hadith, The Book of AL-Iste'ab Vol. 3/1103, a man came to Khalift

> 'Omar and said, "I was in travel away from my wife for two years and when I came back, I found her pregnant." Then 'Omar asked, "Who is around?" If he maybe supposed to stone her! However, Ibn Ma'az said, "Well if you like to stone her, do not stone her baby!" So 'Omar agreed to let her give birth. However, when the woman gave birth to the child, his testicles were out (meaning, he is older than an infant, about 2 years old). The husband came to 'Omar and said, "I swear by Allah. The child is mine, and he looks like me!" So, 'Omar said thanks to Ma'az. If Ma'az had not advised me 'Omar going to hell. Which means, 'Omar accepts the man saying that it is his child, even if he had no sex with her for more than two years, and he was thanking Ma'az for the advice!

مؤمل بن إسماعيل كما رواه
في الاستيعاب 3/1103
أن رجلاً جاء إلى عمر بن الخطاب فقال: يا أمير المؤمنين! إني غبت عن آمرأتي سنتين فجئت وهي حبلى؛ فشاور عمر الناس في رجمها، فقال معاذ بن جبل: يا أمير المؤمنين! إن كان لك عليها سبيل فليس لك على ما في بطنها سبيل؛ فاتركها حتى تضع، فتركها، فوضعت غلاماً قد خرجت ثنيتاه؛ فعرف الرجل الشبه فقال: ابني وربّ الكعبة فقال عمر: عجزت النساء أن يلدن مثل معاذ؛ لو لا معاذ لهلك عمر

An example of judgment regarding the period of pregnancy

In the coming example, we will show you a real judgment made in an Islamic Court and approved by all the Islamic scholars. A judgment in Islam is called a "**Fatwa**" which is an Islamic judgment based on the Qur'an and the stories of Muhammad.

> "Fatwa number 18395. Date: June 27, 2002
>
> Question: What is the judgment regarding the women who had delivered a baby in two years after her husband's death. She is stated as a widow and she never remarried after his death.
>
> Answer: Praise be to Allah and peace into the prophet and his companions. If a woman is divorced or if her husband passed away and he did not remarry after but she gave birth after her husband's death by four years, the son will be considered to belong to the deceased husband. And after she gave birth to the baby she can go and remarry again, and this is according to the sect of Al-Maliki, Al-Shafie, Al-Hanbali, and Al Hanafi sect approved that up to two years only, and the majority of the scholars have this opinion and judgment

based on the hadith which proves that women can be brought up to four years as is mentioned in the book of Al-Daraqani, from Al-Walid Bin Muslim, that Aisha said to Malik Ibn 'Anas; "the maximum time of her pregnancy is two years" so he answered her saying praise be to Allah who said, that? This is our neighbor the wife of Muhammad Ibn 'Ajlan a faithful woman and her husband is a faithful man. She was pregnant three times within 12 years [4 years for each pregnancy]. And based on this the woman who gave birth as your question two years after her husband's death the child belongs to the deceased husband. As long as she did not marry another husband after his death, and this is approved by all Islamic sects.

And the biggest scholar of Islam Zakaria Al-Ansari may Allah bless his soul, said in the book "Asna Al-Ma'talrb" if the husband issued a final divorce order reversal one or canceled his marriage and did not deny the pregnancy of his divorced woman who gave birth for years after his divorce, regardless she Mary and your husband or she a did not after the waiting period is over (which mean the waiting Period can go up to four years) if she agreed that her waiting period is over or she did not agree still the child belong to the first husband(who was born four years after the divorce)."

If you speak Arabic you can read this Fatwa in the following Islamic site www.islamweb.net/fatwa/index.php?page=showfatwa&Option=Fatwald&lang=A&Id=18395

Do Muslims make any videos about this amazing science?
It's very clear that all Islamic scholars of Islam in the last 1400 years until now have the same exact understanding. So where did Mr. Harun got his science and discovery from? It's just a new way of deceiving. Muslims today know that science affects the minds of people and after exhausting every way to convince people to convert to this religion, they now need to use science.

Muslims claim

The region that controls our movements

No indeed! If he does not stop, We will grab him by the forelock, a lying, sinful forelock. (Qur'an, 96:15-16)

The expression "the lying, sinful forelock" in the above verse is most interesting. Research carried out in recent years has revealed that the prefrontal area, which is responsible for the management of particular functions of the brain, falsification in the frontal part of the skull. Scientists only discovered the functions of this area, which the Qur'an pointed out 1,400 years ago,
http://www.miraclesofthequran.com/scientific_52.html

My answer

Control of Movement

> *Qur'an 96:15-16 – Harun Yahya's translation*
>
> *"No indeed! If he does not stop, We will grab him by the forelock, a lying sinful forelock".*

At the end of the Muslim's explanation of this chapter (sura), none of the listed scientists' literature mentioned the word "forelock", but you can find it only in Muslims fabricated articles. after examining the scientists' books and material, these scientists don't support this Sura.
Since nothing was found to substantiate the Muslims
Muslims claim
 claim in the Sura that this is intracranial related, then the conclusion by definition is that this "forelock" is external to the brain. Forelock is referred to as a piece of hair, not intracranial (internal to the head). Many of us have heard the term a "lock" of hair, meaning a piece of hair. Oxfords English Dictionary defines forelock as hair growing just above the forehead.

Do scientists say that the control of movement is in our hair or is this Islamic science?
Looking at Arabic sources such as the (Shaker) English Arabic dictionary, which has 8 Arabic dictionaries, it confirms without a doubt that Sura 96:15-16 indeed refers to a lock of hair growing just above the forehead. This shows that the Muslim who is explaining this Sura is in gross error of its meaning and/or is deliberately trying to deceive his fellow Muslims and non-Muslims.

This following Tafsir shows that forelock is the hair:

Tafsir Al-Jalalayn 96:15

No for sure as punishment for him for his belief, We shall seize him by the forelock, We shall grab, drag him to the Fire by his forelock,

And all Muslims interpretations agree about it, but these new claims are something new with new waves of scientific Qur'an propaganda.

Even one of the proudest name in Islam he agrees that this is the Forelock front hair on the head.

Book of Tafsir Al-Qur'an by Imam Fakher Al-Deen Al-Razi he said: "we will Hold him from his forelock, and drag him in too fire, and word Safi' mean grapping and holding with strength, as He say(Allah):

Qur'an 55:41

"(For) the sinners will be known by their marks: and they will be seized by their forelocks and their feet"

أحدها : لنأخذن بناصيته ولنسحبنه بها إلى النار ، والسفع القبض على الشيء ، وجذبه بشدة ، وهو كقوله : (فيؤخذ بالنواصي والأقدام) [الرحمن : 41].

Tafsir al-Jalalayn, trans. Feras Hamza

"The guilty will be recognized by their mark: which is blackened faces and blue eyes; so, they will be seized by the forelocks and the feet."

Even in Harun Yahya's translation it says:
"We will **grab him by the forelock**, a lying sinful forelock"

It's clear that the verse is speaking about hair.

Qur'an 96:14

أَلَمْ يَعْلَم بِأَنَّ ٱللَّهَ يَرَىٰ

Did he not know that God sees?

Muslims are supposed to understand that Allah knows everything. Apparently, Allah doesn't, according to Muhammad.

Qur'an 96:16

A lying, sinful forelock!

Al-Jalalayn said this is just a description for the sinful forelock of Abu Jahel, Muhammad's uncle. In such terms it's meant figuratively, but what he actually meant was this individual, Abu Jahel.

This is not even about every human. It's about one **individual,** in this case, the uncle of Muhammad.

This Tafsir is talking about Muhammad's uncle, **Abdul Uzza Ibn Abed Al Mut'aleb and Muhammad named him as Abu Lahab which means the father of the flame** and also known as Abu Otbah who died in 624. He was a half-brother of Abdullah bin Abdul-Muttalib, Muhammad's father.

Abdul Uzza, his known nickname later was called Abu Jahl for refusing to accept Islam. Only two uncles of Muhammad accepted Islam after they lost war with him and even Abu Taleb who was like a father to Muhammad. Muslims claim that he accepted Islam in the last moment of his life when he was almost dying. Muhammad was trying hard to push him to accept Islam. Out of nine uncles, two became Muslims and out of six aunts, only one accepted Islam. These three individuals (the two uncles and one aunt) converted to Islam after losing the war against Muhammad. This is more proof that Muhammad was a false man.
And Muhammad men killed his uncle and torture him as we read:

It has been reported by Anas son of. Malik that the Messenger of Allah (Allah pray on him) said (after the encounter at Badr): Who will ascertain for us what has happened to Abu Jahl? Ibn Mas'ud went (to gather this information). He found that the two sons of 'Afra' had struck him and he lay cold at the point of death. He caught him by his beard and said: Art thou Abu Jahl? He said: is there anybody superior to the person you have killed, or it's his people have killed him. Ibn Mas'ud says that, according to Abu Mijlaz, Abu Jahl said: I wish it was someone not a goat shepherd would have killed me. (Sahih Muslim Book 019, Hadith 4434, Book 32, Hadith 144)

And its reported that prophet of Islam was extremely happy for killing him.
As we read in Book of Tafsir Al-Qur'an by Imam Fakher Al-Deen Al-Razi p 24

> *"Son of Massoud when he slit his ear and make thread in it and make dragged to the Messenger of Allah, peace be upon him and Jibril between his hands and he laughs, and says: 'O Muhammad authorized me (to laugh), but we got here his head with the ear, this is what been said in the killing of Abu Jahl"*

Imagine how savage this action, especially if you learn that Abu Jahel, not only his father brother (his uncle) but he was the father of two men was married to Muhammad daughters.

We go back to the claim again;

The fact in here is that the verse itself presents 2 big mistakes!

If somebody doesn't believe that Allah is their god, it doesn't mean they are lying. They are being honest. What does this have to do with lying? If Muhammad's uncle didn't believe in Allah, he wasn't lying. It was just his belief, nothing more.

If a Hindu says to a Christian, "My god is not Christ," can anyone accuse him of lying? No, because this is what this Hindu believes in. Lying is saying something knowing it's not true. Why would Muhammad accuse his uncle of lying when his uncle honestly did not believe in Allah as God and Muhammad as a prophet?

If someone says, "I believe a Satan ate my food," (Like a *jinni* eating a Muslim's food. The Muslims believe in jinn's, who are considered to be creatures made of gas and fire. They even believe Satan have sex with their women) they are in essence not lying because this is something the person truly believes in. As foolish as it seems that someone would actually believe a spirit would eat their food in the first place, and that Satan would have sex with their women, it is still something they faithfully believe in. **"The messenger of Allah said: Do not eat with your left hand, for the Satan eats with his left hand. (Sahih Muslim, Book 023, Hadith 5007)**

Also, the mistake in this verse is the word "forelock." its a very foolish of themselves to make it a scientific miracle. Maybe you don't know what I mean yet. In all Islamic translations of the Qur'an they are using the same word, **forelock,** so it must be that they all agree about the meaning of the word. They are out of their minds. Why?

> *Forelock means the following from all dictionaries:*
>
> *(n. A lock of hair that grows from or falls on the forehead, especially the part of a horse's mane that falls forward between the ears.)*

It's so dumb to say that hair is where our brain is. What science is talking about is the front of the brain, not the hair!!!

Muslims claim

Heart Massage- Miracles of the Qur'an

http://www.miraclesofthequran.com/scientific_102.html

One of the verses *that may be referring to the future* is verse 73 of Surat al-Baqara:

> *Remember when you killed someone and violently accused each other of it, and Allah brought out what you were hiding. We said, 'Hit him with part of it!' In that way Allah gives life to the dead and He shows you His Signs so that hopefully you will understand. (Surat al-Baqara, 72-73)*

Among the meanings of the Arabic term "biba'diha," translated as "with part of it" in the above verse, is "someone or some people." In the context of that meaning, the **verse may be a reference to heart massage, striking the chest from above**, which makes it possible to restart the heart if it has stopped beating. (Allah knows the truth.)

My answer

I cannot believe how some people lie with no shame! This verse, in a miraculous way, became about a heart massage!

This is Harun's translation:
> *"Remember when you killed someone and violently accused each other..."*

1. Notice that he claimed "the **verse may be a reference to heart massage.**" Why would someone say "maybe" if he is certain? But it's very clear he used "maybe" because he has no proof, so he has to mix between science and a maybe.
2. The verse is talking about a dead man, "**Remember when you killed someone and violently**" and not someone who's had a heart attack and survived!
3. Violently mostly by a sharp weapon as sword or knife.
4. This story speaks about Moses. Allah told him to get a cow meat, beat the dead man with it, and he would come back to life. Then he (the dead man) was asked who killed him, so he live for few seconds and dies again. What does this have to do with heart massage?! Read the story in Ibn Kathir:
> *"So, We said, unto them, strike him (the man who was killed) with a piece of it, the cow meat"*

303

http://tafsir.com/default.asp?sid=2&tid=2294

5. Do Muslims believe that if we beat a man with beef meat, the dead will come back to life?
6. Should we start teaching in our hospitals that if somebody dies violently as the verse in the Qur'an states, the medical recommendation is to beat that person with a peace of steak?

It's a very clear lie and totally different from what the verse is about. I wonder if this is real science. This would make the work of an FBI agent much easier to find a murderer out...just hit the corpse with a steak and once it's back to life, get the entire story!

There are many jokes in Harun's website that even kids would find it hard to accept. but we better not waste our time with the silly ones.

Muslims claim

Locusts moving in swarms

> *They will emerge from their graves with downcast eyes, like swarming locusts. (Qur'an, 54:7)*

This verse describes all people's situation in the Hereafter as one resembling swarming locusts. There is great wisdom in this simile.

A great deal of information was obtained about locusts in the twentieth century by conducting wide-ranging studies using micro-cameras. Locust swarms contain huge numbers of individual locusts that behave as a single body.

My answer

I am not sure if the one who made this claim is in good shape or not. No one knows that the locusts come in huge groups except Allah? This is really funny. At the same time, the verse says locusts scattered, not swarming.

The fact is that the Bible says something amazing; that is locusts move by biological control and other means of non-chemical control, which means they have no leader or a king or queen, and this is something that has just been found recently. We read this in the Bible:

Proverbs 30:27

The locusts have no king, yet go they forth all of them by bands;

The verse presents two facts. They move by bands or swarm which is not much of a secret and something anyone can notice. But without a king? Its in one of the bible books written between the tenth and sixth centuries B.C, this discovery took humans about 3,000 years to know?

Still, we do not see Christians making books about this scientific discovery in the Bible. We do not need science to prove God for he does not need their approval.
At the same time, maybe Mr. Harun can make a book about how LOCUSTS fly and are made of gold.

Sahih Al-Bukhari, Book 55, Hadith 604

Allah's Messenger said at the same time as Job was naked from taking a shower, a swarm of gold LOCUSTS fell on him, and he began collecting them in his dress. His Lord called him, 'O Job! Have I not made you rich enough to need what you see? He said, 'Yes, O Lord! However, I cannot discharge with your benefit

To read more visit this site:

www.sciencedaily.com/releases/2008/05/080508132545.htm

History Mistake and False Prophecy

Muslims claim

The Word "Haman" in the Qur'an the name "Haman" mentioned in Egyptian inscriptions

http://www.harunyahya.com/articles/50_the_word_haman.php

Haman is a character whose name is mentioned in the Qur'an, along with the Pharaoh. He is recorded in six different places of the Qur'an as one of the closest men to the Pharaoh.

Before these discoveries, the writings and inscriptions of ancient Egypt could not be understood. The language of ancient Egypt was hieroglyphic, which survived through the ages. However, with the spread of Christianity and other cultural influences in the 2nd and 3rd
Through the decoding of hieroglyph, an important piece of knowledge was revealed: the name "Haman" was indeed mentioned in Egyptian inscriptions.

My answer

The name found was not Haman but rather it was **'Haman** in the Egyptian hieroglyph. It is the same in Hebrew and Arabic. We have the letter ح h which does not exist in the Latin language *"ḥmn-h"*, but the name 'Haman in the Qur'an starts with the letter H same as we read it in latin or english like the word **H**ouse and that would make a big difference.

Name in Qur'an	H	A	M	A	N
hieroglyph	h	m	n	h	

And that's exactly the same with the book referenced by Mr. Harun which he named the New Kingdom Period (Fig. 4).

As you see, this is very bad news for those who made the false claim because the name in both the Qur'an and the Egyptian hieroglyph didn't match at all and the first letter in Egyptian is not even H its ح = ḥ as the pronunciations of this letter is the same as the sound of a snake (hissing).

[Walter Wreszinski, Aegyptische Inschriften aus dem K.K. Hof Museum in Wien]

Let us assume that Mr. Harun is correct and that the name "Haman" is in the ancient Egyptian scripture. Still, that does not make him the high minister of the pharaoh. From the claim of Mr. Harun we take this quotation: *"In the dictionary of "People in the New Kingdom."* It was prepared based on the entire collection of inscriptions. Haman is said to be "the head of stone quarry workers." So he agreed that the name is talking about a simple employee not a government minister as mentioned in all the Islamic books' interpretations, and from **Ibn Kathir, p. 471** we quote:

> The interpretation of Qur'an 40:36 "Allah Almighty said: reporting the arrogance and and unfairness of Pharaoh against Moses peace be upon him, he ordered his *minister Haman* to build a high building".

471تفسير بن كثير ـ صفحة القرآن رقم

يقول تعالى مخبرا عن فرعون، وعتوه ، وتمرده ، وافترائه في تكذيبه موسى ـ عليه السلام ـ أنه أمر وزيره هامان أن يبني له صرحا

So as long as the Muslims agreed that he was "the head of stone quarry workers.", so why Allah is calling him a minster when he is not?

1. If we read the verse itself, it will expose the mistake. As you see, the Pharaoh is asking to build a tower to reach God.
2. Where in the world is this famous tower which a king built to reach to God called *ziggurats*?

Arabic: برج بابل

It's the Babylonians, The Tower of Babel.

Hebrew: מגדל בבל

So the corruption of Muhammad made him move the story, which happened in Iraq and the Babylonians' land, all the way to Egypt.

It's very clear that Muhammad took this story about making a brick from clay to build a tower from the Bible, as we see in:

Genesis 11:1-4 - KJV

> *1 And the whole earth was of one language, and of one speech.*

> *2 And it came to pass, as they journeyed from the east, that they found a plain in the land of Shinar; and they dwelt there.*

> *3 And they said, one to another, Go to, let us make brick, and burn them thoroughly. And they had brick for stone, and slime had they for morter.*

> *4 And they said, Go to, let us build us a city and a tower, whose top may reach unto heaven; and let us make us a name, lest we be scattered abroad upon the face of the whole earth.*

3. At the same time, the verse in the Qur'anis saying that the Pharaoh thinks he is god but why did he want to go up to God?

Here is the verse translated by Mr. Harun himself:

> *"Pharaoh said, 'Council, I do not know of any other god for*

307

*you apart from Me. Haman, kindle a fire for me over the clay
and build me a lofty tower so that perhaps I may be able to
climb up to Moses' god! I consider him a blatant liar.'" (Surat
al-Kasas, 38)*

Here it is in the Bible, book of:

Esther 3:1 - KJV

*After these things did king Ahasuerus promote Haman the
son of Hammedatha the Agagite, and advanced him, and set
his seat above all the princes that were with him.*

It's so clear that Muhammad mixed two stories together and made them
one. Each of these are one is totally different and both are in entirely
separate times too. The story itself is showing the crazy mixed up
knowledge of Muhammad's god, or let us say Muhammad himself. I
challenge Mr. Harun to show us the tower reaching to God that the
Pharaoh built!

Muslims claim

Titles of Egyptian Rulers in the Qur'an

http://www.harunyahya.com/musa12.php
In contrast, the ruler at Moses' time is referred to as the "Pharaoh":

*"We gave Moses nine Clear Signs. Ask the tribe of Israel about
when he came to them and Pharaoh said, to him, 'Moses, I
think you are bewitched.'"*
(The Qur'an, 17:101)}

The rulers of the old dynasty did not use the title. The use of the word
pharaoh as the title of the ruler did not start until the "New Kingdom" era
of Egyptian history. This period started with the 18th dynasty (1539-1292
BC), and by the 20th dynasty (945-730 BC) the word "pharaoh" was
adopted as title of respect.

My answer

The point he is saying here is how Allah knew that the one who ruled at the time of Moses had the title of *Pharaoh* and the one who ruled at the time of Joseph had the title of *King*!

1. Muhammad copied the story from the Bible. The word <u>king</u> in the time of Joseph is mentioned in the Bible.

Genesis 39:20

And Joseph's master took him, and put him into the prison, a place where the king's prisoners were bound: and he was there in the prison.

- ✓ The word *Pharaoh* was used in the time of Joseph and even 300 to 400 years before the time of Joseph. The claim that the word *Pharaoh* was not used until the 20th dynasty (945-730 BC) is not true. You can search yourself for **The pharaohs of Dynasty XVIII** who ruled for about 250 years (him and 1550-1298 BC)
- ✓ Muslims themselves believe that Yusuf (Joseph) lived between 1610 BC - 1500 BC. Mr. Harun Yahya said in his writing that "This period started with the 18th dynasty (1539-1292 BC)", which are false dates. Even that is enough to prove that his claim is false.
- ✓ What's funny is that Muslims think he lived between 1610 to 1500 BC which would mean Joseph lived under the rule of more than one king and was living at the time of the pharaohs as the dates are displayed in Harun Yahya's claim.
- ✓ *Pharaoh* is a word that originally meant the great house. Let's just say that the one who lived in it had the name as owner of the house.
- ✓ Also, in the new kingdom of Egypt, by the year 1479-1425 BC, it became a title and/or name for whoever was the king, but in general that means the name became more adopted in this way. The fact is that even the word *Pharaoh* was used long before that for the kings, but it was not used often. Later it turned into a custom.
- ✓ This can be proven from many books. As an example, the King Amenhotep IV ruled for 17 years and was called *Pharaoh* as a title. That was in the years of 1352-1336 B.C. 18th dynasty, during his lifetime.
- ✓ <u>References,</u> Kuhrt 1995: 186
- ✓ Christopher Bronk Ramsey et al., Radiocarbon-Based Chronology for Dynastic Egypt, Science 18 June 2010: Vol. 328. no. 5985, pp. 1554-1557.
- ✓ Aidan Dodson, Dyan Hilton: The Complete Royal Families of Ancient Egypt. The American University in Cairo Press, London 2004.

✓ All this being said, we have enough proof concerning the false claims made by the Muslims.

✓ To make my final point, I will show something that Muhammad said which proves that Islam and the Qur'an consider the Pharaoh as a name of a man and not a title based on the coming hadith.

Qur'an consider the Pharaoh as a name of a man, not a title.

Sahih Al-Bukhari, Book 57, Hadith 113;
(in Arabic: Hadith 3558).

> *Narrated Abu Musa AL Ash'ari: Allah's Prophet said, "Many amongst men reached perfection but amongst women none reached the perfection except Mary, the daughter of 'Mran and Asiah (Asieya), the woman of Pharaoh. And the superiority of 'Aisha to other women is like flavoring the meat over other dishes.*

صحيح البخاري ـ كتاب فضائل الصحابة ـ يا عائش هذا جبريل يقرئك السلام

3558 حدثنا آدم حدثنا شعبة قال وحدثنا عمرو أخبرنا شعبة عن عمرو بن مرة عن مرة عن أبي موسى الأشعري رضي الله عنه قال قال رسول الله صلى الله عليه وسلم كمل من الرجال كثير ولم يكمل من النساء إلا مريم بنت عمران وآسية امرأة فرعون وفضل عائشة على النساء كفضل الثريد على سائر الطعام

• Notice here that Muhammad is using the name of Asieya, wife of Pharaoh, not of The Pharaoh! This is clear evidence that according to Muhammad and Allah, *Pharaoh* is a name of a man, not a title. This is why it shows in the Qur'an **74 time but no name of that king or the word king for the Pharaoh appear.**

• We have very clear proof, if Pharaoh was a title in the Qur'an why he is counted with individual names as we read in; Qur'an29:32 *And [We destroyed] **Qarun and Pharaoh and Haman. And Moses** had already come to them with clear evidences, and they were arrogant in the land, but they were not out runners [of Our punishment].(* ***Sahih International translation.***

  o As we see he is counting names so if Pharaoh is a title it shouldn't be there, if we replace the word Pharaoh with the meaning of it(King) then the verse will look funny which already is because that will give the true meaning of the verse, *"And [We destroyed] **Qarun and <u>king</u> and Haman, And Moses"***

  o obviously, he is counting names of individuals, and the word king doesn't fit there unless he thought it's a name.

  o Qur'an 38:12 "The people **of Noah** denied before them, and

310

[the people of] **'Aad** and **Pharaoh**, the owner of stakes"
○   Again **Noah, 'Aad, Pharaoh**, there are individuals especially if we notice that the other two names are not even kings.

•   Muhammad said;
"women none reached the perfection except Mary, the daughter of 'Mran and Asiah (Asieya), the woman of Pharaoh.", so we notice here:
  ○   Daughter of 'Mran.
  ○   Wife of Pharaoh.
  ○   To say that it can be fine, if this statement made in the time of Pharaoh, but to say the wife of Pharaoh thousands of years after many Pharaoh died already, how we will know which wife of which Pharaohs she was, the word Pharaoh makes reference to various *pharaohs* (kings of Egypt)?
  ○   Unless he thought Pharaoh is a name of a person, and there is only on Pharaoh, Qur'an (8:52) "Same as **the custom of the people of Pharaoh** and of those before them. They disbelieved in the signs of Allah"
  ○   Qur'an "And a believing man from the family of Pharaoh who concealed his faith said, "Do you kill a man "so he is from the Family of Pharaoh? Family of a king? Which king!

I think the answer is clear, that the word Pharaoh in the Qur'an used as a name of a person not as a king which is an error not the opposite.

Muslims claim

The victory of Byzantium(Romans)

http://www.miraclesofthequran.com/predictions_01.html

Alif, Lam, Mim. The Romans have been defeated in the lowest land, but after their defeat they will be victorious **within three to nine years**. The affair is Allah's from beginning to end. On that day, the believers will rejoice. (Qur'an, 30:1-4)

These verses were revealed around 620, almost 7 years after the idolatrous Persians had severely defeated Christian Byzantium in 613-14, ... The loss of Jerusalem in 614 was particularly traumatic for the Byzantines, for the Church of the Holy Sepulchre was destroyed and the Persians seized the "True Cross," the symbol of Christianity. 174 In addition, the Avars, Slavs,

Another miracle revealed in these verses is the announcement of a geographical fact that could not have been known by anyone at that time: that the Romans had been defeated in the lowest region

----

My answer

If you'd like to read the entire articles, please visit this link:
http://www.miraclesofthequran.com/predictions_01.html

I would like to point out some of the falsification in this article but before I begin, let us quote Mr. Harun:
"...defeated Christian Byzantium in 613-14 took place in the region. The Lake of Lut region,"

All of you can go and search for **the Siege of Jerusalem.**

After the twenty-first day of bombardment, the city's **walls finally broke**, Persians army continually blasted the walls of Jerusalem with ballistas and other military engines.

Read here:
Antiochus Strategos, The Capture of Jerusalem by the Persians in 614 AD,
FREDERICK C. CONYBEARE, English Historical Review 25 (1910) pp. 502-517

The beginning of the struggle of the Persians with the Christians of Jerusalem was on April 15th, in the second indication, of the fourth year of the Emperor Heraclius. They spent twenty days in struggle. And they shot from their ballistas with such violence that on the twenty-first day, they broke down the city wall.

The war was in the city for 21 days before the city fell into the hands of the Persian army.

This was Mr. Harun's claim. I will now demonstrate to you the way he makes his claims, as he always does, by manufacturing a new meaning of the Qur'an.

The word in the Qur'an about the Roman victory is "**bed!**" بضع. This word has the same meaning as "*few*", which is a number between 3 and 9 maximums. As long as Mr. Harun agreed about the date when the verse was revealed to Muhammad, as he said, seven years before 627, this means that the verse was made in 620. This is a great point that Mr.

Harun made to expose his lie. Quoting his words:

"These verses were revealed around 620, almost 7 years after the idolatrous Persians had severely defeated Christian Byzantium in 613-14."

Now I challenge him as well as all the Muslims to give me the source to where it says that Muhammad revealed this verse in the year 620. At the same time, I will show you in the following book the proof that this is absolutely false and it's a shameless lie.

The Location of the Battle

Book of Asbab Al-Nuzul, 1963 Print., Vol. 1, p. 674
The interpreters of the Qur'an said: "King Kissra (the Persian king), sent an army to fight the Romans and he made the leader of the Army his name is Shehrezyaz, and he killed them destroying their cities and towns and cut their olive trees. The Roman Caesar sent the leader by the name of Yuhanes who met with Shehrezyaz in the city of Adhri'at {Izra' (Arabic: أزرع)} and Busra, (adna al-ard) which is the the closest point of the Arabian land, and the Persians were victorious over the Romans, and the news arrived to the prophet".

أسباب النزول
لحسن علي بن أحمد بن محمد بن علي الواحديU أبو
دار الكتب العلمية
م1963سنة النشر:
--- :رقم الطبعة
عدد الأجزاء: جزء واحد
أسباب النزول « سورة الروم » قوله عز وجل " الم غلبت الروم " سورة الروم
. قوله تعالى: (الم غلبت الروم) الآيات
قال المفسرون : بعث كسرى جيشا إلى الروم ، واستعمل عليهم رجلا يسمى شهريراز ، فسار إلى الروم بأهل فارس وظهر - 674
عليهم ، فقتلهم ، وخرب مدائنهم وقطع زيتونهم . [وقد] كان قيصر بعث رجلا يدعى يحنس ، فالتقى مع شهريراز بأذرعات
وبصرى ، وهي أدنى الشام إلى أرض العرب ، فغلب فارس الروم . وبلغ ذلك النبي

You can read the entire story by visiting the Jordanian government's website at: altafsir.com

- ♦ As you read, the battle between both armies was in the city of Basra which is located 120 km (75 miles) from the Dead Sea and is 850 m above the sea level.
- ♦ The city of Izra' is located 136 km (84 miles) from the Dead Sea and its height is 650 m above the sea level.
- ♦ This is clear proof that Mr. Harun lied even about the location as he said: **"The Dead Sea basin where Byzantium was defeated by Persians**. Above is a satellite photograph of the region. **The Lake of Lut region, which is the lowest region of the world, is 395 meters below the sea level."**

♦ It's very obvious that they are trying to make and create the miracle out of nothing. And he said, about the word [Adna] the following: **"This Arabic expression adna al-Ard is interpreted as "a nearby place" in many translations. However, this is not the literal meaning, but rather a figurative interpretation. The word adna, derived from the word dani (low), means "the lowest". The word ard means "the world." therefore, adna al-ard means "the lowest place on Earth."** It's very clear that Mr. Harun is playing a fool's game against those who do not know Arabic. But that will not work for someone like me with Arabic as my first language. I also spent my entire life studying it and studying with it. If you go back and read what I posted for you from the book of **Asbab Al-Nuzul, 1963 Print., Vol. 1, p. 674, the story there explains to us the actual meaning and to quote "(adna al-ard) which is the closest point of the Arabian land."**

➤ This is why all Islamic translations agree nearest Sahih International trans: *"In the nearest land. But they, after their defeat, will overcome."*

➤ **Muhsin Khan** "In **the nearer land** (Syria, Iraq, Jordan, and Palestine), and they, after their defeat, will be victorious."

➤ Pickthall trans"In the **nearer land,** and they, after their defeat will be victorious"

➤ Yusuf Ali trans "In a **land close by**; but they, (even) after (this) defeat of theirs, will soon be victorious-"

We can find the same inside the interpretation of Ibn Kathir Vol. 6, page 303. The Almighty said: "the Roman defeated" and that battle was between the Persians and the Romans where they defeated between Izra' and Busra as reported by Ibn Abbas, and Ikramah, plus many others [of the prophet's companions] in those two cities it is the edge between the land of Syria in the land of Hijaz (Arabia), and Mujahid said it was the nearest between the land of the Romans and the Persians.

303تفسير سورة الروم » تفسير قوله تعالى " الم غلبت الروم "الجزء السادس] ص:
وكانت الواقعة الكائنة بين فارس والروم حين غلبت الروم بين أذرعات وبصرى ، على ما ذكره ابن عباس وعكرمة وغيرهما ،
. وهي طرف بلاد الشام مما يلي بلاد الحجاز . وقال مجاهد : كان ذلك في الجزيرة ، وهي أقرب بلاد الروم من فارس

Isn't it really ridiculous to tell the world that your god Allah reported the fall of Jerusalem 6 years after the real date? What's up with Allah? Was his news reporter using camels?
The people of Mecca had many caravans going to Damascus in Syria. Even Muhammad himself went in caravans to Syria at that time. This included all of Jordan and what was called Palestine.

If we go and see what the last defeat of the Romans was before they became victorious, it was in the year 614 which was the Siege of Jerusalem (614). There was one war after that of the Persians; the failure of a Persian attack on Constantinople, but there was no winner in that attack. Since the only defeat of the Romans before their victory over the Persians was the Siege of Jerusalem (614), and the victory of the Romans was in the year 627, then this means that it was 13 years after and not a few years as the Qur'an claims.

Few = bed' = 3 to 9 بضع as in his translation.
> *Qur'an 30:1-4*
>
> *Alif, Lam, Mim. The Romans have been defeated in the lowest land, but after their defeat they will be victorious within three to nine years. The affair is Allah's from beginning to end. On that day, the believers will rejoice.*

How can we give more proof that the Qur'an speaks about the Siege of Jerusalem? Read with me Mr. Harun's words, not mine!

> *{...the Byzantine Empire and the Persians, when the Byzantines were defeated and lost Jerusalem, had really taken place at the lowest point on earth.}*

And one more quote:
{defeated Christian Byzantium in 613-14.}

I think falsification cannot live long with the truth. This is the answer of the first lie or claim about the prophecy of Muhammad and the victory of the Byzantine. To make my point clear, I will show you that it's funny and impossible that Arabs in Mecca never heard of what was going on in Jerusalem until the year 620, as Harun said, **"These verses were revealed around 620."**

Below, I have listed caravan attacks launched by Muhammad. These raids will tell us how many caravans came and went from Syria each year.

List of some of Muhammad's Caravan Raids coming back from Syria	
First Quraysh caravan attack	March of 623
Quraysh Mecca Caravans: Bowat	April of 623
Quraysh Mecca Caravans: Qharar	May / June 623
Quraysh Mecca Caravans of Wahdan	August of 623
Quraysh Mecca Caravans 2nd Bowat	October of 623

Quraysh Mecca Caravans: Yanbo'	November of 623
Quraysh Mecca Caravans: Nakhalah	December of 623
It's clear that Muhammad's caravan raids took place between Syria and Mecca all year long. How did it take 6 years for the news to come to Mecca and to Muhammad's god Allah?	

On top of that, the one who made this claim surely didn't know nor had read the book before, as even the Qur'an tells us how many trips the people of Mecca did per year!

Qur'an 106:1

For the agreement of security that practiced by the Quraysh,

Qur'an 106:2

protecting their trade caravans during their trading winter and summer trip

Ibn Kathir's interpretation

لائتلافهم واجتماعهم في بلدهم آمنين. وقيل: المراد بذلك ما كانوا يألفونه من الرحلة في الشتاء إلى اليمن، وفي الصيف إلى الشام، في المتاجر وغير ذلك، ثم يرجعون إلى بلدهم آمنين في أسفارهم

We made them (Quraysh) live in their land and we made as the timing of the caravans to set forth in winter and summer, in winter to go to Yemen and in summer they go to Syria.

What we understand from these verses is that the Quraysh tribe (People of Mecca) went on for at least two trips a year. This is enough to prove that it is a false claim. Another proof is that the verse was revealed by Muhammad right after all the people of Mecca had received it. We see this in the interpretation of Qur'an 30:1-4 by **Imam AL-Tabarani:**

"The Kufar of Quraysh was happy to hear that the Romans were defeated and they were saying Muhammad's claim to have the same god as the Christians, so we can defeat Muhammad as the Christians were defeated, and the king of the Romans sent his army when he heard the news about the coming of the Persian army, and they met in Izre' and Busra, which is the nearest location of the land of Syria to the land of the Arabic [the border between the Arabian and non-Arabian land], so the Persians were victorious, and the Persians occupied the city of Jerusalem, which was the center of the

Roman spiritual worship."

It's clear that the verse of Muhammad was made immediately as a response to those who were making fun of the loss of the Romans. Mr. Harun had to play games and make us believe that the verse was given from Allah to Muhammad 6 years later!

Muslims claim

The miracle of 19 in the Qur'an

http://www.miraclesofthequran.com/mathematical_03.html

Another mathematical miracle of the Qur'an is the manner in which the number 19 is numerological encoded in verses. This number is stressed in the words of the Qur'an: "There are nineteen in charge of it." (Qur'an, 74:30), and is encoded in various places in the Book. Some examples of this can be listed as follows:

The Formula consists of 19 letters. Please see following table.

The Qur'an consists of 114 (19 x 6) Suras.

The first Sura to be revealed (Sura 96) is the 19th from the end.

The first verses of the Qur'an to be revealed are the first five verses of Sura 96 and the total number of words in these verses is 19.

My answer

I will answer each photo one by one, to show you how Muslims deceive. If you look at the top of this image, you see that the Muslims are using the artistic writing of Arabic, which is not showing the letter A = ا or *"Alif"*. They know that Westerners don't know Arabic, and those who do may not even notice it. In this form of writing, the letter A always comes in that way; hardly noticeable. It's also making it short, but there is the letter A = ا there, as I will show.

ب	1st letter	ا	8th letter	ا	15th letter
س	2nd letter	ل	9th letter	ل	16th letter
م	3rd letter	ر	10th letter	ر	17th letter
ا	4th letter	ح	11th letter	ح	18th letter
ل	5th letter	م	12th letter	ي	19th letter
ل	6th letter	ا = A	13th letter	م	20th letter
ه	7th letter	ن	14th letter		

13th letter: This is the letter A, or "*Alif*" as spoken in the Arabic tongue. It's made small and in an artistic way, but this is why it's still showing in the word. Why did the Muslims delete it? Well, they have to or else the letter count will end as 20 and then the miracle is smoked!

From Islamic dictionaries, it is called راف العباب الزاخر
This poet from one of Muhammad's best friends, Ka'eb Ibn Malik AL-Ansary said:

We obey the PROPHET AND OBEY GOD; HE IS *AL-RAHMAN*

:كعب بن مالك الأنصاري

نُطِيْعُ نَبِيَّنَا وَنُطِيْعُ رَبَّاً هو الرحمان كان بنا رَؤُوفا

This is how the word is: AL-RAHMAN. This is a print screen taken from the Ministry of Islam, Government website of Saudi Arabia. Go here and see how many time the word appear as I said in one page
http://quran.ksu.edu.sa/tafseer/tanweer/sura19-aya93.html

وتكرير اسم { الرَّحمان } في هذه الآية أربع مرات إيماء إلى أن وصف الرحمان الثابت لله لفظه ، ينافي ادعاء الولد له لأنَّ الرحمان وصف يدلّ على عموم الرَّحمة وتكثُّرها . ومعنى

In the book of Al Qurtbi he said that the word AL-RAHMAN is a hebrowe word as we read in Arabic

وفي تفسير القرطبي عن ابن الأنباري عن المبرد أن الرحمان اسم عبراني نقل إلى العربية قال وأصله بالخاء المعجمة أي فأبدلت خفاؤه حاء مهملة عند أكثر العرب كشأن التغيير في التعريب

"In the interpretation of the verse from Ibn Al-Anbari he said that AL-Rahman, a Hebrew name was transferred to the Arab"

The 1st word inside the bracket is **AL-RAHMAN**. The first claim is gone with the wind! The Muslims today they do write it in the Qur'an but Qur'an never took it off, it shows as a small letter artistically, and as long the Qur'an writer 'Uthman made this way who dare to took back to the way it use to be!

This is one of the most deceptive claims posted in Harun Yahya's website. The fact is, it's not even his work! It was a claim made by an Egyptian man who was killed by Muslims in Arizona. The Khalifa was murdered at Masjid Mosque in Tucson, Arizona for doing two things: 1) deleting verses from the Qur'an to make this number 19 miracle work for him, and 2) for claiming to be the messenger of Allah.

Rashad Khalifa, who received his Ph.D. in biochemistry from Arizona State University and a Ph.D. from the University of California, based his claim on false calculations; sometimes by counting letters as words, and other times counting letters as letters. Add to that he had to say that there were false verses in chapter 9 of the Qur'an, namely verses 128 and 129.

As you see, even the Muslims rejected this false miracle and murdered him, showing the peace of Islam.

I have to ask myself, why is Mr. Harun playing the number 19 game again? Muslims follow their prophet's teaching, which is the war of *deception*.

I think Mr. Harun in a very easy way he has many working for him and they are maybe copy and paste from other Muslims claims. The link below shows 2 photos taken as is from his website:

http://www.miraclesoftheQur'an.com/mathematical_03.html

open the site please to view it

See the و in here? He considered it but did not count it at all! As we see in other next;

خَلَقَ	الَّذِي	رَبَّكَ	ياسْمِ	اقْرَأْ
5th	4th	3ed	2nd	1st word
اقْرَأْ	عَلَقٍ	مِنْ	الْإِنسَانَ	خَلَقَ
10th	9th	8th	7th	6th
عَلَّمَ	الَّذِي	الْأَكْرَمُ	رَبَّكَ	وَ
15th	14th	13th	12th	11th
لَمْ	مَا	الْإِنسَانَ	عَلَّمَ	بِالْقَلَمِ
20th	19th	18th	17th	16th
				يَعْلَمْ
				21th

He is saying that he will not count the و ("**WA**"). This means that the letter "**WA**" و is being added or Allah does not know that we have to take it off now!! Can or does Harun Yahya *DARE* to drop a letter from the Qur'an?!

The letter "**WA**" و is a letter but in that location, it is equal to the word "**And**".

In the coming photo, I will show how they even made two words as one. How? Maybe the two words got married in a Christian church and this made them united?

I will make them both bigger so you can see them and show how Muslims lie and play games!

We will show you from the Qur'an itself that these are not connected and not one word;

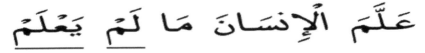

In this photo we see two words, "Lam" (لَم) and "Ya'lem" (يعلم),

but he made the two words into one! Why? So, he could make his dream come true. Changing the numbers of the lotto from your side will not make it real! This one alone, I mean counting two words as one, is enough to destroy all of Harun's or Rashad Khalifa's claims!

The rest of the claim is based on these, so since we have already proved it to be a lie, there is no need to continue proving the false miracle of 19.

How will Allah recognize the Muslims from non-Muslims?

Qur'an 2:134

therefore, We have nominated you a middle nation, that ye may be witnesses against mankind, and that the messenger may be a witness against you. And We have chosen the direction of the qiblah which you previously celebrated only that We might know him whom follower the messenger, from him who turn on his heels against (Allah) In truth. It was a hard trial with the exclusion of for those whom Allah guided. However, it was not Allah's goal that your faith should be in vain, for Allah is merciful to mankind.

وَكَذَلِكَ جَعَلْنَاكُمْ أُمَّةً وَسَطًا لِّتَكُونُوا شُهَدَاءَ عَلَى النَّاسِ وَيَكُونَ الرَّسُولُ عَلَيْكُمْ شَهِيدًا ۚ وَمَا جَعَلْنَا الْقِبْلَةَ الَّتِي كُنتَ عَلَيْهَا إِلَّا لِنَعْلَمَ مَن يَتَّبِعُ الرَّسُولَ مِمَّن يَنقَلِبُ عَلَى عَقِبَيْهِ ۚ وَإِن كَانَتْ لَكَبِيرَةً إِلَّا عَلَى الَّذِينَ هَدَى اللَّهُ ۗ وَمَا كَانَ اللَّهُ لِيُضِيعَ إِيمَانَكُمْ ۚ إِنَّ اللَّهَ بِالنَّاسِ لَرَءُوفٌ رَّحِيمٌ

(سورة البقرة , Al-Ba'qara, Chapter 2, Verse 143)

Let us study this verse carefully and you will notice the following:
* The Kaaba is not a holy place as Muslims claim or even as Allah himself claims in the Qur'an as we read in Yusuf Ali's translation:

Qur'an 5:97

Allah made the Kaaba, the Sacred House, an asylum of security for men, as also the Sacred Months, the animals for offerings, and the garlands that mark them: That ye may know that Allah hath knowledge of what is in the heavens and on earth and that Allah is well acquainted with all things.

Because Allah made it a place of direction for one reason and that is to know who is a Muslim and who's not.
* As long as Allah made it for that reason which is to know who is a Muslim and who's not, it then means that he is all knowledgeable which the Qur'an keeps talking about. If Allah is all-knowing, he doesn't need to know who is a Muslim and who's not a Muslim.

"And We have chosen the direction of the qiblah which you previously celebrated only that We might know him whom follower the messenger, from him who turn on his heels against (Allah)"

- As you see he is making it very clear "**only** that **We might know**" and notice he is saying **we might know?** So, he might know and might not?

Why did Allah make the boys sleep in the cave for more than 309 years?

This story is one more proof that Qur'an is a fairy tale story. Here, Allah tells the story of boys who refused to deny Allah and they ran away for their lives by hiding in the cave and Allah made them fall asleep for an unknown number of years!

So the question here is, why did Allah do this miraculous act? The answer is in the following verses:

Qur'an 18:9-14

⁹ Or do you think that the boys of the cave and the Raqim (Name of a Valley) was of Our wonderful wonders.

¹⁰ when the youths searched for refuge in the cave, they said: Our Lord! Grant us from yourself mercy from, and provide us a right guidance in our affair.

¹¹ So We blocked them from hearing in the cave for a number of years.

¹² Then We raised them up that We might know which of the two parties was most successfully able to calculate the time for which they remained.

¹³ We recount to you their story with the truth; surely, they were youths, which believed in their Lord, and We multiplied them in guidance.

¹⁴ And We supported their hearts with patience, when they stood up and said: Our Lord is the Lord of the heavens and of the earth; we will not call any as god besides Him, for then indeed we should have said a false thing.

ثم بَعَثْنَاهُمْ لِنَعْلَمَ أَيُّ الْحِزْبَيْنِ أَحْصَى لِمَا لَبِثُوا أَمَدًا

(سورة الكهف , Al-Kahf, Chapter 18, Verse 12)

So now after reading these verses together, Allah told us why he performed this amazing funny miracle.

"¹² Then We raised them up that We might know which of the two parties was most successfully able to calculate the time for which they remained." (Qur'an 18:12)

1. Did Allah want to have some fun and see who is better in giving the most accurate number about how many years they slept?
2. Allah wanted to know? Yes, as you see he said, "**that We might**

know" so does that mean Allah will not know until he raises them and asks them? What makes sense is that if Allah already knows he will not have fun getting the correct answer. It is like watching a movie wherein he does not know and he cannot wait to see who of the three boys will give the most accurate number of years.

3. Again, Allah uses the word "**We might know**". So, what's wrong with this Allah that even after they give the answer he still will not know. Or maybe because he does not know which is the correct answer anyway? Or can someone tell me what the phrase "**We might know**" stands for?

4. *On the top of that, what did we learn from this silly story? Are we a bunch of kids being told bedtime stories by grandma?*

5. In the same chapter, we read this:

Qur'an18:18

And you might think they were awake, even though they were asleep, and We made them turn over to the right and the left, their dog stretching forth his two fore-legs on the threshold: if you take a look at them, you would have certainly turned back from them in flight, and would definitely have been occupied with terror of them.

6. I think the story is more exciting now for kids because Allah added a dog with the three boys! But we thought Allah hated the believers who own dogs?

As we read in this hadith:

Sahih Muslim, Book 010, Hadith 3810

Ibn 'Umar Allah blesses him reported: Allah's Messenger ordered to kill all dogs, and he sent Muslim men to the corners of the city of Medina in search for dogs to be killed.

7. Now Allah gives us a description on how the dog stretched his two legs. Remember, this is the god of Islam speaking every word. It should lead to wisdom. The funny and sad part is that Allah made an entire chapter about nothing while he only made **one verse** in the entire Qur'an about **Christ's crucifixion**!

How many boys were there in the cave? When I say Qur'an is a joke I am not just insulting. Read with me please.

سَيَقُولُونَ ثَلَاثَةٌ رَّابِعُهُمْ كَلْبُهُمْ وَيَقُولُونَ خَمْسَةٌ سَادِسُهُمْ كَلْبُهُمْ رَجْمًا بِالْغَيْبِ وَيَقُولُونَ سَبْعَةٌ وَثَامِنُهُمْ كَلْبُهُمْ قُل رَّبِّى Qur'an 18:22 أَعْلَمُ بِعِدَّتِهِم مَّا يَعْلَمُهُمْ إِلَّا قَلِيلٌ فَلَا تُمَارِ فِيهِمْ إِلَّا مِرَاءً ظَاهِرًا وَلَا تَسْتَفْتِ فِيهِم مِّنْهُمْ أَحَدًا

The Logic of the Bible's corruption

"Was entrusted on the protection of Allah's book," Qur'an 5:44

Qur'an 5:44

"We gave the guidance to the prophets to judge by it for those who they believe, by the rabbis and the doctors of law: for to them was entrusted on the protection of Allah's book,"

1. Allah trusted the Rabbis for the protection of his book.
2. The Rabbis were not trustworthy; they did not protect the book.
3. The result: the Torah is corrupted.

According to this, I must ask the following questions:

- Did Allah put his trust in the bad ones?
- Did Allah know that the ones he trusted were bad?
- If Allah knew and trusted those who would do bad to the book, does it mean that he gave it (the book) to them in order to corrupt it?
- This means it was Allah's plan because humans cannot destroy Allah's book if Allah is God! They could only do it if Allah gave permission to do such an act, especially in his Qur'an. He said, no one can change the words of Allah, as it says in the Qur'an:

Al-Anaam, Chapter 6, Verse 34:
"NO one can change and exchange the words of Allah."

- This is even a contradiction of the accusation of corrupting the Torah. How can Allah's book be corrupted when no one can do that according to Qur'an 6:34?
- The Muslims might say that the verse is speaking about the Qur'an, not the Torah!
- Then why is Allah saying, *the words of Allah,* and not *the Qur'an of Allah*, if it's about a special book? He should have named it. Instead he said, *no one can change the words of Allah.* This goes for ALL his words.
- Add to this everyone that has the book! I mean concerning the Rabbis. Only one Rabbi? Two? How about ten? The answer is in the Qur'an:

يَا بَنِي إِسْرَائِيل اذْكُرُوا نِعْمَتِيَ الَّتِي أَنْعَمْتُ عَلَيْكُمْ وَأَوْفُوا بِعَهْدِي أُوفِ بِعَهْدِكُمْ وَإِيَّايَ فَارْهَبُون

سورة البقرة, Al-Baqara, 2:40

Oh, Children of Israel remember my favor upon you (all) and keep your covenant between you and me and I will keep my covenant to you, and fear me.

In another verse, the law of Allah is being given to all of them, not only to the Rabbis, as we see in:

وَ﴿إِذْ أَخَذْنَا مِيثَاقَ بَنِي إِسْرَائِيلَ لَا تَعْبُدُونَ إِلَّا اللَّهَ وَبِالْوَالِدَيْنِ إِحْسَانًا وَذِي الْقُرْبَىٰ وَالْيَتَامَىٰ وَالْمَسَاكِينِ وَقُولُوا لِلنَّاسِ حُسْنًا وَأَقِيمُوا الصَّلَاةَ وَآتُوا الزَّكَاةَ ثُمَّ تَوَلَّيْتُمْ إِلَّا قَلِيلًا مِّنكُمْ وَأَنتُم مُّعْرِضُونَ

سورة البقرة , Al-Baqara, Qur'an 2:83

We took covenant on the children of Israel that worship Allah only, and be good to your parents and family, do the prayer, pay the charity to the poor and orphans and poor, and speak good to others but few of you did that only.

If you look at the last two chapters I posted, you will see that Allah's law is still there. It's not corrupted. The verse is even saying in clear words that a few of the Jews were still practicing Allah's rules. The book is corrupted but they are following the law of Allah? Where did these few Jews get the true law from? As we see in Qur'an 2:38, Allah asked them to follow his rules which are:

Worshipping Allah only
Being good to your parents
Being good to your family
Praying
Paying charity to the poor and orphans
Speaking good to others

Are these rules good to go if the Rabbis follow them? These rules had been given to all the children of Israel, which means:

1. How did *all* the Rabbis turn evil in one day and agreed to corrupt the Torah? Was it all of them? Wasn't there one good Rabbi left in this world who had abstained from doing such action?
2. Did *all* the children of Israel, their men and women, agreed to corrupt the Torah also? Isn't it a funny and exaggerated claim?
3. In Jesus' time, the Torah was not corrupted yet (Muslims claim otherwise) as Qur'an 61:6 states:

When Isa (Jesus) said, "Oh children of Israel, I am a messenger of Allah to you <u>approving the book between my hands</u> and giving the good news of a new prophet that will come after me, his name is Ahmad".

4. If the book of the Jews was good until the time of Jesus as the verse states, this alone proves that it has now become more impossible to corrupt it. Why?

5. The Torah is now in the hands of the Jews and Christians as Christianity had already spread around the world. If the Jews all agreed to corrupt their book, how can all the Christians agree with them too? We know that Christianity was not in good relations with the Jews for a long period of time.

6. It's clear, as we see in Qur'an 61:6 that the whole idea of corruption is about the name Ahmad. Muhammad was trying to push one of the names he called himself into the Torah and Gospel. The only way was to claim a corruption to serve his false prophecies.

7. As long as Muslims believe in predestination as we proved before, this means it was Allah's plan all along, and no one else's, to corrupt the Bible as we see in this hadith:

Fateh AL-Bari Fe Sharih, Sahih Al-Bukhari, book of 'Qadar (BOOK OF DESTINY), p. 497 and Sahih Muslim, Bishare'h AL-Nawai, p. 155:
Allah wrote down the decrees of creation fifty thousand years before He created the heavens and the earth.

How to answer Muslims' claim about Bible corruption

There is an extremely important question we must ask a Muslim when he accuses us of **the corruption of our Book.** First, remember that Muslims consider the Old and New Testament being the book of Allah.

Allah's words vs Allah's words?

- If the Qur'an, Torah, Gospel, and the book of **Psalms** all is his books, so why Allah do not want to protect his books but he favorers the Qur'an over the books of the bible?

This is an important question we demand answer for it from Muslim's! however you will never find someone can answer such a a simple question.

Sahih International Translations
Qur'an 3:3

"He has sent down upon you, [O Muhammad], the Book in truth, confirming what was before it. And He revealed the Torah and the Gospel."

- Do Allah like the Qur'an and hate the rest of his books The Torah, and The Gospel?
- Is his Qur'an is better than his other books?
- If he will not protect all these books, and he is obviously not interested in protecting his other books what is the point to send it?

Allah will make Qur'an better than his Qur'an?

The madness of Islam logic is endless in the coming verse we will see one of the most stupid statement can be made by someone claim be God!

Qur'an 2:106

"Whatever verse we abrogate or cause it to be forgotten except that We will make something better than it or similar to it. Do you not know that Allah is over all things competent?"

Please read this verse above carefully this is an extremely important verse, actually this verse alone is enough to make millions leave Islam is they got to understand it.

What we understand from the Qur'an verse above is;
1. Allah has miscellaneous quality if his own Qur'an.
2. There are bad verses, and better ones.
3. But don't worry Allah will make you forget the bad one and he will come with better one?
4. It's clear Allah maybe when he is in a bad mode his writing is not good and he produce bad text.
5. So, he will go over It again and he will say to himself {oh no this is bad I'd better make something better, and make them forget how stupid the previous one, before mankind notices how foolish I am!}
6. Allah will make us forget the Qur'an is he going to forget it too?
7. If yes Allah can't be God if no so what is the point of making us forgetting the verses?
8. Can the Qur'an (the word of god) be destroyed?
9. Well according to this verse yes.
10. But this means Qur'an is not protected and Allah himself is the

first to act destroying his own words.
11. Can the Qur'an be forgotten?
12. The answer yes Allah will make us forget his Qur'an.
13. Allah will make us lose memory when its come to the bad verse only!
14. By the way what are these bad verses Allah causes us to forget?
15. Maybe the breastfeeding or suckling for an adult man by adult woman in Islam? But it's not working we still remember it as well as Muslims.
16. In this story, we will read one of the most ridiculous teaching which one day was a verse in the Qur'anitself as an order from Allah to do.

"' A'isha (Allah be pleased with her) reported that Sahla bint Suhail came to Allah's Apostle (may peace be upon him) and said:

Messenger of Allah, I see on the face of Abu Hudhaifa (signs of disgust) on entering of Salim (who is an ally) into (our house), whereupon Allah's prophet said: Suckle him. She said: How can I suckle him as he is a grown-up man? Allah's Messenger smiled and said: I know he is a grown-up man? 'and the Messenger of Allah's laughed." (Sahih Muslim, Book 17, Hadith 33)

17. This was one day a verse in the Qur'an but guess who made it gone, if it is not Allah then who?

Even A Goat can destroy the words of Allah!

Is this true? YES

"('A'isha) said:

There was revealed (verses) in the Holy Qur'an ten clear suckling's, and then another verse of five clear suckling's." (Book 17, Hadith 31)

accordingly, the Qur'an use to have Tow verses;
1. one verse about Man should suckle an adult woman breast for Ten times (not in the same time like in one suckle till he is satisfied.
2. Then a new verse came from Allah to make **Five** times suckling instead of **Ten**.
3. However, I will not about this stupid teaching much I will leave it for my coming book, but why we can't find these verses in the Qur'an we have to day?

4.   The answer the Goat eat it!

Sunan Ibn Majah, Hadith 1944:

"Aisha said: 'the verse of stoning and of suckling an adult man ten times was revealed, and they were on a paper kept under my bed. When the Messenger of Allah dies and we were occupied by his death, a Goat entered and ate away the paper.'"

This story alone is showing us how crazy it's to believe that Allah is the true God.

Now I am not done yet with this verse;
Qur'an 2:106

"Whatever verse we abrogate or cause it to be forgotten except that We will make something better than it or similar to it. Do you not know that Allah is over all things competent?"

There is an important point I did not speak about in this verse yet which is this part;

"Except that We will make something better than it **or similar to it.**"

Allah will cause us to forget a verse so he will make a verse is Similar to it???

That is really kind of mental disorder from Allah to say but do not Muslims and Qur'an claim that Allah is all wise?
Let us think about it;
1.   in the beginning, we did ask questions about Allah will abrogate or cause to forget verses because according to him(Allah) he will make something better.
2.   But not in this case because he is saying "or to make verse which is similar of it"
3.   if if its similar of the older verse so what is the point of making something similar?
4.   Similar mean nothing real change and it's not better but a twin of the old verse he would like us to forget?
5.   Obviously, there is no point here at all its foolish action.
6.   So, what is the secret behind this?
7.   The answer is easy, Muhammad each time he tries to recite a verse he told before he makes mistakes, and it's not the same as

the one he claims to be reciting again by adding words or missing words.

8. To the point he had to come with such a verse as an excuse to explain why he forgot it.
9. And that explains why Muhammad told the Muslims if you remember Allah send him **seven Qur'an**, go back to refresh your memory.

Was the Bible of Allah corrupted by his will or against his will?

When asked this question, a Muslim has to respond to one of two answers:

A)   By Allah's will. This **makes it Allah's fault**. This puts Allah in partnership with Satan in doing an evil work. Actually, it makes Allah the devil himself as he arms Satan with strong tools used to deceive people with.
B)   Against Allah's will. This means it's impossible for Allah to be God as he is too weak to protect a few pages of a book... his own book!

Either way, Allah is not fit for the job of being God.

Advice for Christians about debating Muslims

1. Remember, do not defend the Bible when a Muslim says your Bible is corrupted. The Muslim is talking about Allah's bible, not ours. Why would you defend a book that's not yours anyway?
2. If he says, "Your Bible is corrupted!" Answer this: "You mean the bible of Allah?" Be sure to make him answer with yes because it's an Allah's book as stated in Qur'an 45:16, Qur'an 40:53, Qur'an 5:46, and Qur'an 57:27. You will then see that the Muslims would be shocked of how ridiculous his claim is. After all, he is trying to prove to you that his god got screwed up and his book was corrupted. For me, this book is not mine and this god is not mine. Why would I defend it? I simply agree with the Muslims that his god's bible is corrupted by answering this: "You know what? I agree with you! Your Allah got screwed up and his book is corrupted!" Then you will silence the claim and he will try to change the topic.
3. Then ask the Muslim why couldn't Allah protect his bible? He will not give you an answer but he will surely reply: "The Christians and the Jews corrupted the book."
4. Ask him, "I would like to know who it is that destroyed your god's word. Can you give me a name for the one who beat the power and strength of your god Allah?"

Sacrifice in Islam

Why do Muslims practice such act? I will show you a Muslim's demonstrations and claims.

Islam, My Only Choice
by Khwaja Kamal-ud-Din
Founder of the Woking Muslim Mission, England, and 'The Islamic Review'
in Chapter 2
The author of the book said:

Muslims do observe sacrifice, but not to appease Divine wrath. One of the objects is to "Feed the poor man who is contented, and the beggar" (22:36). This institution also supplies an occasion for being benevolent to others, and it is a symbol of the religion of God; as the Qur'an says, we have to submit to His will as the animals under the knife have to submit to ours. And then a verse on the subject in the following thundering words denudes sacrifices of the merits that had been attached to them by other religions - such as the propitiation of Divine anger:

"Not their flesh, nor their blood, reaches God, but to Him is acceptable the guarding (against evil) on your part; thus has He made them subservient to you, that you may magnify God because He has guided you aright; and give good news to those who do good (to others)." (22:37)
http://www.muslim.org/islam/choice/choice.htm

End of quotation
....

Is this true? Let us find out:

The author said: "Muslims do observe sacrifice, but **not to appease Divine wrath**."

to "Feed the poor man who is contented, and the beggar" (22:36)

That statement is based on deception.
In fact, Islam has at least five kinds of sacrifice;

1. Allah asking Abraham for human sacrifice (his son). (Qur'an 73:102).
2. Allah himself giving great sacrifice as ransom for Abraham son, (Qur'an 73:107).
3. Muslims seek forgiveness by giving sacrifices for

individual or for the sake of other family member or for forgiveness of all Muslims as one nation, as we read in Shaykh Ibn 'Uthaemeen he said: in the book AlSharh AlMumtie' (5/275) we quot; "There is no limit to how many people may share in the reward. The Prophet offered a sacrifice on behalf of his entire Muslim nation" or in Al-Tirmidhi (hadith 1505).

4. A Muslim sacrifices himself for the sake of Allah to get into paradise as we read; Volume 5, Book 59, Number 600: "Narrated by Mujahid: I said to Ibn 'Umar, "I want to migrate to Al-Sham." He said, "There is no migration, but Jihad for the sake of Allah. Go and sacrifice yourself for Jihad, and if you find an opportunity for Jihad (stay there) otherwise, come back."

Qur'an 2:244 "And fight in the cause of Allah and know that Allah is Hearing and Knowing."

Qur'an 4:74 "So let those fight in the cause of Allah who sacrifices the life of this world for the Hereafter, and he who fights in the cause of Allah and might be killed or achieves victory - We eventually grant him a magnificent reward."

5. **Muslims sacrifice you** for the sake of making his God happy so he can go to haven by killing whomsoever do no't accept Islam. **Qur'an 9:29 "Fight those who do not believe in Allah or in the Last Day"**

Allah's severe penalty can be avoided by sacrifice
Qur'an 3:183

"Those who said: Surely Allah took an oath from us that we should not believe in any messenger until he brings us an sacrifice which the fire consumes. Say: Indeed, there came to you messengers before me with clear evidence and with that which you requested; why then did you kill them if you are truthful"

The word قربان 'Qurban translates as **offering**. In Yusuf Ali's translation, it translates to **sacrifices**. Now in Qur'an 3:183, we would notice few important things.

1. Allah first told the Jews not to accept any prophet unless he provides sacrifices and then Allah accepted these sacrifices by

sending fire (holy fire!) from Heavens.

2. Allah approved what the Jews said and eventually he sent the fire to consume the sacrifices.

3. The Jews killed the prophets who provided signs! Notice in here how foolish this argument is. The Jews will not accept a person for prophet-hood unless this person makes sacrifices and Allah sends a fire to consume it yet the Jews killed him?! Why they will do if he did whatsoever they asked for?

4. Why couldn't the Qur'an provide a name of one of the prophet-hood that was killed after giving an offering to which Allah then sends his holy fire to consume the sacrifices?

5. And the most important question: why didn't Muhammad make a sacrifice to which Allah would send his fire and consume it since Allah ordered not ever to accept a prophet among the prophet-hood unless he provides with a sign?

6. Therefore, the Jews had every right to reject Muhammad because he fail to provide such a significant sign.

7. Based on that rule, did the Jews behave inappropriately by following Allah's commands?

8. What's wrong with this god Allah? You become a criminal even when you do his will.

The author of the book said:
"Muslims do observe sacrifice, but **not to appease Divine wrath**."

> to "Feed the poor man who is contented, and the beggar"
> (Qur'an 22:36)

1. Was the fire a homeless fire?
2. Hungry fire?
3. Homeless hungry fire coming from heaven?
4. Even in heaven there is homelessness!

For sure now it's clear that Muslims cannot accept a homeless fire! They will say this is made to be a significant sign in order to prove the prophet-hood of a person. This was done once which means it was only done to perform and examine. It was not an act practiced to seek forgiveness.

Therefore, its time to show more proof that all of these sacrifices in Islam were not made as signs but as a practice.

> Qur'an 5:27
>
> Tell to them the true story of the two sons of Adam. Behold!
> they each provided a sacrifice (to Allah) but It was accepted

from one, but not from the other. Then he said(Cain): "I will slay thee." (Allah) only doth accept of the sacrifice of those who are righteous.

Interpretation of AL-Zama'khshary

هما ابنا آدم لصلبه قابيل وهابيل، أوحى الله إلى آدم أن يزوّج كل واحد منهما توأمة الآخر، وكانت توأمة قابيل أجمل واسمها (إقليما) فحسد عليها أخاه وسخط. فقال لهما آدم: قرّبا قرباناً، فمن أيكما تقبل زوّجها، فتقبل قربان هابيل بأن نزلت نار فأكلته؛ فازداد قابيل حسداً وسخطاً، وتوعده بالقتل.

"Adam has two sons from his seeds, so Allah inspired Adam to make each one of the boys marry his twin sister. And the twin sister of Able was more beautiful which made Cain jealous. Therefore, Adam said: each one of you, make a sacrifice to Allah; the one whose sacrifice is accepted by Allah, will marry her."

﴿ واتل عَلَيْهِمْ نَبَأَ ٱبْنَيْ ءَادَمَ بِٱلْحَقِّ إِذْ قَرَّبَا قُرْبَاناً فَتُقُبِّلَ مِن أَحَدِهِمَا وَلَمْ يُتَقَبَّلْ مِنَ ٱلْآخَرِ قَالَ لَأَقْتُلَنَّكَ قَالَ إِنَّمَا يَتَقَبَّلُ ٱللَّهُ مِنَ ٱلْمُتَّقِينَ ﴾

Tafsir (interpretation) of Al-Jalalayn Qur'an 5:27

In addition to recite, O Muhammad, to your community the account of the two male children of Adam, Abel and Cain, how both and each one of them offered a sacrifice to Allah. In the case of Abel was a male sheep (a ram), and in the case of Cain were green crops. One of both offerings was accepted, namely Able's, when a fire came down from heaven and consumed his offering (the ram). Cain's offering not being accepted, he became angry and undisclosed his jealousy until Adam left on pilgrimage. Cain said to him (Abel): 'I will certainly murder you,' and Abel replied, Why? to which Cain responded: 'Because your offering was exclusively accepted'. Abel said: Allah only accepts offerings from god-fearing witnesses.

To see Muslims trans go to www.altafsir.com.

So, what we understand from this story according to Muhammad is:

1. Adam is a prophet inspired by Allah in finding solutions to everyday life problems.
2. Sacrifices were given to fulfill a request, in order to receive an answer and a blessing as an approval from Allah.
3. "(Allah) doth accept of the sacrifice of those who are righteous.
4. Allah only accepts sacrifices from righteous men as all Muslims are righteous.
5. The fact is that you can offer a sacrifice on behalf of someone

else, as stated in the hadith of Sahih Al-Bukhari, Book 6, Hadith 293:

6. Allah's Messenger sacrificed some cows on behalf of his wives.

7. Sacrifices started taking place from the time of Adam, as Islam copied from the Bible.

Genesis 4:3 - KJV

And in process of time it came to pass, that Cain brought of the fruit of the ground an offering unto the LORD.⁴ And Abel, he also brought of the firstlings of his flock and of the fat thereof. And the LORD had respect unto Abel and to his offering: ⁵ But unto Cain and to his offering he had not respect. And Cain was very wroth, and his countenance fell.

1. Therefor it's not about feeding the poor at all. Allah is not hungry or homeless, is he? Allah took the sacrifices into himself.
2. Why is it that in Islam, Allah never accepted any sacrifices but rams?
3. Clearly, Allah is not a vegetarian. Why has he always requested blood sacrifices but not green crops as Cain did?
4. Christians believe that the sacrifices performed in the Bible represent the coming of Christ where Jesus Christ shed his blood, Him being *the* ultimate sacrifice in behalf of all human kind. He *is* the unblemished and spotless lamb sacrificed for mankind.
5. In Islam, what does the bloodshed of a ram as a sacrifice represent for Allah?
6. Allah made his decision about the marriage of Abel and his twin sister on what basis?
7. Both sons gave offerings to Allah, therefore both were equally good men in seeking Allah's approval.
8. However, it's clear that the ram and only the ram was acceptable before Allah. We will prove that with more evidence.

This hadith (Muhammad's speech) is very clear:

"Moreover, if anyone of you is sick or has a skin illness of his head, and must shave, He must pay money and either fast or feed the poor, or offer a sacrifice."

(Qur'an 2:196, Sahih Al-Bukhari, Book 59, hadith 504)

1. All the above actions are needed to recover from sickness.
2. A Muslim must pay money, and either fast or feed the poor, or

offer a sacrifice.

3. Notice offering is distinguished from blood sacrifice in Muhammad's statement.
4. So, there's a clear distinction between feeding the poor and offering a sacrifice.
5. This means that sickness in Islam is a result of Allah's anger. You therefore need to remove Allah's anger on you if you want to be healed from the sickness.

"(Allah) doth accept of the sacrifice of those who are righteous.

Qur'an 66:4-5

4 If yet both of you repent to Allah, your hearts will indeed incline. However, if ye back each other against Muhammad, truly Allah is his Protector, and Jibrel (Gabriel), and every righteous one among those who believe, and the angels will support him.

5 It will possibly be, if he divorces all of you, that Allah will award him better consorts in exchange of you, they who submit their will, who are Muslims, who are devout, who turn to Allah in repentance, who worship (in humility), who travel and fast, - previously married or virgins.

These verses give us a clear understanding that Muhammad's wives are not righteous. Even the Qur'an considers them as "kufar" and disbelievers as if they were Muhammad's enemies to the point that Muhammad needs Allah, the angels and every righteous Muslim to back him up. Therefore, how and why did Muhammad offer a sacrifice on behalf of his bad wives while at the same time, Allah asks Muslims not to make a sacrifice on anybody's behalf?

Sahih Al-Bukhari, Book 6, Hadith 293

"Allah's Messenger sacrificed some cows on behalf of his wives."

Basically, it means that my own good action brought the other person a reward! In this case, what happens to this verse:

Qur'an 6:164

Say: What! Shall I look for a Lord another one then Allah? And He is the Lord of all things; and no soul does evil but against itself, and no bearer of burden shall bear the burden of another; then to your Lord is your return for judgment, afterword's He will be the judge between you in your arguments.

Qur'an 2:48

Protect yourself from that day (Day of Judgment) when no soul can be useful to another soul and no intercession will be accepted, and no help will come from anyone.

We previously saw Allah giving a sacrifice on behalf of Abraham but in that case, was it for the forgiveness of Abraham's sin or was it about something else? Does Muhammad himself even know? In the last hadith, Muhammad sacrificed a cow on behalf of his wives as an intercession. Can this be an evident proof for the Christian faith that Jesus Christ sacrificed Himself on behalf of all mankind as a pure loving gesture in order for us to be forgiven? As we saw, Muhammad himself practiced the act of sacrificing on behalf of his wives! The most important difference I see between Christ's sacrifice and Muhammad's is that Jesus did so for the entire world whereas Muhammad did so for himself, being a person who only thought about his own house, and not others.

Sacrifices of blood is a must in Mecca pilgrimage to complete Allah requirement

Qur'an 2:196

"And complete the pilgrimage (you Muslims) . But if you are detained, then offer what can be obtained with ease of sacrificial animals. And do not shave your heads until the sacrificial animal has reached its place of slaughter."

Even Allah makes Sacrifices

و فَدَيْنَاهُ بِذِبْحٍ عَظِيمٍ

Qur'an 37:102-107 Yusuf Ali's translation

102 Then, when (the son) reached (the age of) (serious) work with him, he said: "O my son! I see in vision that I offer thee in sacrifice: Now see what is thy view!" (The son) said: "O my father! Do as thou art commanded: thou will find me, if Allah so wills one practicing Patience and Constancy!" 103 So when they had both submitted their wills (to Allah), and he had laid him prostrate on his forehead (for sacrifice), 104 We called out to him "O Abraham! 105 "Thou hast already fulfilled the vision!" - thus indeed do We reward those who do right. 106 For this was obviously a trial- 107 And We ransomed him with

337

a momentous sacrifice:

This story proves that Allah Himself gives sacrifice and it is just proper that we should ask why! Let us study this chapter and we will notice many extreme mistakes.

- First of all, Allah did not order Abraham to sacrifice his son at all. It was a dream: *"O my son! I see in vision that I offer thee in sacrifice: Now see what is thy view!"*
- It was Abraham's offer (as a Muslim): "I offer thee in sacrifice". It was not ordered by Allah.
- Muslims sacrifice humans as an offer from themselves.
- The verse shows a bad mistake on how Abraham made an offer from himself as the verse says that it was a trial:
  "For this was obviously a trial".
- This means that Allah made Abraham see this vision and it translated by Abraham mistakenly as it's just a vision as it's his own offering to Allah when it's Allah order.
- This shows bad communication between Allah and his prophet. Therefore, Allah cannot be the real God.
- Because Abraham thinks it's his offer and Allah thinks it's his order.
- Abraham passes the trial but still Allah is in need of requesting the sacrifice.
- Allah himself sent his offer.
- Not only humans give offering to God, but God makes offering to God,

"And We ransomed him with a momentous sacrifice:"
- God's sacrifice is not from earth. It's from heaven.
- Why didn't Allah send a sacrifice of a ram from earth?
- Do Allah breed rams in heaven?
- Why did Allah call the ram م "Azeem" which means **Great**?
- Why didn't Allah ever call other living beings "Azeem"?

When you offer sacrifices to Allah, he helps you

فَلَوْلَا نَصَرَهُمُ الَّذِينَ اتَّخَذُوا مِن دُونِ اللَّهِ قُرْبَانًا آلِهَةً بَلْ ضَلُّوا عَنْهُمْ وَذَلِكَ إِفْكُهُمْ وَمَا كَانُوا يَفْتَرُونَ
(سورة الأحقاف , Al-Ahqaf, Chapter 46, Verse 28)

I could not find one Islamic translation of the verse to the word in bold: قُرْبَانًا "Quraban" which means sacrifice.

"Why couldn't their gods help them? Those who gave a sacrifice to other gods instead of Allah. It is because these gods are fake and are their inventions. (Qur'an 46: 28)

Let us read this verse carefully and see what Allah is trying to tell us:

- The person who makes a sacrifice to a god other than Allah is seeking help from the wrong god.
- Giving offerings is a way to get help and make Allah happy with you. Therefore, Allah loves sacrifices.
- Making sacrifices is the same as paying the Islamic god. It's not about giving a gift to someone you care about or love, but it's a must to get his attention.
- But this again means that the Muslims claim, that sacrifices are not meant to cool down the anger of their god Allah, is false.
- Allah, as Muhammad claimed, did not help those who didn't offer him sacrifices. This angered Allah and not only did he not help them out but he made them lose war and their very lives for not giving him (Allah) any offerings.

Qur'an 22:37 - Muhammad H. Shakir's

There does not reach Allah their flesh nor their blood, but to Him is acceptable the guarding (against evil) on your part; thus, has He made them subservient to you, that you may magnify Allah because He has guided you aright; and give good news to those who do good (to others).

- This verse contradicts Qur'an 5:27 where Allah accepted and the Ram of Abel's and send fire to take it to heaven. **"fire came down from the heaven and consumed his offering"**
- Shedding blood protects you against evil "but to Him is acceptable the guarding (against evil) on your part"
- You make sacrifices to **magnify Allah** "thus has He made them subservient to you, that you may **magnify Allah because He has guided you aright**"

Now there are problems in this verse. Since it says Allah does not accept any kind of sacrifice offered to him, the story in Qur'an 3:183 would be a contradiction as the following verse states that Allah accepted the ram into heaven as he always has done for each of his messengers.

Qur'an 3:183

Those who said: Surely Allah took an oath from us that we should not believe in any messenger until he brings us an sacrifice which the fire consumes. Say: Indeed, there came to you messengers before me with clear evidence and with that which you requested; why then did you kill them if you are truthful?

And it's a contradiction to the story of Abraham too:

Qur'an 5:27

"Tell to them the true story of the two sons of Adam. Behold! they each provided a sacrifice (to Allah) but It was accepted from one, but not from the other. Then he said(Cain): "I will slay thee." (Allah) only doth accept of the sacrifice of those who are righteous."

It's so clear that Allah accepts sacrifices as his own way to show who he likes or dislikes, and this was his own idea. Yet he accepted only the blood shed ram only.

So I think we showed enough evidence proving that the Muslims claim, what is called Qur'an Scientific discoveries is nothing but fabrication either about not making sacrifices to pacify Allah's anger or to seek his help, are absolutely false.

Now we almost done with this book and my coming book would be about Muhammad and the Ancient legends & Islam, we did expose many stories Muhammad took from others like **"The Legends of The Jews"**, but are we the first to find out about it?
The answer NO; even the Arab in the time of Muhammad they were the first to know about it, and that due the spread of these stories in the Arab culture.

"It is true we were promised this, - we and our fathers before (us): these are nothing but tales of the ancients."

Qur'an 27:68 Yusuf Ali

This is why the Arab told Muhammad according to the Qur'an many times your Qur'an is the tale of the ancient as we read in about 9 locations in the Qur'an 68:15 / 83:13 / 46:17 / 27:68 / 25:5 / 23:83 / 16:24 / 8:31 /6:25

"That, when Our revelations are recited unto him, he saith: Mere legends of the ancestors."

Qur'an 68:15 | إِذَا تُتْلَىٰ عَلَيْهِ آيَاتُنَا قَالَ أَسَاطِيرُ الْأَوَّلِينَ

....

Qur'an and Scientific miraculous claims taken from and **we quoted from their site;**

www.harunyahya.com miraclesofthequran.com

***

I pray Muslims will read my words carefully the objective of the book is to help Christians, and Muslims or whoever is searching for the truthfulness of God, I end my book with my favorite verse in the bible;

"And ye shall know the truth, and the truth shall make you free." John 8:32

May The Lord bless us all.

The author: Christian Prince. ©

To contact https://www.patreon.com/ChristianPrince

www.facebook.com/TheChristianprince/

www.investigateislam.com

13173428R00195

Printed in Germany
by Amazon Distribution
GmbH, Leipzig